Polidoro da Caravaggio

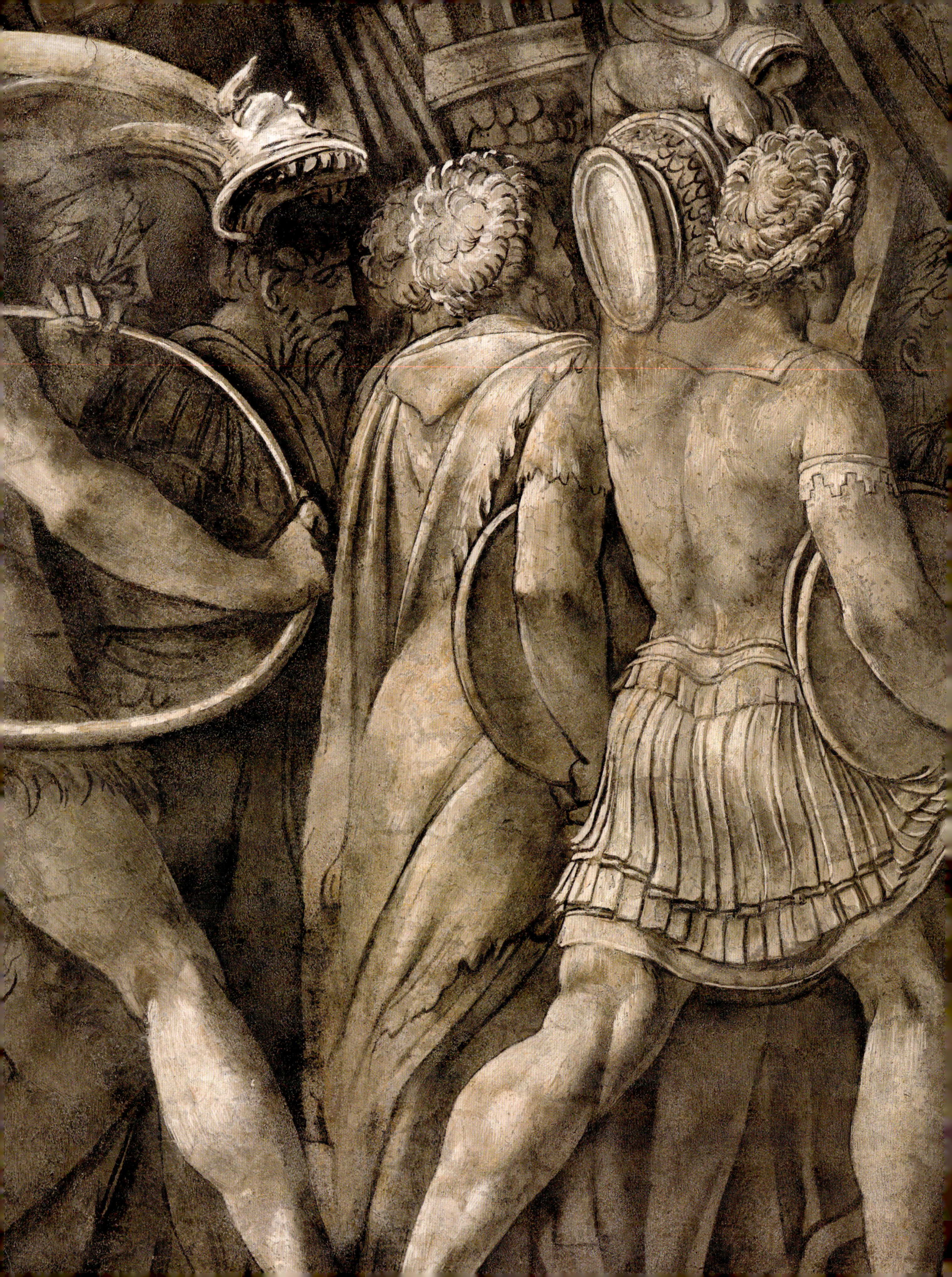

Polidoro da Caravaggio

David Franklin

Yale University Press   New Haven and London

First published by Yale University Press 2018

302 Temple Street, P.O. Box 209040, New Haven, CT 06520-9040

47 Bedford Square, London WC1B 3DP

yalebooks.com / yalebooks.co.uk

ISBN 978-0-300-22389-7

Library of Congress Control Number: 2017954550

10 9 8 7 6 5 4 3 2 1

2022 2021 2020 2019 2018

Cover design and book layout: GradeDesign.com

Printed in China

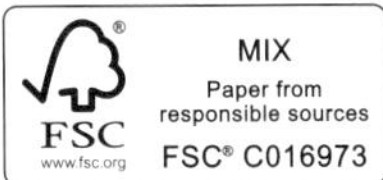

Editorial Note

In the absence of extensive documentation, securely dating works by Polidoro da Caravaggio on stylistic grounds alone is difficult. In some cases it would be guesswork even to propose a useful range. Dates of works of art have therefore been omitted from the captions, but are suggested where possible in the main text. See also the Chronology on page 152 for a documented timeline.

Illustrations

Jacket, front: detail of fig. 1.28; jacket, back: detail of fresco in San Silvestro al Quirinale, Rome; page 2: detail of fig. 2.16; page 6: detail of fig. 3.17; page 8: detail of fig. 1.3; page 10: detail of fig. 1.22

Photographic Acknowledgements

Jörg P. Anders: figs 2.33, 4.4, 4.18; © British Museum: figs 1.17, 1.29, 2.5, 2.24, 2.34, 2.37, 4.2, 4.3, 4.19, 4.27, 6.13; Mauro Coen: figs 2.13–2.16; Steven H. Crossot, 2014: fig. 2.26; Enrico Fontolan: figs 1.5–1.14, 1.21–1.25, 1.27, 1.28, 2.1, 2.7, 2.9–2.12, 2.23, jacket front and back; © Frequin Photos, Voorburg: fig. 2.3; © Her Majesty Queen Elizabeth II, 2017: figs 1.20, 3.8, 3.15, 3.16, 3.18–3.23; © R.M.N.: figs 1.1, 1.33, 4.11; Arnaldo Soares: fig. 2.38; © Elke Walford: fig. 1.30

For Antonia Reiner

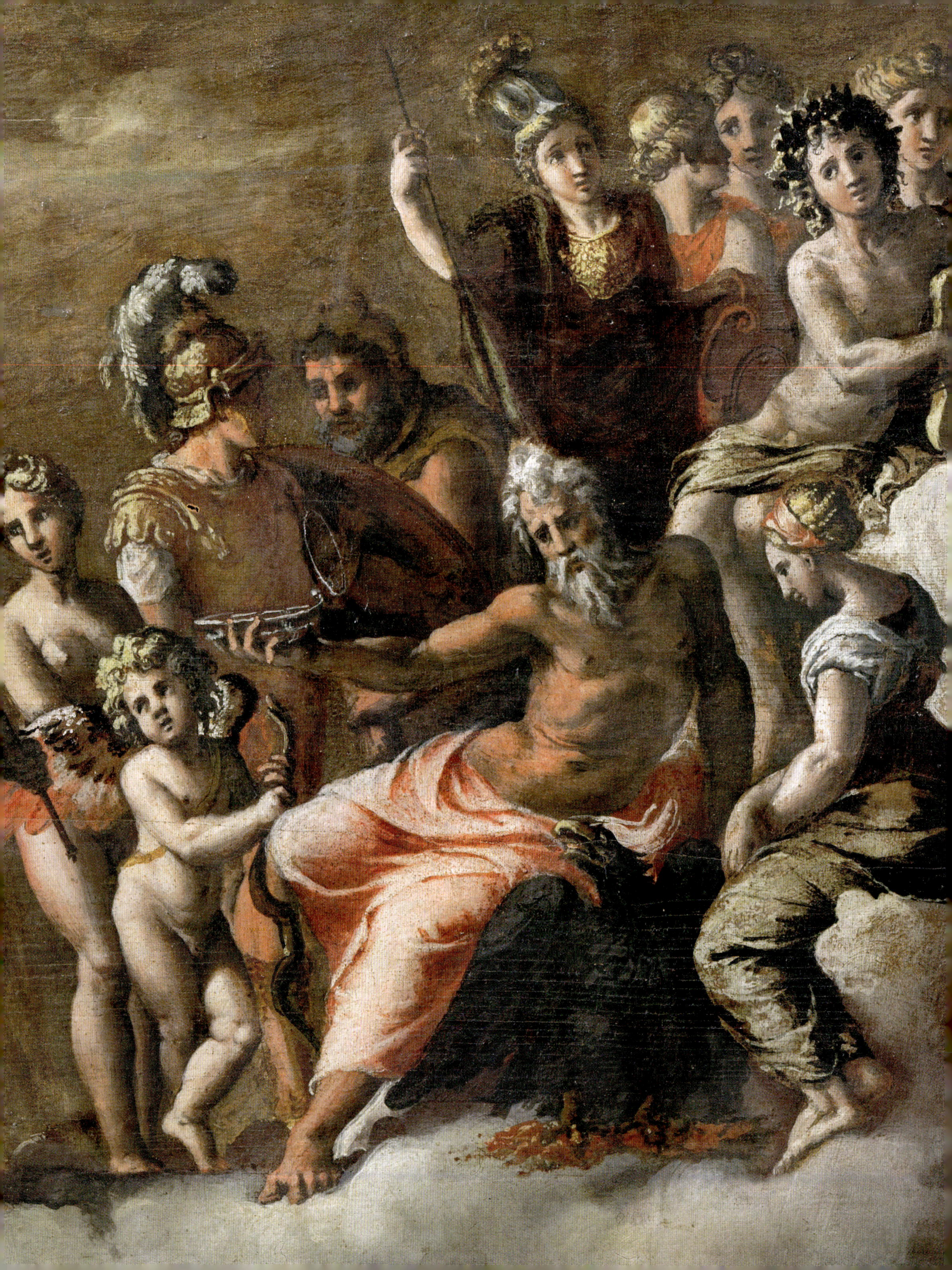

Contents

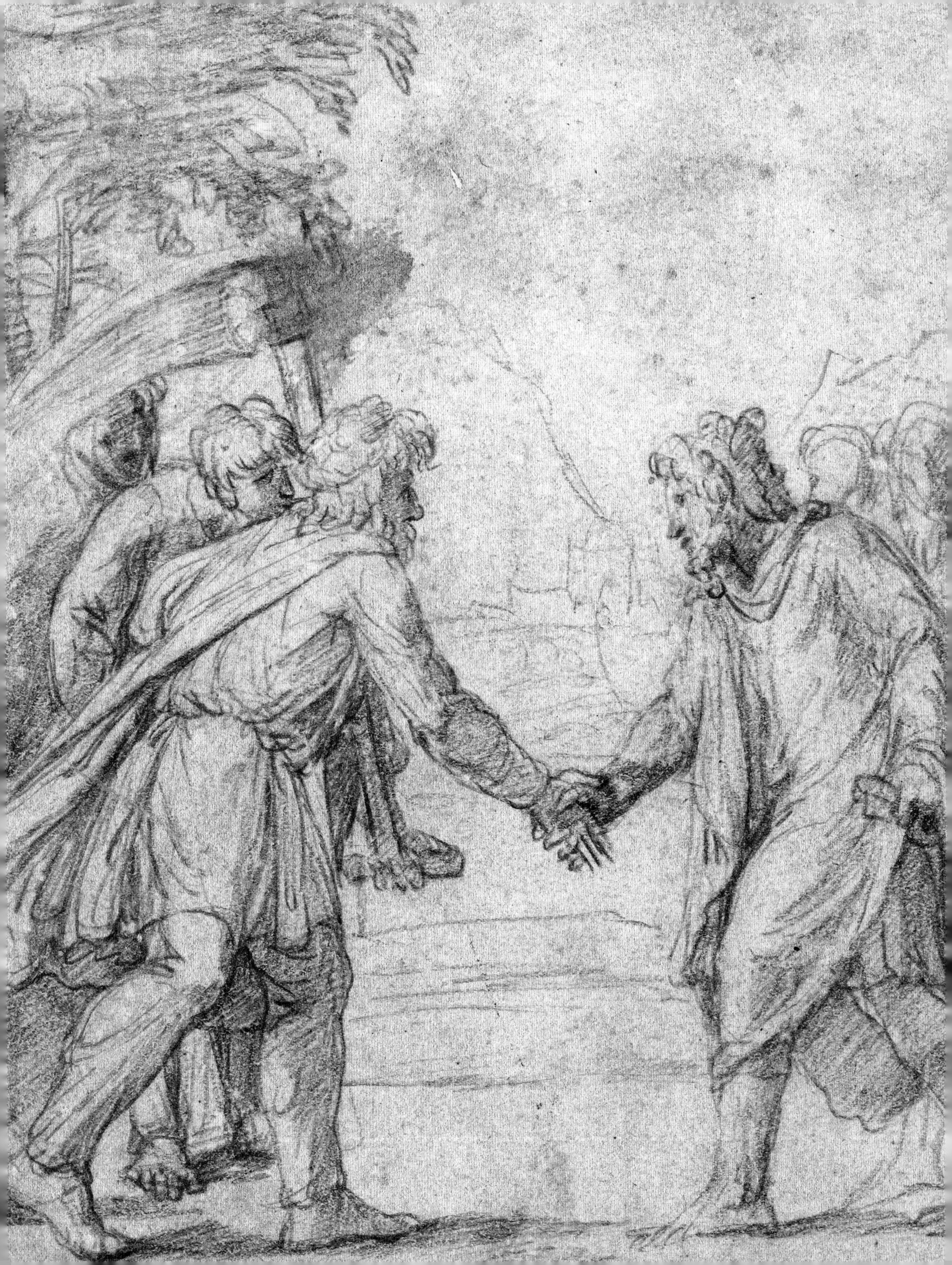

Acknowledgements

For their generous assistance in different ways the author wishes to thank, in alphabetical order, the following friends and colleagues: Antonina Affronti, Simone Andreoni, Emily Antler, Carmen Bambach, Sylvain Bellenger, Kent Brainerd, Julian Brooks, Andrew Butterfield, Cyndie Campbell, Lester Carissmi, Eugene Carroll, Davide Cermignani, Martin Clayton, Mauro Coen, Karen Colby, Roberto Contini, Dominique Cordellier, Giorgio Corsi, Gino Corti, Phillipe Costamagna, Nelda Damiano, Peter Dawson, Marina De Carolis, Sylvie Deswarte-Rosa, Mark Eastment, Rhoda Eitel-Porter, Christopher Etheridge, Marzia Faietti, Fanny Fioravanti, Enrico Fontolan, Giuliana Forti, Gordon Franklin, Roman Franklin, Thomas Franklin, Charlotte Gere, Achim Gnann, Catherine Goguel, Jean Goldman, Charlotte Grievson, Stephen Gritt, Suzanne Haddad, Florian Harb, Francis Haskell, Tom Henry, Michael Hirst, Jane Horvitz, David Jaffe, Paul Joannides, Ingrid Kastel, Alice Kennedy-Owen, Elizabeth Kieven, Dagmar Korbacher, Monique Kornell, Erich Lessing, Julie Levac, Catherine Loisel, Antonella Longo-Turri, Hannah Lyons, David McTavish, Giorgio Marini, Camilla Marking, Patrick Matthiesen, Minna Moore Ede, Jennifer Morris, Jane Munro, Arnold Nesselrath, Jennifer Nicoll, Alessandro Nova, Patrizia Piscitello, Myril Pouncey, Antonia Reiner, Patricia Rubin, Agata Rutkowska, Marga Sanchez, Sebastian Schutze, Margaret Shufeldt, Donatella Spagnolo, Jesse Stewart, Maria Stijkel, Jacqueline Thalmann, David Thomson, Nicholas Turner, Claire Van Cleave, Murray Waddington, Louis Waldman, Aidan Weston Lewis, Catherine Whistler, Clovis Whitfield, Lucy Whittaker, Michelle Wilson and Nigel Wilson.

Extra special thanks are due to Linda Wolk-Simon, Hugo Chapman, David Ekserdjian and Rick Scorza for reading different chapters and making many pertinent comments. Thanks as well to Judy Spours for her sensitive and careful edit of the text. I am most deeply grateful to Sophie Oliver for her meticulous attention to every detail of the publication. I would also like to single out the tremendous effort of Johannes Roell and his colleagues at the Hertziana Library in Rome, to whom I am indebted for their assistance with some new photography in Rome. The book never would have been published without the constant support and inspiration of Gillian Malpass.

Research on the book commenced at All Souls College, Oxford, where I was fortunate to have held a post-doctoral fellowship from 1994 to 1998. I remain profoundly grateful to the Warden and Fellows of the College for providing the crucible in which this text was first contemplated. Further dedicated research was conducted at the Hertziana Library in 2009 and I am again especially grateful to the Director and staff of that institution for their kind assistance during that period.

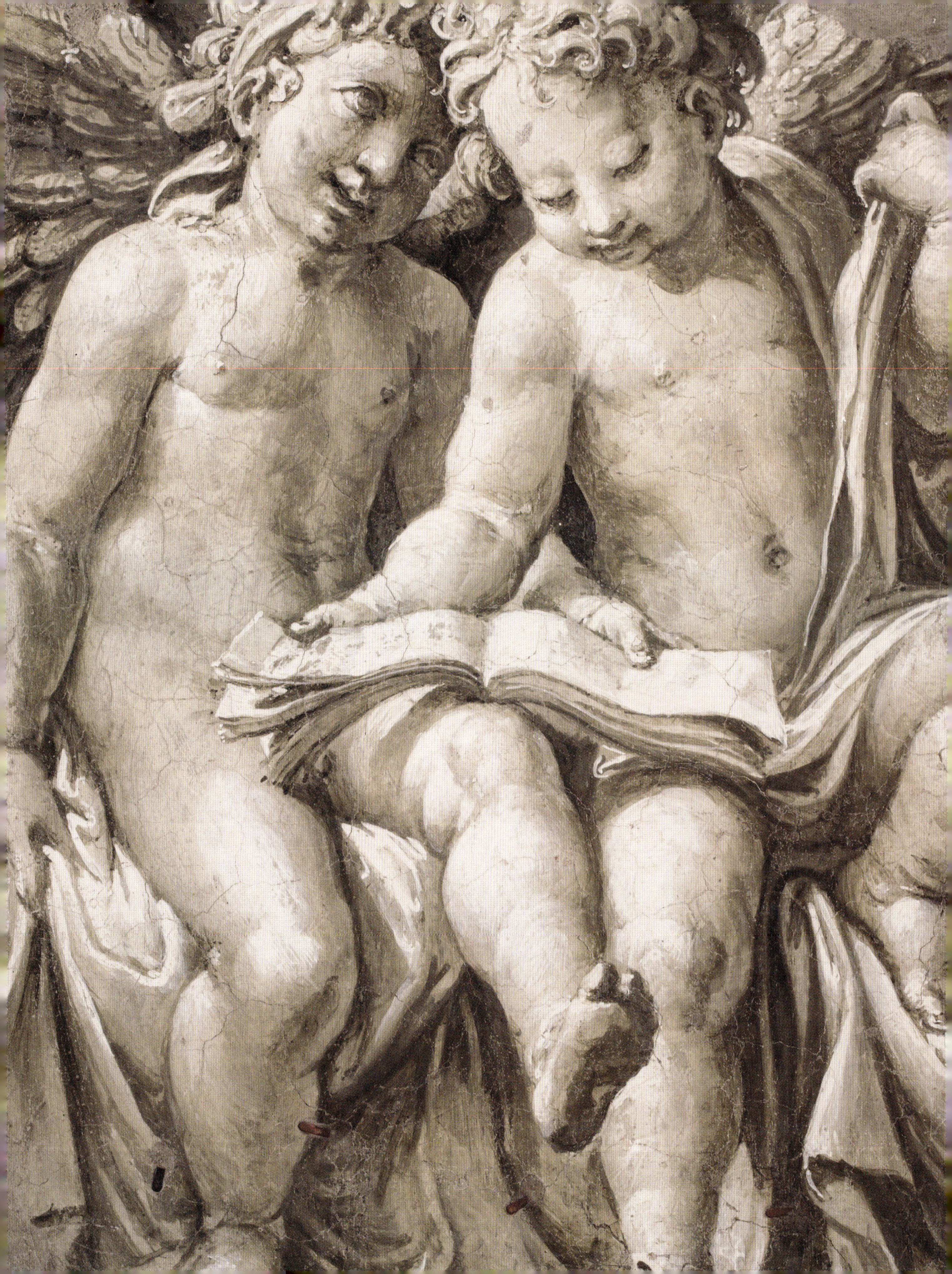

Preface

Polidoro da Caravaggio has not been treated well by time, in spite of his close association with one of the most famous artists of any period – Raphael. This is primarily because most of his significant early commissions were for exterior palace facades in Rome that have perished almost without exception, the designs for which are now preserved in drawn and printed copies of varying quality. Consequently, the original character of all this public work is difficult to appreciate. For these commissions Polidoro apparently collaborated with a painter of Florentine heritage called Maturino, who is himself a complete mystery and his specific role in the design or execution of any of these frescoes is unclear. (Maturino had trained with Raphael too and this makes it even harder to separate their hands in surviving drawings and paintings.) It has proved convenient to discuss their production under Polidoro's name alone, but this must distort the truth.

An examination of Polidoro's career is not helped either by his having spent the last 15 years of his life active in Sicily, a region for which there are few surviving primary sources from earlier periods and one that had a somewhat delayed historiography of the arts. His output there is also not easy to unravel. The study of Polidoro's later work suffers from the opposite problem to that of the facades. Many originals appear to survive but these are so unusual in style and technique that the attributions of some may well remain permanently controversial. It is difficult to identify a Renaissance painter, with the exception perhaps of Botticelli, whose career is so neatly split in two opposite directions, from the sophisticated and often playfully secular to the troublingly religious without contemporary parallel.

Finally, the chronology of Polidoro's paintings and particularly his drawings is unusually difficult to establish on stylistic grounds alone, and his undocumented work presents some thorny connoisseurship decisions. Sadly there are few documents and secure dates for his life and work to offer assistance. Therefore, although Polidoro was as individually talented as any of his contemporaries, and among the two or three most influential on later generations in Rome alone, his art is the hardest to assess. He has certainly been under-appreciated since the physical decline of his work, which was already apparent by the seventeenth century. How many sixteenth-century artists had access to the Sistine Chapel and Vatican Stanze? Polidoro's outdoor frescoes were accessible to all. A fuller comprehension of his huge achievement will also indirectly help us to appreciate Raphael's later style in Rome and the type of master he was for his many workshop assistants.

Rather than repeating much of the catalogue of drawings and Roman facades included in Pierluigi Leone de Castris's definitive monograph of 2001 – the benchmark for all future treatments of the artist – a synthetic chronological account is presented here in an attempt to provide a readable introduction to Polidoro's more public production to stimulate future research. It remains important to define his graphic corpus, and while there is still work to be done in this regard, a few comments about attribution will be made in different parts of the book. Even if Polidoro will never now achieve the popular acclaim of his better-known compatriot born later in the sixteenth century, Michelangelo Merisi da Caravaggio, he nonetheless deserves to be fully brought back into the mainstream of art history.

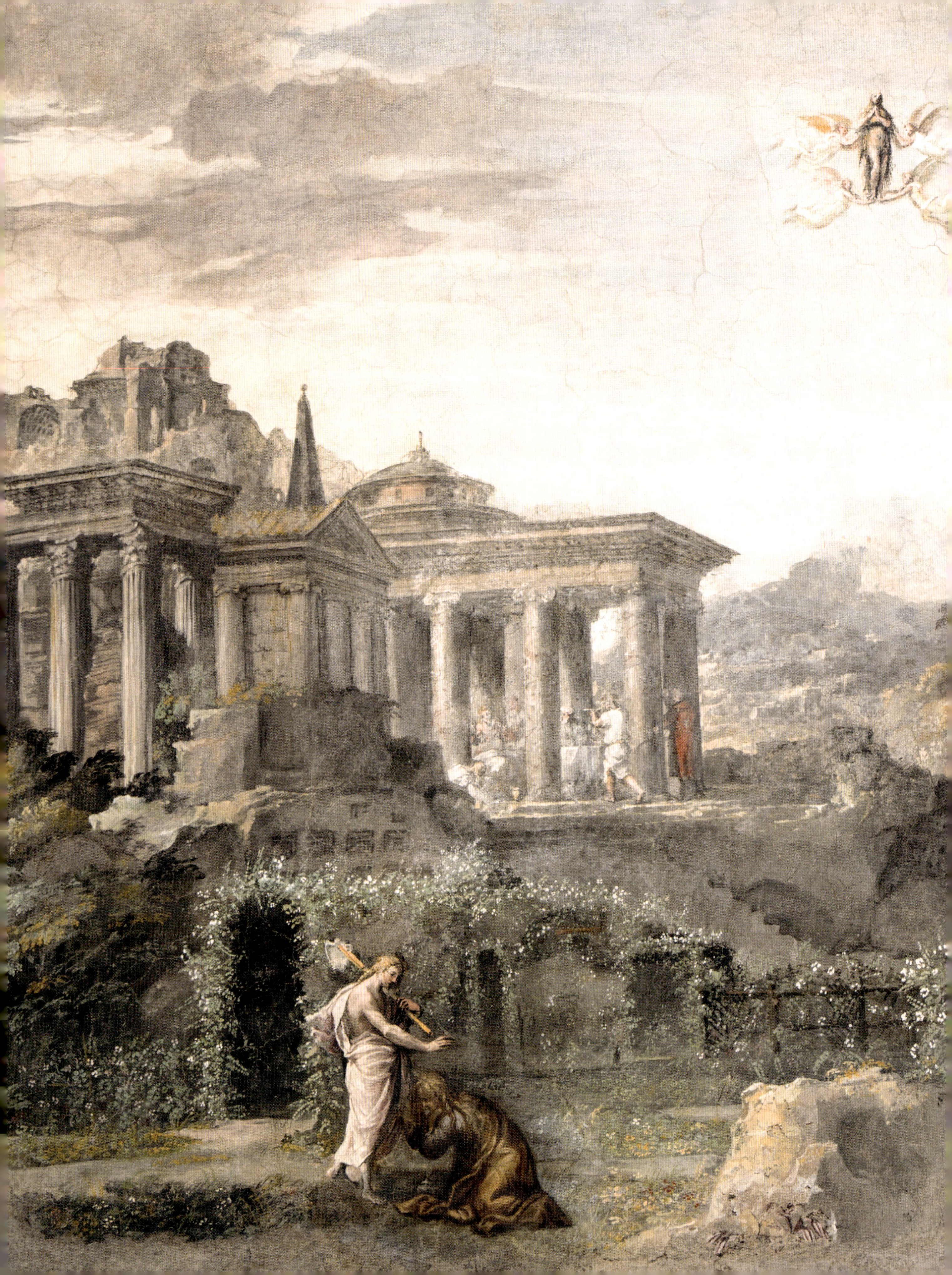

1   Rome

Polidoro da Caravaggio's birth date is not known for certain. According to a manuscript written around the mid-eighteenth century by a Cremonese scholar named Giambattista Biffi, the artist was born in 1490.[1] Given that the source of this statement was an antiquarian from his own northern Italy, the opinion should be given weight – he may have had access to a document subsequently lost – but the claim cannot otherwise be confirmed. Most scholars instead accept a later date of about 1498–1500, based on the internal logic of Giorgio Vasari's presentation of events in the artist's biography in the *Lives of the Artists*, according to which Polidoro, aged 18, came from the north of Italy as a foreigner to work as a menial plasterer in Raphael's studio in the Vatican Loggia.[2] This would put his birth at around 1500, considering that the decoration of the Loggia was definitely in progress by 1518 and finished before the summer of 1519.[3] This date neatly balances Vasari's other claim that the artist died in Messina, in Sicily, in 1543 at the age of 44. While Vasari never visited Sicily, he did go south as far as Naples in 1544, only a year after Polidoro's presumed death in Messina, and he may have heard news

of it then. Some scholars have considered, however, a death date of 1543 too advanced because Polidoro is last documented in 1535, but there is a body of work that could occupy this final period of his life, so this concern is misplaced. Another piece of relevant evidence is found in a letter of *c*.1523–4 in which Polidoro is referred to as '*iovane assai*' (very young), which would imply that a birth date around 1499 is more realistic than that of 1490.[4]

The acceptance of the more advanced of the two proposed birth dates has implications for our knowledge of the artist's likeness. The evidence suggests that the so-called self-portraits of Polidoro, known from drawings inscribed by the Portuguese artist and theorist Francesco de Hollanda, including an example in the Lugt Foundation (fig. 1.1), are questionable as the man represented is too old given that the studies were almost certainly produced in Rome before the Sack of 1527.[5] It appears that De Hollanda collected drawings like this one by Polidoro during his visit to Rome around 1538–40. A related sketch in the Louvre (fig. 1.2) is relevant here as it is formed of two sheets joined by a collector at a later date and features a man, apparently not a self-portrait, viewed from behind and looking down, as if he is sketching the irregularly cut

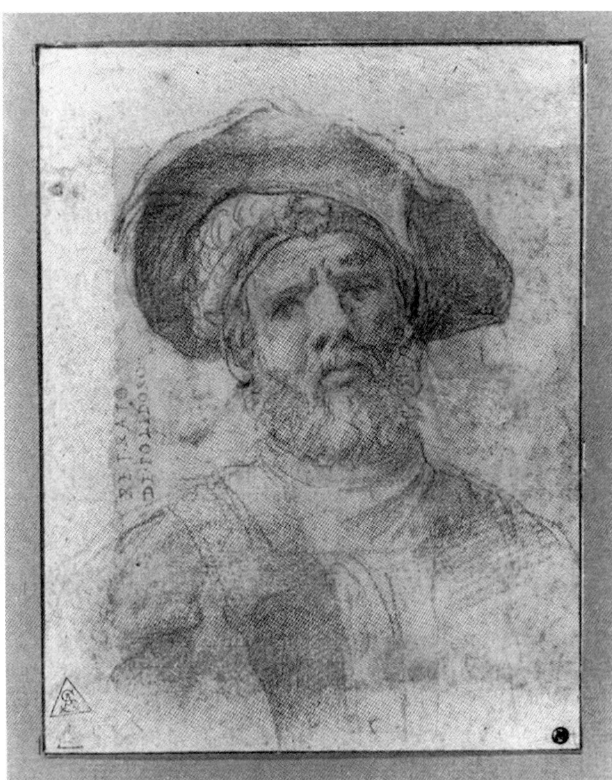

1.1 *Portrait of a Man*. Red chalk on laid paper, 13 × 10.2 cm. Fondation Custodia (Lugt Foundation), Paris

antique fragment of an outstretched arm and pointing finger on the other sheet positioned above his head.

The first surviving credible document containing his name, one of 1524, refers to Polidoro from Caravaggio and so the place of his birth is not in dispute. That his surname was Caldara is harder to confirm, although it is attested by the record of a signature on a now lost painting of the *Adoration of the Shepherds*, once in a private collection in Frankfurt, which also suggests he had been knighted ('*Eques*', or knight, is inscribed on the work), and by the Lombard artist and writer Giovanni Paolo Lomazzo in his treatise published in 1584.[6] It cannot even be established if the artist's birth name was 'Polidoro' but, to speculate, it was possibly given to him as a sobriquet while, as a promising young artist, he was immersed in ancient art. According to Pliny the Elder in his *Natural History*, one of the sculptors of the *Laocoön*, discovered in Rome as recently as 1506, was Polydorus of Rhodes.[7] Polydorus was also the name of the son of Priam, murdered by Achilles, as mentioned in Homer's *Iliad*.

The town of Caravaggio is located in Lombardy in the northern Italian province of Bergamo, and it is naturally tempting to detect a strain of Lombard realism in aspects of Polidoro's style, especially his predilection for genre drawings and landscape, even though he was never active there and his career apparently commenced in the Vatican within Raphael's workshop.[8] Polidoro did have connections with Lombard-born patrons at different periods of his career and this indicates that he was at least identified by his origins and benefited from them. There were many artists from that region living in Rome with whom he would have had contact, traditionally working more often as architects, sculptors, carpenters and stonemasons than as painters. The emergence of a second painter from Caravaggio nearly a century later provided another major exception to this pattern.

The first notice of a Polidoro da Caravaggio in Rome falls in 1517 in a document paraphrased by Domenico Gnoli, but unfortunately it cannot be confirmed as the scholar provided no source, and the potential implications of this data must be left in suspense.[9] Possibly based on a census document, Gnoli stated that this Polidoro was then renting a house in the Santa Lucia alle Botteghe Oscure quarter in Rome's Pigna district, which included the Pantheon, and that his father was one of the many Lombard stonemasons working in the city. A 'Polidoro *pintore*' is mentioned in 1517 in the documents of the confraternity of the Gonfalone for his part in the production of a Passion play performed at the Colosseum but, again, it is not certain that this is our artist.[10]

In looking for Polidoro's earliest identifiable work we must search in the decorations of the Vatican Loggia, the so-called 'Bible of Raphael'. It appears that Giovanni da Udine acted as the main supervisor of the ornamental sections, while Giulio Romano translated Raphael's designs and directed the painting. Even though the Loggia was a collaboration, it was one of the most important monuments for Raphael's later reputation. Baldassare Castiglione's letter to Isabella d'Este of 16 June 1519 attests that work on an unspecified painted loggia by Raphael, assumed to be that in the Vatican, including stucco-work executed '*alla anticha*', was fully concluded.[11] The completion of the Vatican Loggia thus overlapped towards the end of the 1510s with the decoration of Villa Farnesina in Rome, which was certainly finished by the start of January 1519, but there is no hint in Vasari that Polidoro assisted the group on this second, equally ambitious project.

The assumption that Polidoro first emerged around 1518, working on the Vatican Loggia as part of Raphael's talented and eclectic assembly of artists of varying ages and nationalities – starting as a humble assistant, before graduating to stucco-work and grotesques, and finally as a figure painter trusted with his own narrative – is a seductive hypothesis. No better theory has been presented. It must be admitted, however, that Polidoro is not cited in any documents for the Loggia decorations, nor are many of the other presumed collaborators, and deciphering the various hands in these frescoes from stylistic analysis alone is difficult due to the corporate nature of the commission. Further, except for the effaced lower register with horizontal biblical narratives treated in faux bronze monochrome, there was no extensive grisaille fresco in the Loggia either, the type of painting on which Polidoro eventually based his career in Rome. Nonetheless, it is in the Vatican Loggia that the artist's stylistic roots will have to be located. The space consists of 13 square bays originally open to the elements on one side and nothing survives in particularly good condition. Each bay contains four Old Testament narratives, except for the last bay, which concludes with representations from the New Testament. Bold handling, vigorous forms and bright acidic colours distinguish the painted decorations. Below the narratives in the Loggia, arches, piers and pilasters faced with stucco-work are interspersed with yet more frescoes containing a plethora of plant and animal forms, as well as copies of antiquities – a virtual encyclopedia of visual motifs that Polidoro absorbed first-hand as a young artist. Indeed, it was the most complete transcription of ancient imagery in one venue to date. Importantly for his artistic formation, the Loggia also housed a gallery of ancient sculpture, as well as careful reproductions and spirited interpretations in stucco.

Raphael, who was made responsible for assessing the value of newly discovered ancient stone in Rome by Pope Leo X in 1515, provided another inspiration for Polidoro's attraction to antique objects. The historian and collector Paolo Giovio, in a brief biography of Raphael of the mid-1520s, praised the artist for his efforts in measuring the surviving ancient architecture in Rome in order to aid

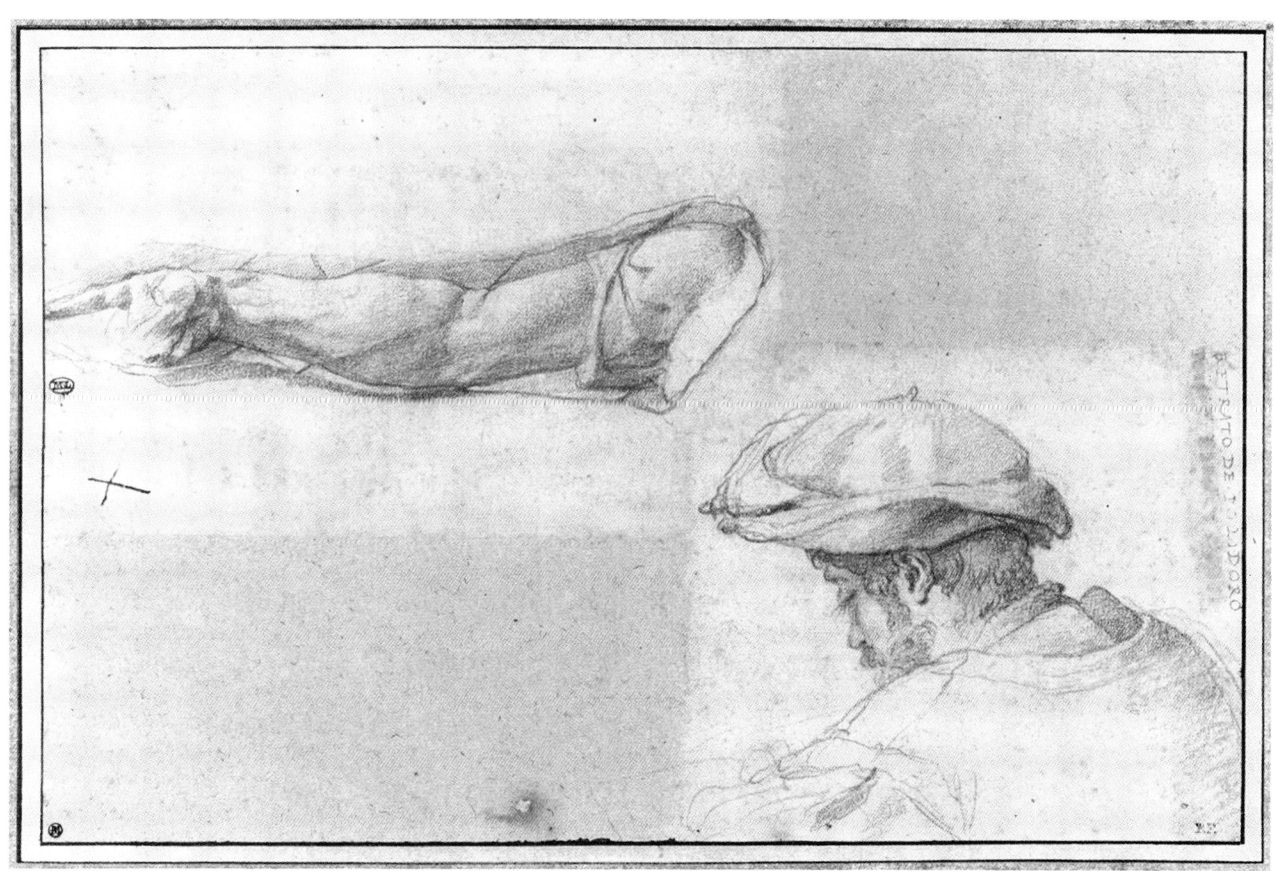

1.2 *Portrait of a Man and Study after the Antique.* Red chalk on laid paper, 16.5 × 25.8 cm. Musée du Louvre, Paris, Cabinet de Dessins

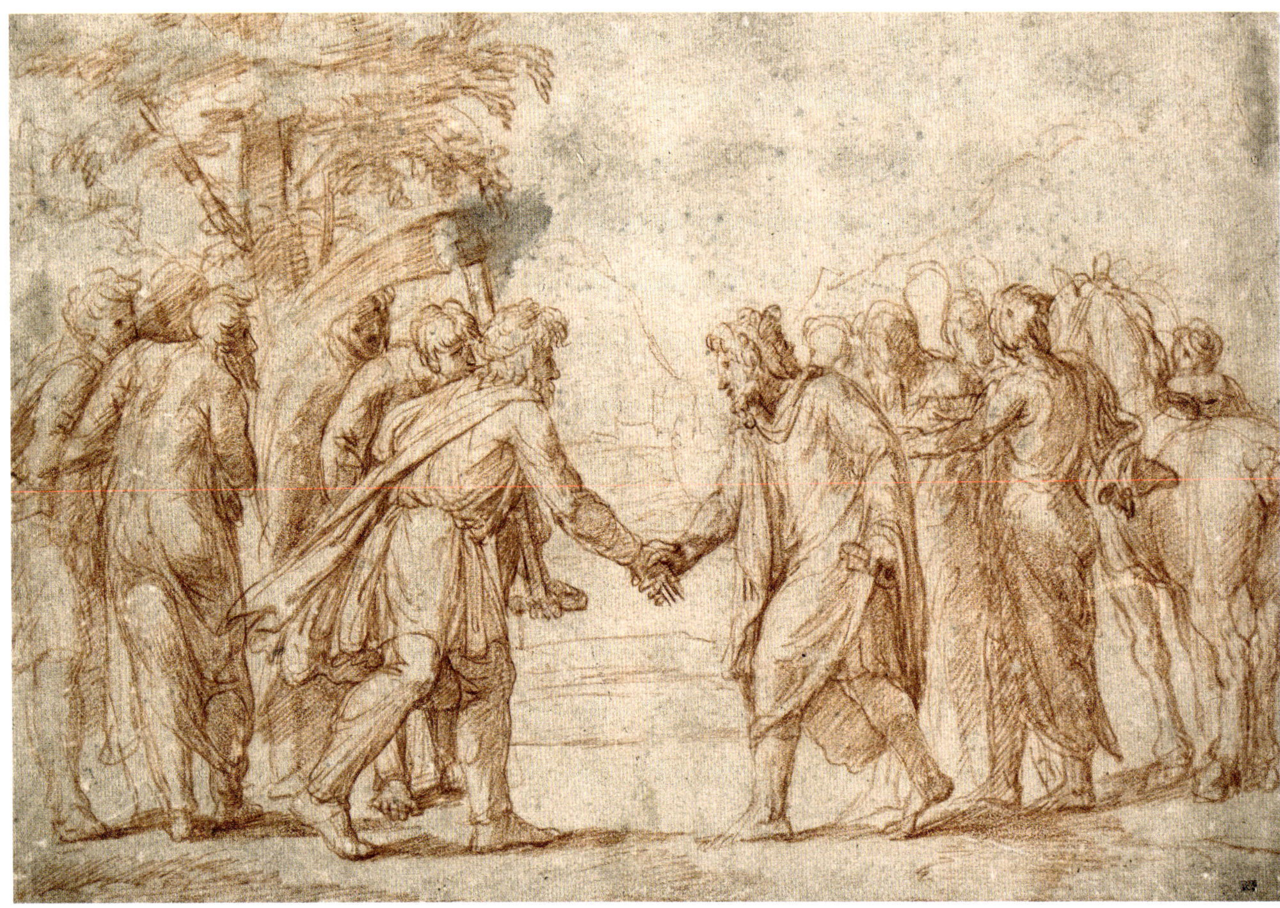

1.3 *The Meeting of Janus and Saturn*. Red chalk on laid paper, 19.8 × 28.5 cm. Musée du Louvre, Paris, Cabinet de Dessins

the reconstruction of the old city, and one can imagine this impressing the young Polidoro.[12] Raphael and Giovanni da Udine are known to have visited the Domus Aurea, the Golden House of Nero, discovered in the 1490s under the Esquiline Hill.[13] This palace was the most celebrated and accessible depository for ancient painting in the city. Two different graffiti with the words 'Caravagio' and 'Caravazo P', possibly evidence of Polidoro's own youthful experience of the site, have been deciphered there.[14]

The last works Raphael executed in Rome before his early death were frescoes for the four reception rooms of the papal palace. They met with spontaneous acceptance from his many supporters. According to Cardinal Bibbiena, Leo X preferred the figure of *Justice* painted in oil on the wall of the Sala di Costantino (Raphael's last major project) to any other fresco in the Stanze, and stated that it was possibly the greatest work done since ancient times.[15] So wrote Sebastiano del Piombo to Michelangelo in a letter of 3 July 1520. Giovio, writing in his biography of Raphael, pointed out that while the Sala di Costantino

was only begun by the artist, it in no way signalled a decline in skill or reputation. Polidoro was thus active at a still dynamic, increasingly diverse moment for the bottega, only gradually affected by the death of the master. Raphael's followers after his death exerted considerable control on patronage in Rome and Polidoro would fully exploit that dynamic.

Polidoro's early years nonetheless remain hard to unravel. His precise relationship with Raphael's principal assistants – Giulio, Gianfrancesco Penni and Giovanni da Udine – is vexed. Whether Polidoro was one of their subordinates for an extended period, namely one of the collective *giovani* of the master repeatedly cited in the archival documents, is an open question. It seems plausible that Polidoro and the Florentine Perino del Vaga developed together in Raphael's workshop in the Vatican Loggia at around the same date, towards the end of the 1510s. Polidoro's slower rise can be contrasted with that of Perino, born in 1501, as the Lombard was certainly older and less precocious. Inevitably, attributions have been proposed for Polidoro from the later products of Raphael's bottega, including the grisaille *basamento* (lower register) of the Sala di Costantino, but just as inevitably one has to doubt them; until it is certain when he achieved some stylistic autonomy, it is impossible to identify his hand.[16] One fact is indisputable: his experience of this artistic crucible led to his specialisation in fresco, narrowing to facade painting in monochrome, a type attempted sporadically by other Raphael acolytes, such as Penni, Pellegrino da Modena, Vincenzo Tamagni and Perino. For Polidoro their production supplied the means to advance and differentiate himself as an artist in a complex work environment that intensified with Raphael's death in 1520.

Despite the obvious formal debt evident from the artist's secure works, it is impossible to know how long Polidoro remained linked to Raphael's bottega following the master's sudden death, at which point Giulio and Penni assumed leadership roles. The most compelling case for some extended relationship is provided by the frescoes from Villa Lante on the Janiculum Hill (later removed and installed in Palazzo Zuccari, now the Bibliotheca Hertziana). A drawing by Polidoro, now in the Louvre, clearly relates to one of the frescoes. It features a rarely depicted subject from the foundation myth of Rome, *The Meeting of Janus and Saturn* (figs 1.3 and 1.4).[17] Vasari attributed all the frescoes to Giulio, although some subcontracting was necessary when he went to Mantua in the autumn of 1524.

The Louvre drawing is most significant as one of the few securely datable examples from Polidoro's Roman period. Executed in a style already recognisable as typical of the artist, red chalk is applied in heavy, thick lines that lend the drawing an agitated quality and negate the description of details. The design is based on a simple division into two groups with the resonant handshake between the protagonists, the Roman god Janus, the first king of Latium, and the protector Saturn, who brought agriculture to the region, isolated in the centre for dramatic effect. That the drawing is preparatory for the fresco and that both are by Polidoro has been universally accepted, but the relationship between these two iterations of the composition is problematic, for the painted treatment of the scene is much more static and inelegant than the drawn study. It contains fewer bodies and their proportions are stunted in comparison with the more characteristically attenuated ones in the drawing. The ambitious torsions Polidoro employed for some of the marginal figures are abandoned in the fresco. Even if we accept that the drawing was made in preparation for this fresco and not another secular project by Polidoro, the painting cannot have been executed by him. Indeed his entire participation at Villa Lante must be in doubt other than his role as designer in selected cases such as this, presumably at the behest of one of the more senior followers of Raphael, like Penni or the absent Giulio. The tight, pristine handling and confectionary colours

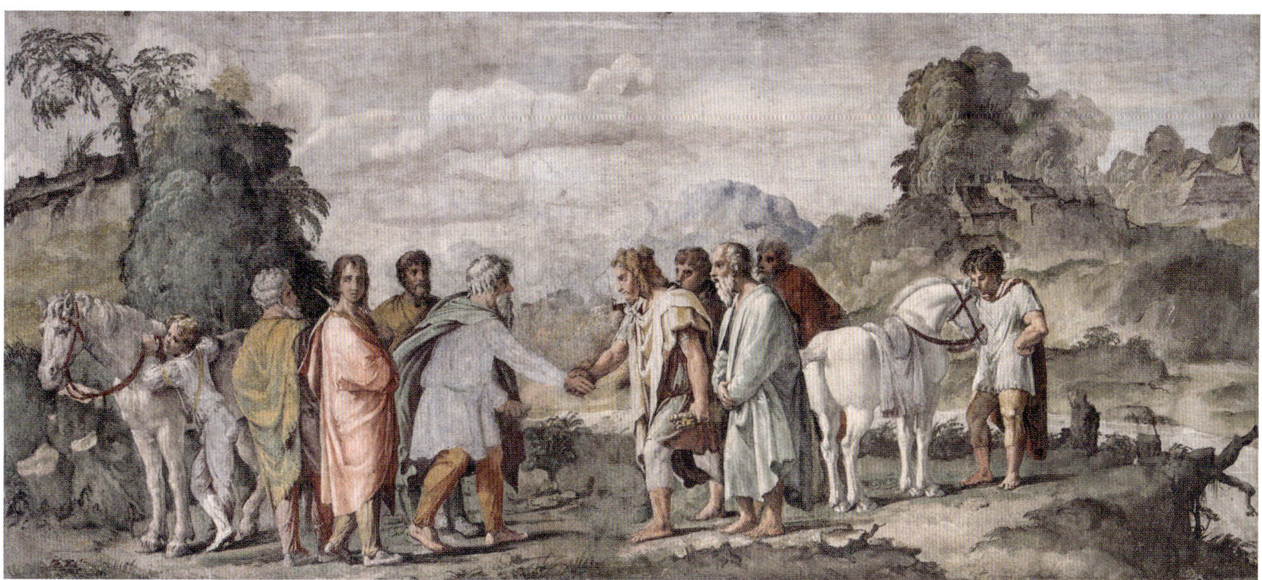

1.4 Workshop of Giulio Romano, *The Meeting of Janus and Saturn*. Fresco. Bibliotheca Hertziana, Rome

of the Villa Lante frescoes as executed seem foreign to Polidoro's bolder sensibility. Even if Polidoro occasionally collaborated with Raphael's followers as a designer after 1520, as this example attests, he was already independent by this date. Polidoro would have been emulating Raphael's own practice in distributing drawings to other artists. This particular case, which at first glance seems definitive because of the relation between drawing and painting, is symbolic of the challenge in unravelling Polidoro's ties to Raphael's workshop.

The earliest surviving independent works by Polidoro that we can consider documented are the frescoes in a front room on the second floor of the grand palace of Melchiorre Baldassini at Via delle Coppelle, 35, now the Istituto Luigi Sturzo.[18] This is where an examination of Polidoro's art truly commences. While less typical of his overall Roman production for being an interior and painted in colour, this cycle offers a better idea of Polidoro's earlier style than any of the very few surviving exterior facade frescoes, which are all in yet poorer states of preservation, where still extant. These paintings can be attributed to Polidoro based in part on a brief passage in Vasari's life of the artist stating that he worked both on the interior and exterior of this palace near the church of Sant'Agostino.[19] In part because the citation does not include any titles for the ten narrative frescoes, their subject matter remains somewhat mysterious, even if the attribution to Polidoro is secure enough.

In the case of a private commission for a palace interior one can assume that it was commenced prior to the death of the patron, the distinguished university professor of civil law and consistorial lawyer from Naples, Melchiorre Baldassini, who was employed by Popes Leo X and Adrian VI. The subject matter of the external frescoes was no doubt important for presenting the image of a donor with aspirations to a Roman lineage not actually present in his genealogy. Indeed, the arcane nature of the subjects seems an almost over-extravagant attempt to demonstrate this in an erudite way that few, if any but the patron, could have fully understood. Based on a reading of a census document of 1517–18, Christoph Frommel hypothesised that the palace, which Pietro Bembo memorably described as the 'la più bella e meglio fatta che sia in Roma', was built according to the designs of the Florentine architect Antonio da Sangallo the Younger in the period 1516–19.[20]

(As a compelling aside, the palace was later acquired by Giovanni della Casa, who owned the Rosso Fiorentino painting of the dead Christ, *Pietà with Four Angels*, now in the Museum of Fine Arts, Boston.) The construction was certainly completed by July 1522 when Baldassini made reference to his new palace and 'studio' in his will.[21] And so the frescoes must have been executed sometime within a six-year period between about 1519 and the patron's death in 1525. A date in the early 1520s, however, would fit with the chronology of Vasari's life of Polidoro, placing the work among his first independent efforts. It is just possible therefore that the patron had Raphael in mind for supervising the entire painted decoration, but with his death it had to be realised by major followers all active in the Loggia as well, including Giovanni da Udine, Perino del Vaga and Polidoro. In any case, the painted work in the Baldassini palace can be understood as a direct extension of the Vatican Stanze after Raphael's death.

The decoration of a medium-sized room with a wooden ceiling, possibly the patron's study, is the only extant work at Palazzo Baldassini attributable to Polidoro (figs 1.5–1.14). The room is located next to the main reception space, which was painted with ancient subjects by Perino alone in the same period: the *Judgement of Zaleucus* and *Tarquinius Priscus and the Augur Attius Navius*. Found towards the middle of the palace front, the position of Polidoro's work protected it somewhat from the damage even more obviously suffered by Perino's frescoes in a larger room of the *piano nobile* on an exposed corner of the building. Still, Polidoro's murals also deteriorated – the skies on one long wall had turned black, which one assumes was not the original intent – but have since been fully restored. Unlike Perino's frescoes they were never removed from the walls. The only natural light falls from the pair of windows on the facade wall. On the two shorter walls the projecting beams are real while the others are fictive, although some of the framing elements have been completely repainted. The two scenes on the interior facade and the two on the opposite surface feature a pair of putti with the Baldassini coat of arms containing golden eagles and griffins with three black bands. Each of the longer side walls has three separate scenes, making a total of ten narratives for the entire room.

The unusual subject matter of the Baldassini frescoes may never receive full elucidation but, as supported by our

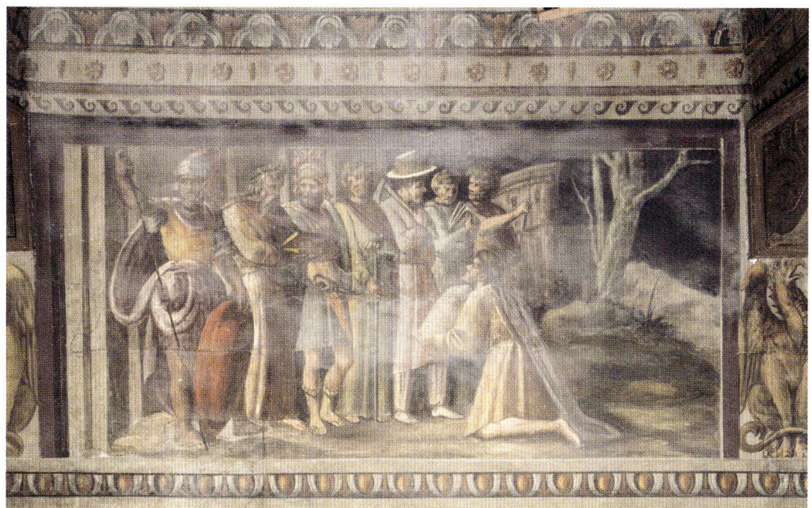

1.5

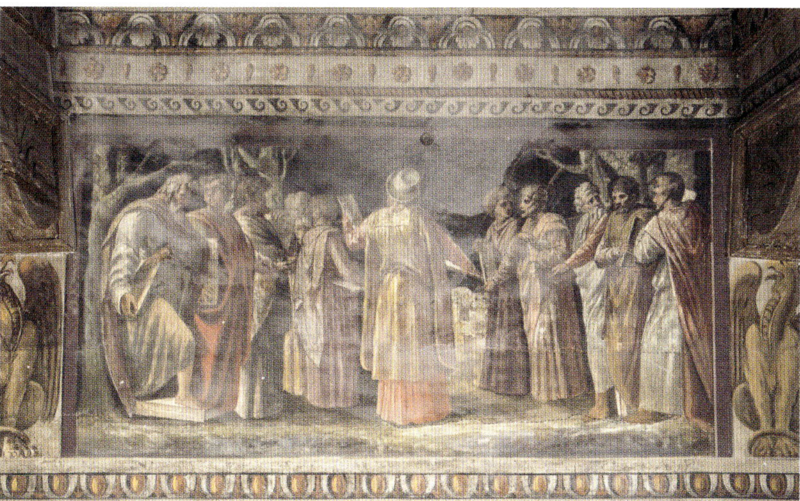

1.6

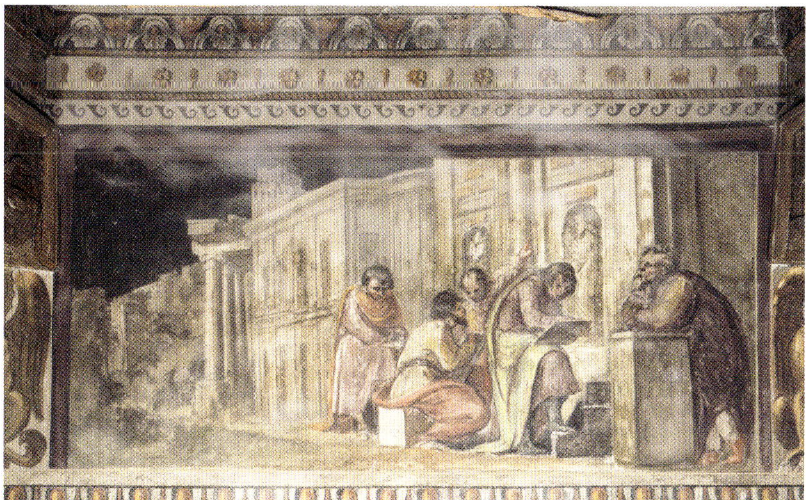

1.7

ABOVE AND PAGES 20–22: 1.5–1.14 Various ancient scenes. Frescoes. Palazzo Baldassini, Rome

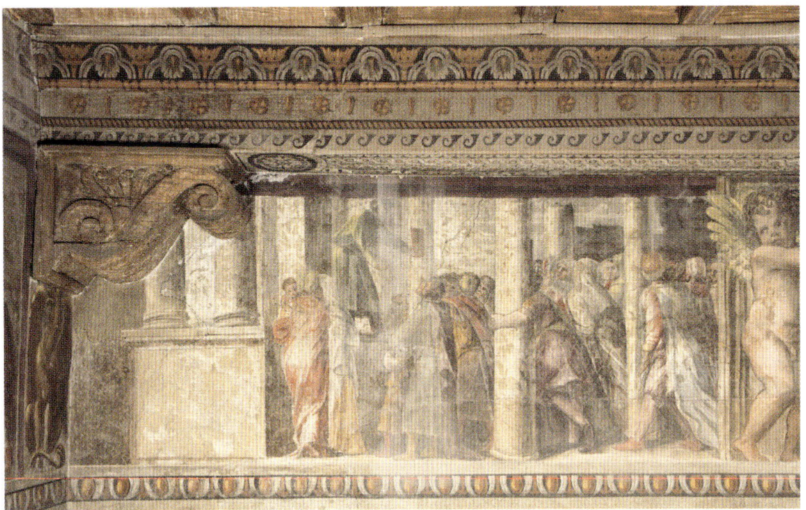

1.8

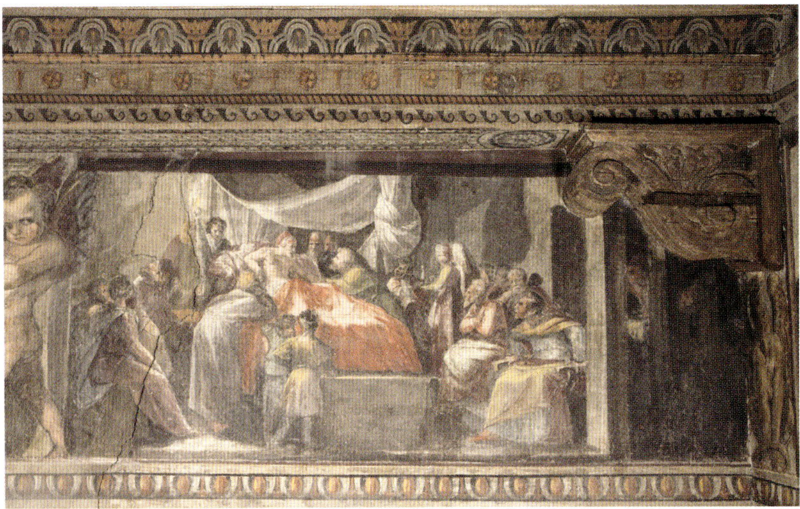

1.9

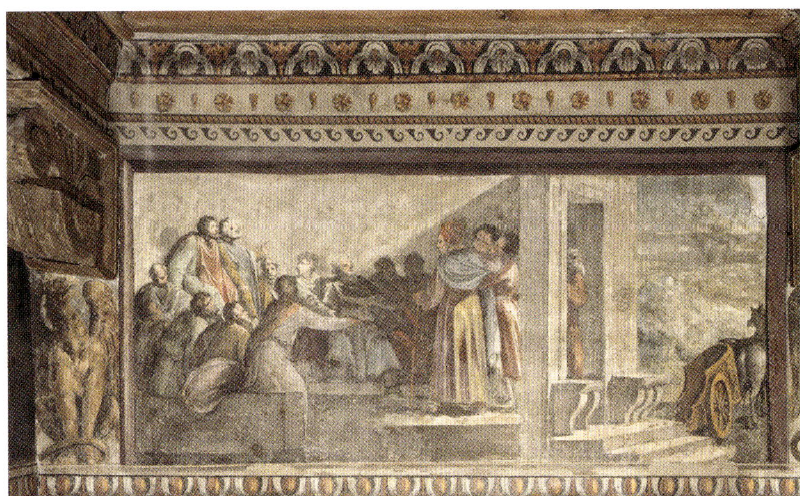

1.10

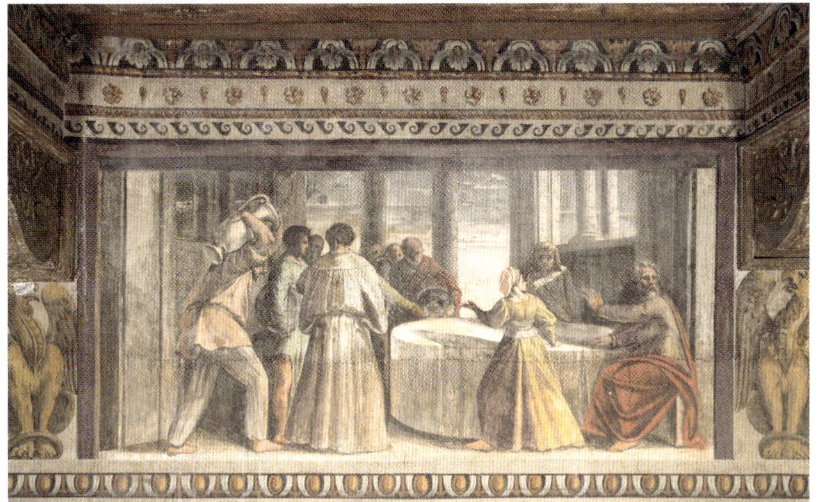

1.11

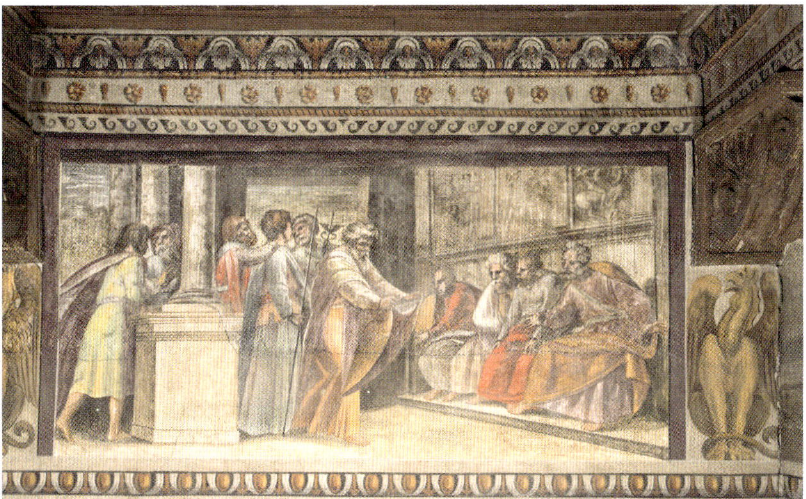

1.12

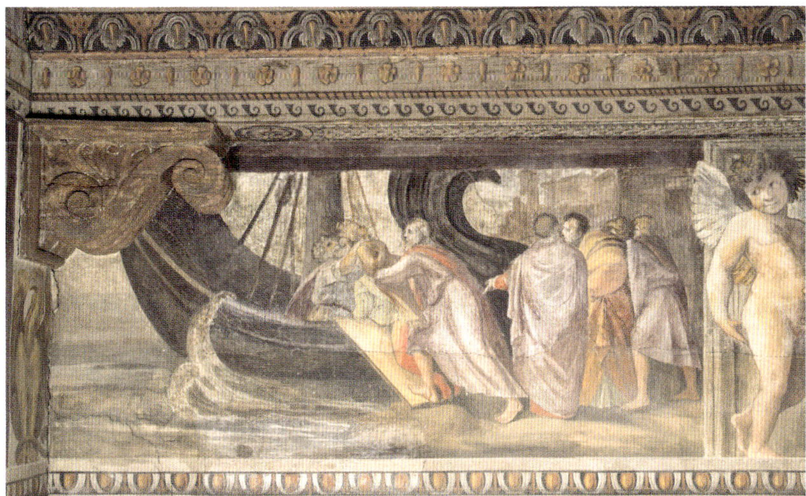

1.13

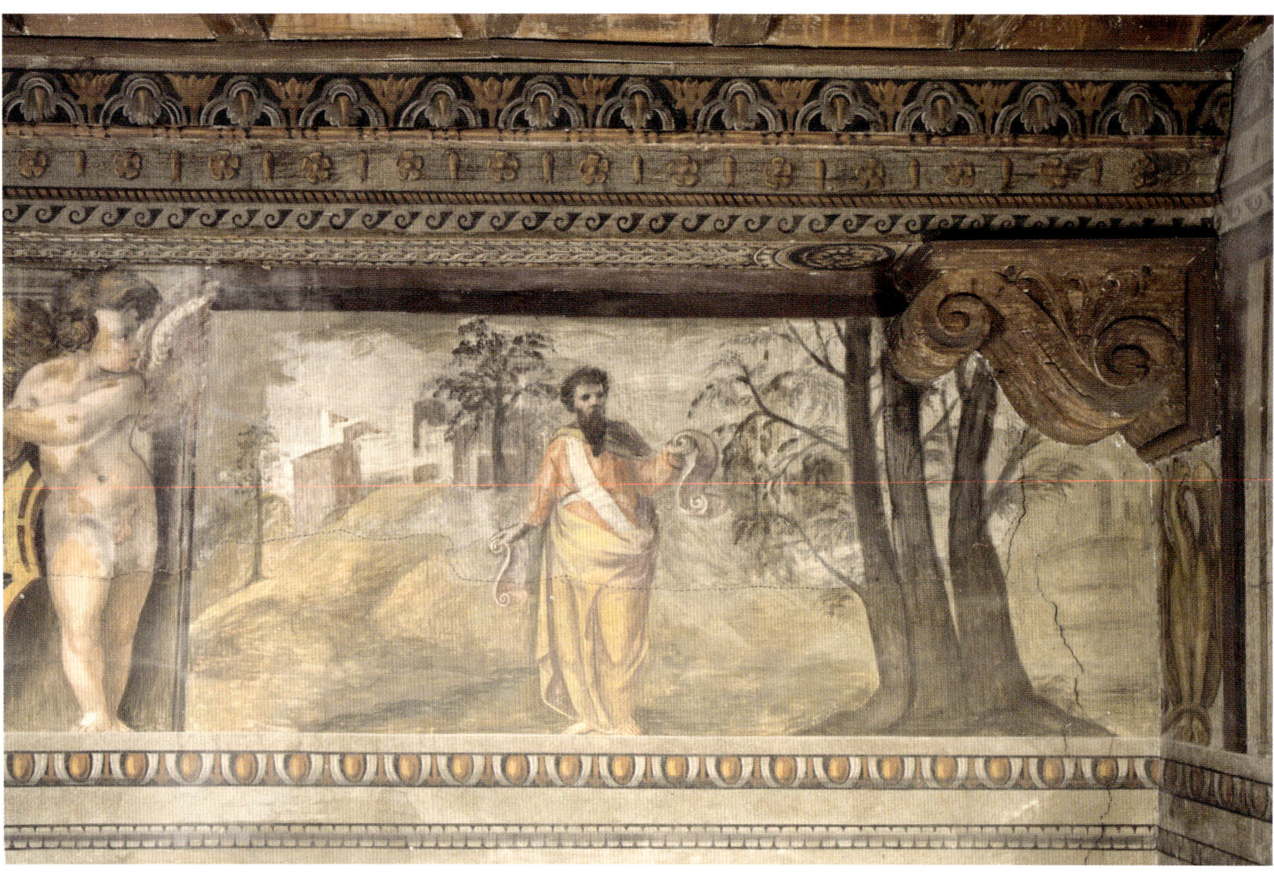

1.14

knowledge of the patron's biography, it is evident they depict various stories from the ancients illustrating the evolution of Roman law, as in a visual compendium. Some subject choices are clearly unique and without precedent, or apparent legacy, in the history of art, thus requiring considerable formal invention on the part of the artist. This degree of fearless ambition that artists emerging from Raphael's orbit felt in expressing original narratives is worth stressing in itself. As Linda Wolk-Simon has pointed out, Livy in his *Ab Urbe Condita* described how a group of ten citizens were responsible for bringing the law of the Twelve Tables, the basis of the law of the Roman Republic, to Rome from Greece and this may be illustrated in the one fresco in which a tablet is presented before the Roman citizenry, represented by seven different types (fig. 1.5).[22] A second scene appears to feature the distribution of the Twelve Tables among various ancient jurists (fig. 1.6). As these laws derived from the Athenian Solon, he is likely the single bearded figure holding scrolls represented in yet another field (fig. 1.14). There is also a deathbed vignette sometimes identified as the *Death of Socrates* or the *Death*

of Pericles (fig. 1.9), which Wolk-Simon has instead proposed might depict the last testament of the Greek Spartan king Eudamidas, as told by Lucian in his *Toxaris: A Dialogue of Friendship*.[23] The only drawing by Polidoro surviving for this decoration relates to this fresco, a double-sided red chalk compositional sheet in Washington (fig. 1.15).[24] Rapidly drawn, the principal sketch on the recto reveals the U-shaped design with an open centre with great clarity, but also gives a richer sense of the charged emotional quality of the image than the extant fresco, compromised by poor condition. Because of its pedagogical subject matter, it is tantalising to link a red chalk drawing of academics occupied in a disputation, now in Lille (fig. 1.16), to the Baldassini decorations (fig. 1.7), even if the composition seems too expansive for the small fields in the palace. The composition combines references to Raphael's famous fresco in the Vatican Stanze with the electric vigour of the Stanza d'Eliodoro, reminding us where Polidoro was drawing ideas from for the Baldassini frescoes.[25] To continue: the scene of an embarking ship onto which figures carry a statue, possibly that of the

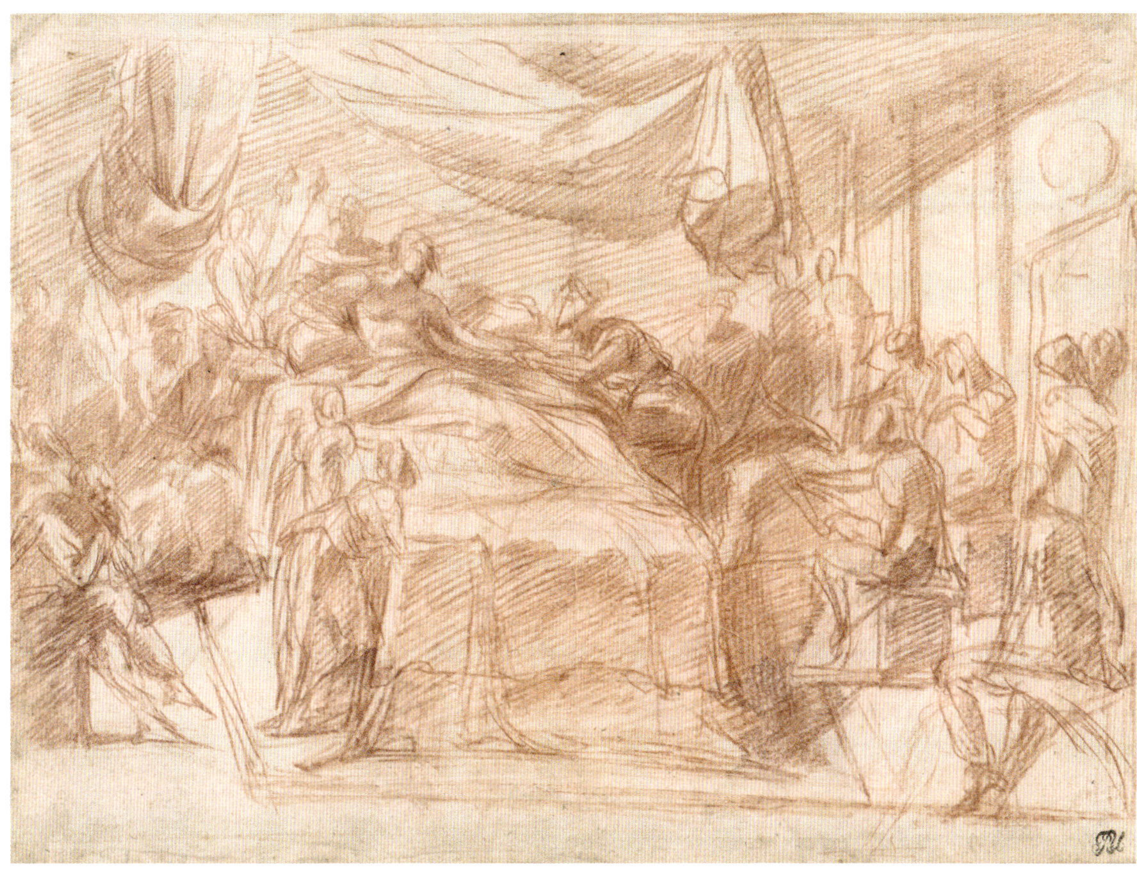

1.15 *Deathbed Scene*. Red chalk on laid paper, 21 × 29 cm. National Gallery of Art, Washington, DC

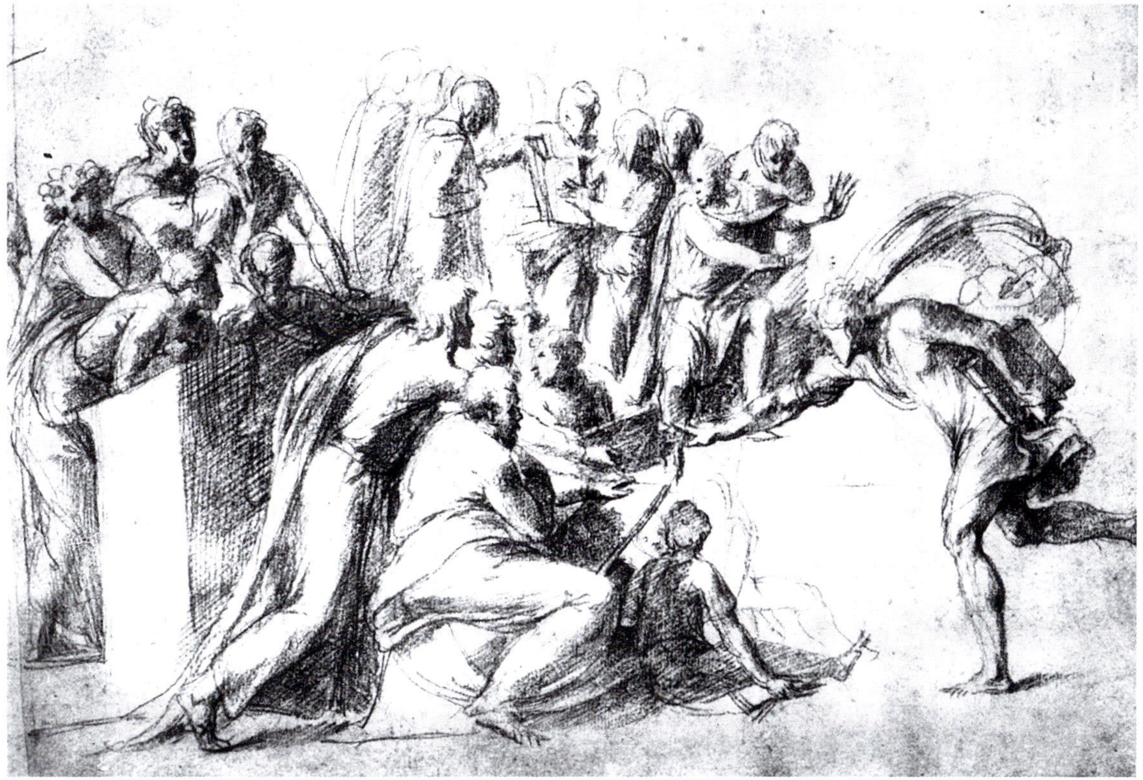

1.16 *Disputation Scene*. Red chalk on laid paper, 18.1 × 27 cm. Musée des Beaux-Arts, Lille

mother goddess Cybele being transported to Rome from Pergamum, is also related by Livy, as suggested by Maria Celeste Cola (fig. 1.13).[26] Beyond these four frescoes it becomes even more speculative but the core subjects that seem to stress the public, societal nature of law can be described. For example, a figure in one fresco holds up a drapery, apparently some form of ancient proof, before a panel of four judges (fig. 1.12). There is a banquet scene during which a figure reacts suddenly to something outside the space (fig. 1.11); an image with a chariot possibly heralding a journey (fig. 1.10); one with an orator speaking before a crowd (fig. 1.8); and a representation of a group of students with a rather distracted instructor (fig. 1.7).

In formal terms the Baldassini frescoes are comparable to those in the Vatican Loggia, with the stress on variety, density and circulatory designs, populated with sturdy figurines. The exception is the field containing the single male with a long dark beard, perhaps Solon as has been suggested, standing precariously on the edge of the space. Those scenes furthest from the window seem to be of higher quality and feature more elaborate designs, indicating perhaps that Polidoro left the work on the interior facade wall to assistants, anticipating that those frescoes would perish the most rapidly, although again the poor state of preservation does not allow for a definitive formal analysis of any part.

Polidoro's paintings are distinguished by an unembellished directness and intensity, differentiating them from the work of other artists inspired by Raphael. By contrast, Perino's Baldassini frescoes are more sedate and purified. Polidoro's frescoes display a powerful treatment of light that is equally unusual, like a seared twilight against pale, scoured skies, as is the bold, polychromatic colour scheme.

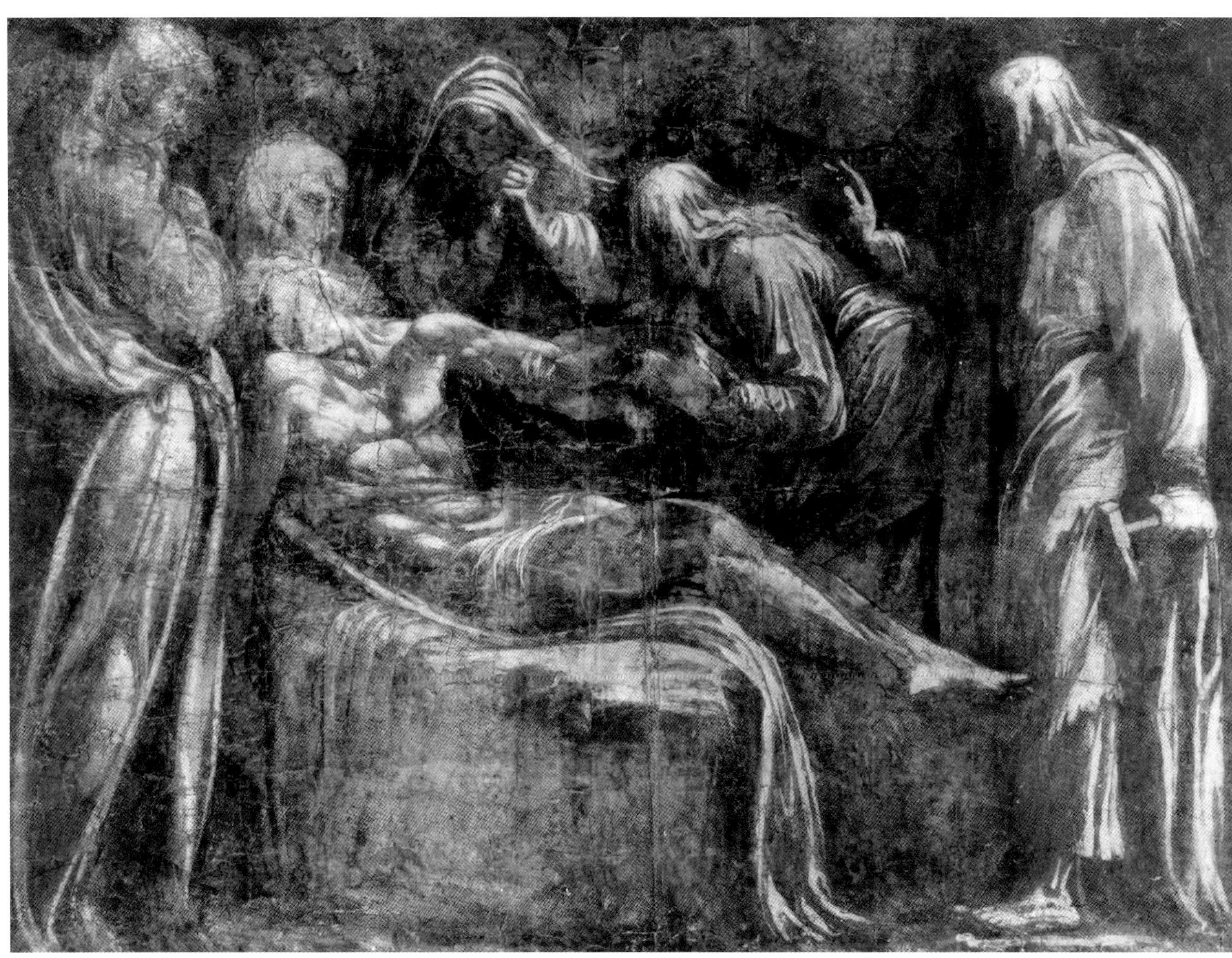

1.17 *Pietà*. Brush drawing in brown washes, heightened with white on two sheets of vertically joined paper, some pricking, 55 × 76 cm. British Museum, London

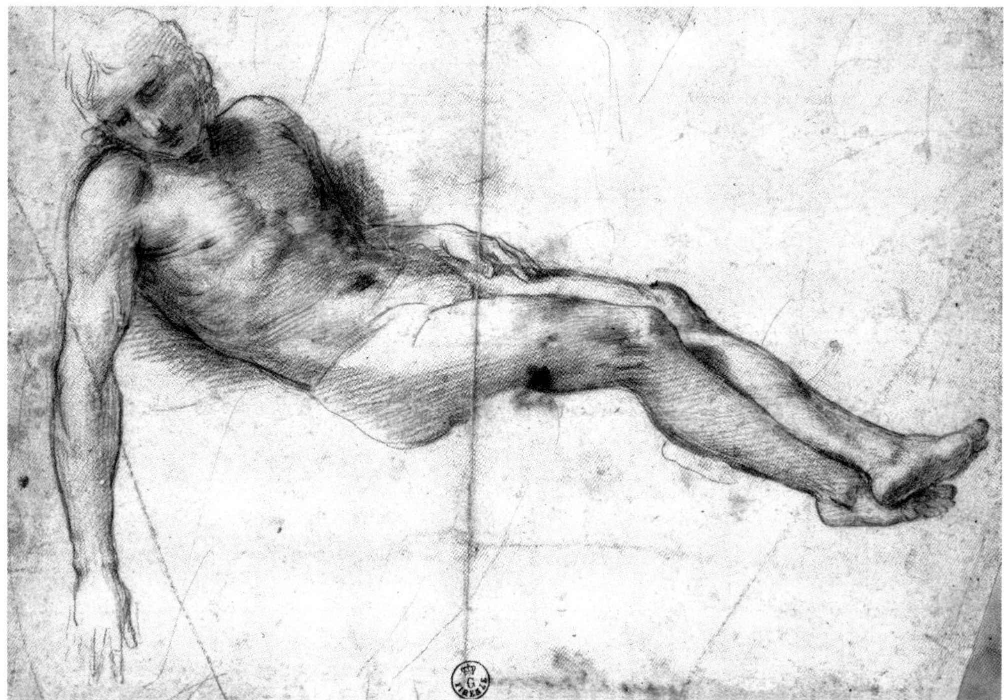

1.18 *Male Nude*. Red chalk, stylus and traces of black chalk on laid paper, 15.5 × 22.4 cm. Gabinetto Disegni e Stampe degli Uffizi, Florence

Again, they allow us to appreciate the strength of relief that the facades in Rome must originally have had. Polidoro's style, from the evidence of Palazzo Baldassini, already seems surprisingly distant from Raphael's not long after his death, and makes one further question how close it ever was. Polidoro's preference for monochrome is exposed in the dominant grey architectural backdrops – the neutral ground on top of which he introduced a palette of scintillating colours. The chariot scene is especially effective, with a dramatic spotlight quality that anticipates early seventeenth-century painting in Rome, like that of another Caravaggio in the Contarelli chapel in San Luigi dei Francesi (located not far from this palace, incidentally).

One other collaborative work from this earlier Roman period is Polidoro's contribution to the Martelli altar featuring Jacopo Sansovino's sculpture of the *Virgin and Child* in the church of Sant'Agostino, only a few paces from Palazzo Baldassini.[27] Documents for the entire commission indicate a date from 1516, with the principal sculpture, the so-called *Madonna del Parto*, visible only by 1521. Like the sculptor, the Martelli traced their origins to Tuscany, which would account for his selection as principal artist. It was presumably Sansovino who then subcontracted the painting in the chapel to the Lombard

Polidoro in the manner of a patron, not least because the ostensible commissioner of the entire complex, Giovan Francesco Martelli, was already dead. Presumably with Raphael's painting of Isaiah accompanied by two muscular children in the same church in mind, Vasari made a point of being scathingly critical of the now destroyed putti holding a cloth of honour that Polidoro frescoed in colour in the highest part of the Martelli chapel. The writer did, however, praise a *pietà*, one assumes painted by Polidoro in his more adept monochrome technique, for which a scale drawing survives in the British Museum (fig. 1.17), likely an earlier effort produced contemporaneously with the installation of Sansovino's marble.[28] It must have served as an altar frontal. The attribute of a hammer (*martello*) held by the figure at the right alludes to the patron's family name. It is an auxiliary cartoon on two sheets of joined paper, the contours pricked during the execution, but rather miraculously preserved given its partly functional nature. Any background has been lost and a few figures survive only as pricking. The handling appears rough, even considering the damage, and certain areas are merely thick washes, although some white heightening survives in a thinly varied application. The box-like design is highly structured, with the two outside figures turned inwards to frame the action. The elongated pose of Christ is more elegant than usual for Polidoro, which can be explained in part by its source in an ancient model – the *Bed of Polyclitus*, as supported by an attractively silken drawing in the Uffizi (fig. 1.18).[29] Formerly attributed to Raphael, Rosso and Jacopo Pontormo, until Philip Pouncey recognised its true paternity, the drawing studies the figure alone in a feathery red chalk handled nervously but to a shimmering finish. The broader composition is hinted at by only a few schematic lines above and below the body. The soothingly graceful emotion recalls Raphael's style almost more than any other Polidoro image.

It is documented that Polidoro travelled to Naples sometime before March 1524, where he worked to his strengths and painted a facade and loggia with motifs specifically based on the Column of Trajan, according to the local humanist Pietro Summonte in an informative letter to the Venetian connoisseur Marcantonio Michiel.[30] More specifically, Polidoro likely went there as early as 1522, after the election of the austere, reform-minded Fleming Adrian VI to the papacy in January of that year – an event that, combined with a plague, motivated many artists to abandon Rome temporarily to seek employment elsewhere. The fact of this solitary visit south is especially telling because it implies an independence from the surviving members of Raphael's workshop already by that date, and a definite cleavage. This sojourn away from Rome may be paralleled with Perino's visit to Florence at the same time, although whether Polidoro caused the same polemic among artists in Naples as his colleague did in Florence by very publicly importing the latest foreign style is not recorded, but seems unlikely considering the warm reception he later received. Nothing Polidoro might have produced there can be identified with certainty but the visit is nonetheless significant as he was to return to Naples later, and it foreshadows a yet more challenging time in his life. Why he went to Naples in particular may well be traced to Baldassini, who was born there, and could have provided key introductions.

Polidoro and Perino returned to Rome, like so many other artists, with the cessation of plague and the election in November 1523 of the new pope, Clement VII, following the death of Adrian VI that September. The opportunities in Rome had improved markedly, if only elusively as it

transpired, with the appointment of a Medici pope and the upcoming Jubilee in 1525. It was a hopeful, even buoyant moment promising a new Golden Age, harkening back to the glorious papacies of Julius II and Leo X. Ironically, Giulio Romano's departure around that point from Rome to Mantua symbolically signalled the collapse of the initial powerful wave of Raphael's legacy and also allowed others to achieve prominence, at least temporarily. An abundance of talented artists arrived in Rome, some for the first time, including many Tuscans attracted by the Florentine pope, such as Benvenuto Cellini and Rosso, while Parmigianino came from his native Emilia – but all had limited if any official success during this period of real crisis in Rome. Polidoro at least enjoyed serious glimpses of it.

Polidoro sustained his career during this competitive period largely by continuing to fresco palace facades, but he did take on a few other commissions. One rare fixed point is a papal commission for three ovals depicting the Passion of Christ, executed in rock crystal (and signed) by Valerio Belli, a specialist carver in glass from Vicenza, and now preserved in the Museo Sacro of the Vatican (fig. 1.19). It has been reasonably assumed that these engraved crystal intaglios were produced as part of the base of a glass crucifix ordered by Pope Clement VII, and described by Vasari as a 'croce di cristallo divina'.[31] Payments to Belli of the astronomical sum of 1,111 ducats survive for this work of 1524–5, thus the date of the drawing is reasonably secure.

Only one preparatory sketch by Polidoro has been identified for this expensive order, but it is among his most spectacular drawings of any period. Preserved at Windsor Castle (fig. 1.20), it represents the entire composition of the *Betrayal of Christ*, a story told in all four Gospels.[32] The other subjects depicted on this luxury object are Christ Carrying the Cross and the Entombment, likely all designed by Polidoro, even if graphic evidence is lacking. The Windsor sheet is drawn in brush with brown and grey washes, with added white heightening, on a prepared dark blue paper. It presumably served as a *modello* – the final drawing made for the glass – as it is so complete, even if, not surprisingly given the inherent intricacy of carving on crystal, the finished work is more restrained in style. It provides an example of Polidoro's richest and most elaborate graphic technique, prior to the Sack of Rome in May 1527. The glass medium may have inspired the especially dense graphic approach. Formerly

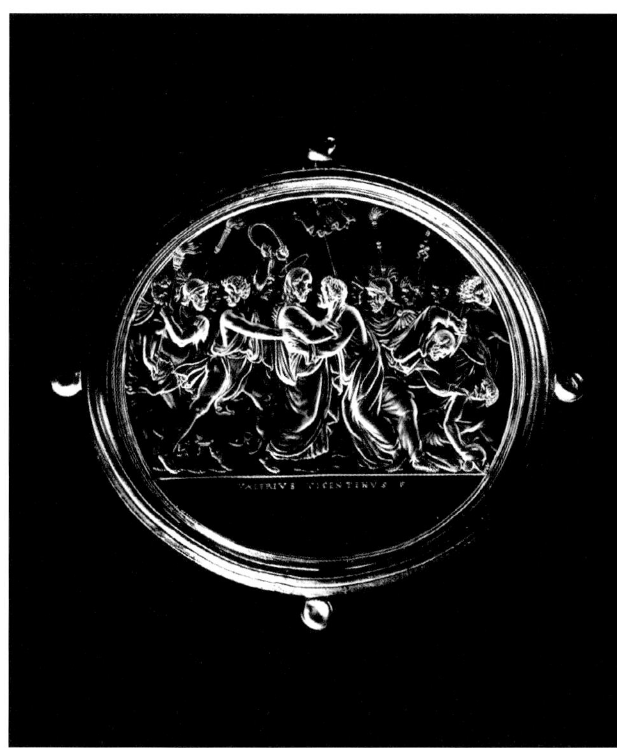

1.19 Valerio Belli, *Betrayal of Christ*. Rock crystal, 11.5 × 12.5 cm (oval). Museo Sacro, Vatican

attributed to the Ferrarese artist Benvenuto Garofalo, and once owned by the eighteenth-century British watercolourist Paul Sandby, the drawing's attribution to Polidoro, first proposed by Frederick Antal, is convincing, although surprisingly it has not always been accepted. The vivacious, rather suffocating and staccato design, peopled with agitated, muscular figures, is typical of the artist. For dramatic purposes, Christ, who blesses his betrayer as the rope descends around his neck, is placed just off the central axis. The handling of the heightening in thin, ragged lines is distinctive to Polidoro, as are the stumpy figures with dishevelled hair and triangular faces. Notable, too, are the internal light sources, which indicate that this is a night scene and account for the dark paper. This taste for nocturnal representations was increasingly prevalent among Polidoro's contemporaries in Rome during the period – it was by then an ostentatious artistic trope – and specifically this example recalls Raphael's bold experiments in various parts of the Vatican Stanze, such as the *Liberation of Saint Peter*. The youth looking out towards the viewer at the far right edge is also a quotation from

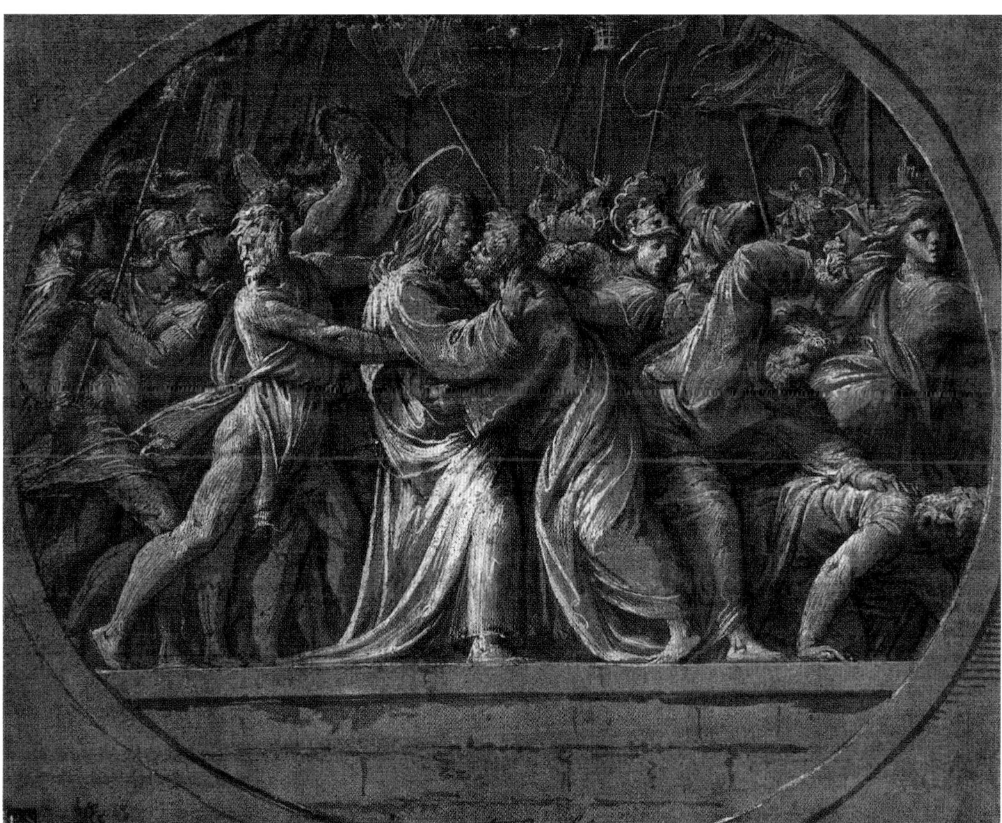

1.20 *Betrayal of Christ*. Pen and brown ink, and brown and grey washes, with white heightening on blue prepared paper, 21.2 × 26.3 cm. Royal Collection, Windsor Castle

Raphael. Given that the glass crucifix was a papal commission, the partial dependence on Raphael, an artist who operated so successfully in the Vatican, may have a strategic purpose rather than forming an explicit homage.

Polidoro did not only receive commissions in Rome to paint subjects from ancient history and mythology. One ecclesiastical assignment, mentioned by Vasari, in a small chapel to the right in the church of Sant'Eustachio remains mysterious, frustratingly so as extant drawings, doubtless made for it, exist in Polidoro's corpus but cannot yet be associated with it.[33] What do survive are decorations for the chapel of Fra Mariano Fetti in the church of San Silvestro a Monte Cavallo, later 'al Quirinale', controlled by the Dominicans since 1507 thanks to Pope Julius II, and partly renovated under Fetti's supervision, apparently concluded in 1524.[34] Born in Florence in 1460 (later dying in Rome in 1531), Fra Mariano Fetti was a notorious wit and confidante of the Medici popes – one of the great complex and contradictory personalities of the age, who received an admirable mention in the first volume of Castiglione's *Book of the Courtier* (1528). With the death of the architect Donato Bramante, Leo X made him *piombatore*, keeper of the papal seal, a distinguished charge that required him to become a member of the Cistercian Order, although he remained at the more hospitable San Silvestro al Quirinale.

To judge on the basis of its confident style it seems this chapel (fig. 1.21) was decorated after the artist's return from his first Naples sojourn, even as late as 1526 and into 1527. The project is not dated but some hitherto unnoticed payments in the papal accounts of 47 ducats in the summer of 1526 to a 'Polidoro', not identified by profession, may be linked to this commission as it is known that Clement VII supported Fra Mariano financially for expenses related to the church.[35] That the payments were distributed by no less a pivotal figure than the apostolic secretary Pier Polo Marzi further stresses the direct linkage to Clement. If this interpretation is correct, the document allows that this commission was not only an emulation of papal patronage on Fra Mariano's part, to display allegiance, but also a Medici papal direct initiative favouring one of Raphael's former students and providing a burial chapel for a loyal court celebrity. The resplendent tiled floor of the chapel, manufactured with Medici emblems by the Florentine sculptor Luca della Robbia the Younger, was

even given to Fra Mariano by Pope Leo X, unused remnants apparently from the Vatican Loggia. Yet the *piombatore* certainly approved of Polidoro's style and influenced his selection as, according to Vasari, he also decorated the patron's house and private garden with *cosette*, minor decorations, now lost.[36] In this area of the garden, later praised for its splendour by no less a critic than Pietro Aretino, Fra Mariano commissioned the Sienese artist Baldassare Peruzzi in this same period to fresco the apparition of the Virgin and Child to the Cistercian saint Bernard of Clairvaux in a landscape predicated on a close canopy of trees, also lost but recorded in a print.[37] Fra Mariano had enjoyed cordial relations too with Raphael himself. The Frate owned the paintings of Saints Peter and Paul, now in the Vatican, initiated but abandoned in Rome by a fellow Dominican, Fra Bartolomeo, that Raphael apparently completed. These panels were eventually placed on the high altar of San Silvestro al Quirinale. That someone who admired Raphael's style would turn to this particular bottega assistant to execute major work is itself telling about the perception of Polidoro's high promise in Rome after 1520.

There is no evidence at any point in his career that, like Raphael or Giulio, Polidoro had higher social aspirations, but he did work for some of the greatest patrons of the period in Rome. Excepting the Vatican Loggia, Villa Lante frescoes and Belli glass crucifix, with all of which he was only partly involved, it was primarily through this commission for Fra Mariano that he approached the most elevated of papal circles. Not surprisingly, because of his more consistent preoccupation with facade frescoes, it was these that put Polidoro most often in the papal orbit.

At San Silvestro al Quirinale Polidoro revealed himself as a more adaptable painter, even if the chapel decoration was in fresco and so in harmony with his technical prowess. The saturated appearance of the paint and introduction of very dark pigments, even black, suggest that Polidoro introduced oil into the medium in a progressive, hybrid manner of fresco with which Raphael had also experimented in the Sala di Costantino just before his sudden death in 1520.[38] His willingness to go beyond the purity of traditional *buon fresco* reveals a sophisticated use of the medium also evident in the Roman facade paintings. Even more than the Baldassini frescoes, this chapel is essential for reconstructing the surfaces of the palace

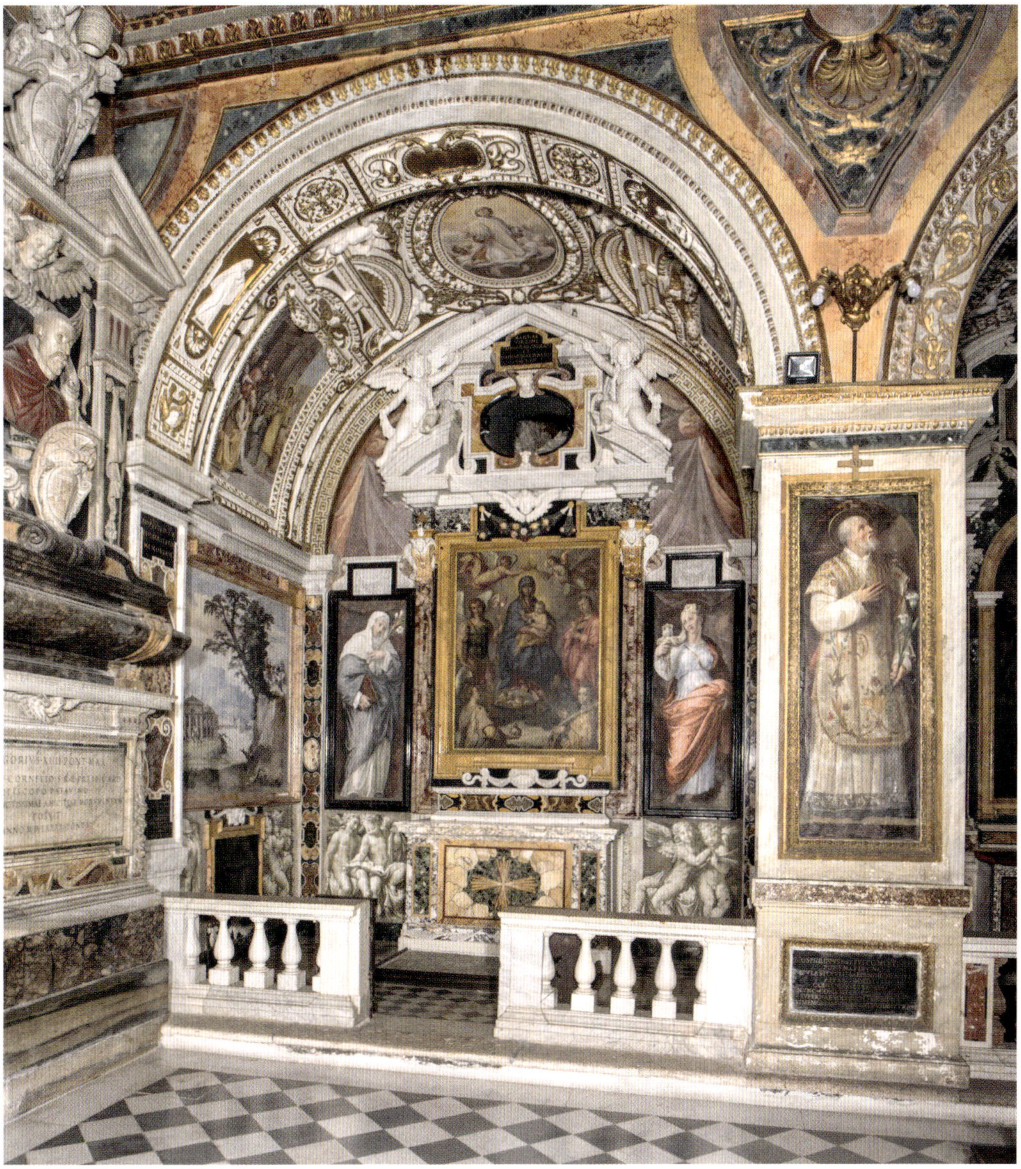

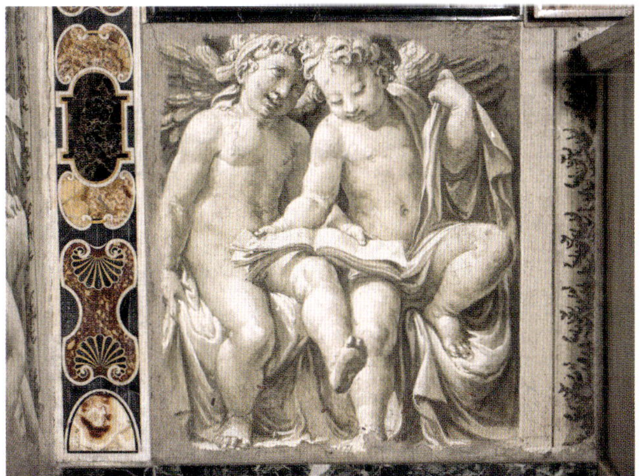
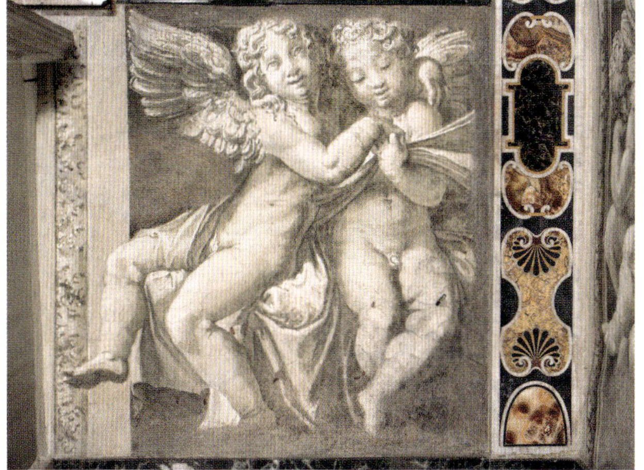

1.21 General view of the Fetti Chapel. Fresco. San Silvestro al Quirinale, Rome

1.22–1.23 Putti in the Fetti Chapel. Frescoes, each 103 × 71.3 cm. San Silvestro al Quirinale, Rome

facades that are, with a very few damaged exceptions, entirely lost, preserving as it does monumental examples of Polidoro's Roman frescoes, relatively easily viewed. Sadly, however, the San Silvestro al Quirinale frescoes are only slightly better preserved than those in Palazzo Baldassini and display extensive damage from moisture and repainting to judge by the dense, compacted surfaces.

The church originally had more chapels at the front, but when the street was lowered and enlarged in the nineteenth century this necessitated their destruction and the addition of a new facade, so Polidoro's chapel was not the first in order but the second. How subject the architectural fabric of this space was to the renovations of the site introduced by Fra Mariano is uncertain but Polidoro introduced novel elements into the decoration.

The chapel dedication was to Saint Catherine of Siena, according to Fra Mariano's will of 1529, so she presumably also featured in the lost altarpiece.[39] As the subject of the Mystic Marriage of Saint Catherine was depicted by Polidoro in a lateral fresco, the altarpiece was presumably a traditional *sacra conversazione* type with the Virgin and Christ Child and standing saints. To judge by an inscription dated 1518 there was an image of the Virgin somewhere in the chapel, perhaps a medieval icon, significant enough for Leo X to grant indulgences to any visitor, as recorded in this tablet.[40] The dedication was later changed to the Virgin Mary, according to the sale document of 1602, when rights to the chapel were acquired by Cardinal Jacopo Sannesio and the painting completed by Cavaliere d'Arpino.[41] The chapel is also

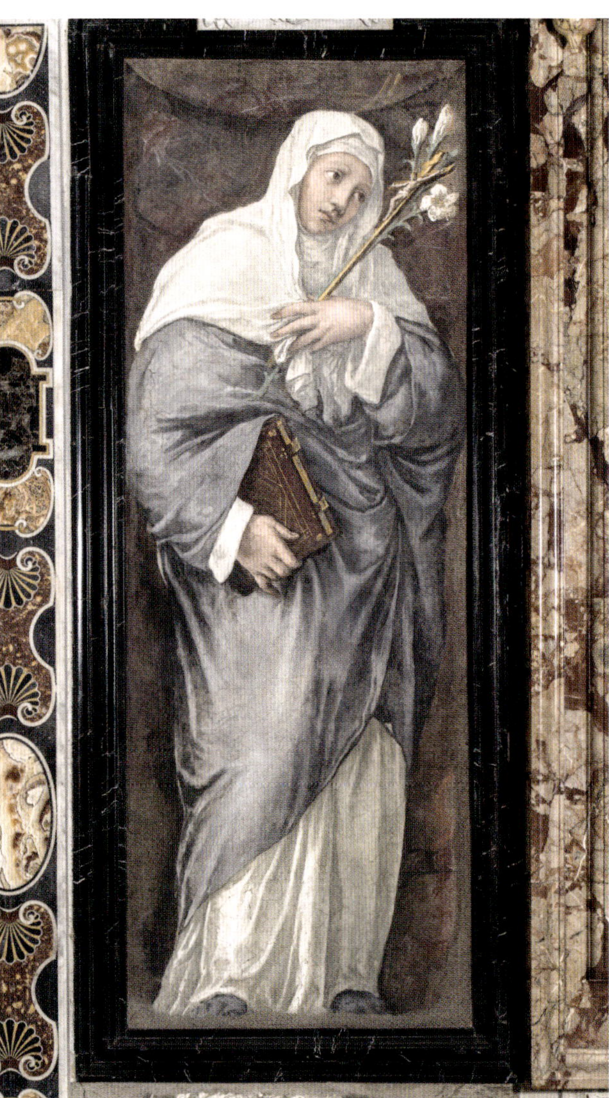
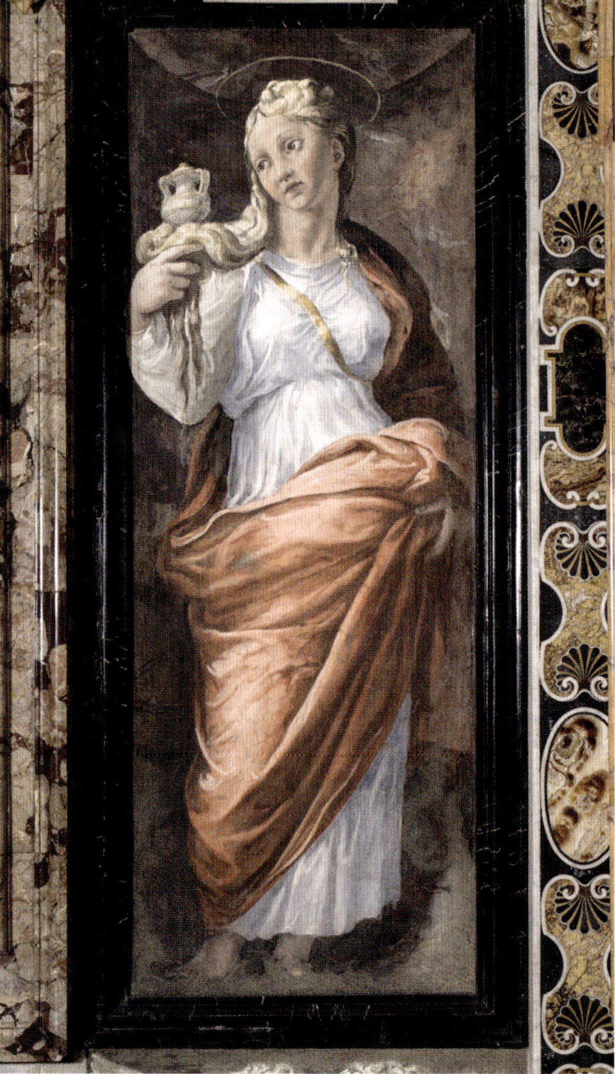

1.24–1.25 *Saint Catherine* and *Saint Mary Magdalen*. Frescoes, each approximately 165 × 60 cm. San Silvestro al Quirinale, Rome

considerably changed architecturally, with ostentatious marble cladding. The original altarpiece, now lost or unidentified, had already been painted by the Florentine artist and occasional partner of Fra Bartolomeo, Mariotto Albertinelli, according to Vasari's testimony.[42] Fra Mariano would have known well Fra Bartolomeo's interpretation of the theme of the Mystic Marriage in an altarpiece, now in Palazzo Pitti, painted for the church of San Marco in Florence. Polidoro was required to fresco the two saints on each side of the main field – Catherine of Siena to the viewer's left (fig. 1.24) and Mary Magdalen to the right (fig. 1.25), as well as two lateral murals with scenes from the lives of these protagonists, which have survived (figs 1.27 and 1.28). The space also features six pairs of life-size mourning but highly animated putti (see figs 1.22 and 1.23) in fictive square recesses in the lower register. Nude but seated on a drapery, one putto holds an extinguished torch, and a companion turns away in unbearable sadness, while others sing in unison from partbooks. Although grisaille elements are a traditional feature of chapels, these putti explicitly further evoke marble sculptures included on the exteriors of Roman chapels, often on the balustrades, as well as ancient sarcophagi that could include them in supporting roles, holding garlands, for example. Because of their subsidiary role the artist represented them with the greatest flexibility of poses in the entire decoration. Although painted in close proximity to the negative events of the Sack of Rome, it appears that Polidoro completed all the work required of him in this space, right down to the *basamento*.

Both saints direct their glances at the altar area. Catherine was included as a Dominican, reflecting the order controlling the church and the onomastic saint of the chapel. Her Tuscan origins would also have been meaningful to Fra Mariano, Pier Polo Marzi and Clement VII. Catherine further resonated with the papacy, as during her lifetime the future saint played a decisive role in its return from exile in Avignon to Rome during the period of the so-called Babylonian Captivity of the Papacy in the fourteenth century. The marble frame of the altarpiece and other surrounds, later added by Cardinal Sannesio, distort the appearance of the main chapel wall. The wall supports of the frescoes are buckling and their original edges were cropped, but the saints were depicted in shallow fictive niches in variegated dark marble. Although their poses are different, these thick-limbed, robust saints, life-sized and posed frontally, recall the female virtues flanking the narratives in the Sala di Costantino.

Dressed in her canonical black and white habit, Catherine brandishes her attribute of white lilies, along with a crucifix. The stem of the cross, twisted outwards, is placed directly over her heart, while in her right hand she elegantly holds a red book with more gilt detailing, partly protected by her drapery. Her body is weightless and animated as if she is swooning with emotion, and her head is elegantly inclined at a 45-degree angle to transmit an endearing state of tenderness and receptiveness.

The figure of Mary Magdalen is more monumental than Catherine, and she has a more irregular contour and outwardly expressive, even agitated emotional quality, approaching pathos in an antique manner. With an almost uncomfortably twisted hand the Magdalen holds her attribute, an ointment jar, among the rope-like tresses of her hair. The abundant piece of red drapery wrapped around her body introduces an unstable element to the pose, but the strap holding it in place also reveals her sanctity because it is made of a precious gold. Her blue

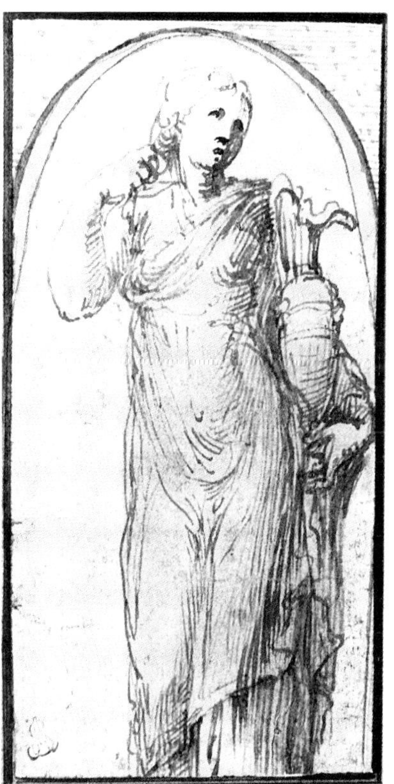

1.26 *Study for the Magdalen*. Pen and brown ink on laid paper, 11.2 × 5.8 cm. Albertina, Vienna

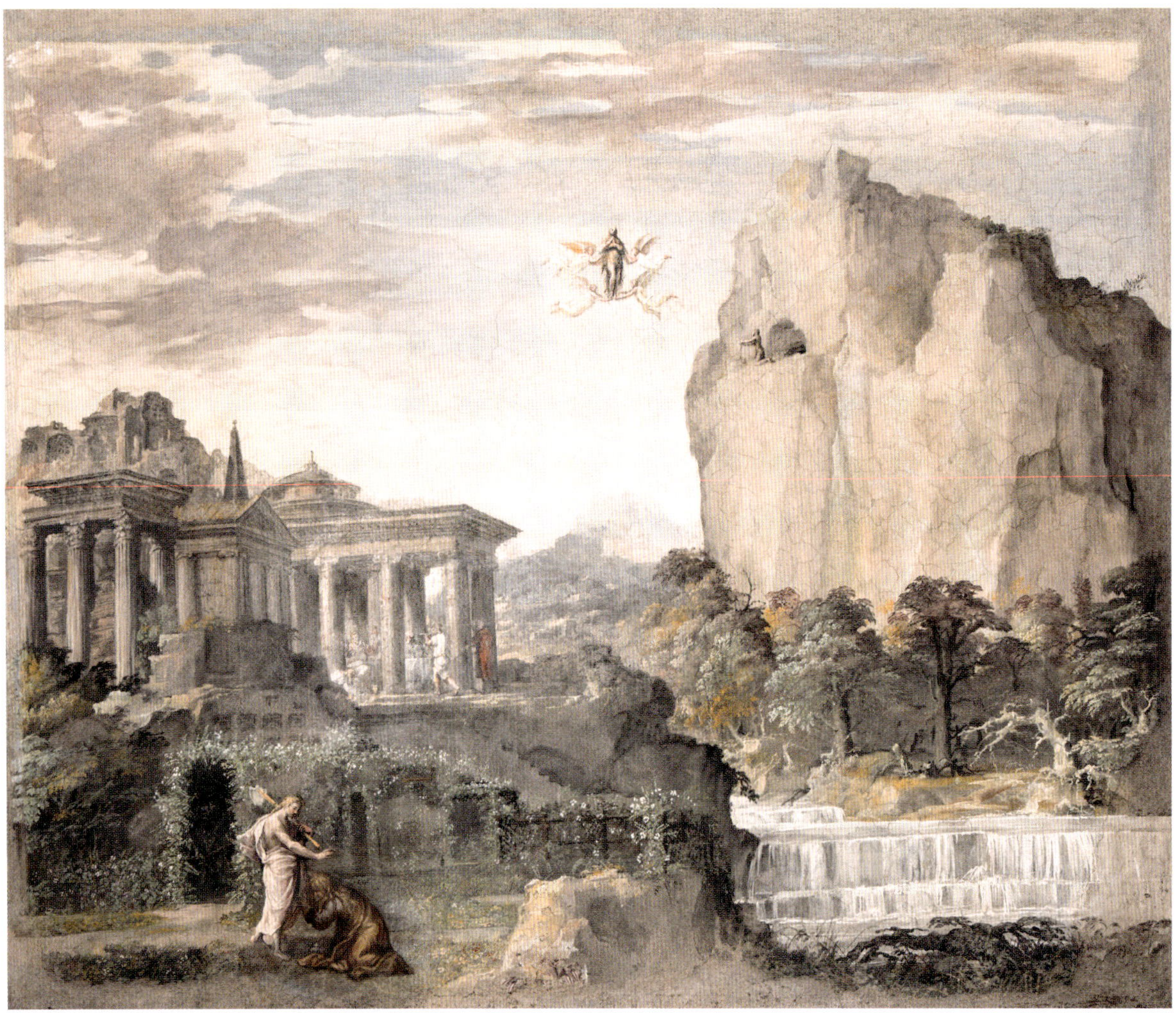

1.27 *Scenes from the Life of Saint Mary Magdalen*. Fresco, 165 × 205 cm. San Silvestro al Quirinale, Rome

tunic has the colour and texture of quartz. An exquisite pen and ink drawing in Vienna (fig. 1.26), possibly an early preparatory study for this figure, reveals a more sensuous, elegant side to Polidoro's depiction of women, rarely so explicit.[43] The motif of the woman holding her hair, an allusion to the washing of Christ's feet, is more accentuated here than in the fresco.

Like the two saints, the compositions of both narrative scenes are accented towards the altar end of the chapel. The introduction of supporting *storie*, or narratives, frescoed and framed on the side walls, is a lateral format that was to become common in Roman churches well into the seventeenth century. This is not only one of the first examples but also one of the most original for the inverse stress on landscape at the expense of the figures. The fresco with stories from the life of Mary Magdalen (fig. 1.27) features three discrete subjects: the Noli Me Tangere in the immediate foreground, the Magdalen Anointing Christ's Feet in the House of Simon the Pharisee in the middle ground and the Death and Assumption of the saint in the upper centre.[44] The scenes are treated on different scales and levels in the pictorial field and the order of events is not sequential, so it can be presumed that the patron requested that the more iconic scene of the Noli Me Tangere be represented the most prominently. The main protagonists appear in a cultivated bower with flowers resembling snowflakes, where Christ disguised as a gardener supporting a shovel on his shoulder stays the kneeling Magdalen with his right arm extending over her head. In this treatment they form a compact shape in the broad pictorial field as Christ faces the saint and blesses her like a supplicant before an altar. Her ointment jar appears again as an attribute. The figures tend still to be disposed outwards near to the picture plane, not absorbed

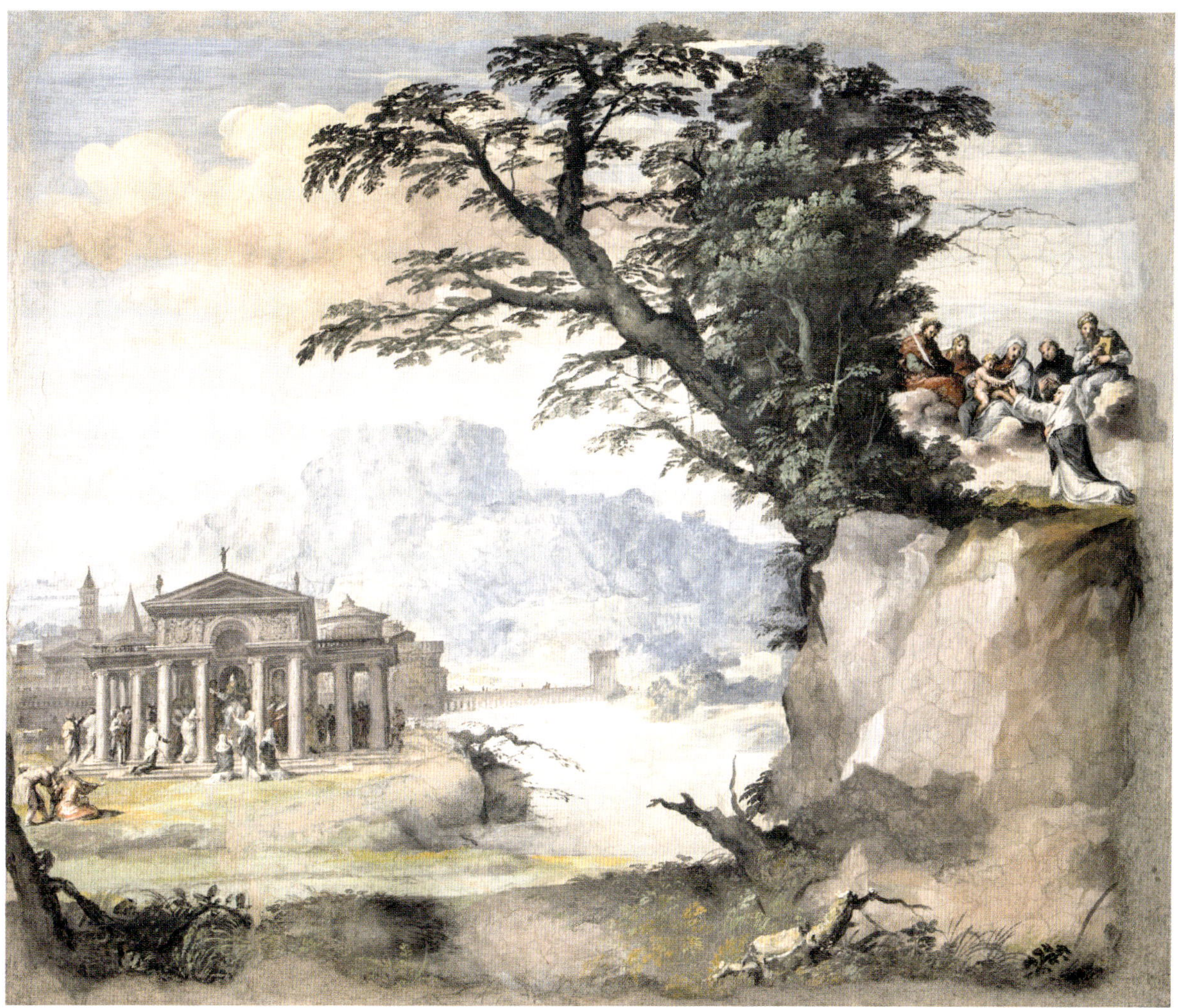

1.28 *Scenes from the Life of Saint Catherine of Siena*. Fresco, 165 × 205 cm. San Silvestro al Quirinale, Rome

by the landscape, and so Polidoro respected some traditional conventions in representing the religious subject matter. The image of the Magdalen washing and anointing Christ's feet with her sinner's tears and hair in the house of Simon the Pharisee is placed directly above in a sumptuous classical temple with marble columns. The presentation has the aspect of a theatre set with buildings arranged in profile, including semi-ruined structures behind. This fresco is particularly celebrated for the near complete dominance of landscape elements like the trees and prominent waterfall, which are as solid as the architecture and suggest a vision of nature not supported by direct observation but by pure fantasy and the impetus to create a beautiful design. The inclusion of the pyramid and obelisk betrays an element of antiquarian research inspired by Raphael and establishes the setting in ancient times contemporary with Christ in a general attempt at

historical reconstruction. Finally, at the top centre of the scene the tiny figure of the Magdalen with long dishevelled hair is assumed into heaven, assisted by the angels who attended her for many years. She apparently appears again, hermit-like and alone, outside a cave facing the sky and worshipping a tall thin cross near the summit of a formidable mountain – in Provence, according to her legend.

The narrative fresco relating to the Dominican saint Catherine of Siena (fig. 1.28) illustrates only two stories but shares with the other image of Mary Magdalen a structured organisation with clear spatial relationships. It is banded with the darkest forms in a wooded foreground area, with browns and oranges; a lighter middle ground with pale greens and yellows in a field, including a tranquil body of water with a toll bridge; and, lightest, the background with a pale blue mountain. A prominent tree on the rocky outcrop divides the picture space into two unequal halves.

The unnaturally sharp outlines that split the pictorial field are again reminiscent of flat screens on a stage set. Like its counterpart, the fresco is ethereal and contains a glimmering light over a mysterious horizon. The scene closest to the foreground features the Mystic Marriage of Saint Catherine to the Christ Child, with Mary and four additional seated figures, namely Saint Paul, a youthful John the Evangelist and Saint Dominic, and King David with a harp, two on each side. It was this spiritual encounter with Christ that inspired Caterina Benincasa, as she was then known, to devote herself to good works on behalf of the church. The other scene depicted here by Polidoro – the elaborate architecture in the middle ground, mirroring that of the Magdalen fresco – features Pope Urban VI receiving Saint Catherine in Rome in November 1378.[45] Polidoro is true to the textual authority, Blessed Raymond of Capua's life of the saint, also his source for the Mystic Marriage scene, in showing her accompanied by a number of devout followers on her pilgrimage to Rome. There she preached loyalty to the pope and his cardinals in the face of the Schism of the Catholic Church, a barely veiled contemporary reference, one assumes, to the rise of Protestantism in Germany. This was an uncommon subject for art and, not surprisingly, Vasari only specifically mentioned that the chapel included scenes from the biography of the Magdalen and did not appear to comprehend the Saint Catherine stories. The Medici coat of arms with the *palle* (balls) on the facade of the fictive architecture brings to mind the documents in which a 'Polidoro' is paid for an unidentified purpose related to this church in the papal accounts for 1526. With the production of so many facades taking place concurrently, as discussed in the next chapter, there was, inevitably, a concentration on Roman history and mythological subjects in Polidoro's corpus in Rome; and even where he engaged with religious themes, as in San Silvestro, the work is haunted by ancient spectres.

One of the most original aspects of the lateral frescoes in the San Silvestro chapel, as noted earlier, is the dominating landscape and the correspondingly diminished figure scale.[46] As often pointed out, both the style and stress in Polidoro's landscapes at once look back to antiquity and are prophetic of art of the later sixteenth century and beyond. Painters like Annibale Carracci and Domenichino attentively studied these walls to great profit. The inspiration

for this unusual approach to nature came less from the real world and more from a desire to recreate the tenor of antique art, providing the filter through which Polidoro saw his surroundings empirically. Polidoro was familiar with the few precious remains of ancient painting in and around Rome, especially the Golden House of Nero, but given how little survived and in what poor condition we must not neglect to ascribe this innovation in landscape representation to Polidoro too. The landscapes at San Silvestro are treated with considerable breadth and delicacy, very like the backgrounds in the later Stanze by Raphael in the Vatican, some of which were reprised in the Loggia. Although the condition of the frescoes is poor and compromised by restoration, it is still possible to appreciate Polidoro's virtuoso handling, with a fluency and freedom approximating wash drawing, but with denser areas as well.

There is little contemporary literary evidence for attitudes towards the representation of landscape at this time, but it was a skill commonly associated with Northern European painters throughout the sixteenth century, and for an Italian trained in Rome, Polidoro made a heterodox artistic choice with this emphasis in the Eternal City.[47] And yet to judge by Philostratus' *Imagines*, the ancients took pleasure in landscape in painting and so this taste could equally be regarded as antiquarian and in part inspired by classical literature. It does not seem necessary to believe that Northern artists such as Jan van Scorel passing fleetingly through Rome affected him, even if there is some logic to that proposal. In parallel to the religious subjects in Fra Mariano's chapel, a Polidoro drawing featuring a mythological subject from this period – the *Abduction of Ganymede* in the British Museum (fig. 1.29) – exhibits the same balance between diminutive figures and a prominent expansive landscape by blending contemporary architecture with classical ruins as in the San Silvestro narratives.[48] He did not differentiate in his innovative approach between religious and secular subjects. Polidoro's painted landscapes are not especially analytical or descriptive but imaginative and attractive, creating compellingly beautiful and dramatic views, always with a deep vista, and unconcerned with registering realistic effects. The artist's advanced skill at producing landscape upset the conventional balance between subject matter and setting, privileging the latter – the natural world. This would also indicate that he was

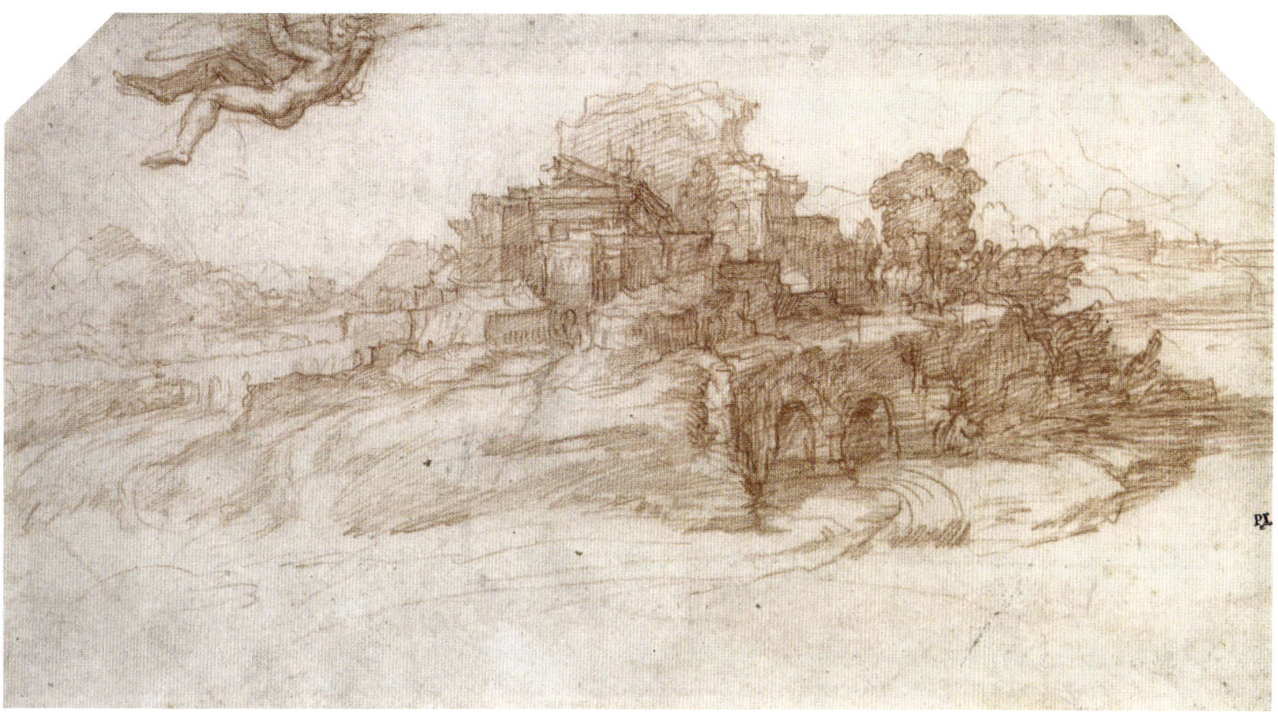

1.29 *Abduction of Ganymede*. Red chalk on laid paper, 15 × 28.1 cm. British Museum, London

taught to specialise in such depictions during his time in Raphael's workshop and, indeed, landscapes are a prominent feature of the Vatican Loggia and of some of the frescoes in the Stanze. In its virtuoso representation of the variety of the visible world, including skies, on a walled surface, the concentration on landscape in fresco painting might be further classed as a challenge to the more restricted possibilities of sculpture, which also locates Polidoro's achievement in the conventional language of Italian humanist courts and writers like Castiglione.[49]

The novel representation of landscape was another development in Rome by accomplished young artists, not just Polidoro, but also Parmigianino and Perino del Vaga. The Venetian artist transplanted to Rome, Sebastiano del Piombo, also merits mention here. Drawings like the Hamburg *Raising of Lazarus* (fig. 1.30) reveal Polidoro again approaching a religious narrative with a broad emphasis on the surrounding natural world but always with a background architectural component. The conception is markedly different from Sebastiano's painting of the same subject, now in London's National Gallery, executed close to the same date. The intended destination and purpose of the Hamburg study is unknown but it was perhaps also meant for a lateral fresco in a chapel. Polidoro also treated landscape yet more exclusively in mysterious drawings

such as one in the Uffizi (fig. 1.31), which may be an even purer example of the genre because the figures seem mere accessories. The individual may be a weary pilgrim slumped under a tree before a dramatic cityscape blending modern architecture with ruins, but the intent of such a drawing is unclear. Muted, with a sense of foreboding and handled with an impasto so thick it is now cracking in places, the sketch may well contain no pen, only melting white heightening and briskly applied washes that appear almost electrified. Its technical and conceptual originality, which nonetheless seem to have roots in Raphael's metal point technique, can hardly be overstressed.

If bringing greater significance to landscape was one of Polidoro's original contributions to the art of this period in Rome, so was genre drawing, if in an entirely private arena. Due to their apparent informality, his genre drawings can present issues of attribution and interpretation.[50] Among the most secure from the Roman period is another sheet once collected by Francesco de Hollanda, now in Vienna (fig. 1.32).[51] This red chalk drawing represents a group of contemporary women washing, drying and carrying laundry. As none of the individual studies coherently interrelate it has the appearance, perhaps misleading, of having been assembled from separate studies rather than done directly from life outdoors in a single

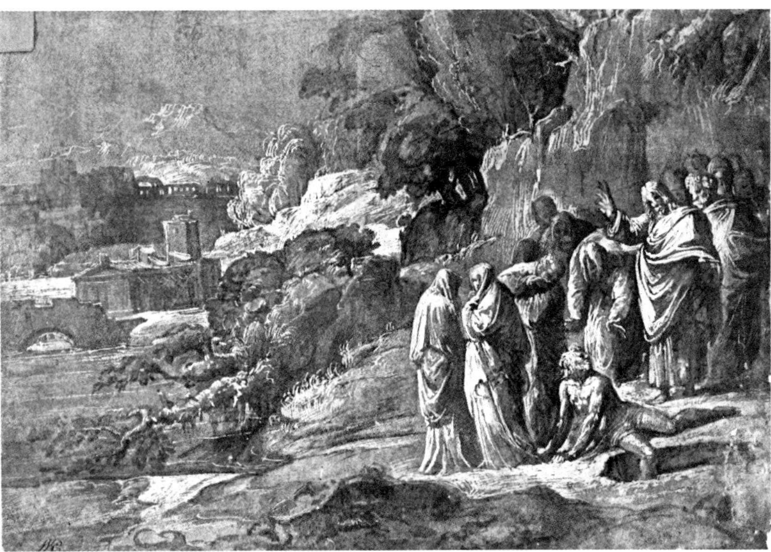

1.30 *Raising of Lazarus*. Pen and brown ink, and brown wash, with white heightening on laid paper, 20.6 × 28.7 cm. Kunsthalle, Hamburg

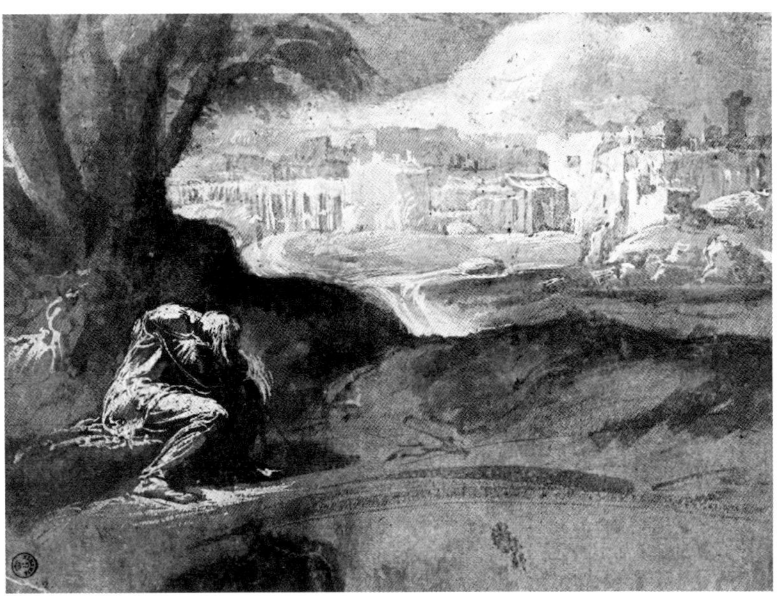

1.31 *Landscape with a Slumped Figure*. Point of brush, grey-brown wash, with white heightening on brown prepared paper, 20.4 × 26.9 cm. Gabinetto Disegni e Stampe degli Uffizi, Florence

session. This is not to imply that the drawing is rigid or mechanical in handling, for it contains a sense of urgency because of the many pentimenti and the haphazard arrangement of bodies on the sheet. Although such images contrast markedly with Polidoro's characteristic Roman facade paintings of antique and mythological subject matter, there is a dignified and exalted quality to the expressions and poses of these figures seen from all angles and worked up to different degrees, which tends to blur the distinction between pure genre and compositional study. Presumably the vibrant physical activity of these women provided a general inspiration for the artist's narrative paintings, and was one of his motivations for training his hand through spontaneous sketches like the example in Vienna, among others. A parallel drawing in the Ashmolean, Oxford, featuring these women may instead depict the Gathering of Manna. Polidoro's genre drawings are indicative of the unusually comprehensive range of his artistic interests in Rome and his basic visual curiosity, as in another work involving some unusually agitated readers at a table, now

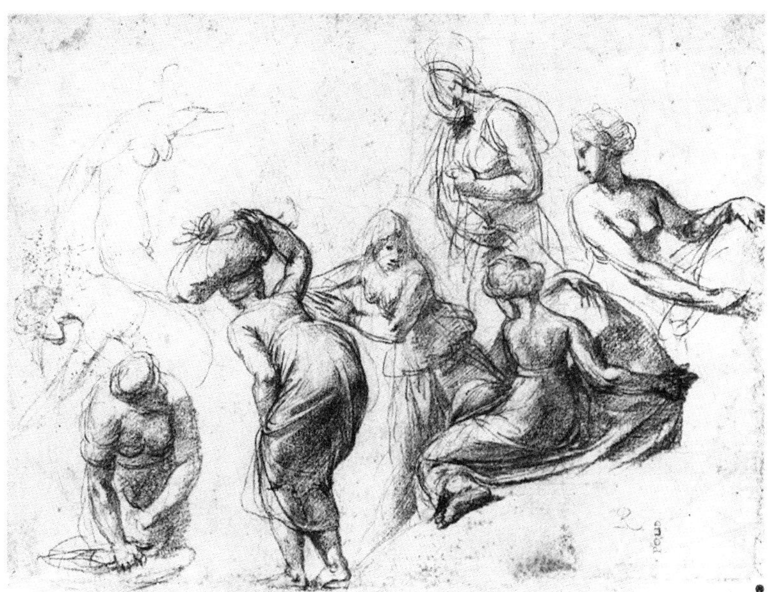

1.32 *Genre Studies*. Red chalk on laid paper, 20.7 × 28.5 cm. Albertina, Vienna

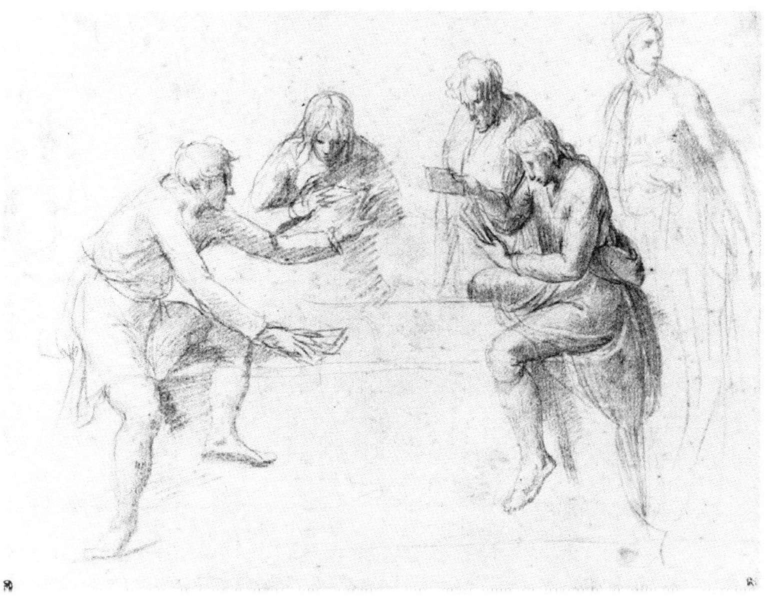

1.33 *Genre Study*. Red chalk on laid paper, 16.7 × 21.1 cm. Musée du Louvre, Paris, Cabinet de Dessins

in the Louvre (fig. 1.33), which anticipates the work of his compatriot the Baroque painter Caravaggio by almost a century.[52] He continued to create such drawings throughout his life, although his concerns when in Sicily tellingly shift from women and children in moments of work and leisure to quotidian religious life. Sometimes drawn on both sides of a sheet of paper, attesting to the artist's economy and spontaneity in making them, the relatively large number that have survived is indicative of their private nature as opposed to commissioned works: they were not consumed and discarded by his workshop. Their novel charm would also have made them desirable for the first collectors of drawings, as attested to by De Hollanda's interest within a couple of decades of their creation.

More so than the eclectic group of projects discussed here, including the Palazzo Baldassini and San Silvestro al Quirinale frescoes, Polidoro's career in Rome was distinguished and defined by the numerous facades he painted with an enigmatic colleague from Florence named Maturino. These will be considered in the next chapter.

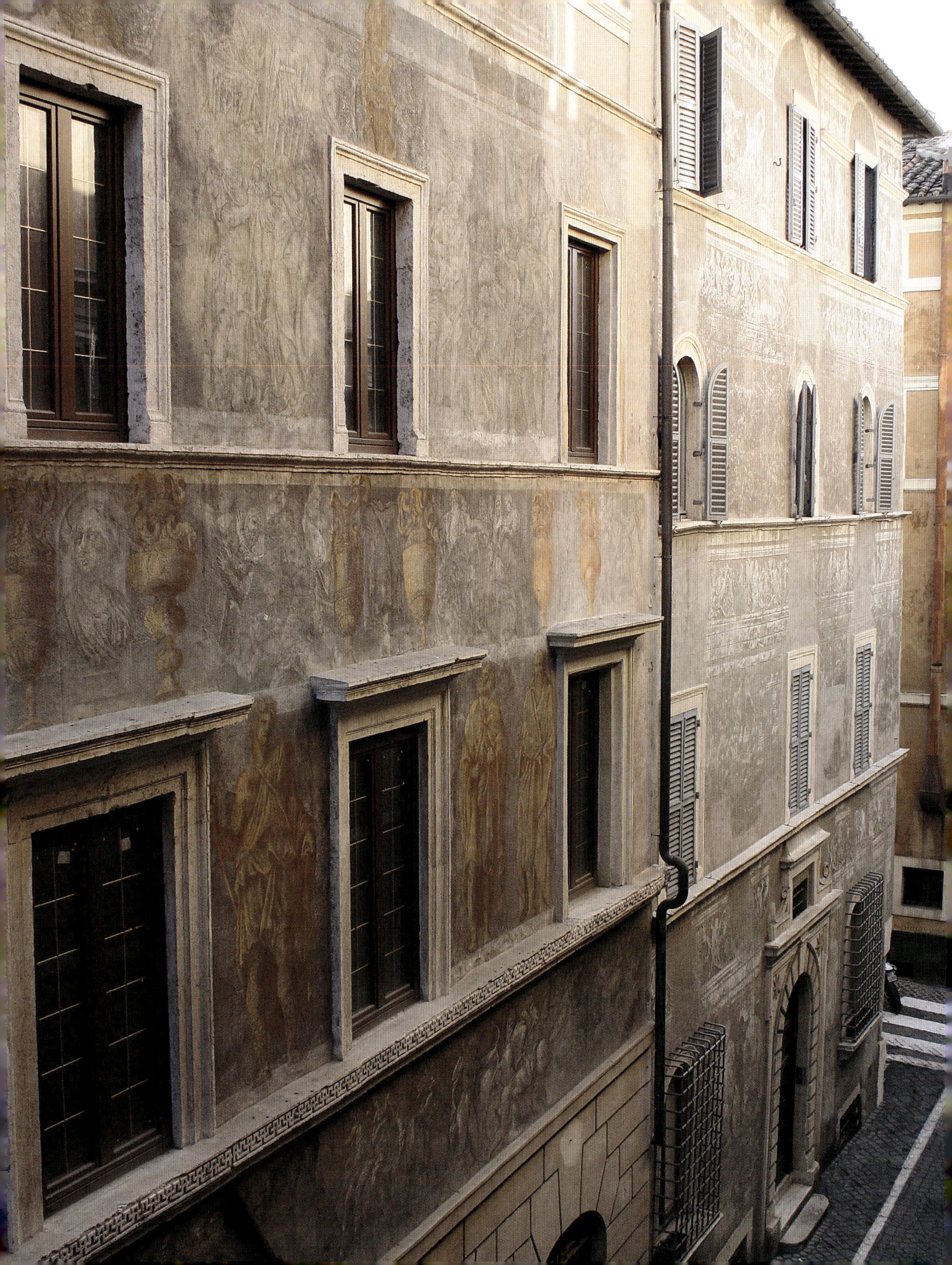

2 'A particular Genius for Freezes':[1] The Facades

Polidoro specialised in the frescoing of palace facades in Rome, working in collaboration with an artist of Florentine heritage who remains enigmatic and is known simply as Maturino. Such is the enormous importance of their works that they merit separate treatment. Vasari wrote, albeit with some exaggeration, that there was 'no apartment, palace, garden, or villa in Rome that does not contain some work by Polidoro and Maturino'.[2] His descriptions of these facades distributed around Rome inspired some of his most exuberant writing in the entire *Lives* as he attempted, almost breathlessly at times, to match their visual density in words, often without knowing the ancient stories depicted. The pair painted between 40 and 50 facades around Rome, all prior to the sack of the city in May 1527, when, according to Vasari, Maturino died of the plague. Maturino was one of several Florentine-born artists Raphael attracted to his workshop, including Gianfrancesco Penni, Perino del Vaga and the sculptor Lorenzetto, and he must have encountered Polidoro there. Their collaborative approach to these almost exclusively urban frescoes presumably respected

2.1 Palazzo Milesi, Rome

a procedure Polidoro first learnt in accordance with Raphael's practice. There is no evidence for this, but it seems likely that Polidoro was involved more as a master designer of the frescoes while Maturino acted as the technical specialist in their execution. But for the purposes of the present study, facade frescoes are referred to as the work of Polidoro alone, as unjust as this is to Maturino.

These exteriors have now, with two very partial exceptions remaining *in situ*, been erased due to exposure to the elements. The other frescoes were on buildings and walls long since whitewashed, remade or destroyed. A thoroughly accurate reconstruction of all the facades, and even their locations in many cases, is no longer possible. So, ironically, although they were initially accessible to all artists by virtue of their external and public nature, their exposed setting was also responsible for their gradual but inevitable destruction, something sadly already acknowledged within a century of their execution. These monumental decorations covering the entire walls on which they were painted, interrupted only by the real windows and doors, must be reassembled from prints and drawn copies that are, fortunately, abundant. Pietro da Cortona's sketchbook represents an apogee in

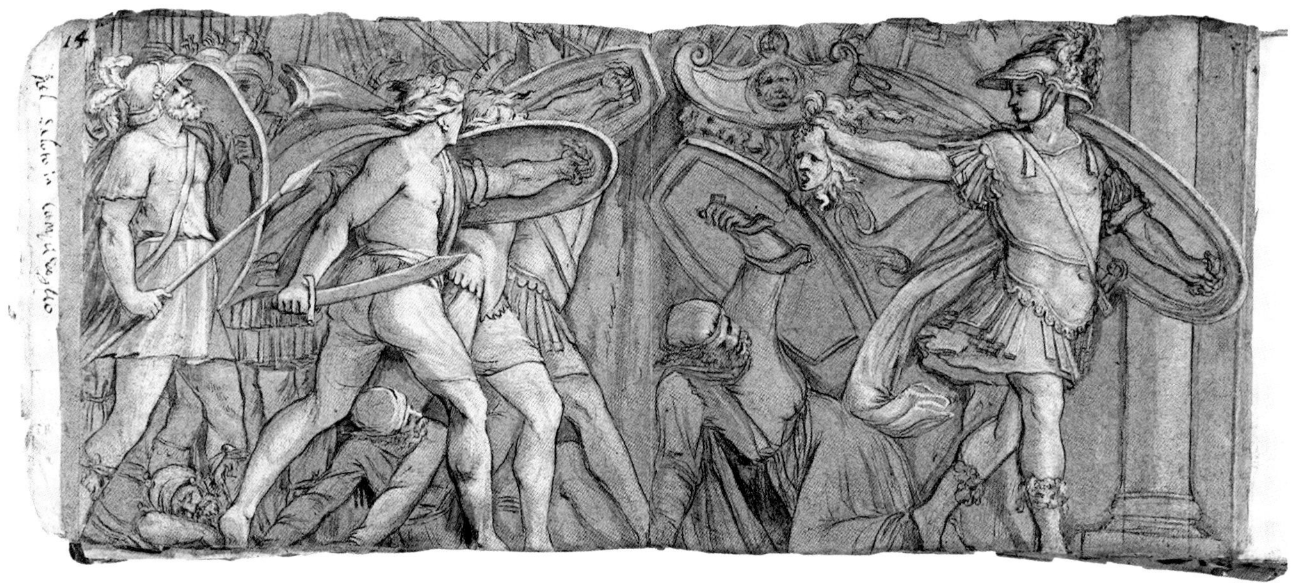

2.2 Pietro da Cortona, Copy after the Casino del Bufalo facade. Graphite and chalk on grey laid paper, 23 × 17 cm. Royal Ontario Museum, Toronto

terms of quality (fig. 2.2) but many are more amateur and will remain forever anonymous. Polidoro became the most copied and, arguably, the most influential artist active in Rome during the 1520s. Beyond the scope of the present study, this is a worthy historiographical exercise in itself: Polidoro's impact on non-Italian artists, including great ones like Rubens, for example, can hardly be underestimated, even relative to the influence of Raphael and Michelangelo. The fact that the frescoes were executed in monochrome only added to the ease with which they could be recorded in drawings, especially by the less experienced. Of course, the paintings' imagination and elaborateness deepened interest in them, and they became pattern-books for successive generations of artists of all levels of skill, something akin to a perpetually open art gallery, to adapt John Gere's phrase.[3] And so Polidoro, a non-Roman by birth, very soon became an emblem of the Renaissance in Rome – his name virtually inseparable from figurative antique art. One might say he was a reader, editor, translator and illustrator of the ancient world, providing a classical visual index for the literate and illiterate alike. Romano Alberti and Federico Zuccaro, writing for the academy in Rome in a text published in 1604, mention students drawing from the antique and from Polidoro's facades as fundamentally the same exercise.[4] Ironically, Polidoro's work of this nature was less permanent than the sculpture of the ancients that he emulated.

Copies are the main evidence for Polidoro's facades. It is striking how frequently the name 'Polidoro', or less frequently 'Maturino', is inscribed on the drawn copies, more a brand name or identification of a souvenir than an attempt to simulate or falsify an attribution. Some later artists certainly used Vasari's biography as an imperfect guide to locating the frescoes. Without copies the very subject of Polidoro's frescoes would be almost completely opaque. These reproductions, especially those published by Northern European printmakers, allowed the designs to survive as models for future generations, but as replicas they inevitably defuse the power of the original frescoes. When examining these representations of Polidoro's monumental frescoes, which range from the outright crude to the harmonious, it is not surprising to find that his style is linked by modern scholars to the elegant and graceful characteristics of a Roman 'Mannerism'.[5] Yet it was the more dramatic and formal aspects of these paintings that attracted artists in the first place and were the ones emphasised in early written sources. For Lomazzo, for example, in his treatise of 1584, Polidoro is governed by Mars, the god of war, and his element is *forma*.[6] Similarly, Federico Zuccaro, in depicting Mars in an artistic hierarchy intended for Palazzo Zuccari, apparently gave the god the features of Polidoro as portrayed in the equally fanciful woodcut portrait in Vasari's *Lives*, in which he holds a partly rolled-up drawing of a facade design (fig. 2.3).[7] Alongside a partisan Taddeo Zuccaro, only Raphael and

Michelangelo were represented with Polidoro in this
review of illustrious predecessors, impactful evidence
for the artist's continuing great fame around 1600.

These facade paintings represent the apogee of the
genre rather than its origins. Raphael's own output supplied
some limited precedents for Polidoro's, but were different
in nature, and the master would have regarded this as a
secondary genre. Sadly none of his models survives, nor
do the ephemeral decorations of the period that would have
been further contemporary prototypes. Raphael designed
lavish decorations in stucco for the facade of Palazzo
Battiferro in Rome, located near the church of San Luigi
dei Francesi, and for the then newly constructed Palazzo
Branconio dell'Aquila in the Roman Borgo, both more
elaborate and sumptuous than anything Polidoro and
Maturino ever attempted.[8] An assistant of Raphael's from
Siena named Vincenzo Tamagni, who had, like Polidoro,
begun his career working in the Vatican Loggia, frescoed
a frieze that included the nine Muses near Palazzo Branconio,
again as mentioned by Vasari.[9] Vasari recorded that Penni
executed a facade in grisaille on Monte Giordano near Ponte
Sant'Angelo.[10] Perino painted a facade explicitly in the style
of Polidoro, again according to Vasari, at Palazzo Millini,
near Santa Maria dell'Anima.[11] Baldassare Peruzzi, a more
senior artist who was never a pupil of Raphael's but was
influenced by his style as a painter, also provided specific
precedents and parallels for Polidoro's facades, as Vasari
recognised.[12] Indeed, more than Raphael himself or any
other pupil, Peruzzi was the most serious rival to Polidoro
in Rome in this genre. While little survives recording the
original appearance of these other facades, some of which
included colour, it can nonetheless be assumed that Raphael's
instruction prepared other students in his workshop in
addition to Polidoro to exploit the genre and elevate what
was a relatively minor, utilitarian art form. Even recognising
the disparate recent precedents for facade painting in Italy,
Polidoro made this format his own by the sheer number
and quality of his efforts, assisted by Maturino. One rare
instance of frescoes on the facade of a church was San
Pietro in Vincoli, where scenes from the life of Saint Peter
and prophets are recorded, but otherwise outdoor
production was concentrated exclusively on palaces.[13]
It was an example Vasari himself copied, reminding us that
his descriptions of Polidoro in his *Lives* were sometimes
supported by his own careful illustrative record (fig. 2.4).[14]

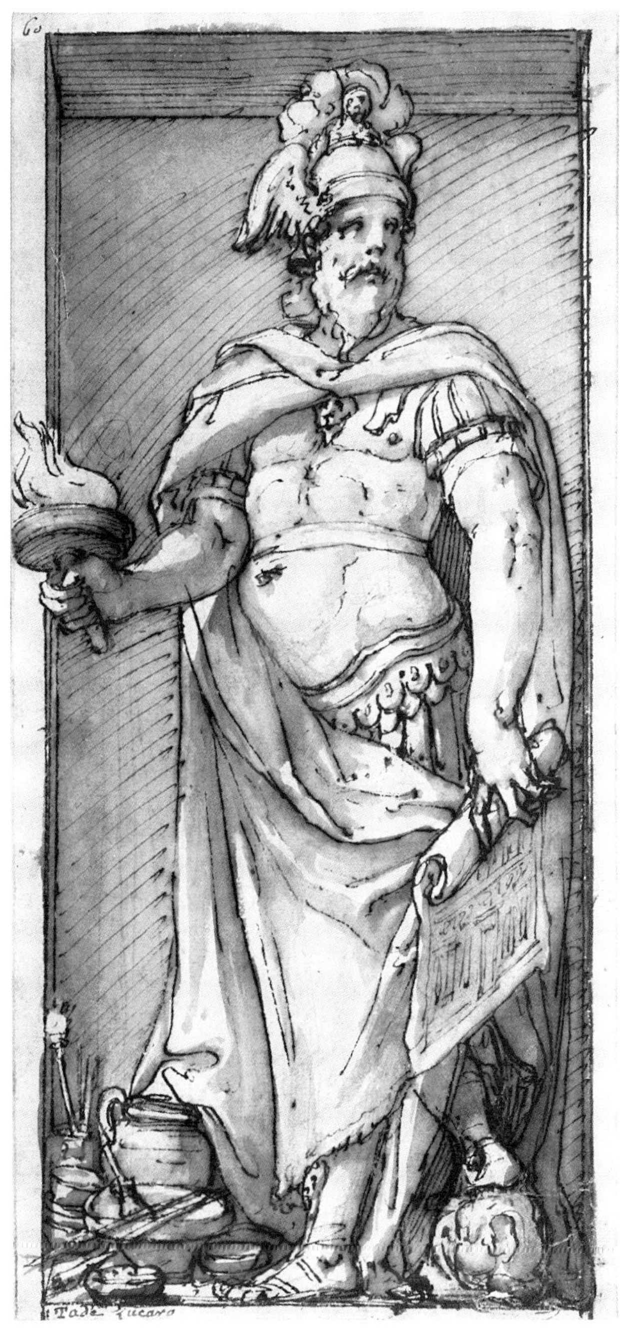

2.3 Copy after Federico Zuccaro, *Mars*, c.1600. Pen and brown ink,
and brown wash, over black chalk on laid paper, 26.9 × 13.8 cm.
Museum Boijmans Van Beuningen, Rotterdam

Given the number of facades executed, Polidoro
presumably brought his own evolving expertise even to
the selection of subjects, many of which were undeniably
rare, sometimes unprecedented in Renaissance art, in a
period when the study of Rome's own history was starting
to be addressed in contemporary scholarship. Polidoro
was employed because of his particular skill in filling these

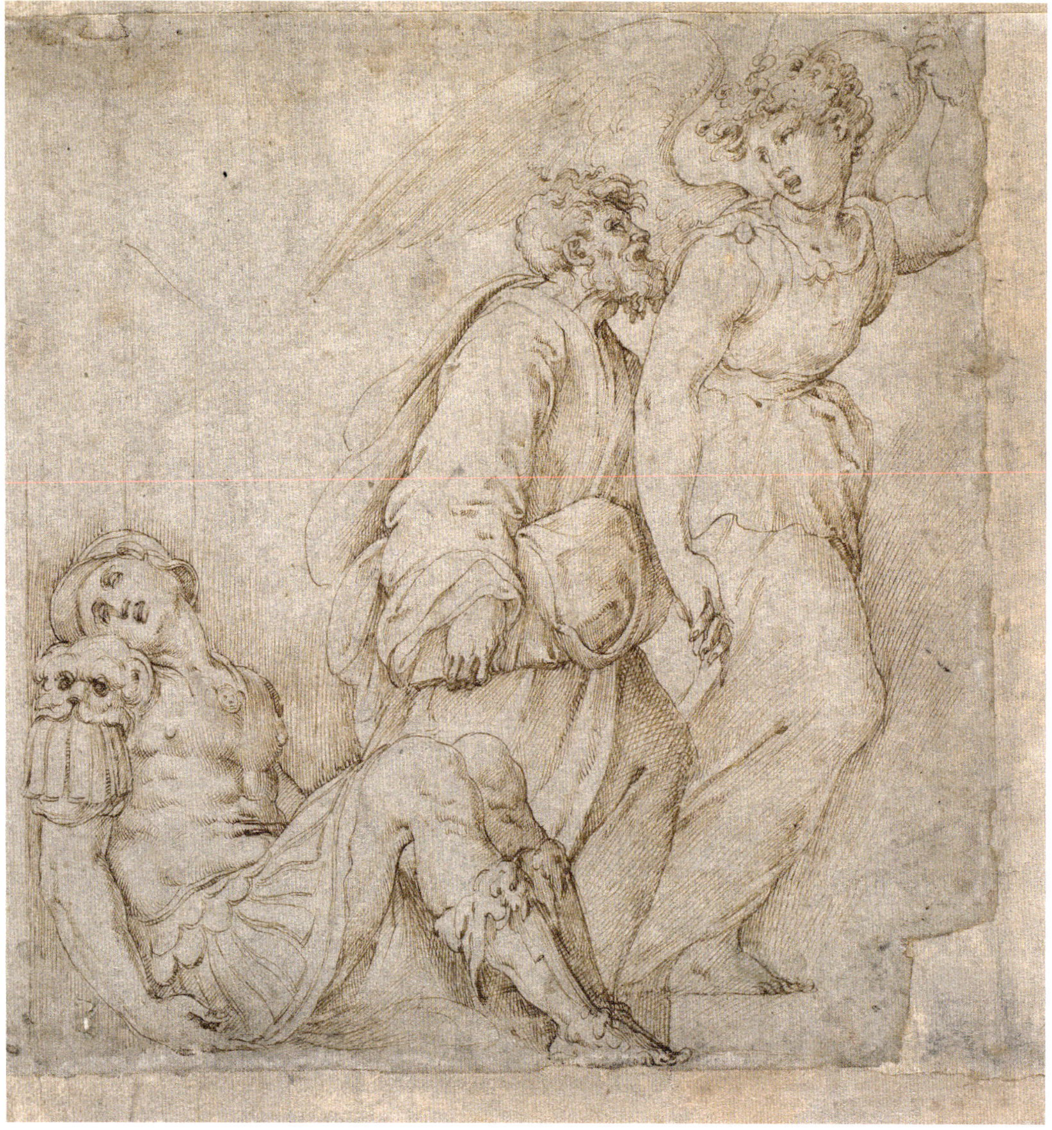

2.4 Giorgio Vasari, after Polidoro, *The Liberation of Saint Peter*. Pen and brown ink over black chalk on laid paper, 21 × 20.4 cm. National Gallery of Canada, Ottawa

spaces with images based on classical mythology and early Roman history, often interspersed with single figures representing historical or allegorical characters. So often in the Renaissance period, a gap exists between an artist's typically modest education and the learning required to elaborate such themes. Many of the ancient texts would have been available in Italian translation by the 1520s but whether, as seems more likely, Polidoro had a learned humanist friend to assist him at times with subjects is open to speculation. Some frescoes could be topical, such as those on the Palazzo Capranica facade, which made reference to Pope Leo X and can therefore be dated to before 1521, and which featured religious virtues, a

personification of Rome and images related to contemporary Turkish conflicts.[15] As one of the responsibilities of the college there was to teach theology, the facade signposted the activities inside.

The role his patrons played in the selection of particular subjects and themes for their facades is difficult to reconstruct in the absence of explicit documentation. While owners of the buildings are traceable in some cases – around a quarter of the examples – in the majority of cases we lack direct knowledge of actual patronage, making it difficult to interpret them beyond their basic identification. The fact that the names of the patrons were not often recorded is itself evidence for the ephemeral nature of external facade painting. Excluding those patrons who may have simply been attracted to Polidoro's style, the facades were commissioned by a few indigenous Roman families, Florentine expatriates and members of the papal court presumably trying to impress the Florentine popes with the artist's link to Raphael, and other Italian settlers in the city seeking to create a spontaneous Roman lineage.

In general terms the facades glorify and dignify patrons with reference to an illustrious civic past and enrich their city palaces, one of their more valuable possessions, with the illusion of wealth and sophistication. These public frescoes declared and located ownership for particular families in a complex and shifting urban environment and some ancient, if not the most distinguished, Roman families like the Bufalo and the Naro were attracted to them. Given the private nature of most elite art patronage, the bold public nature of the frescoes was unusual and may even have discouraged more reticent and venerable families from considering them, including the baronials. Polidoro's patrons were an eclectic mixture of old and new families in Rome. Cardinal Agostino Spinola, the Genoese-born Bishop of Perugia, almost certainly commissioned a facade from Polidoro for his palace in Via di Parione because of the patron's loyalty to the Medici popes and respect for the memory of Raphael.[16] Spinola had earlier commissioned work from Raphael's 'master' Perugino and was later represented as a cardinal in Raphael's *Mass at Bolsena* in the Vatican Stanze. The especially brutal execution of an early betrayer of Rome, Tarpeia, by soldiers with their shields, frescoed on his palace, was of an appropriately severe moral tone for this ecclesiastic veering into secular patronage. The Piedmontese Cardinal Alberto Serra's facade in Via dei Coronari represents a similar case of a foreign-born member of the Curia displaying loyalty to the Medici through association. The partnership with Maturino may also help to account for the marked popularity among Florentines of this pair of painters. The facades of the Cepperelli family near Piazza Farnese, the Gaddi in Via Maschera d'Oro, the Boniauguri near Santa Maria sopra Minerva, and that of Cardinal Francesco Soderini at what is now Palazzo Altemps, near Sant'Agostino, supply instances of Florentine appropriation of ancient Roman subjects in a domestic situation and a very contemporary desire to associate with

Medici papal domination and further assert Florentine dominance, by now well established in the city. When one considers how much power in Rome was possessed by foreign-born residents, especially the Florentines, this desire to establish a visual index of the ancient city may appear superficial, not to mention unmerited – a forthright attempt to claim a more elevated social status and to demonstrate family roots extending back to antiquity; a mythologising declaration of lineage. The case of the Lombard Giovanni Antonio Milesi's facade is an example of this type, even if members of the family had settled in Rome during the previous century. This observation is significant for Polidoro rarely explicitly quoted from ancient sources, for many of his clients had no legitimate claims among their own collections to appropriate famous works. A more generalised approach was clearly permissible, especially in a public setting. However misleading, for relatively new families to Rome this proclamation of a collection of antiquities nonetheless transmitted an air of the genuine, just as the ephemeral character of fresco undermined the apparent permanence of the buildings they promoted.

How a particular location conditioned subject choices for the frescoes in Rome can be difficult to determine, but was often a direct motivation. In some cases, as with an image of Romulus tracing the walls of Rome with his plough on the Boniauguri family facade, Polidoro made explicit, albeit general, reference to the city, although other narratives involving augury evoke the patron's name, as Rolf Kultzen has pointed out.[17] The subjects identify the place like the attributes of a saint. In a comparable instance the subject was even more localised to a particular spot – the facade in Campo Marzio with scenes from the life of Ancus Marcius, the Roman warrior king who expanded the territory of the ancient city.[18]

Vasari outlined in the technical preface to the *Lives* what could easily be a description of Polidoro's work:

> Monochromes according to the painters are a kind
> of picture that has a closer relation to drawing than
> to work in colour because it has been derived from
> copying marble statues and figures in bronze
> and various sorts of stone; and artists have been
> accustomed to decorate in monochrome the façades
> of palaces and houses, giving these a semblance other

than the reality, and making them appear to be built
of marble or stone, with the decorative groups actually
carved in relief; or indeed they may imitate particular
sorts of marble, and porphyry, serpentine, and red
and grey granite and other stones, or bronze, according
to the taste, arranging them in many divisions.[19]

In addition to fresco, the other common technique for facade
painting was sgraffito, which had the advantage of being
more water-resistant, as described in Vasari's text and easily
visible on the palace at Via Maschera d'Oro, no. 9, adjacent
to Polidoro's partially extant facade of Palazzo Milesi. This
less sophisticated technique did not so strongly preoccupy
him, however, although Vasari celebrated one usage of it,

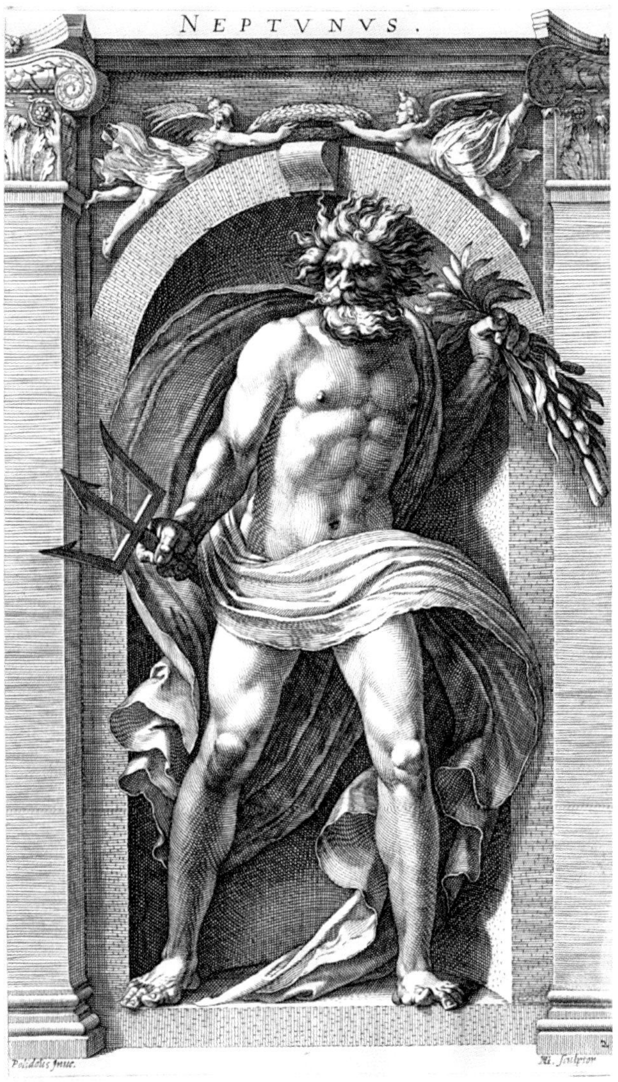

2.5 Hendrick Goltzius, after Polidoro, *Neptune*. Engraving,
35.8 × 21.5 cm. British Museum, London

now lost, at Palazzo Baldassini and mentioned another
in the Borgo Nuovo, close to the Vatican.[20]

Monochrome painting was a branch of ornament that
Raphael encouraged his pupils to cultivate to a supreme
standard. This was on the whole not prominent in fresco
but was more so in the *basamento* areas of large-scale
decorations like the Vatican Loggia and parts of the
Stanze. Elsewhere, even a canvas like Raphael's portrait
of Castiglione, now in the Louvre, can be interpreted
in formal terms as a bravura exercise in monochrome
painting. Examples by Giulio Romano, such as the
panel of *Abundance*, also in the Louvre, for the cover
of a small *Holy Family* by Raphael, represent the zenith
of this technique. It is highly polished in finish and there
is a virtuoso attempt to represent a variety of different
precious materials, as in a *trompe l'œil*. Polidoro always
operated at the other extreme – much more broadly and
with greater expediency whether in fresco or on panel,
as if the technique liberated his brush – rather than
seeking discipline and immaculate finish. Monochrome,
however it was handled, aimed to simulate sculpture in
paint for the depiction not just of stone but of bronze and
other more precious materials, providing a swift illusion
of reality. It was typically employed for secular subjects,
as well as pure ornament, and so had overtly pagan
overtones. Pliny the Elder attested that the earliest
painters worked in a monochrome technique, thus also
giving it the imprimatur of antiquity and even a
primitiveness that in Polidoro's day must have been
judged as sophisticated.[21] It is not difficult to imagine
Polidoro's exposure to Pliny's writings in Raphael's
workshop. Leon Battista Alberti reinforced this in citing
an ancient painter named Aglaophon who used only black
and white in his work.[22] Leonardo's comment in his notes
that 'the crown of the science of painting comes from the
use of shadows and light' is not explicitly about monochrome
but nonetheless signals the integral nature of this approach
in this period, as the first goal of a painter was to create
a three-dimensional body on a flat surface.[23] It is relevant
that Pliny also attests that paintings were occasionally
displayed outdoors in ancient Rome. The strength and
restrictiveness of a technique absent of colour had moral
connotations when treating subjects with potent messages,
along with the more obvious heroic military associations,
retrieving past Roman glory for contemporary Rome.

Monochrome was a pragmatic option for ease of execution of these monumental and complex commissions, for it averted the need to make colour choices. Although giving great impact, such facade decorations were more economical for patrons and correspondingly lower down in the artistic hierarchy. They also permitted a relatively swift execution, which meant that Polidoro and Maturino could deliver many commissions in a period in which delay marred the careers of many of the greatest artists, including Michelangelo and Parmigianino. It would appear that in Rome Polidoro never painted a monochrome on an independent format, a panel or canvas, only in fresco on the facades, where he introduced these representations into monumental architecture and produced assertive images in a distracting, not always hospitable urban environment. By coincidence perhaps, in two cases Polidoro frescoed palace facades very near churches in which he painted chapels, Sant'Eustachio and San Silvestro al Quirinale, so the exterior paintings provided a prelude to the works inside in what would have been a highly unusual visual experience for spectators in Rome. The facade near San Silvestro, featuring eight gods in niches eventually engraved by Hendrick Goltzius (fig. 2.5) and influential on no less a master than Bernini, must date, to judge by its confidently advanced style, to after 1524, and so is close in date to the decoration of the church interior.[24]

A tangible idea of the original appearance of the facades is gained from the mere two that partially survive *in situ*: Palazzo Milesi in Via Maschera d'Oro, recently restored, and that of Palazzo Ricci, some of which is also recorded in an early black and white photograph revealing heavy repainting (fig. 2.6). Both have come down to us in rather discouraging states of preservation and only Palazzo Milesi, located near the church of San Salvatore in Lauro, is anything like complete in terms of surface cover (fig. 2.1).[25] Close-up photographs reveal the blemished surfaces but equally contain memories of truly wondrous background and ornamental details, including Polidoro's version of the style of ancient triumphal column he would have tried to study (fig. 2.7). The street takes its very name from a facade decoration featuring a memorable detail of a gold mask supported by a putto. Adding to the impact of this facade Polidoro also frescoed the exterior of the recently completed Palazzo Gaddi, opposite the Milesi,

with what must have been extraordinary scenes of a naval battle, presented in a long horizontal field, together with others featuring Alexander the Great, but the naval battle is recorded only in copies.[26] Over nine bays wide, this was one of the largest and most ambitious facades the artist ever undertook. The prominent Florentine banker Luigi Gaddi had also been a patron of Parmigianino's in the same period. The presence on this facade of the arms of Pope Clement VII, adjacent to Gaddi's own, allows for a relatively more precise dating between 1524 and 1527.

Milesi, who was buried in the church of Sant'Agostino, originated from the region of Bergamo and was one of Polidoro's most supportive patrons: the artist later wrote to him from Sicily in 1528, as will be discussed. Milesi had close connections to Popes Leo X and Clement VII. The entire Milesi facade was also commemorated in a later print by Ernesto Maccari (fig. 2.8), while the scenes in the most visually accessible lower band were engraved later in the century by printmakers who felt compelled to record Polidoro's frescoes as they did antiquities: Goltzius, Jan Saenredam and Cherubino Alberti. They feature stories

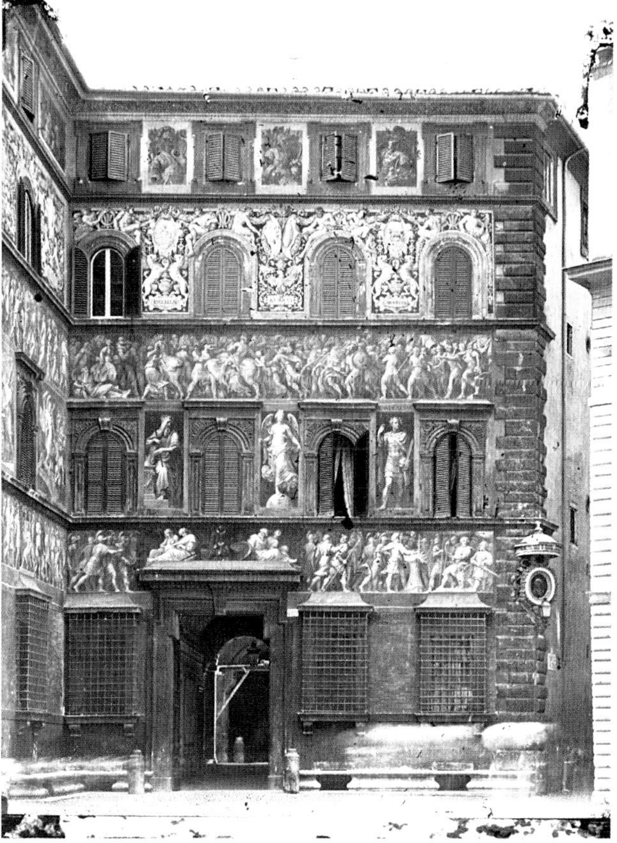

2.6 Palazzo Ricci, Rome. Historical photograph

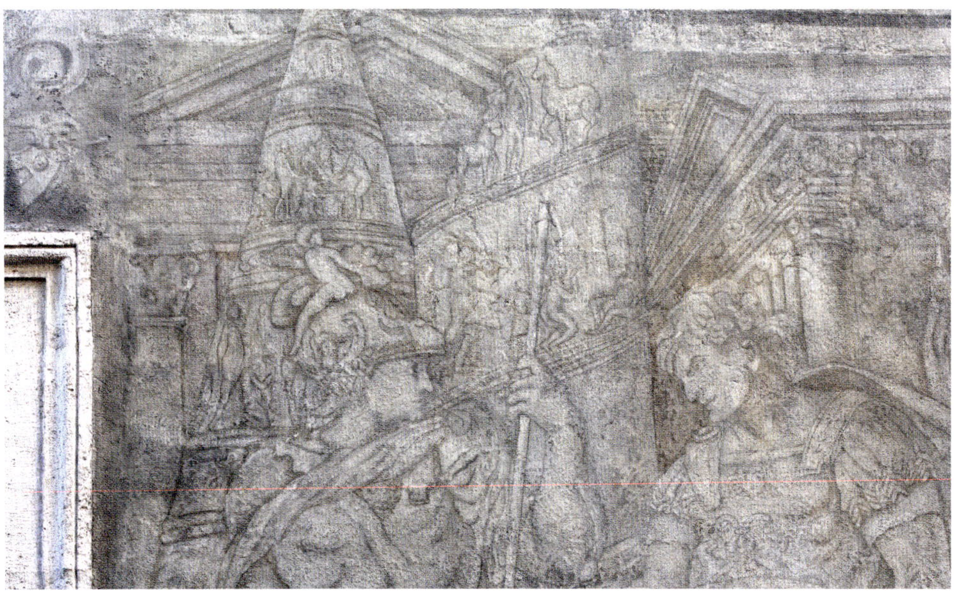

2.7 Palazzo Milesi, Rome, detail of triumphal column

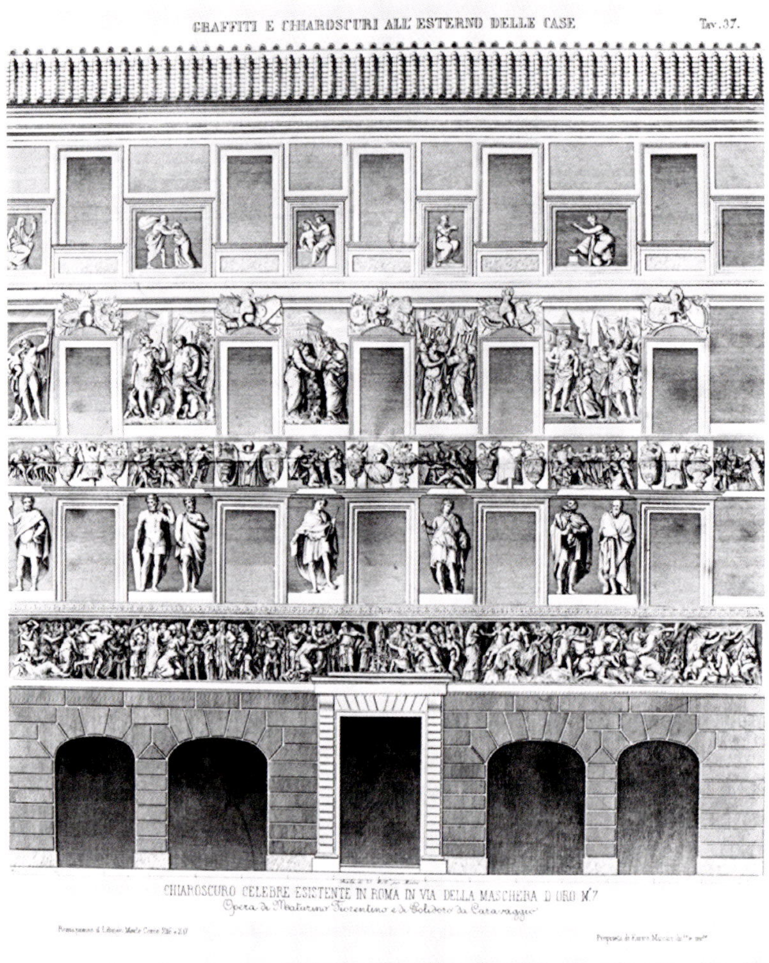

2.8 Ernesto Maccari, Print after Palazzo Milesi, from E. Maccari, *Graffiti e chiaroscuro esistenti nell'esterno delle case di Roma* (1885)

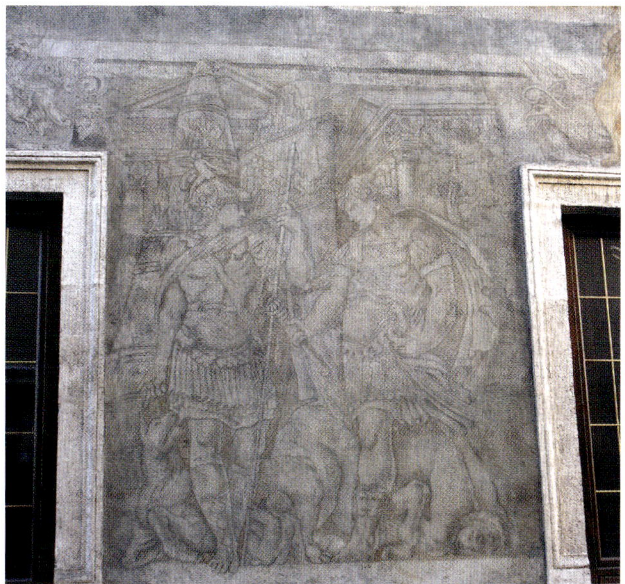
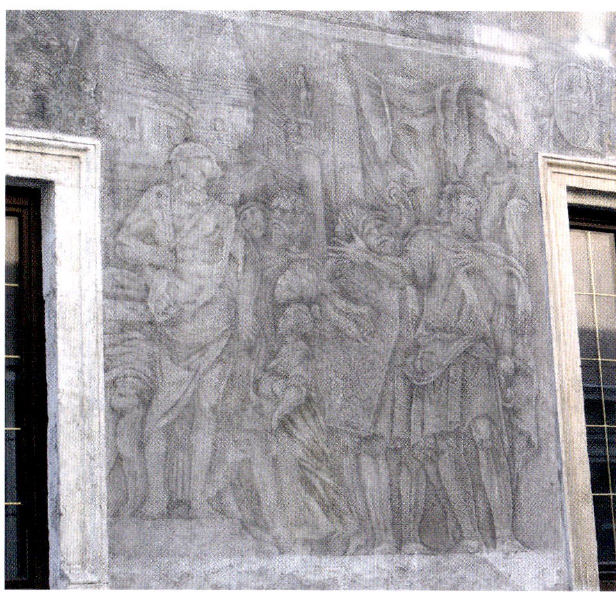

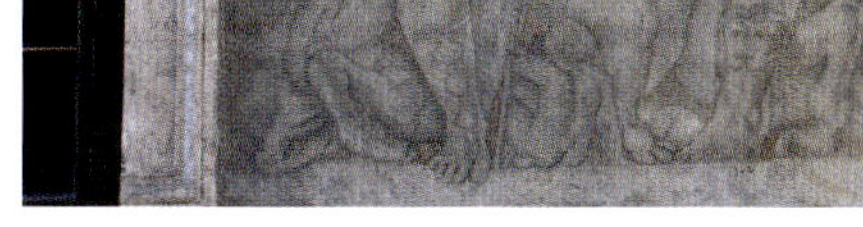

2.9–2.10 Palazzo Milesi, Rome, two details

from the myth told by Ovid of Niobe and the Niobids, murdered by Apollo and his sister Artemis after Niobe boasted of having more children than their mother – the tragic images by which this facade was most readily recalled, including also, rather incongruously, a Rape of the Sabines from the very early history of Rome. The death of Niobe's last daughter, huddled in her lap at the left edge of the lower compartment, is undeniably moving and there is no doubt that Polidoro successfully transmitted emotion in some scenes, in contrast to the more muted nature of other narratives, inspired more by Raphael's art than by ancient examples. The facade is arranged in five horizontal bands of different heights and with a mixture of figure scales, starting above the doorway, and is accentuated as the dramatic stories unfold without framing lines to divide them (figs 2.9 and 2.10). This method of depicting narrative in strip form was a common device in ancient art, in particular on the great columns distributed around Rome. It is still possible to appreciate how the narratives in monochrome contrasted decoratively with the single figures in imitation bronze. Mainly facing forwards, the characters use the real architecture as a platform on which to stand and Polidoro adapted the design to the actual breaks in the structure. He represented them on a larger scale near the top and in more simplified compositions, finally without backgrounds, so there was an explicit attempt at illusionism and adjustments for viewing distance. One second-floor

figure in bronze addresses the viewer directly and adds to the sense of wonderment in the visual experience. Yet the amount of sheer detail reminds the spectator not just of the complex richness of these decorations but of their ornamental preciousness too. Because of the narrow street, it is impossible to examine a facade like this in one glance; unity comes only from an accumulation of details. The various ancient subjects, not all of which interrelate thematically, further stress that overall cohesion was not possible. Polidoro was not therefore compelled to recreate entire episodes of ancient art but rather he was able to quote in a narrower, more expedient and episodic manner, in contrast to the unified treatment of Raphael's narratives. Unusually the Milesi facade included a female bust on a pedestal in the exact middle (fig. 2.23), hinting at a donor portrait in the guise of an ancient statue, but the precise intent remains mysterious.

Less of Polidoro's work survives even in a damaged state at Palazzo Ricci, or Palazzo Ricci-Paracciani, near Via Giulia (figs 2.11 and 2.12).[27] At the time Polidoro decorated the building it was apparently owned by the Florentine family who paid for its construction – the Calcagni. The Ricci family only acquired it later, in 1576. Palazzo Ricci presents two facades to the public. On the right wall the lower band is still decipherable, with soldiers and a river god in bronze above the main portal. The left wall, like the Palazzo Milesi facade, contains five levels, but only one is at all visible, with a boat arriving at the left

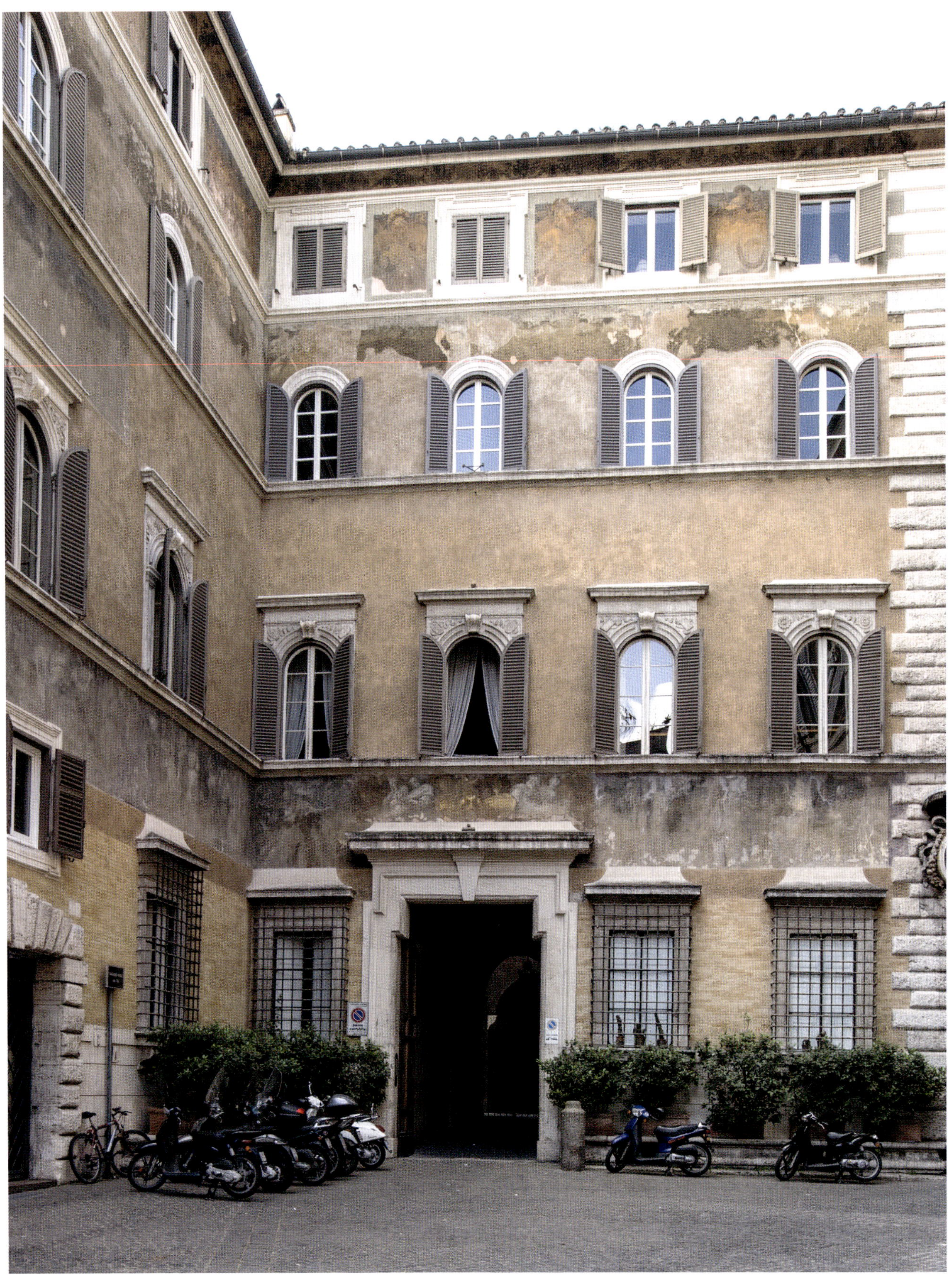

2.11 Palazzo Ricci, Rome

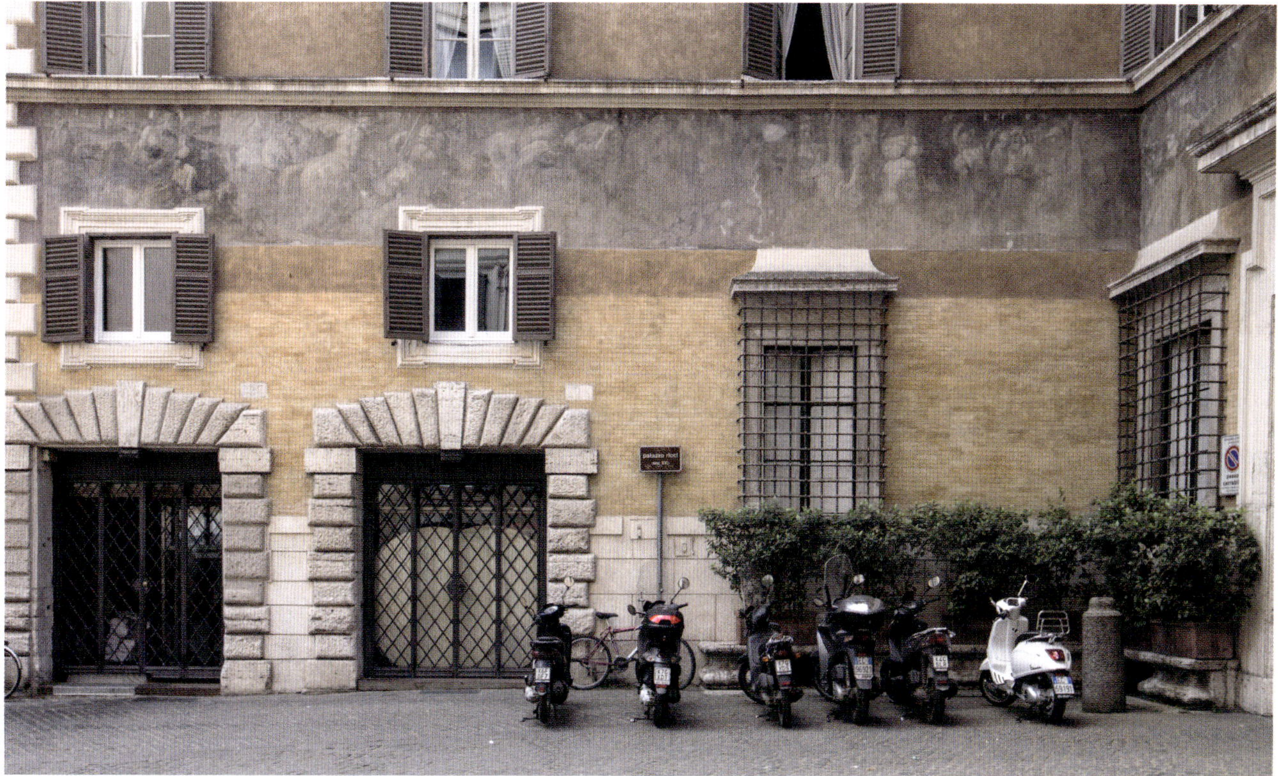

2.12 Palazzo Ricci, Rome, detail of left facade

margin. The most celebrated narratives from the history of ancient Rome featured the Rape of the Sabines, as well as the scholar-hero of the Roman Republic against the Etruscans, Gaius Mucius Scaevola – the ghostly trace of whom is visible on the lower section of the right facade.

Two other sets of fragments from the facades by Polidoro survive in museums in Rome and allow for a closer examination than the few other extant pieces, even if their display in such intimate settings cannot represent their original disposition. Part of one decoration is installed in four separated sections (figs 2.13–2.16) in the Galleria Nazionale d'Arte Antica, Palazzo Barberini, in Rome.[28] Although these were removed from the wall on Piazza Madama as early as 1633 by Cardinal Antonio Barberini, their condition is still much compromised by later retouching and they appear oddly mummified as images. They are true fragments: engravings by Cherubino Alberti portray sections that have been lost; and for large sections we are dependent on the same types of prints and copies to reconstruct the facade, which represents the unusually spectacular triumph of the consul Aemilius Paulus, who defeated the Macedonians and brought all Greece under the

domination of Rome. Vasari mentions other stories of ancient Rome frescoed on this facade without troubling himself to specify them precisely, and one imagines that many observers would have struggled to identify them too. The hero in this case appears accompanied by an angel and one of his generals in a massive, finely decorated chariot pulled by horses that seems to echo the triumph on the Marcus Aurelius relief then on the Capitol in Rome (fig. 2.15). The powerfully stark forms and relentlessly repeated, almost automated rhythms of Polidoro's design are still perceivable, even in the stencil-like remnant that survives, in an unusual combination of energy and ponderousness. These historic figures have a compelling anonymity, often viewed from behind, rarely making direct eye contact with one another, remote somehow even from themselves. Most strikingly, it is possible to appreciate how close these frescoes are to Polidoro's denser style of drawing in pen and ink with an independent overlay of white gouache, by comparing the remnant with, for example, the equally processional *Christ's Entry into Jerusalem* in the Uffizi (fig. 2.17).[29] The facades are like monumental wash drawings in their breadth and tonality, based on a

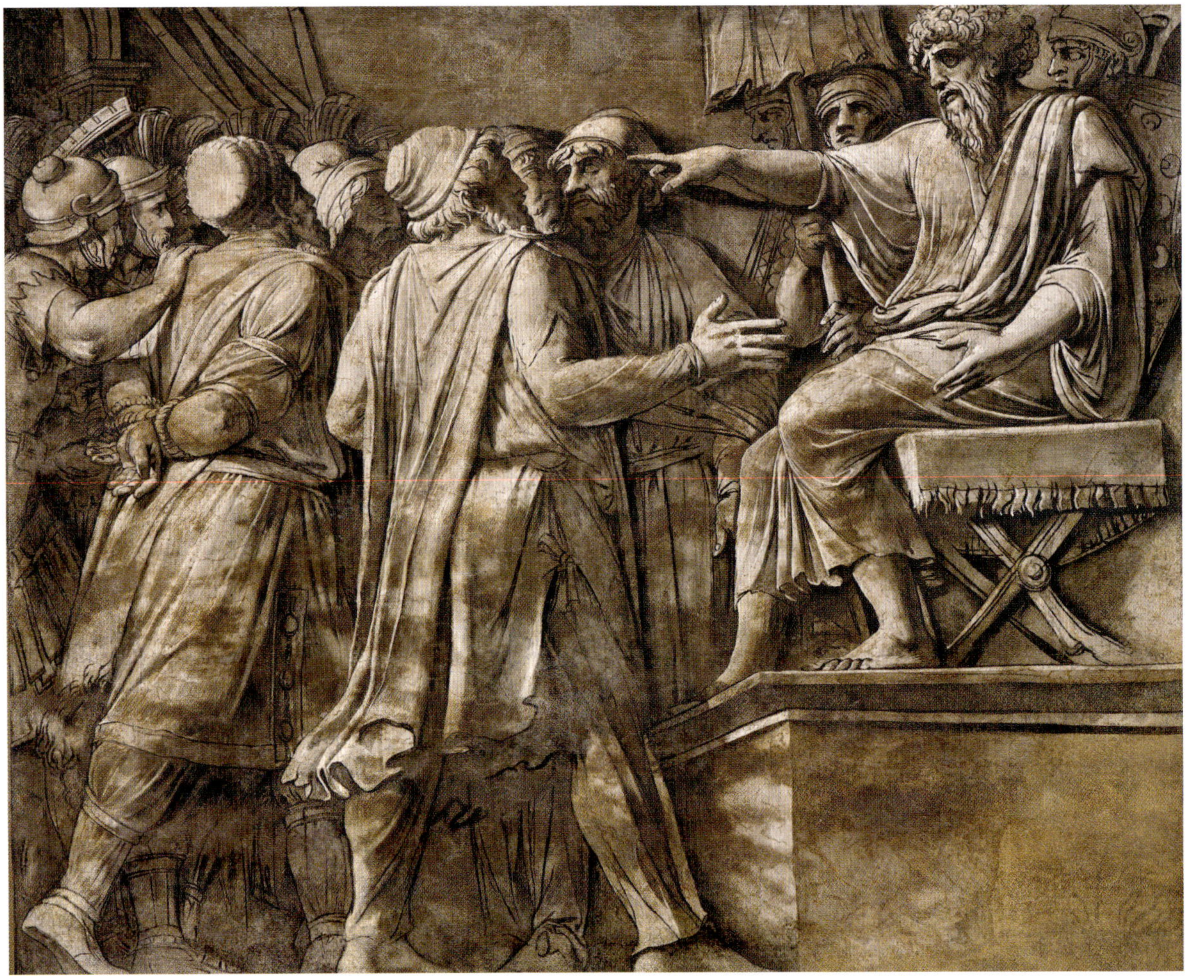

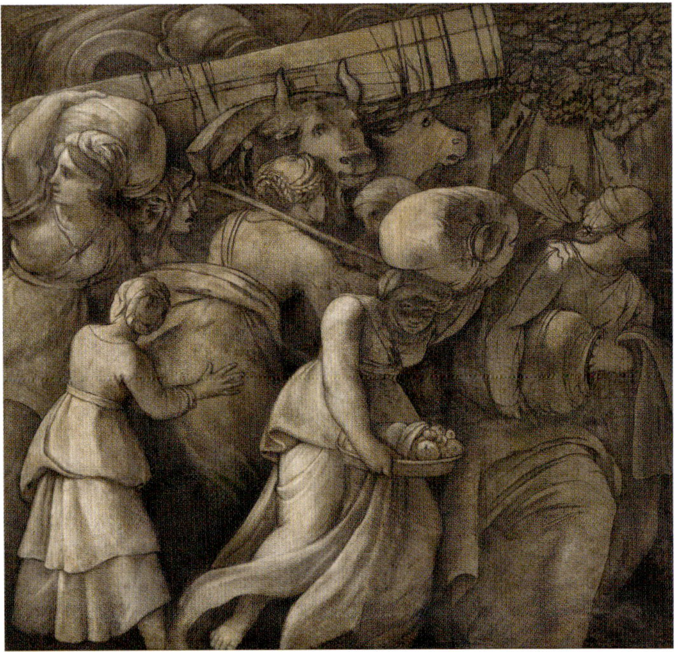

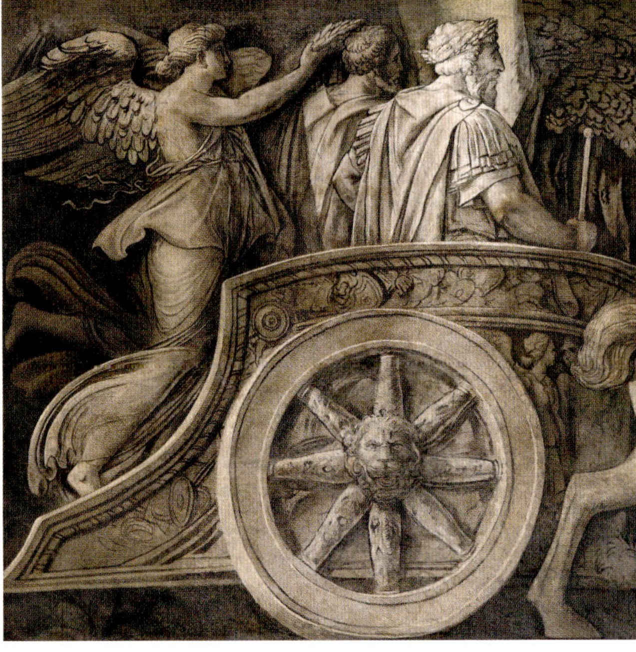

2.13–2.16 Detached frescoes from a palace on Piazza Madama, Rome. Galleria Nazionale d'Arte Antica, Palazzo Barberini, Rome

TOP: *Seated Ruler*, 200 × 220 cm. **ABOVE:** *Women in Flight*, 170 × 165 cm. *Two Parts of a Triumphal Frieze*, 175 × 290 cm; 175 × 280 cm

sharp contrast between black and white. Their surfaces are not static as in so many of the anonymous copies, but pulsating and active. One is reminded of Pietro Leone Casella's assessment of Polidoro as, above all, an artist who was 'brisk and vehement'.[30] The visual decorum of these outdoor locations allowed for a broader approach in all senses. The novelty in Polidoro transposing the sophistication and prestige of monumental narratives, some of which were traceable in subject if not arrangement to Raphael, to generally accessible public spaces must itself have attracted viewers, the vast majority of whom could never visit the papal apartments nor experience painting of this formal sophistication outside of churches.

Another example was found on a facade of the *casino* (garden pavilion) of the new Palazzo Bufalo, located near the Trevi Fountain and the church of Sant'Andrea delle Fratte, where Polidoro produced a scheme derived mainly from Ovid's *Metamorphoses*.[31] Unlike the others discussed, this facade was in one of the most celebrated garden settings of Renaissance Rome, not far from where the *Laocoön* sculpture was unearthed in 1506, a reminder that Polidoro not only represented antiquities magically made whole but also tantalisingly anticipated what might still be underground, the ancient past as contemporary art.

The Bufalo traced their origins to Florence but by Polidoro's time had been resident in Rome for more than two centuries.[32] In this case, we have some information about their interests that expands our appreciation of the paintings, including knowledge of a major collection of antiquities carefully arranged inside their palace and in the garden. Polidoro's decoration served as a backdrop for the ancient pieces, as a miraculous fictive extension of the real objects, but his images also referenced and augmented the meaning of the exhibited collection in a specific way.[33] Here dry quotation from ancient art was replaced by a clever reenactment of the ancient vocabulary in dialogue with some originals. In 1885, when the area was razed for the construction of Via del Tritone, six frescoes surviving from the garden facade of the *casino* were removed, transferred to canvas supports and taken to Palazzo Braschi, which now houses the Museo di Roma (figs 2.18–2.21). Several narratives draw upon the stories related by Ovid of the demi-god Perseus, including the Liberation of Andromeda, the Defeat of the Rival Suitors, their Marriage, as well as an image of his mother Danaë on another facade on the property. Individual fields showing Fortune and Venus survive in a damaged state. Also coded to reinforce the main narratives, another single figure of Mars has been entirely destroyed. The frescoes were

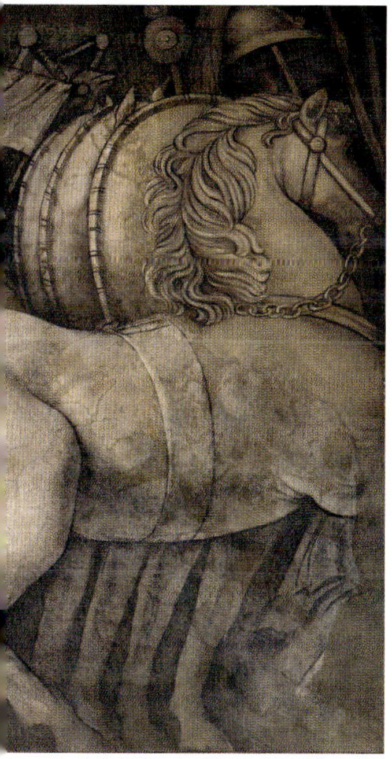

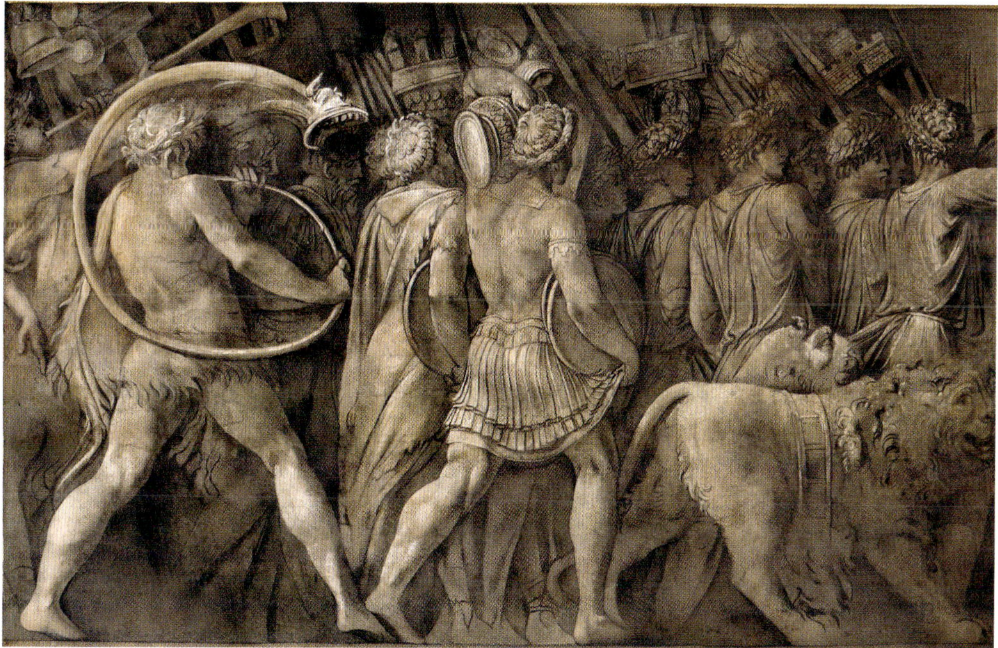

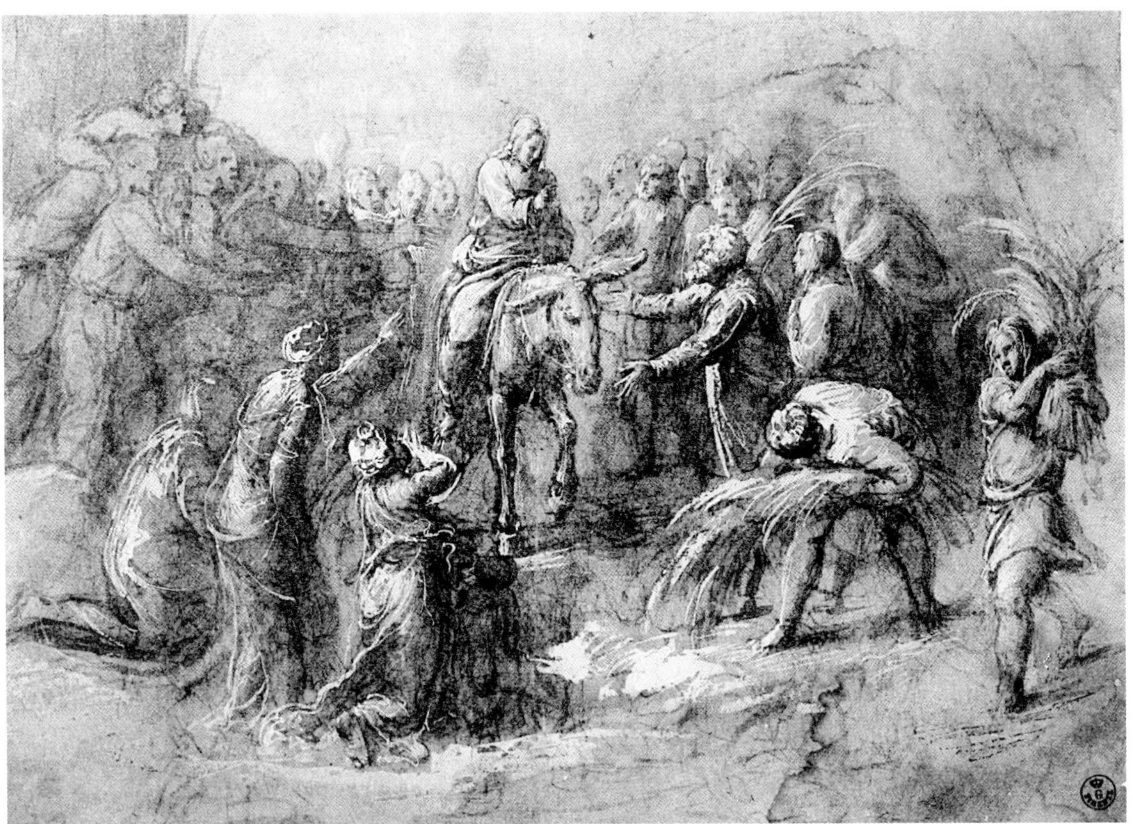

2.17 *Christ's Entry into Jerusalem.* Pen and brown ink, and brown wash, with white heightening on brown prepared paper, 19.6 × 28 cm. Gabinetto Disegni e Stampe degli Uffizi, Florence

arranged on three levels of different heights and widths on the facade with an open loggia on the top level. They were engraved in the sixteenth century by Cherubino Alberti, and also much later recorded overall in a print by Maccari (fig. 2.22). An image of the Poets and Muses on Mount Helicon was also an extension of the real-life experience of the pastoral in this particular suburban area, a site that apparently contained a spectacular fountain and was located not far from a Roman aqueduct, the so-called Acqua Vergine.

In general there is a distinct uniformity and formulaic quality to all the facade decorations. They represent something of an 'unstyled' style, as the artist distilled not just the fragmentary nature of most ancient art but a disparate variety of styles into one perfectly homogenous end result.[34] And so, given the number that have been lost, it is reasonable to offer a summary of their formal appearance. Polidoro's facades are distinguished by vital majestic compositions predicated on direct action and emotion. High-pitched drama and vivacious, adrenalised movement were typically introduced, evidence for

Polidoro's unrivalled ability among Raphael's followers in the depiction of vigorous motion and tactile form. In the narrative fields, density produces great dramatic force, while characters overlap and faces are often hidden to evoke overwhelmingly powerful reactions. The scenes are compactly treated and essentially planar in arrangement, with little or no foreshortening and with dense, rhythmic repetitions on the surface. Despite Polidoro's prowess in the genre, landscape is not normally a feature, presumably because it rarely occurred in ancient relief sculpture. One exception is the extraordinary treatment of the landscape around Andromeda in the Bufalo frescoes. Individual bodies give the impression of being vibrantly alive and yet rather chastened and rigid at the same time, as if to reinforce the fact that while the source for the figure style and subject matter was the art of the ancients, they have been brought to life by means of paint. Facial features and gestures are exaggerated in order to make them legible from a distance. The variety and sense of *horror vacui* of the facades fully echo the ancient source material that provided the voracious Polidoro with an index for

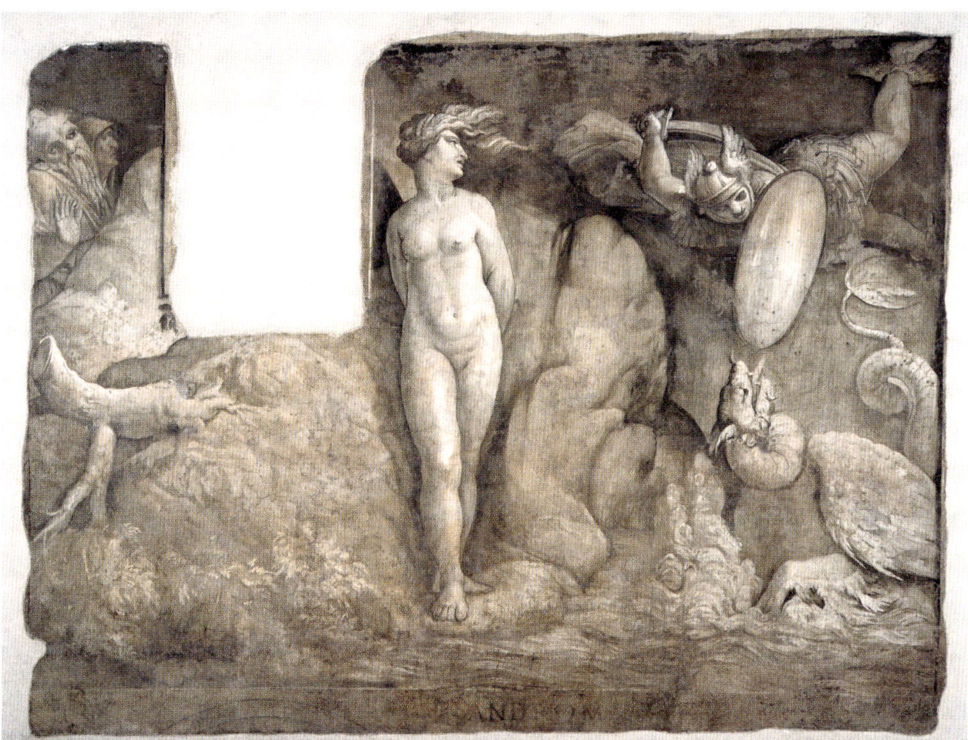

2.18

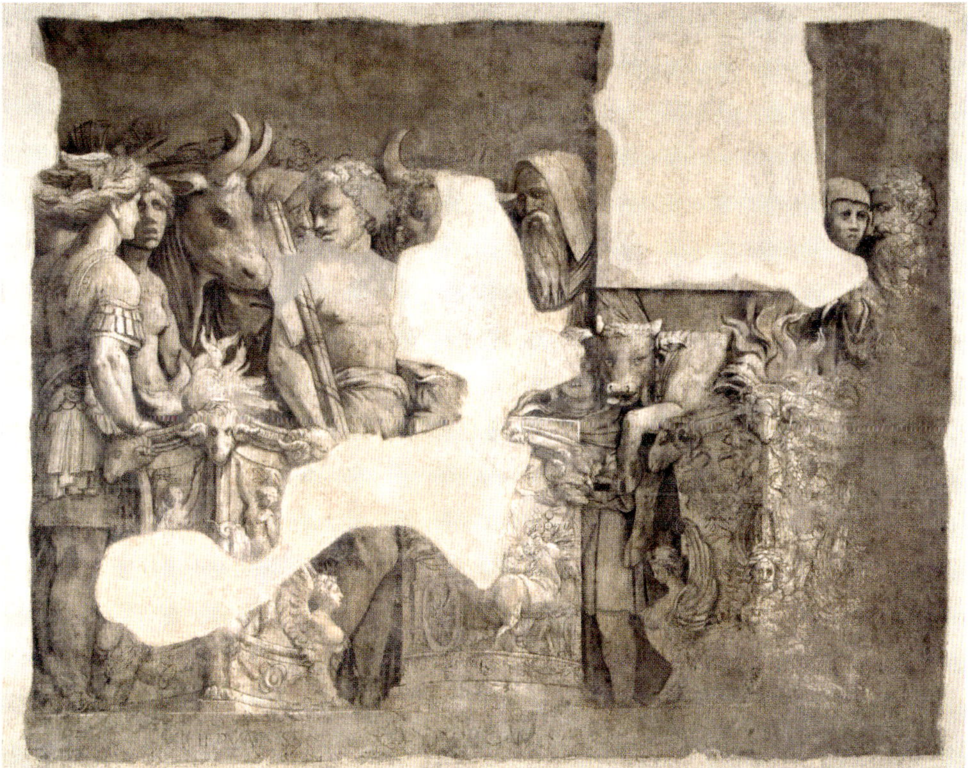

2.19

ABOVE AND OVERLEAF: Detached frescoes from Casino del Bufalo transferred to canvas. Comune di Roma – Sovrintendenza Capitolina ai beni culturali – Museo di Roma **2.18** *Perseus Liberating Andromeda*, 212 × 286 cm | **2.19** *The Marriage of Perseus and Andromeda*, 206 × 266 cm | **2.20** *Perseus with the Men of Polydecte*, 148 × 286 cm | **2.21** *Parnassus*, 148 × 285 cm

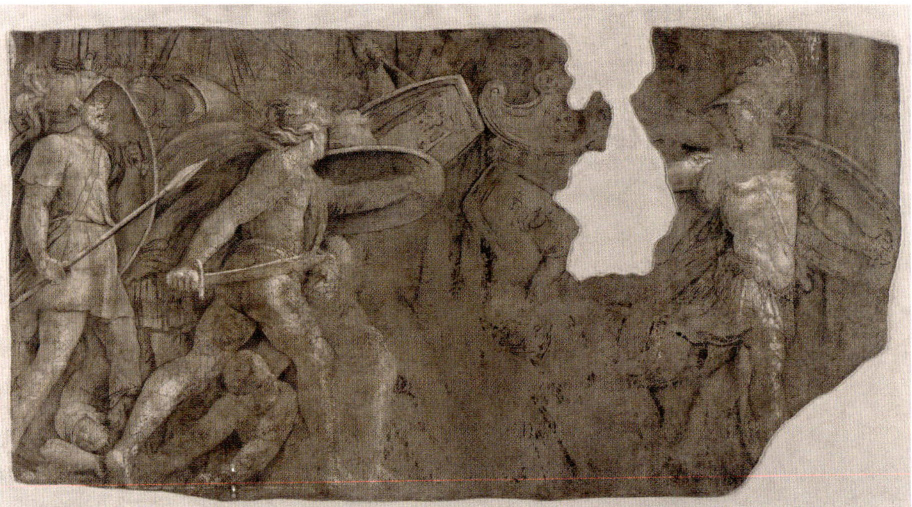

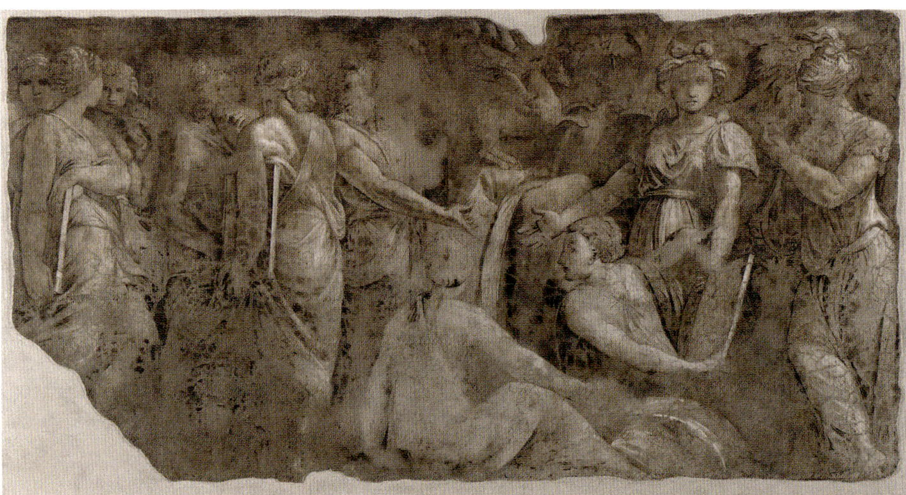

storytelling – sculptural reliefs, sarcophagi and triumphal arches – as he recovered the heroes of the ancient world. By depicting these fictive reliefs and statues on the facades Polidoro attempted to create an overall sense of wonder in passersby, who would appear to stand in the presence of some antique art miraculously intact and perfectly preserved in fresco – a false statement of a collecting history. A pretence to possession of these invented objects was a stronger motivation, it appears, than any enlightenment or ethical lessons derived from the subjects. That actual ancient sculptures were sometimes embedded into different tiers on the facades of palaces and churches only enhanced this alchemy. The rewarding of more sophisticated viewers who might identify known originals had no purpose in such a public setting, which also helps explain

why direct quotations of ancient works are few. When we recall too that modern Rome existed as a fragment of a city, not unlike today, the facades presented a visual unity that was itself striking and contemporary. When viewed in direct sunlight many spectators must have thought they were hallucinating or stepping back in time.

All the facades were painted in fresco and in monochrome, an inexpensive substitute for the marble and bronze they simulated. The fact that fresco allowed a defined amount of wall to be prepared and executed on any given day encouraged the separation of the subject matter into distinct fields. The reduction in colour scheme was inspired by a desire to emulate ancient sculpture, as opposed to the appearance of what little ancient Roman painting remained, or descriptions of it. From examples

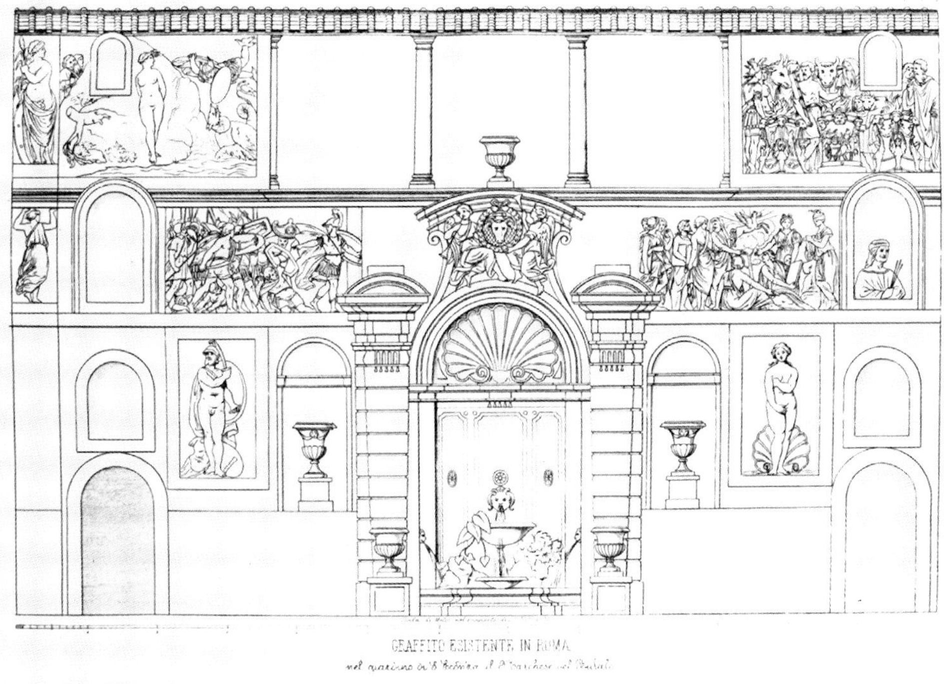

2.22 Ernesto Maccari, Print after the Casino del Bufalo facade

that survive it appears Polidoro often outlined figures with incisions made with a sharp instrument directly into the plaster, a technique carried out with an extraordinary confidence, almost reckless at times. There is evidence that some cartoons were also used and similarly transferred through indirect incisions of varying precision with a stylus into wet plaster, rather than the more laborious pouncing technique.[35] The main inspiration is that of ancient relief sculpture, in which a real shadow is cast on the flat ground by the figural elements: the greater the projection, the darker the shadow. Polidoro imitated these sources by developing a simple and reliable method with three distinct parts, working quickly and efficiently out of doors before the plaster dried. He introduced a dark brownish (not black) ground in the frescoes that served as a middle tone. The fluid outlines with black pigment act as the shadows. This was then overlaid with a brilliant white made from crushed travertine stone for the highlights, and so emulated how sculptures are viewed rather than the reality of how they were carved. The technique is entirely loyal, then, to the perception of sculpture – as opposed to painting – in representing a variety of visual experiences. The effect is not polished but consistently broad and uniform, with open hatching marks, an exceptional vigour and urgency, and no requirement for meticulous detail.

While Polidoro frescoed some new buildings like Palazzo Gaddi, in many cases he ornamented older architecture to modernise its appearance. Polidoro adeptly exploited the actual architecture of the facades in order to create illusion, in particular through his reliance on the ledges as platforms, but also occasionally for hands and feet to dangle fictively and playfully over the edges. At the same time he did not necessarily make adjustments for figure scale because the requisite banding in architectural storeys made this difficult and the views are artificial. In most cases it would have been physically impossible for viewers to study the subjects on the most elevated levels in any detail. Otherwise he seems to have favoured simple framing without much articulation and the appearance of reliefs applied to a modern building rather than the illusion of an architectural facade. Even within the narratives, a sense of levity and copiousness is found in the decorative elements; rather than attempting to create faux architecture, Polidoro sought overall visual splendour. Apparently he did not have the ability to follow Raphael's interest in architecture. His renditions of sculpture are adhered to the facades not inserted into the spaces. What he did

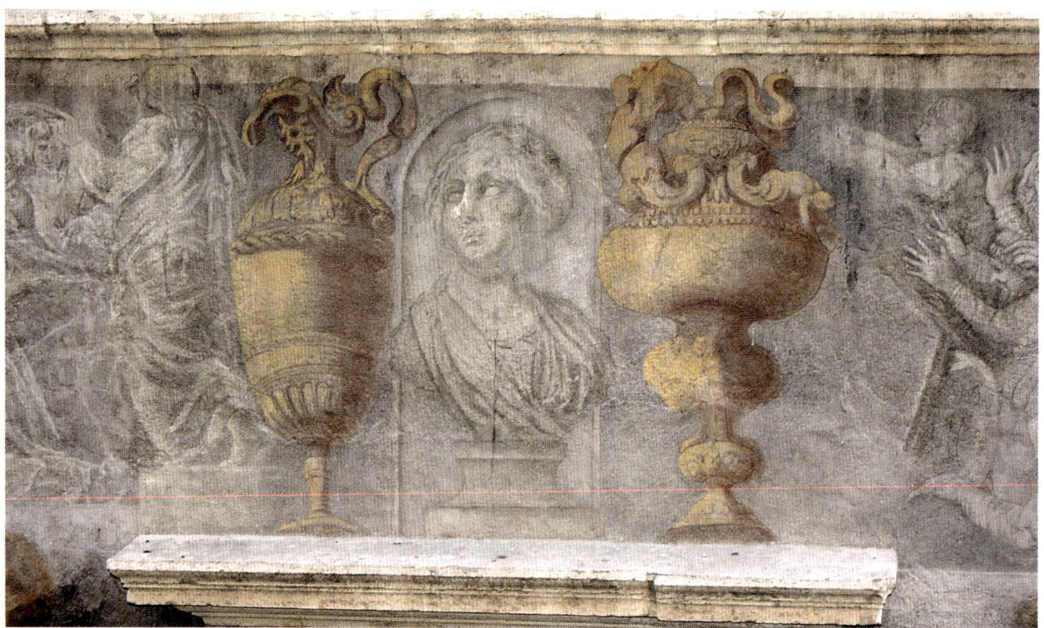

2.23 Palazzo Milesi, Rome, ornamental detail

indulge in, however, are subsidiary decorations containing arms and trophies of the type derived from ancient monuments to provide contrast with the narratives and single figures. His contribution to the history of ornament was as profound and far-reaching as that of narrative because often the decorations were copied on their own, separate from the subject fields. Polidoro also often conveniently portrayed the decorations in self-contained areas (fig. 2.23), frequently presented on a scale more monumental than any figures.

These facades offered Polidoro the chance to quote directly from antique sculptures, but he was selective, generally limiting himself to more dramatic, even violent themes rather than searching for reasoned canons of proportion or beauty as Raphael had tended to do. His decorations were, however, more varied and impassioned than the antique sources and often emotionally moving in interpretation. After all, although the subject matter was ancient, antique art and the versions of it that circulated in Raphael's workshop, or were recorded in prints by engravers like Marcantonio Raimondi during Polidoro's youth, rarely provided specific models for the variety of subjects the artist had to invent. As much as it revived a distant heroic past, there was expediency in Polidoro's use of the ancient art available around him in Rome, as he needed a plentiful repertoire of forms for his many facade decorations. This was a period when awareness of

archeology and preservation was just beginning to intensify, and artists had a particular role to play as experts whose opinion was respected. Simultaneously, the popes were aggressively ravaging ancient sites for precious building materials. Explicit quotations are rarer than might initially be expected and those that are there were generally thoroughly absorbed and transformed through the process of preparatory drawing before they were realised in fresco. Many of the sources Polidoro would have required had already been identified and reconceived in Raphael's workshop for locations like the Vatican Loggia or Sala di Costantino, or in prints, secular and religious, so in many cases he did not even have to return to the originals for particular poses or compositional formulae. Vasari noted a specific source on a facade near San Jacopo featuring two river gods, Nile and Tiber, from the Vatican Belvedere, but scholars have struggled to identify anything else so explicit.[36] The reliefs on the Column of Trajan were another crucial source for Polidoro, as Vasari recognised, and he also identified the quotation of a wounded Scipio from the structure on a lost facade near the Castel Sant'Angelo.[37] This image survives in an exquisite engraving by Saenredam (fig. 2.24).

Rather than attempting accurate and honest reconstructions, Polidoro absorbed his surroundings so deeply that he preferred to be interpretative and evocative in his engagement with antique art, while elaborating a consistent personal style in public spaces. He created substitutes for ancient art rather than providing literal replicas, and quotations were modified by the time they were painted. In holding this attitude of respect mingled with defiance, Polidoro was not unusual among his fellow artists in both retrieving the past and at the same time using it as a springboard for innovation. He did not rediscover a lost art so much as find his own style within it. This creative blending of accuracy and total invention was typical of his contemporaries, and entirely counter to the precepts of archeologists.[38] The notion of the virtuoso, expressive challenge of improving on ancient sculptures, especially fragmentary ones, was described by Vasari in his life of Lorenzetto when writing about Palazzo della Valle, where modern sculptors had performed restorations: 'Antiquities thus restored certainly possess more grace than imperfect specimens.'[39] This attitude is encapsulated in literary terms by Lodovico Castelvetro, who in recounting the difficulty of contriving a written plot from actual events said he preferred to embellish his writing, giving the analogy of Michelangelo completing the missing beard of a freshly excavated statue of a river god with his own creation of an elegant knot.[40]

In literature it is a much older, venerated notion utilised, for example, by Dante in Canto X of *Purgatorio* in describing some stone reliefs as surpassing the work of the great Polycletus. Implicit in this attitude was the desire to understand, equal and modernise, but also to surpass ancient works and so not be intimidated by prototypes.

Fundamentally Polidoro's facades are triumphs of *disegno*, meaning both drawing and design, at the expense of colour, while the importance of lighting, both natural and artificial, was not neglected as it was unified across a given building. In view of the plethora of inventions recorded on the facades, it would be intriguing to know if Polidoro was ever approached by a printmaker to consider collaborating on transforming his designs into prints, as Raphael and later Rosso, Parmigianino and Perino all did in Rome. This would seem natural given his preference for design, but there is no evidence for it from that period.

Polidoro's prolific output in this genre reveals that he was unusually resourceful and efficient in four areas: as a student of the ancients, draughtsman, fresco painter and composer of historical narratives. His grounding in Raphael's workshop was instrumental for developing all these skills. The wealth of physical description and complexity in the

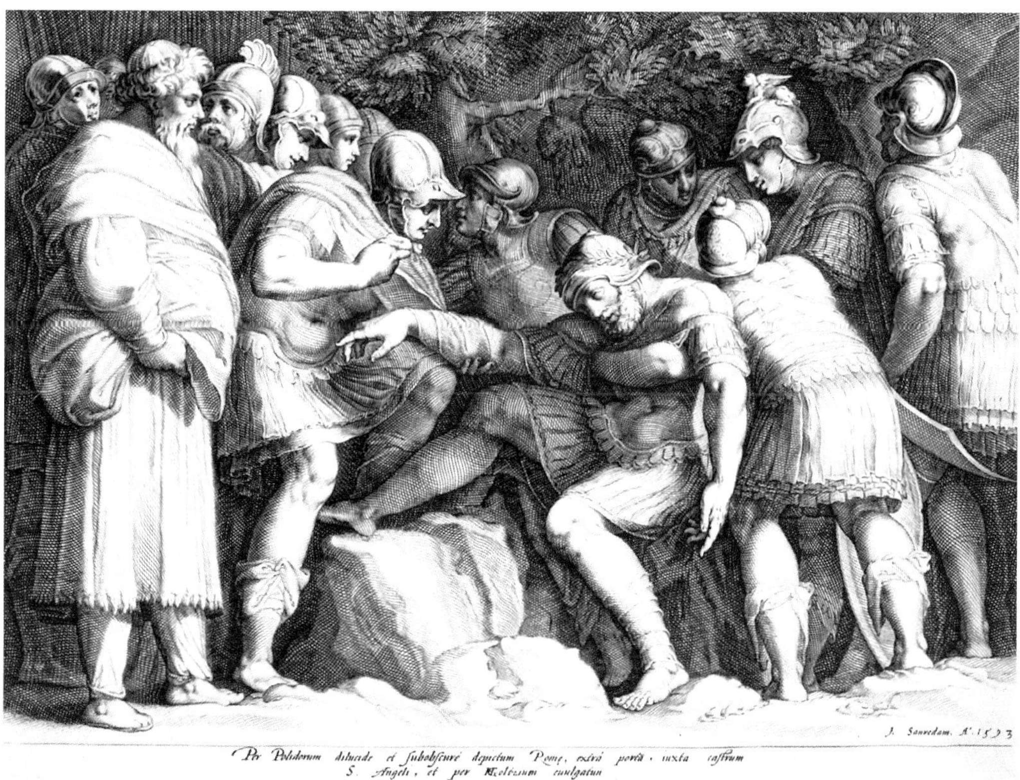

2.24 Jan Saenredam, after Polidoro, *Wounded Scipio*. Engraving, 25.5 × 34.8 cm. British Museum, London

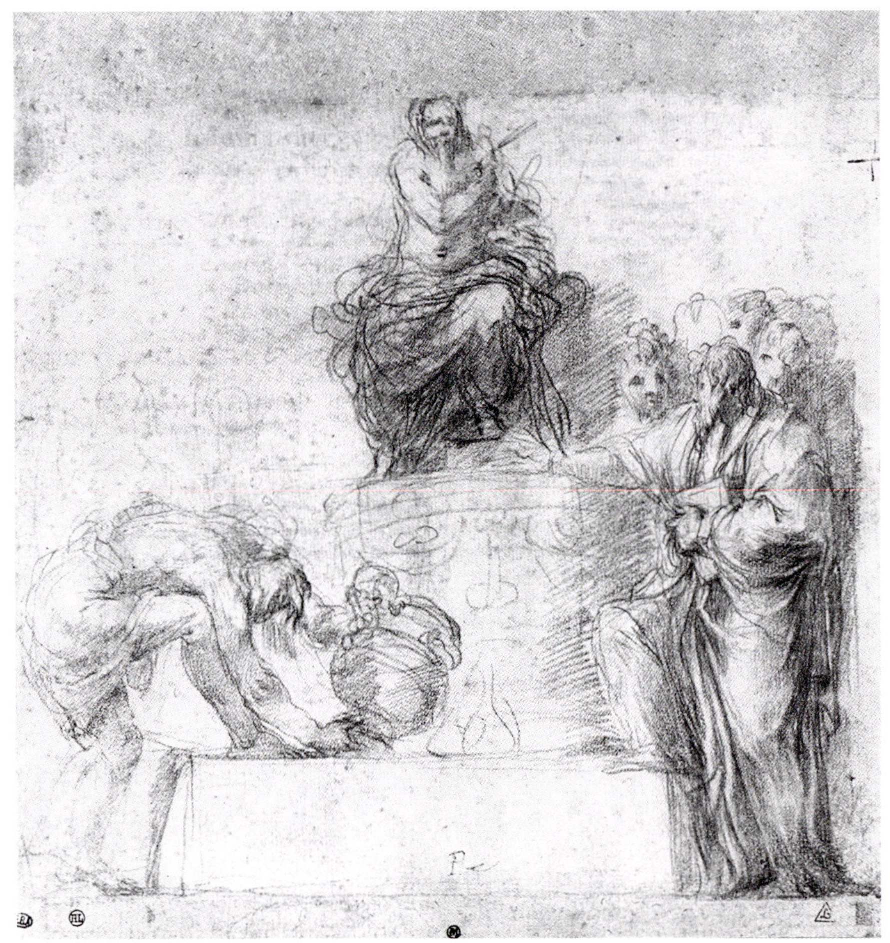

2.25 *Sacrifice to Jove*. Red chalk on laid paper, 20.3 × 19.3 cm. École Nationale Supérieure des Beaux-Arts, Paris

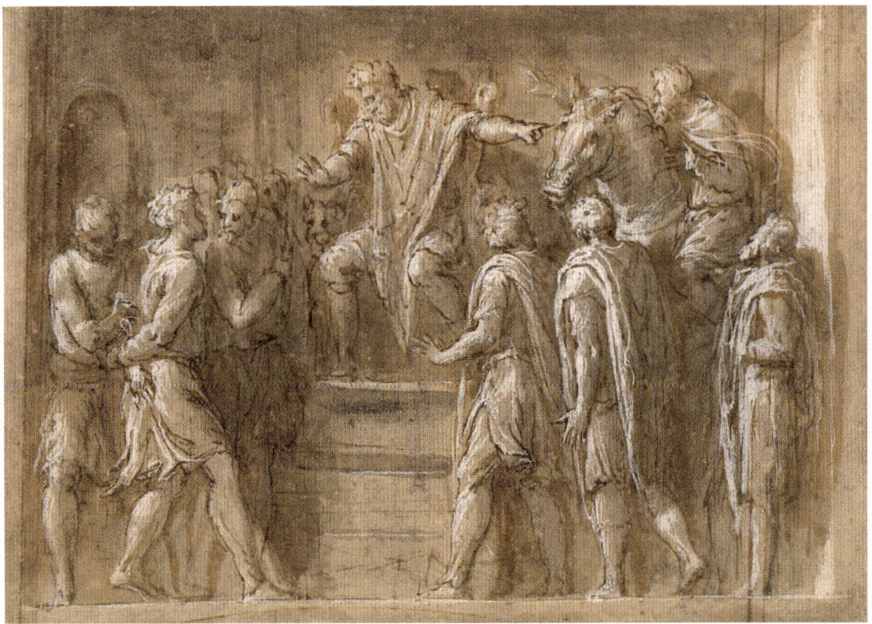

2.26 *Prisoner Brought Before a Judge (Condemnation of Perillus?)*. Pen and brown ink, brown wash, heightened with white gouache, over black chalk, on laid paper, 16.5 × 23.2 cm. Morgan Library, New York

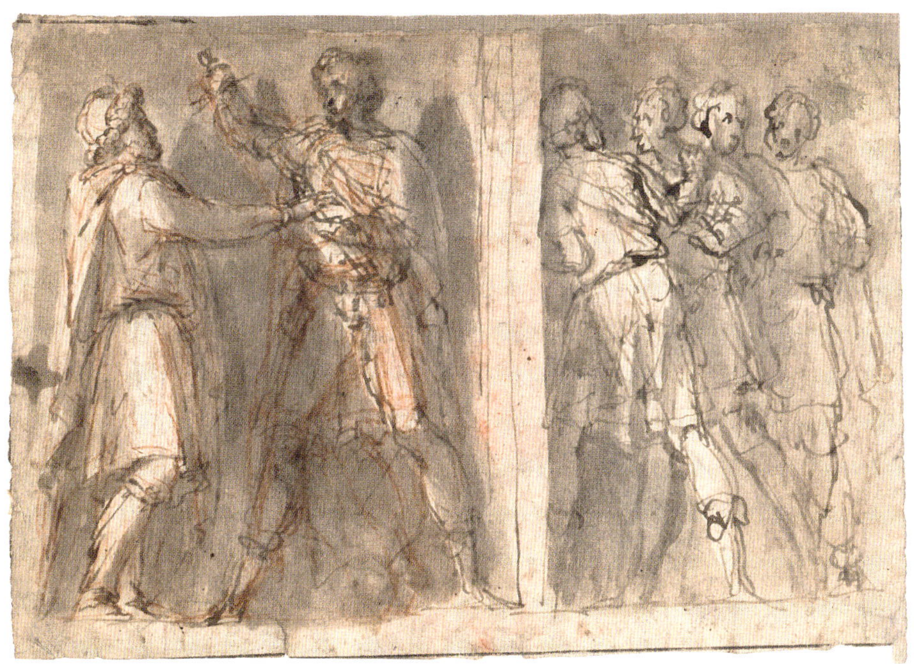

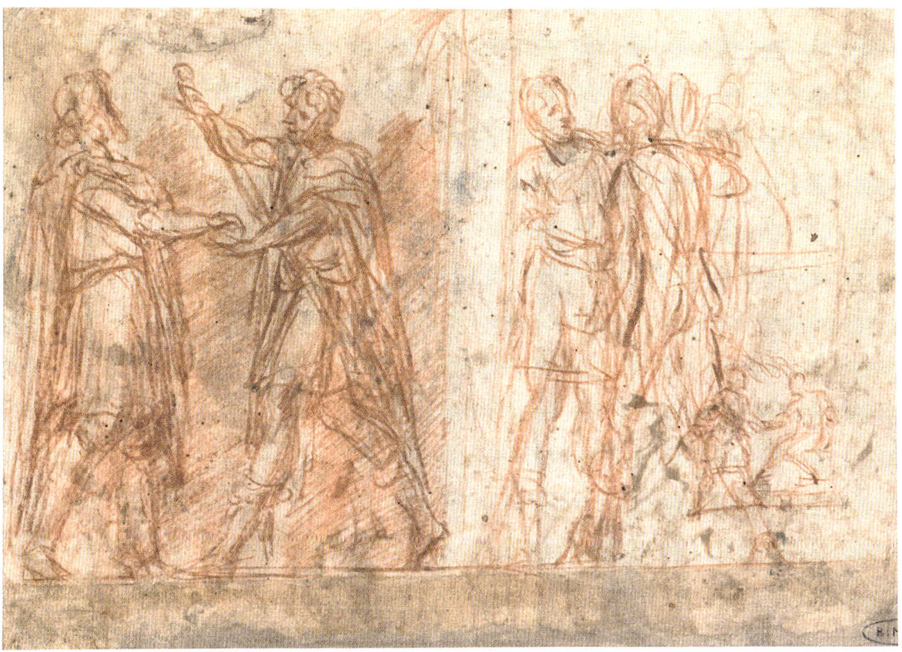

2.27–2.28 *Caio Mario at Minturno.* Pen and brown ink, and brown wash (recto)/red chalk (verso), on laid paper, 16.1 × 23.9 cm. Rijksmuseum, Amsterdam

organisation of these frescoes imply considerable planning, research and invention but, curiously, despite the relatively plentiful survival of the artist's drawings, few secure preparatory sketches survive for the facades, suggesting near wholesale destruction. Given the functional nature of the drawings in the workshop, it is possible that assistants executing the work used and discarded them after the master handed them over. Or perhaps we need look no further than the devastation wrought by the Sack of Rome, when the rebelling troops of Emperor Charles V ravaged the city.

As few as six autograph drawings related to the facades appear to have survived and they can be examined together to provide some insight into the artist's planning process,

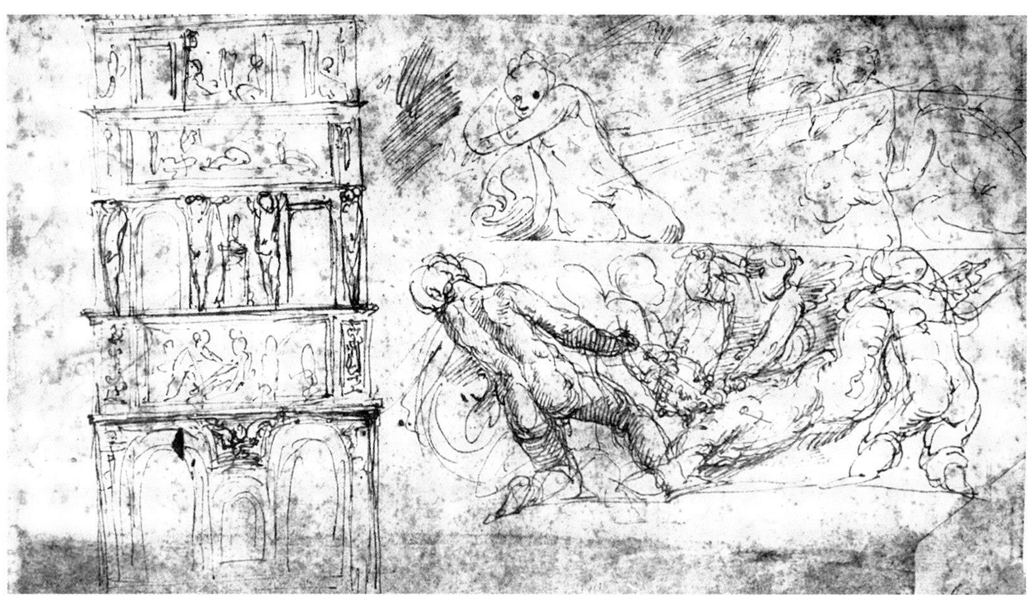
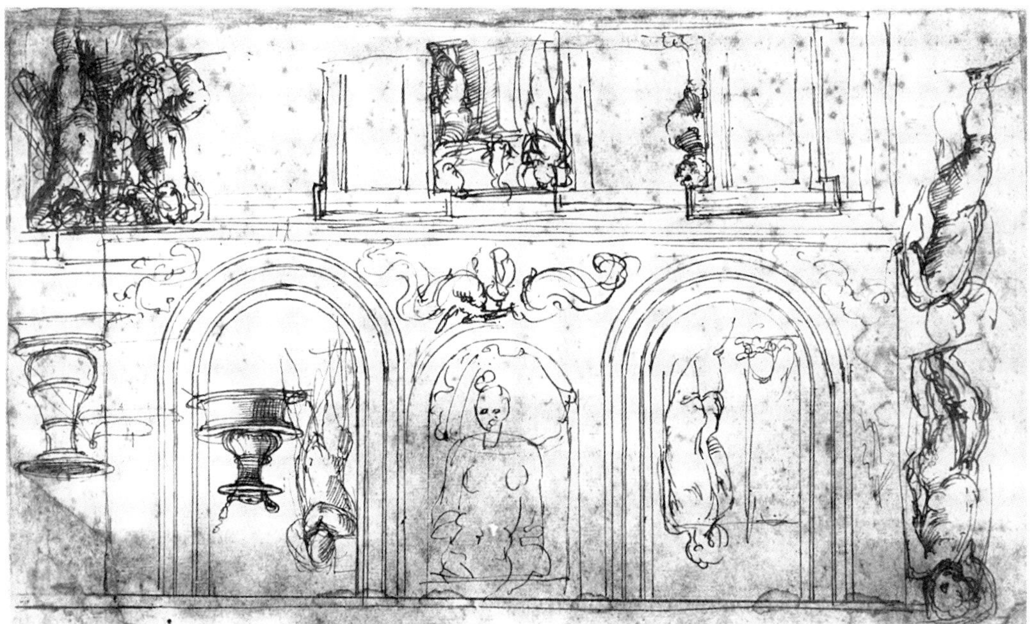

2.29–2.30 *Studies for a Facade.* Pen and brown ink on laid paper, 16.1 × 26.7 cm. Goethe-Nationalmuseum, Weimar

which must have been elaborate and systematic. The most resolved is the *Sacrifice to Jove* in red chalk in the École des Beaux-Arts in Paris (fig. 2.25), which can be linked directly to a square field once on the second level of the facade of Palazzo Gaddi.[41] It is a mature Roman drawing and therefore datable to the pontificate of Clement VII. Jupiter, the king of the gods, appears seated on a platform with a circular pedestal, with his attribute, the eagle, visible to the right. The crowd is placed to the right, and one figure comes forward holding a book and gestures across as if to signal the start of the sacrifice. The purpose of the drawing

was to establish the position of the figures and the lack of ornament is notable. It is distinguished by a mixture of furious, circulating lines, while other strokes are more carved out, the red chalk pressed into the paper to reinforce contours. The light is shimmering and out of focus, as if the artist were studying the play of sun and shadow out of doors. The figures have an elongated, languid quality and elegance that were not always translated in the finished works.

One of the other autograph drawings to be linked, in this case more tentatively, to a recorded facade decoration

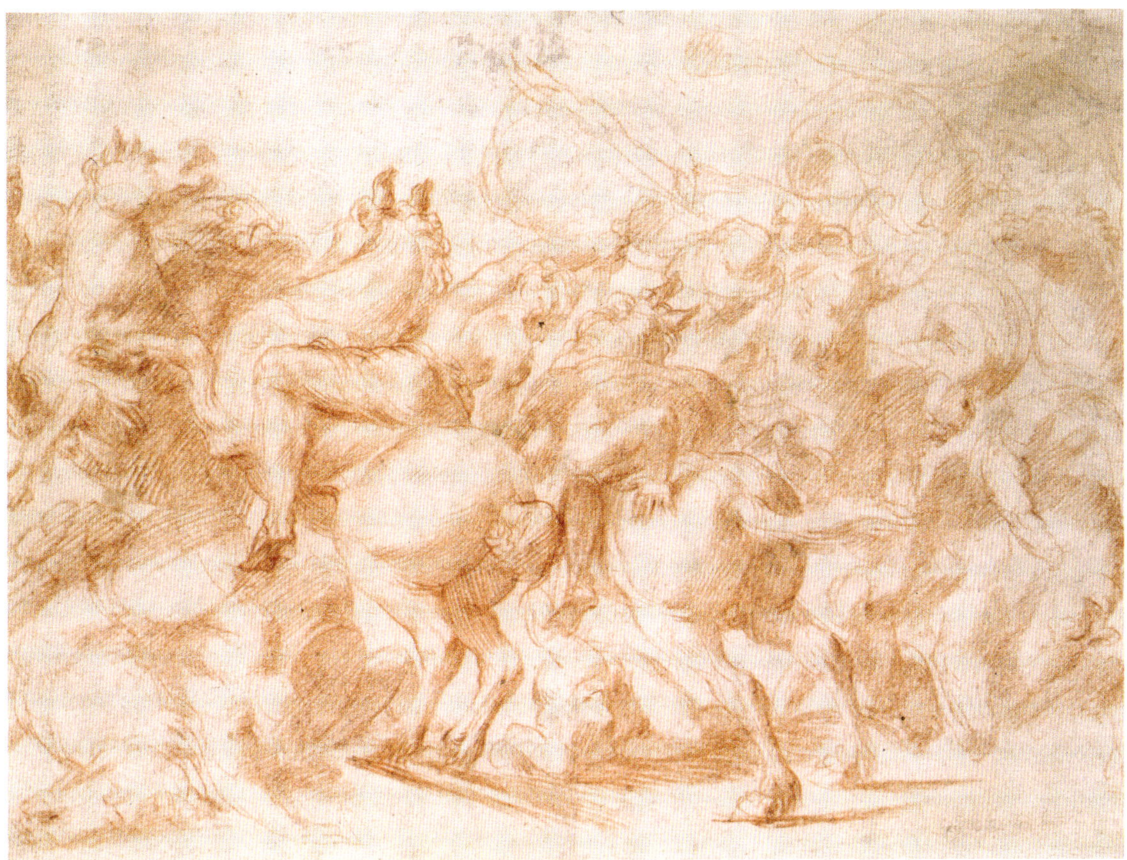

2.31 *Cavalry Battle*. Red chalk on laid paper, 20.2 × 28.4 cm. Agnes Etherington Art Centre, Kingston, Ontario

is a sheet in the Morgan Library (fig. 2.26).[42] It has been connected to a lost fresco on a facade of Via dei Coronari, Rome, thought to have been ordered by Cardinal Alberto Serra, depicting a narrative with a shocking moral. The story is from Ovid and relates how the inventor Perillus created a horrific instrument of torture to be used by Phalaris, tyrant of Sicily: essentially a bronze bull large enough to contain a person, who would bellow like a bull as the object heated up. Phalaris condemned Perillus to be its first victim. The image of Perillus entering the animal is known from copies and prints, and Vasari's account further allows that there was a second image related to the Morgan sheet, that of Phalaris ordering the execution. Usefully the drawing is in pen and ink rather than the chalk of the *Sacrifice to Jove* drawing, so it allows us to appreciate another side of the artist's approach as a designer. Polidoro introduced an abundant and almost electrified white heightening to study the brilliant outdoor light. The design is rather loose and planar, recalling the Palazzo Baldassini designs, suggesting a date closer to 1520 than 1527, which would also distance it from the Serra facade, likely executed during the papacy

of Clement VII. While the reliance on ancient sculptural reliefs is self-evident, the sheer energy is the artist's own.

A double-sided drawing in the Rijksmuseum in Amsterdam (figs 2.27 and 2.28) was recently identified by Leone de Castris, who overturned an attribution to a Spanish painter later active in Rome and Naples, Pedro Ruviale, and related it to a facade outside the Porta Castello.[43] Executed in an agitated pen and ink with abbreviated, almost misdirected lines and loose washes to evoke the shadows, at the limits of the artist's graphic technique, the sheet illustrates the story in Plutarch of Caio Mario at Minturno. The abundant use of wash is again used to interpret the exaggerated light and dark of the natural light in Rome. This is a type of drawing Polidoro must have produced in great numbers for himself to fix compact narrative ideas on paper, a personal shorthand before pursuing other more finished studies to resolve designs. The rough condition, including bad staining, may indicate the artist's own use of the drawing rather than the neglect of collectors. Both sides of the paper are used equally and what is now the verso may have originally been the recto

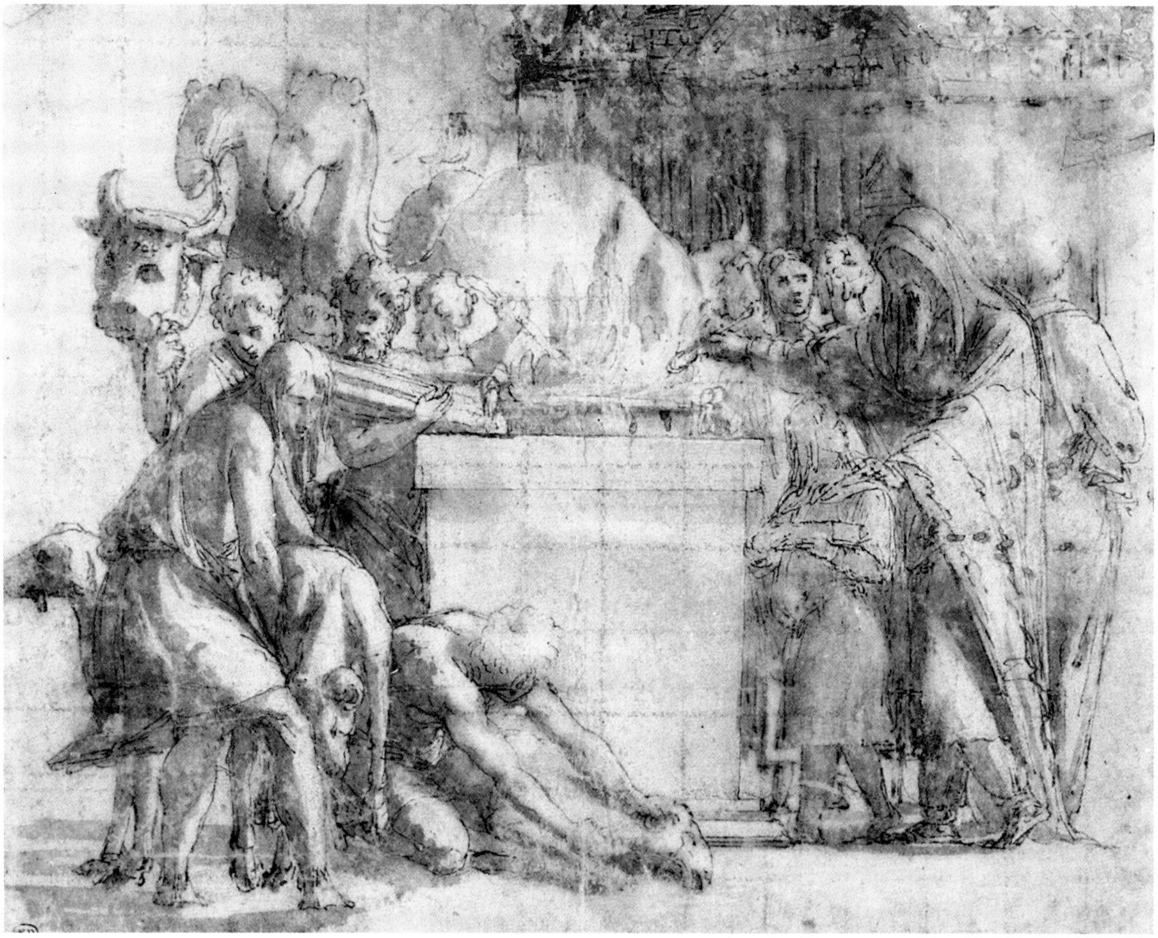

2.32 *Scene of Sacrifice*. Pen and brown ink, brown wash, with white heightening, squared in black chalk, 18.1 × 23.1 cm. Whereabouts unknown

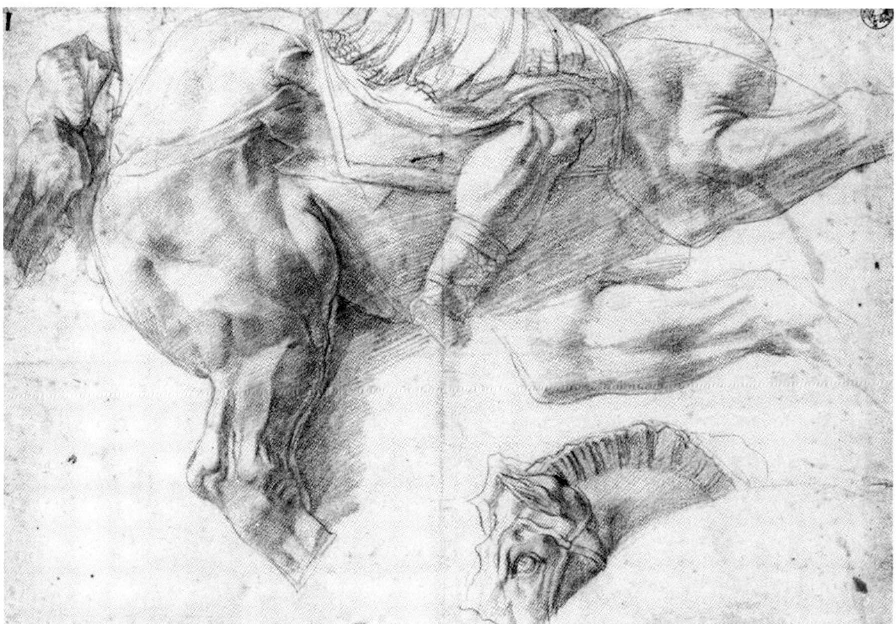

2.33 *Studies after the Antique*. Red chalk on laid paper, 18.9 × 28.1 cm. Staatliche Museen zu Berlin, Kupferstichkabinett

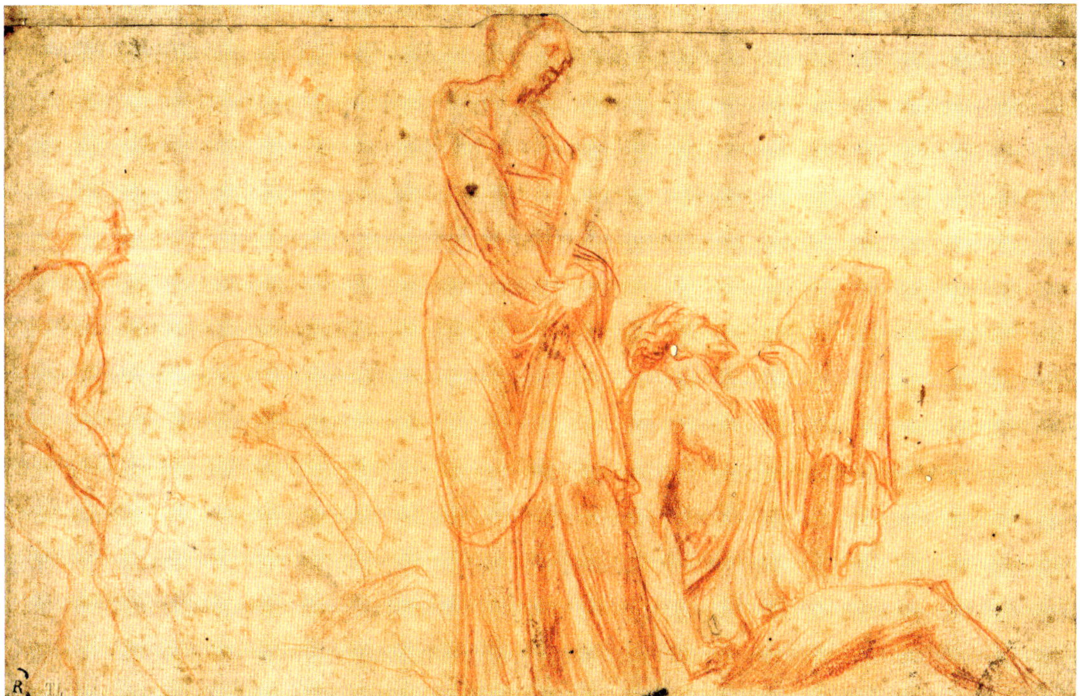

2.34 *Copy after the Antique.* Red chalk on laid paper, 17 × 26.7 cm. British Museum, London

as it is more resolved. The verso, drawn entirely in red chalk, is an important touchstone for the attribution of other relatively free and coarse studies in that medium by Polidoro. A dating in his mid-to-late Roman period seems likely.

Once owned by Goethe, the drawings for a fourth facade by Polidoro are in Weimar (figs 2.29 and 2.30).[44] It is uncertain for which facade they were produced but they are nonetheless useful in that they relate to an entire building – a unique survival. The assured handling, with swirling lines, also suggests they are of the mature Roman period. A study for a narrow facade on five levels, the recto includes a general view as well as details of the narrative and ornamentation. Caryatids appear in the central zone. To the side it depicts separately, with great drama, a scene with putti beating a satyr, a story from Philostratus and a subject Polidoro returned to in Naples in a painting now at Windsor Castle (fig. 3.20).[45] The verso revisits the ground level of the building and another level, but on the sheet turned upside down. More specifically, it reveals further details, including two dolphins and a figure in a shell niche, presumably Venus or Galatea. The drawing is briskly handled in pen and ink, with scribbling, swirling lines betraying the artist's spontaneous creativity.

Also in this group, a red chalk drawing of an unidentified cavalry battle survives in Kingston, Ontario (fig. 2.31).[46]

Given its subject matter, this seems likely to be a study for a narrative detail on a facade, although it has not been connected to any known work. In any event, it is an excellent example of the impact of Raphael's consummate red chalk drawing style on the younger Polidoro – although with a more violent, savage edge, to judge by the twisted bodies – and would place the study closer to 1520 than 1527. His knowledge of antiquity provided him with the appetite and excuse to be unrestrained.

Yet more difficult to discuss, as it is untraced, is a pen and ink drawing of a *Scene of Sacrifice* (fig. 2.32) with an imposing circulatory design, last on the market in 2003.[47] Attributed by Paul Joannides, it appears to be squared and seems characteristic of Polidoro's sharp handling of the pen, although whether it is a damaged original or a copy after a lost drawing rather than one made directly from a facade is uncertain. The squaring might incline us to believe it is an autograph working drawing. The looping, calligraphic quality of the lines may also indicate a very late Roman date, even though the design is unadventurously based on Raphael's *Sacrifice of Noah* in the Vatican Loggia.

In this context it might be claimed that Polidoro made numerous drawings after ancient art as study material. Evidence for this supposition is typically complex, and as with the preparatory studies for the facades, much has

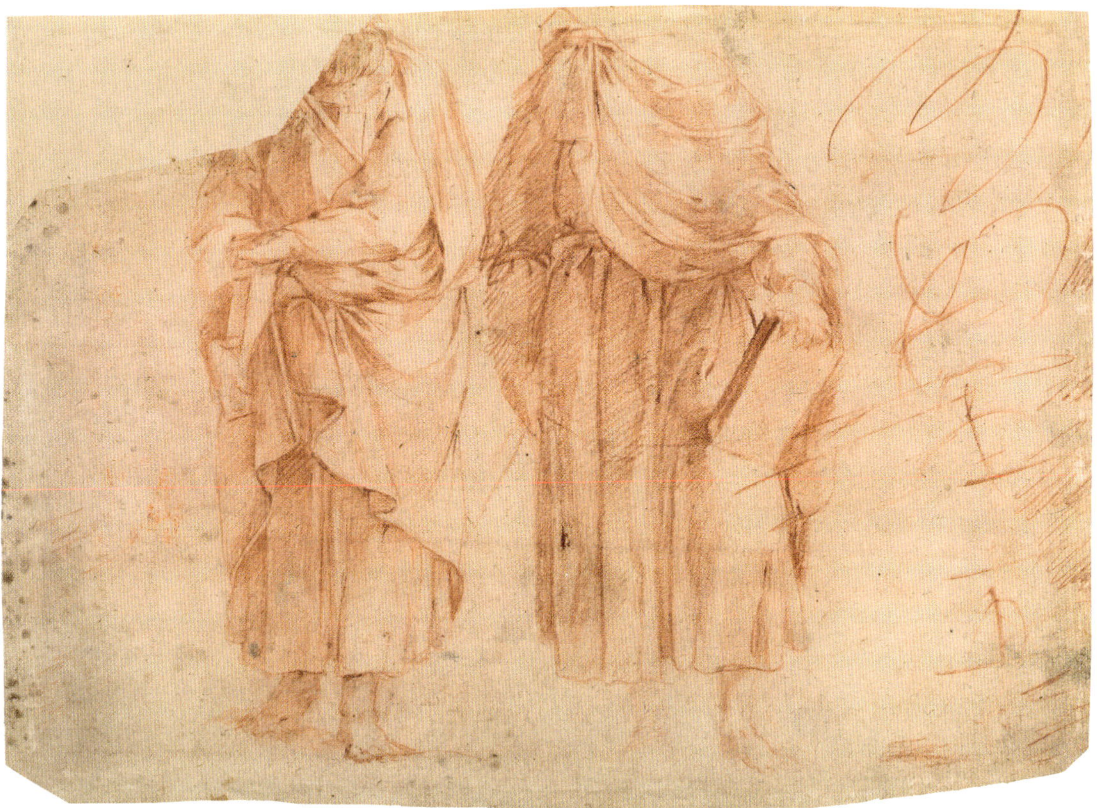

presumably been lost. Traditional connoisseurship is required to make sense of the subject, not least because Polidoro is a near automatic attribution for this type of drawing and the received corpus is certainly overstated. One of the few more convincing attributions to Polidoro, in this case traditional, is a drawing in Berlin (fig. 2.33). Finely modelled in a silky red chalk, it can be recognised as a copy after part of a battle sarcophagus that was later in the collection at Villa Ludovisi, including a soldier on a rearing horse, captured in an attractive agile light that accentuates the musculature of man and animal, as if to bring the stone alive.[48] A small number of other drawings after the antique, handled in a smooth red chalk and including figures with broad outlines and angular features, have been attributed to Polidoro but with varying degrees of plausibility. Presumably the drawing of a sculptural arm attached to the portrait drawing in the Louvre is autograph (fig. 1.2). Similarly, one in the British Museum that copies part of a sarcophagus featuring a scene from Euripedes' *Iphigenia in Tauris* appears close enough to Polidoro's hand to be accepted (fig. 2.34).[49] A double-sided

example certainly by Polidoro in the Courtauld Gallery (figs 2.35 and 2.36) appears to copy in red chalk three bands of marine-based ornament, but until it can be linked to a specific prototype it could as easily be described as an original invention and thus represents another challenge in studying this body of drawings.[50] The briskness of the drawing could indicate invention. The two standing male figures on the recto, who appear to be bathed in outdoor light, could be saints or prophets similar to those portrayed on the facade of San Pietro in Vincoli rather than classical characters. One rare sheet of pen and ink drawings in the British Museum contains a copy after a single Fate from a Meleager sarcophagus (top left), among various studies, mainly genre and religious, that clinch the attribution to the artist (fig. 2.37).[51]

The attribution of copy drawings by their very nature tends to be more difficult, and only through other characteristic sketches on the sheet can one feel confident. Perhaps it is the relative lack of such studies, as opposed to what the few that survive can tell us, that is surprising. Again, the chaos of the Sack of Rome may be the culprit.

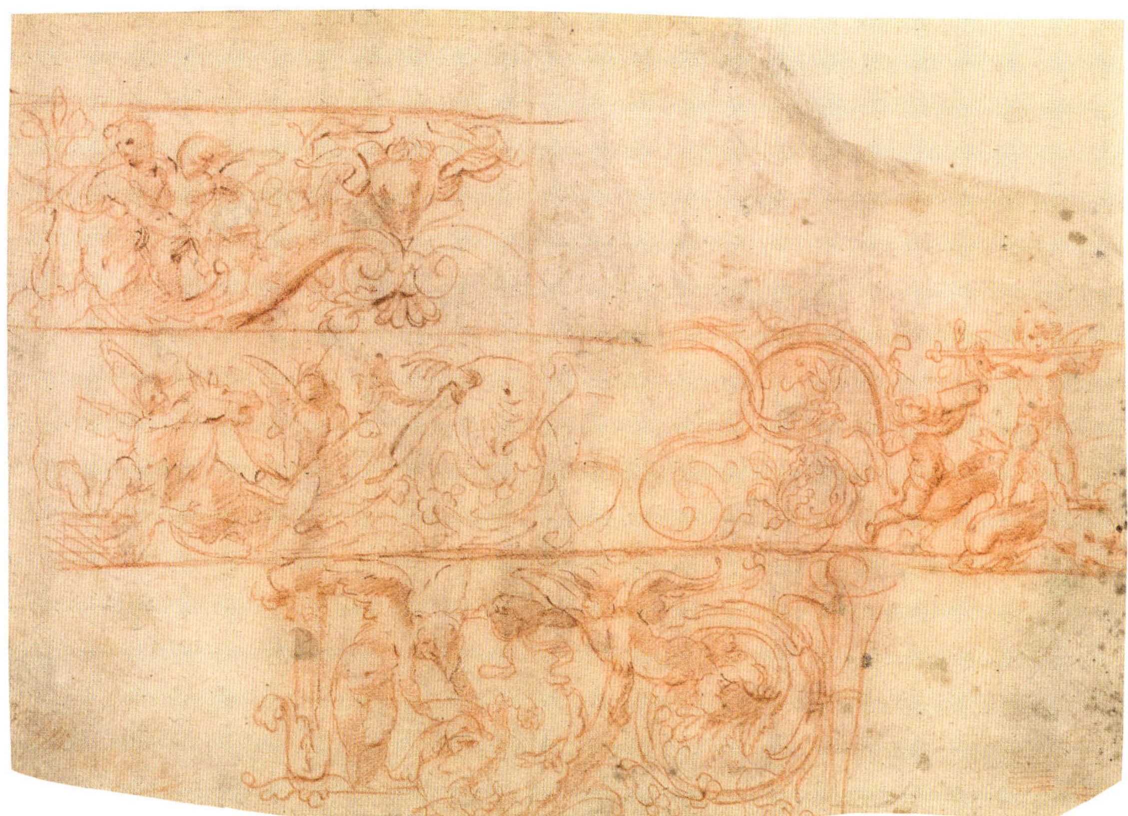

At the time Polidoro was resident in Rome his source material was readily accessible, which may have made him more casual about producing his own copies. His relationship to ancient motifs seems to have been personal and expedient, and none of his studies appears intended to be part of systematic record-keeping or a didactic exercise for members of his workshop. Although his knowledge of ancient art in Rome was extensive, how he transposed motifs into his fresco decorations cannot literally be documented and scholars are left to locate those models already modified and absorbed into finished works through the inventive alchemy of preparatory drawing. One truly exceptional drawing in Lisbon (fig. 2.38) supplies a sense of Polidoro traversing the city, in this case ambitiously recording ancient Roman ruins from a distance, probably those of the Castrense amphitheatre, near Santa Croce in Gerusalemme, but characteristically concentrating as much on the broader landscape with a dominant, exuberant tree in the foreground.[52] Drawings like this would have prepared him for the treatment of background architecture combining ancient and modern

found in surviving paintings such as those on the side walls of the chapel in San Silvestro al Quirinale.

In approaching the antique, sixteenth-century painters like Polidoro had to contend with a challenge that was less of an issue for sculptors and architects. The near complete loss of ancient paintings, apart from the more decorative type in the Golden House of Nero on the Esquiline Hill, meant that there were considerably fewer for them to imitate.[53] Although the search for pictorial designs could be supplemented with coins, gems and even mosaics, as well as sculptural reliefs, painters had not nearly the same number or range of direct models that were available to sculptors. All the facade decorations thus represent a fully creative transformation: sculpture as the source for painting. The main exception was grotesque-type decoration, but this was one branch of painting with which Polidoro was generally less preoccupied, even though its implementation was ubiquitous in decorations emanating from Raphael's workshop. Presumably he regarded this as a different specialisation, simultaneously scholarly and delightful, although a drawing in Budapest

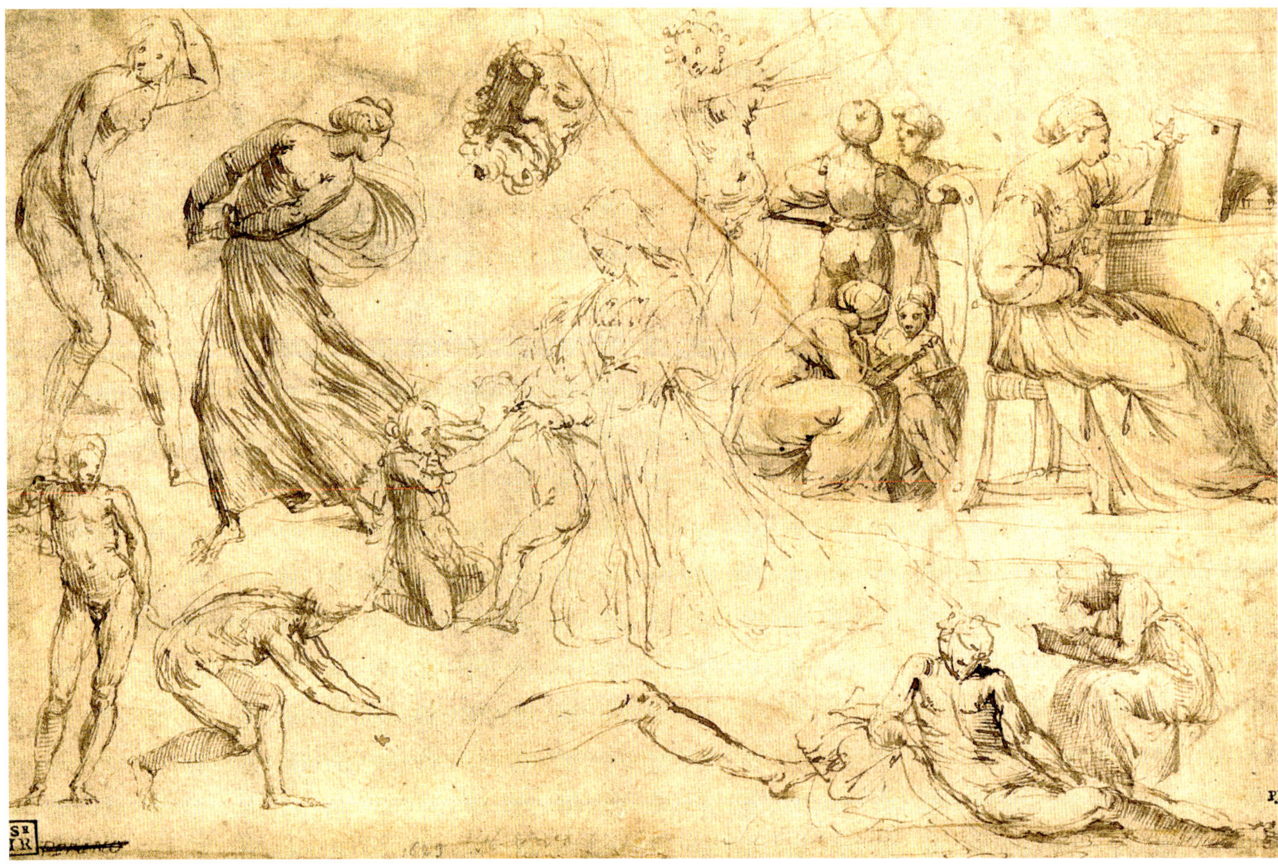

2.37 *Figure from a Sarcophagus and Genre Scenes.* Pen and brown ink, and brown wash, on laid paper, 21.4 × 32.8 cm. British Museum, London

for a complex architectural interior featuring two simulated ancient busts and a scene of Bacchus on his chariot in a lunette reveals that he was perfectly adept at it (fig. 2.39).[54] This highly complete drawing is as close to a reinvention of the Vatican Loggia as any recorded in Polidoro's extant work but, sadly, it cannot be related to any known commission despite its evident ambition. With no precise large-scale ancient paintings surviving as models, with the exception of grotesques, a modern artist felt more obvious pressure to invent than a sculptor, and Polidoro thrived on this creative challenge. He preferred to exploit the potential power of antique vocabulary rather than engage in literal reconstructions of the sort sometimes attempted by other members of Raphael's workshop, as in the subsidiary scenes on the vault of the Stanza d'Eliodoro in the Vatican. Polidoro was never able to develop in Rome along this more antiquarian path, and it is notable in this regard how few inscriptions appear on the facades indicating their relevance for the history of language and literature. Given his specialisation in this genre of secular facade painting, it may have been a

natural progression for him had he remained in the city, as it was a generation later for another artist devoted to the recreation of antiquity, Pirro Ligorio.[55]

Polidoro's output in Rome reveals how an artist closely aware of Raphael at a time that turned out to be the end of his career filtered the master's work in a way that was very different to the more commonly received perceptions of the artist from Urbino, celebrated for his fluid elegance and lucid, engaging narratives. Compared to the late followers of Raphael, Polidoro's expression is more earnest and brusque, though with its own remote, lapidary beauty. Certainly in contrast to Perino del Vaga (or even Parmigianino, who was never in Raphael's workshop), Polidoro looked at Raphael's art in a more oblique manner, seeking to distil and amplify its inherent power rather than use its purely technical features or potential for idealisation. To this extent Polidoro's uniquely rugged later style in Sicily will seem less baffling. Polidoro in Rome selected and rigorously refined merely one facet of the contribution of Raphael, an artist never admired for an interest in violence. In such naturally gifted artists

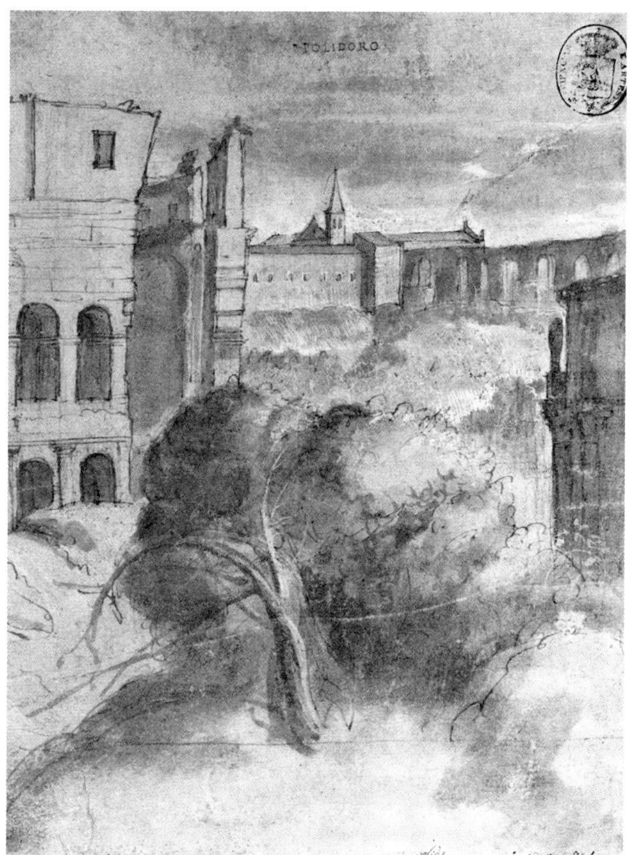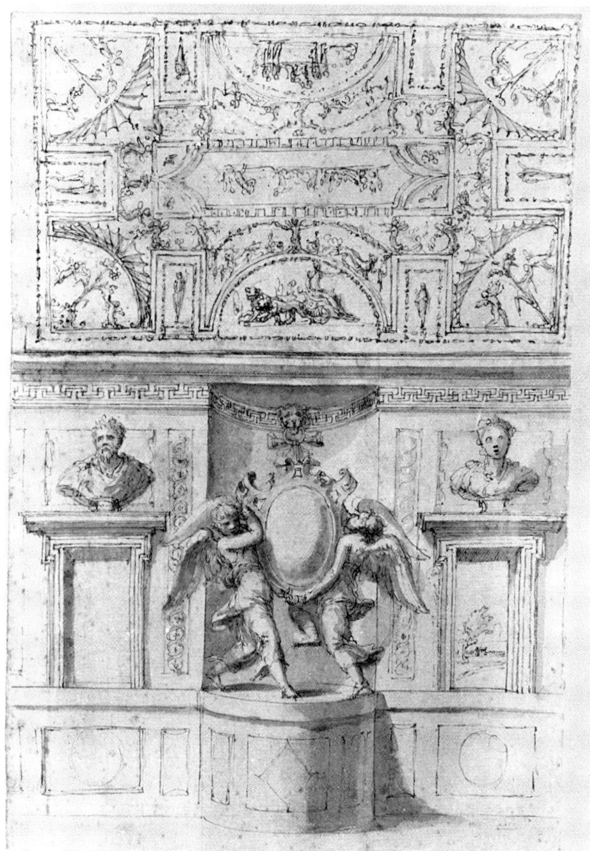

2.38 *Landscape*. Pen and brown ink, and brown wash, with white heightening on brown washed paper, 27.4 × 20.4 cm. Museu Nacional de Arte Antiga, Lisbon
2.39 *Study for a Decoration*. Pen and brown ink, and brown wash, on laid paper, 32.1 × 21.7 cm. Svépmuvészeti Múzeum, Budapest

as Polidoro and Perino, the competition between students of Raphael in Rome encouraged even greater specialisation in refining motifs observed in the master's corpus. This affected how Polidoro approached the ancients as well, eliminating some more lyrical facets of potential interest.

Polidoro rapidly achieved a decisive and distinctive style because of the highly public nature of his main output in Rome. This tendency was partly the result of the sheer scale of the task – to decorate the palace facades, which would only have been possible with a premeditated, pragmatic, even reductive approach, and so it is appropriate that the hand of Maturino remains indistinguishable from that of Polidoro. Valiant attempts to identify a graphic style for Maturino based on old inscriptions on drawings remain inconclusive. The relative absence of surviving drawings for the facades, and the real difficulty of establishing a chronology for them based on style alone, are indicative of the repetitive formal nature of the facade decorations, produced in a solid, consistent style reminiscent of, but never slavishly reproducing, the antique.

The Sack of Rome of 1527 was the unfortunate sudden catalyst for Polidoro's move to the south of Italy, alongside a forced independence with the loss at that time of his colleague Maturino, and distance from a context sympathetic to his initial strengths as an artist as they had by then developed. He could not have been fully prepared for other environments, particularly that of Sicily, given the almost complete lack of conventional religious art in his corpus and correspondingly the relative absence of opportunities to produce work with classical subject matter. The irony of his creating so many images of Roman glory and heroism in the years leading up to the devastation of May 1527 was perhaps not lost on a few of the more sophisticated invading soldiers.

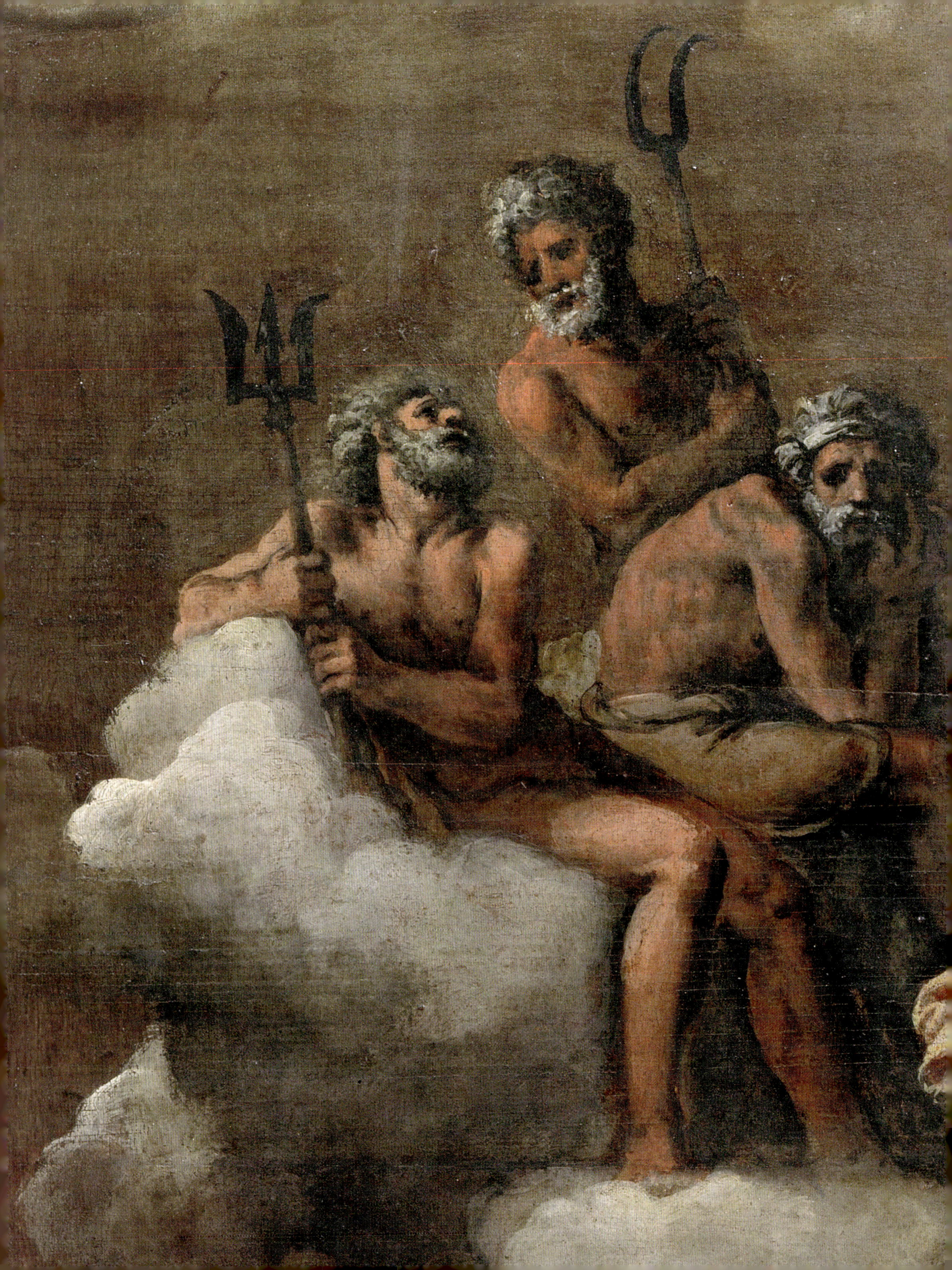

3 Flight to Naples

After the Sack of Rome, Polidoro fled to Naples, where he would remain until the following year. Vasari wrote melodramatically that the artist nearly died of starvation because of the lack of respect among Neapolitans for good painting.[1] In this case Vasari was not at all fair about patronage in the city, where there was an aristocratic class devoted to collecting and a sophisticated cultural milieu anchored by the Accademia Pontaniana, as well as acclaimed local writers like Jacopo Sannazzaro, who had been represented in no less a setting than Raphael's fresco of *Parnassus* in the Vatican. One of Polidoro's patrons during his first visit to Naples, before 1524, was Ludovico Montalto, a member of Sannazzaro's circle. Vasari's view of Neapolitan taste betrays his own veiled prejudice, based on negative personal experience and a failure to change the direction of the local art scene as much as he had hoped while he was working there in the mid-1540s.[2] Nonetheless, Polidoro suddenly faced new issues in his career, resident in a less cosmopolitan city, doubtless traumatised by the attack on Rome and having lost his long-standing partner Maturino.

Certainly the Neapolitans would have been familiar with a style related to Raphael's, and to that extent it is not difficult to imagine them well-disposed in principle towards an artist like Polidoro. One major altarpiece by Raphael came to Naples after its completion around 1514, well preceding Polidoro: the so-called *Madonna of the Fish*, installed in a chapel owned by Giambattista del Doce and dedicated to Saint Jerome in the church of San Domenico (fig. 3.1).[3] It had a deep influence on painters there, especially Andrea Sabatini, the 'Raphael of Naples'. There had been other prior contact between Raphael's workshop and Naples too. For example, the master sent an assistant, probably Giulio Romano, in 1518 to make a drawing in preparation for Raphael's portrait of the wife of the Neapolitan viceroy, Isabel de Requesens y Enríquez de Cardona-Anglesola, not Giovanna of Aragon as formerly thought.[4] (The painting that was produced, now in the Louvre, was sent to France, not back to Naples.) It is possible that Polidoro's brief time in Naples overlapped with that of Gianfrancesco Penni, one of Raphael's major assistants, who apparently went there after the Sack of Rome. Penni then travelled to Ischia to visit Alfonso d'Avalos, Marchese del Vasto, carrying the first painted

Detail of fig. 3.17

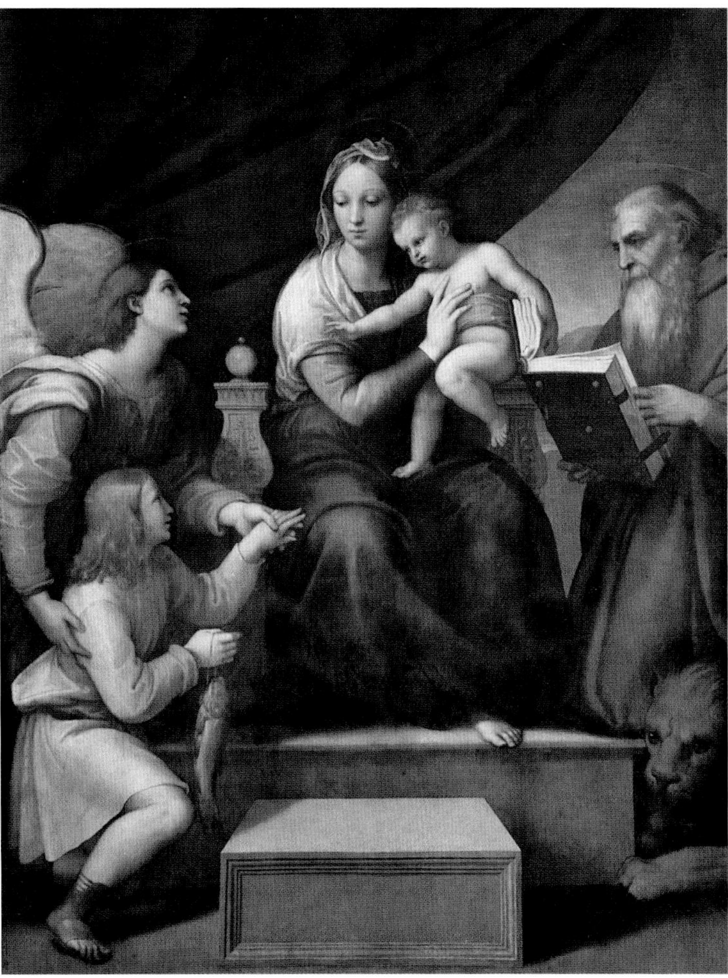

3.1 Raphael, *Madonna of the Fish*. Oil on panel transferred to canvas, 215 × 158 cm. Museo del Prado, Madrid

copy after Raphael's famous *Transfiguration*, which was eventually placed in the church of the Hospital of the Incurables in Naples in the early 1530s.[5] That Polidoro and Penni even travelled to Naples together cannot be ruled out. Penni executed unspecified works for a Florentine merchant based there, Tommaso Cambi, and remained in the city until he died, according to Vasari, probably in 1528. One of Penni's own pupils, Leonardo Grazia, from Pistoia, painted a now lost *Stoning of Saint Stephen* for Diomede Carafa, Bishop of Ariano in Campania, and also the high altarpiece of Monte Oliveto, replaced soon after by Vasari himself. Grazia did not die in Naples as early as 1528 as Vasari claimed, since it has been shown that he was still active during the 1540s. Polidoro's sojourn in Naples corresponds, therefore, to a period of persistent revival of Raphael's style by several artists directly familiar with the master's prototypes.

Polidoro's experience in Naples during his visit before 1524, when he had opportunity to paint the secular decorations for which he was best known, and the strength of his contacts, presumably account for his decision to flee there after the Sack of Rome, as opposed to going north towards his birthplace in Lombardy. It was likely his intention to return to Rome, and the suspicion arises that he was hovering in Naples as he had done during the pontificate of Adrian VI a year or two earlier, anticipating a chance to make his way back to the papal city. If this is true, he soon lost hope and elected to go much further south, where he had apparently never been before, presumably as reports reached him that the situation in Rome under a beleaguered Clement VII would not improve. Polidoro is recorded once in Naples, on 19 November 1527, in a document revealing a degree of local recognition, as it calls upon him as an expert, reflecting the respect that many of the great artists leaving

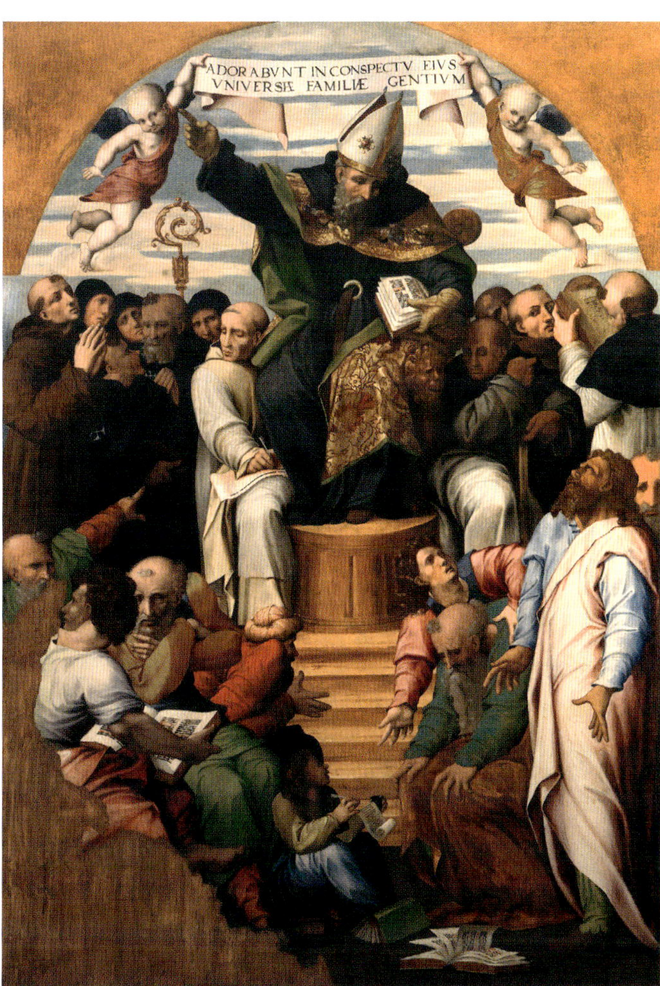

3.2 Marco Cardisco, *Disputa*. Oil on panel, 356 × 246 cm. Museo di Capodimonte, Naples

Rome after the Sack received in their refuges.[6] This contract was for a frame for the high altarpiece of the church of Sant'Agostino alla Zecca (Maggiore) and Polidoro is mentioned as an adjudicator, along with a minor painter from Pistoia, Bartolomeo Guelfo, who had been active in the Naples region for several decades. The painting, surviving in the Capodimonte (fig. 3.2), was eventually executed in the early 1530s by the Calabrese artist Marco Cardisco, possibly from Polidoro's design, as one early source suggested.[7] The towering centralised composition and the powerful gesticulations and animated faces of the densely grouped figures unquestionably reflect the style of Polidoro's Roman facades, although as he independently judged part of the work for value, presumably he had no part in the execution.

According to Vasari, Polidoro's first commission in Naples was the figure of Saint Peter near the high altar of the later church of Santa Maria delle Grazie a Caponapoli.[8] The church still exists but the work is lost and no extant drawings relate to it. Later sources mention that the painting was installed to the left of the high altar of this church, which was founded in 1447 and controlled by the Order of the Hermits of Saint Jerome of the Blessed Peter of Pisa. The principal patron was, however, the confraternity of the Bianchi della Giustizia (the White Robes of Justice), created as recently as 1519. A later writer, the 'Vasari of Naples', Bernardo de Dominici, proposed that Andrea Sabatini introduced Polidoro to this group and acted as an intermediary for the commission out of kindness to his celebrated, but displaced and temporarily impoverished, colleague from Rome.[9] Vasari's account of Polidoro's time in Naples reinforces the view that work was subcontracted to him by other painters who respected him, and that he would even allow paintings like this single saint to be

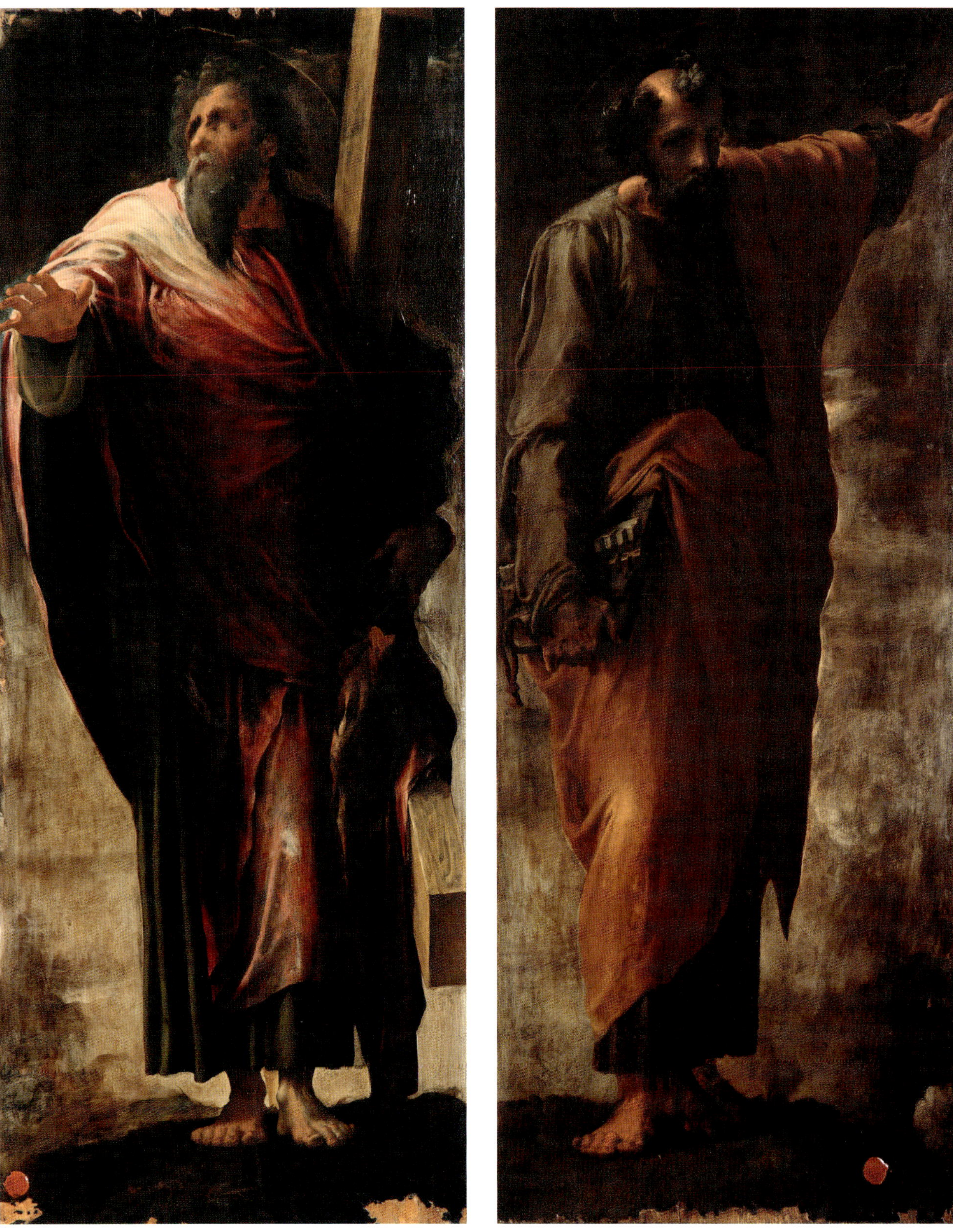

3.3–3.4 *Saint Andrew*. Oil on panel, 140 × 64 cm | *Saint Peter*. Oil on panel, 142.5 × 63 cm. Museo di Capodimonte, Naples

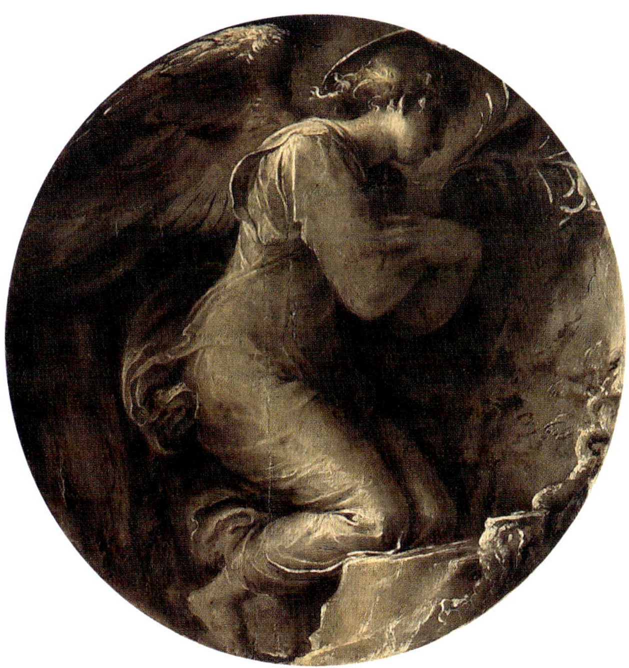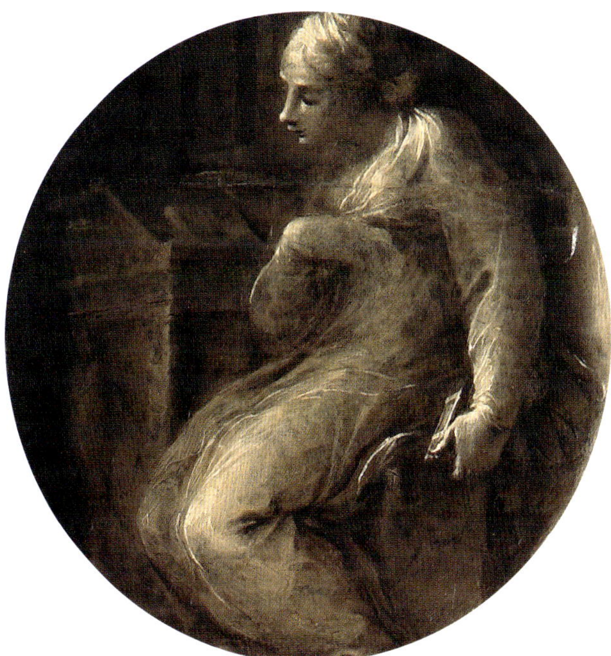

3.5–3.6 *Annunciation*. Oil on panel, each 36 cm diameter. Museo di Capodimonte, Naples

executed by another artist after his designs. Given that Sabatini was active elsewhere in the church, he may well have assisted with its completion. Assuming it was a fresco, it would probably have been obliterated during the Baroque remodelling of the church. Although the main altar was not dedicated to Peter, according to legend he had consolidated his popularity by preaching and performing miracles in Naples, so Polidoro's commission to depict him near the prestigious high altar of this church is entirely understandable.[10]

Following his description of the work featuring Saint Peter, Vasari relates how Polidoro decorated two different altars in another church: 'for Sant'Angelo, beside the Pescheria at Naples, a little panel in oils, containing a Madonna and some naked figures of souls in torment, which is held to be most beautiful, but more for the drawing than for the colouring; and likewise some pictures for the Chapel of the high altar, each with a single full-length figure.'[11] The church of Sant'Angelo in Pescheria, on the coastline near present-day Via Marina, was enlarged in 1526 to honour a medieval icon of the Virgin, originally located on an outside wall nearby. All Polidoro's surviving public paintings from his Neapolitan period were produced for this modest church controlled by the corporation of fishmongers, whose image of the Virgin was thought to have performed miracles during the plague year of 1526.

The site was known as the Pescheria al Mercato or Pietra del Pesce, or – more significantly for our purposes, because of the Marian imagery in Polidoro's drawings for the principal altarpiece – Santa Maria delle Grazie alla Pescheria. The reference to *pietra*, or stone, is found in a text by Virgil that describes how a rock carved with the sign of a fish was placed there, miraculously making the surrounding waters teem with sea life.[12] The church, which was levelled as recently as 1968, was dedicated to both the Archangel Michael and Santa Maria delle Grazie, if Vasari is to be believed.

Unfortunately, although he must have visited the site in person, Vasari's published account of the Pescheria decorations is too vague to permit a firm reconstruction of the high altar, and the surviving paintings and related drawings present conflicting evidence. There are five extant paintings with a provenance to the church, all now in the Capodimonte in Naples: two symmetrical panels featuring *Saint Andrew* and *Saint Peter*, two tondi depicting an *Annunciation*, and an *Entombment* (figs 3.3–3.7). Polidoro was likely responsible for the decoration around the venerated icon that became the high altarpiece, as well as producing a separate smaller panel for a side chapel.

A compositional drawing, now at Windsor Castle, records an original idea for the high altarpiece (fig. 3.8).[13] The sketch shows a unified field, with the icon framed in a simple moulding supported by four monumental angels, with the artist's initial ideas for the protector saints of the fishmongers, Peter and Andrew, flanking souls in the cleansing River of Purgatory. This more ambitious approach was discarded, presumably because it was too expensive to pay for the construction of such an elaborate surround. Instead, the artist altered the scheme to a polyptych format, as the saints are executed on separate panels. There is also evidence in other preparatory drawings, in particular the recto of one in a loosely handled red chalk in the Fitzwilliam Museum in Cambridge (fig. 3.9; formerly Gere Collection), that the saints were then intended to be tightly framed and so executed on their individual supports, as is apparent especially in the drawing of Saint Andrew.

The altar was dismantled within a century of its completion; in 1624, Cesare d'Engenio Caracciolo, in his work *Napoli Sacra*, could describe only the two apostles. This source mentions that there had been 'molt'altre figure per ornamento' on the high altar but that the confraternity had brazenly sold them.[14] Unfortunately, the passage does not provide more specific subjects. The most probable assumption is that they included the souls in Purgatory below the miraculous Virgin, of which we have no visual evidence outside of the Windsor drawing. D'Engenio's account reinforces the belief that Polidoro painted not a unified field like that recorded in the Windsor sheet, but a polyptych, parts of which would have been easily dispersed. Carlo Celano's later description of 1692 is explicit that the two saints were painted on separate panels, and an examination of their edges reveals without question that they were executed on independent supports, but in his guidebook the previously overlooked *Annunciation* tondi are for the first time cited on the high altar too.[15]

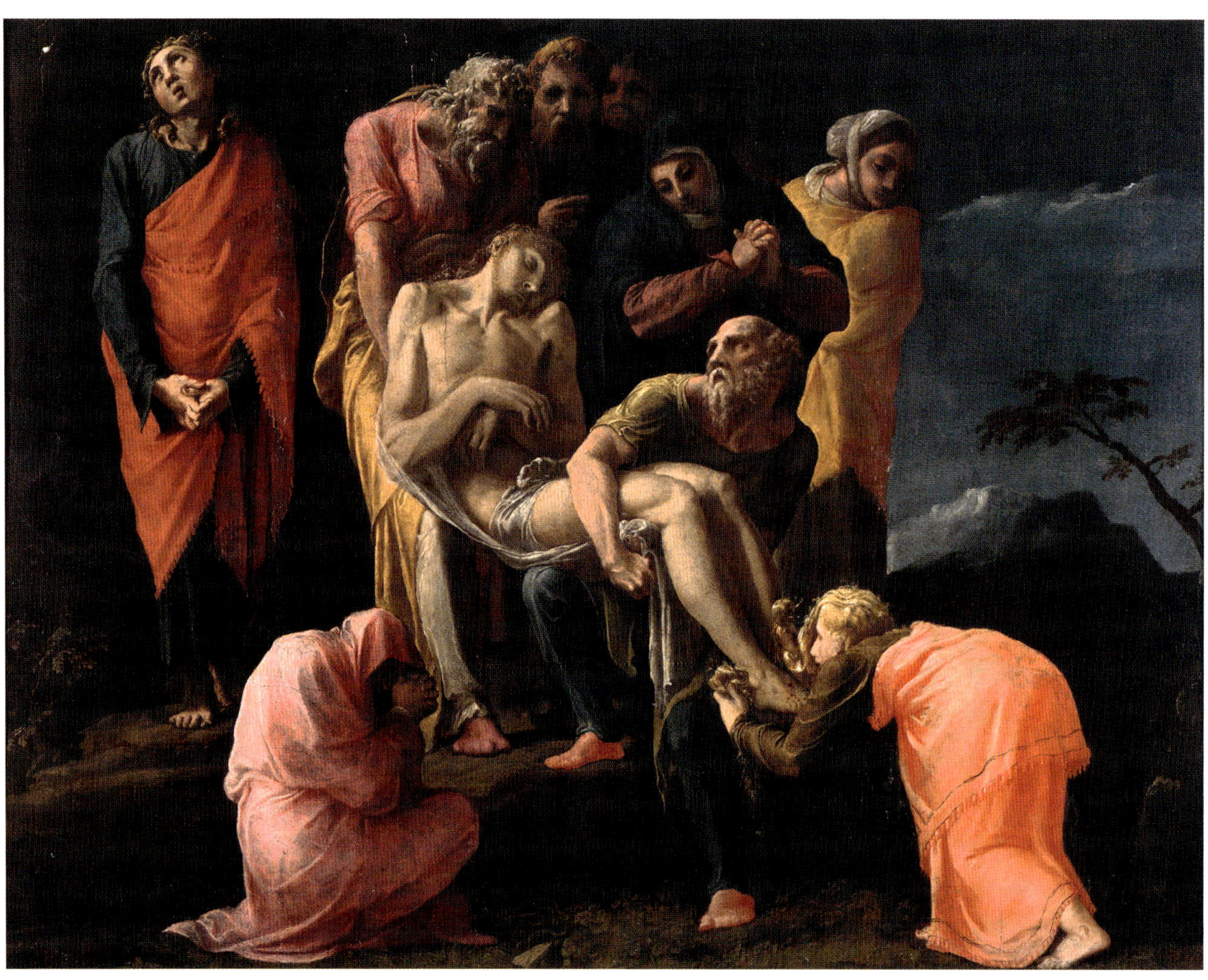

3.7 *Entombment*. Oil on panel, 81 × 106 cm. Museo di Capodimonte, Naples

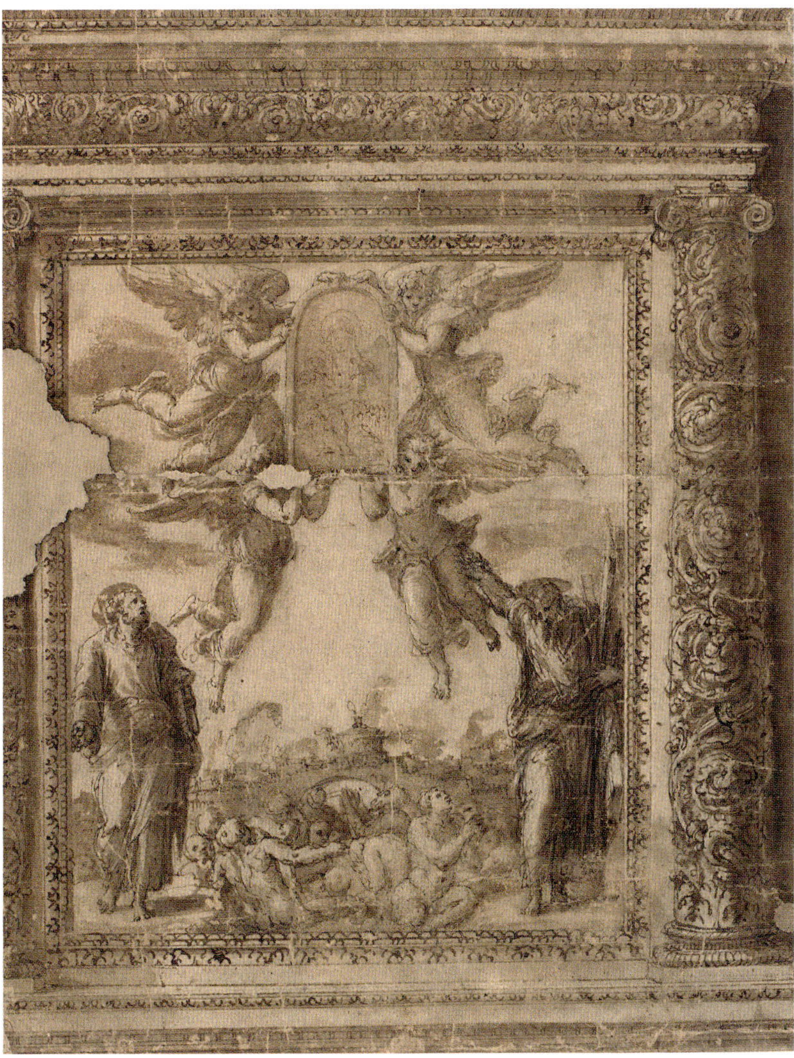

3.8 *Study for the Pescheria Altarpiece*. Pen and brown ink, and brown wash, with some white heightening, and stylus and rule for the architecture, all over traces of black chalk on cream paper, 26 × 20.6 cm. Royal Collection, Windsor Castle

Polidoro's *Saint Andrew* is dressed in a light green cloak covered by raspberry drapery – the canonical colours that he shared with Saint Paul. He is depicted with his traditional attributes, a wooden X-shaped cross and some fish. The first apostle of Christ to be designated, Andrew was a suitable patron of this church, having been a fisherman himself. Christ asked Andrew and another Galilean who also happened to be his brother, Peter, to go with him and be a 'fisher of men', long a celebrated metaphor. In the painting, Andrew steps forward on his left leg, while gesturing with his right hand to acknowledge the worshipper and glancing up dynamically over his shoulder towards the icon. From the verso of the Fitzwilliam drawing it is apparent that Polidoro

reconceived the pose, basing it, as if by a memory reflex, on the figure of Aristotle in Raphael's *School of Athens*, although the comportment is intensified through Polidoro's absorption of the style of the master's late *Transfiguration*. The saint's cloak contains tightly spaced, irregular folds cascading like rivulets, actively rushing like water around an obstacle. His tunic, by way of contrast, has more strictly vertical and deeply cut folds resembling the flutes of a column.

Contrary to his approach to the Roman facades, Polidoro avoided frontal poses even for these single figures, as befits their secondary importance in the decoration, and both saints are angled into depth and stand on pedestals naturally formed from the actual

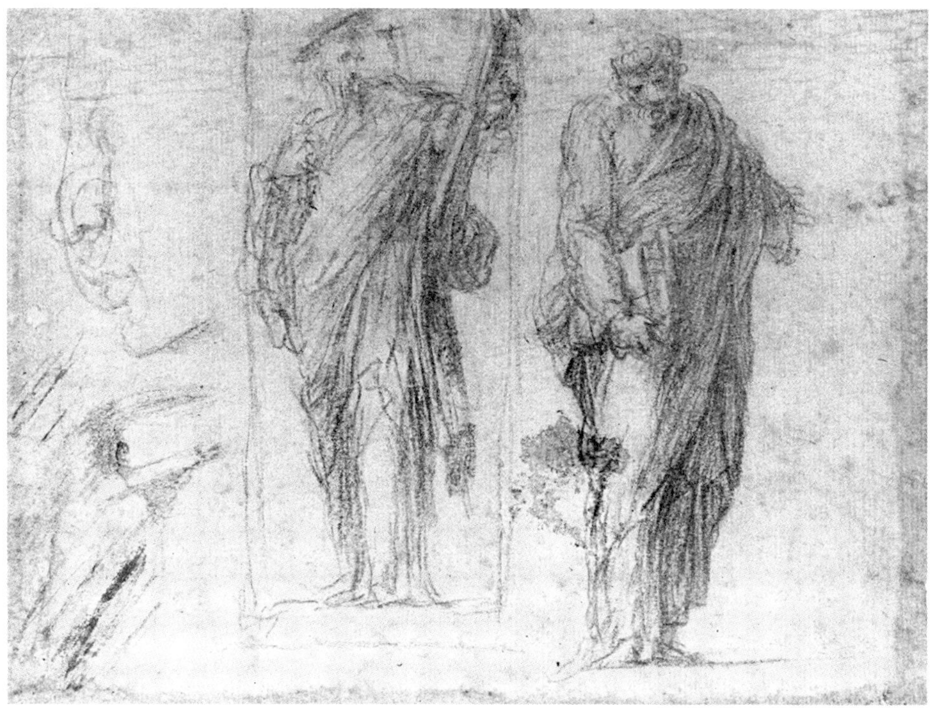

3.9 *Studies of Two Saints for the Pescheria Altarpiece, and a Head Study.* Red chalk on laid paper, 9.8 × 13.8 cm.
Fitzwilliam Museum, Cambridge

ground. Yet visual decorum demanded some symmetry for the two characters, as they function as subsidiary framing figures on the altar. The pose of Peter relates to that of his companion, especially in the lower half, but through various adjustments it was made more relaxed. Peter's knotted hands are more expressive, just as his drapery is more dishevelled. For dramatic purposes he slouches, as if supporting a weight of emotion, as he gestures back into the picture and towards the miraculous icon, while looking directly and engagingly at the viewer. Peter's facial expression is piercing and more commanding than Andrew's, in part because of the portrait-like features. This intervention was typical of Polidoro, who rarely relied on familiar types, creating fresh characterisations for all his saints. Peter holds his attribute at his side, two keys joined together with a red tassel, along with some books that awkwardly push up his orange outer cloak, under which he wears an olive tunic – a colour that Polidoro favoured in this period but one that was not canonical for this saint. This Peter naturally provides our closest indication of what the saint depicted at Santa Maria delle Grazie a Caponapoli might have looked like. Whether the fishmongers of Naples appreciated their good fortune in owning one of the most sophisticated reinterpretations of Roman *all'antica*

painting in a religious format ever created, not to mention work imported from an artist familiar to papal Roman circles, cannot be known.

These markedly vertical panels feature an aqueous handling that anticipates painting of the seventeenth century in Naples, such as that of Bernardo Cavallino. It would seem that Polidoro's relative lack of experience with oil on panel, as opposed to fresco, inspired the liberated handling. The backgrounds are vaporous and insubstantial, although the light falling from the left is directed and intense enough to yield sharp contrasts of light and shade on the figures. Significantly enough for their attributions, this warm subterranean light – the glow of the fiery waters of Purgatory – anticipates Polidoro's much less composed later paintings produced at Messina, in Sicily.

Even more than the saints, the small tondi representing the two components of the *Annunciation*, also surviving in the Capodimonte, develop the formal and emotional qualities of refinement and restraint in Polidoro's art. Indeed, they are his most elegant and tender paintings. The fluid, attenuated poses of the figures are each arranged to echo the circular support, and even Archangel Gabriel's lily bends obediently to follow the direction of

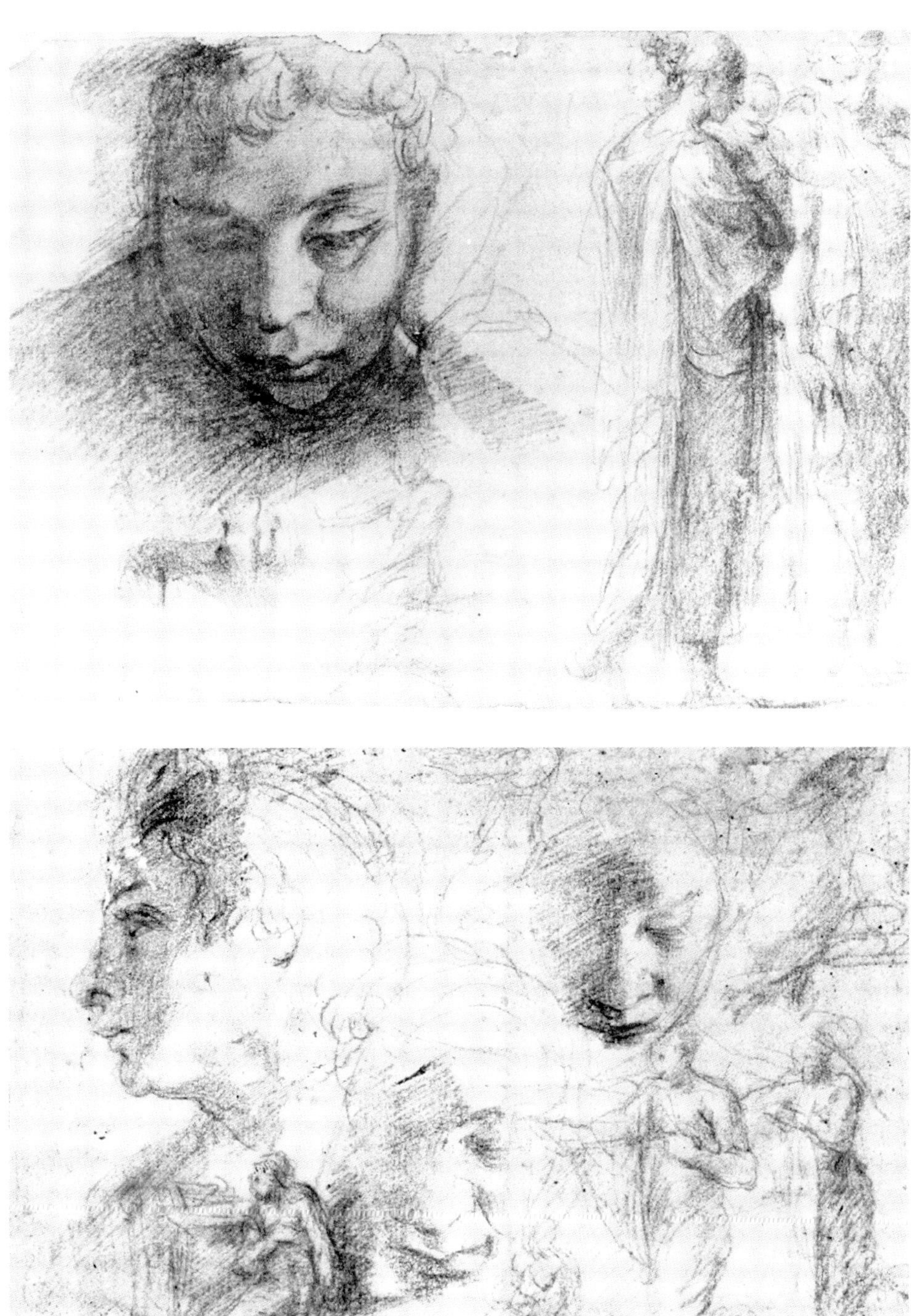

3.10–3.11 *Figure Studies and an Annunciation*. Red chalk on laid paper, 11 × 15.6 cm. Fitzwilliam Museum, Cambridge. From the Gow and Rylands funds with a contribution from the National Art Collections Fund, 2003

the frame. The Virgin's unusual pose may be described as a collapsed 'S'-curve, in which the diagonal angle of her torso seems deliberately arranged to bisect the circular support. To relate the two figures visually, Gabriel assumes the reverse pose as his knees extend towards the Virgin's. The curves in the angel's body are, however, much tauter than those of the undulant Virgin, who receives the divine message of the 'Ave Maria'. Remarkably, Polidoro placed the young angel in an entirely natural setting, kneeling on a flat stone or possibly a tree stump, as opposed to the more conventional interior. The Virgin swoons on a bench before a prie-dieu, in a more traditional interior.

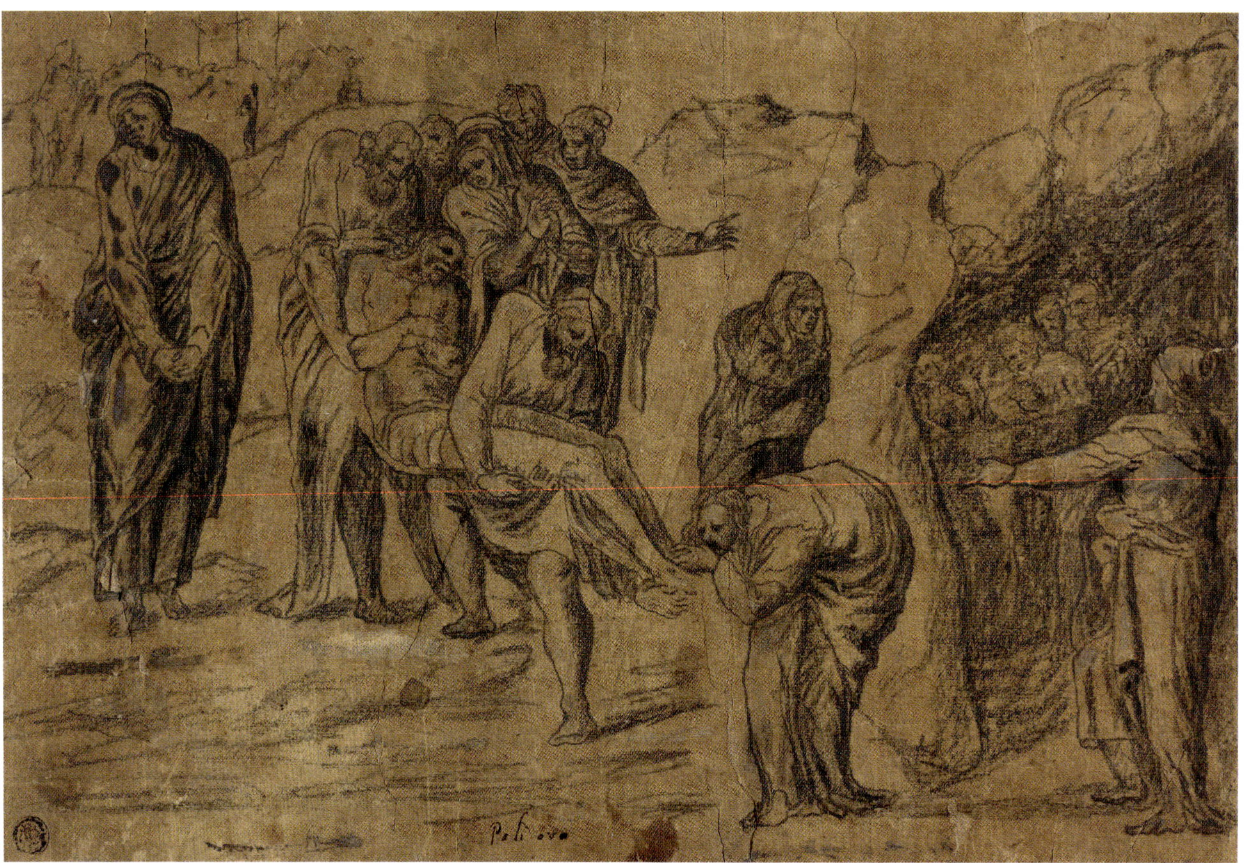

3.12 Copy after Polidoro, *Entombment*. Charcoal and white heightening on laid paper, 22.2 × 32.8 cm. Art Institute of Chicago, Leonora Hall Gurley Memorial Collection

Her feline morphology is distinctive to Polidoro's middle career: the little chin is round and recessed, while the mouth is delicate with a markedly protruding upper lip. The nose is contrastingly prominent and thick, the brows are marked and the forehead high and curved. All these qualities are, if anything, more accentuated in the smoulderingly beautiful double-sided drawing in red chalk formerly in the Pouncey Collection that includes studies for the paintings (figs 3.10 and 3.11). Especially relevant here is the pose of the Virgin, which is shown to have begun as something more outwardly reactive, reminiscent of figures on the Roman facades.[16] The verso of the drawing contains what appears to be a genre study of two women, one holding a child, except they are in classical dress and the interpretation becomes, typically for Polidoro, vexed. Both characters are distinctly youthful, reflecting Polidoro's seldom-displayed interest in graceful representation, as opposed to the more powerful, virile formal qualities that had distinguished his Roman art.

The *Annunciation* panels must have been placed, as was conventional, in the highest part of the altar frame. Their technique is grisaille simulating stone, and so is continuous with the artist's preferred and most successful pictorial type, from his early period in Rome, although the use of the technique here reflects mostly the subsidiary nature of the images and not a classicising motivation. It provides the means to visualise his consummate technique in the absence of any surviving examples from his Roman corpus in a decent state of preservation. It is notable that the handling is not overtly gestural or broad but superficial, and that the highlights are as crisp and vitreous as frost. These tondi are the most exquisite, jewel-like paintings that Polidoro ever produced, but their spare, purified quality, like that of an antique cameo, keeps them from seeming too decorative or precious. These formal aspects are echoed in the moving facial expressions of the characters. Separated by the width of the central altarpiece, the two protagonists seem to voice a question and an answer, and through downcast heads transmit the divine message telepathically rather than via outward gestures.

One other work survives with a provenance in the Pescheria church – the *Entombment*, also in the Capodimonte. This may be the painting referred to as a Deposition from the Cross, cited in the same church for the first time in an eighteenth-century edition of Celano's guide to Naples.[17] There is otherwise no evidence that it was made for an altar in this church, or indeed for Naples, although to judge on stylistic grounds, as it compares so well to the other panels from the Pescheria altarpiece, the possibility that it is the work Celano mentioned, and was therefore executed for that location in around 1527–8, is tantalisingly real. If so, the original placement and function of the picture are open to dispute. It may have been produced for this church as an independent small-scale altarpiece, aligned horizontally with the main altar. However, judging by an analogous Giovan Filippo Criscuolo altarpiece in Gaeta, in Lazio, of about the same date, it was more likely set above the icon in the upper central section of the altarpiece complex as part of the main polyptych itself, respecting a conventional local format.[18] Certainly its particular viewpoint indicates a work meant to be seen from below and so it is not likely to have been an altar frontal.

The picture represents the dead Christ carried down a steep hillside to the tomb. The direction of the movement appears to be towards the lower right corner, but this is unimportant as the focus is less upon the narrative than the body of Christ supported on the winding sheet in the centre of the space. Christ's arms remain rigid and flat across his stomach, the angular pose recalling the Crucifixion. A full-length Saint John the Evangelist stands with his hands interlocked in front of him and his head tilted in anguish, just as he was earlier isolated at the base of the cross. Less conventionally, the Virgin appears without physical support, clasping her hands in front of her body while looking down at the corpse, appearing to be an independent witness in the dense central group rather than a focal point herself. Dressed in her canonical colours she appears as the older woman appropriate to this moment in the Passion cycle.

Polidoro related the story of Christ's Entombment in his more typical, overtly expressive manner. This is particularly apparent not only in the elongated, gnarled

body of the Saviour but also in some of the subsidiary figures. For example, the Magdalen, who washes the blood from Christ's feet with her hair.[19] Another Mary, dressed only in a shaded pink robe, huddles in the left corner and clasps her hands to her face as if to blind herself from witnessing the terrible scene; like most of the figures she is solitary in her response to the traumatic event.

Painted on a horizontal panel, the *Entombment*, with its compact design and small figures balanced in the space, most recalls the narratives in the Vatican Loggia. Overall, however, Polidoro's response to a traditional subject was typically unprecedented. The activity takes place at an angle to the picture plane, a subtle alignment of figures that implies movement and avoids insistent frontality. The preponderant vertical accents stabilise the design so that the sentinel-like mourners of John the Evangelist and Mary bracket the main group, while two other Maries firmly establish the lower corners of the figural composition with hunched and compacted bodies. The image is approached from a low angle to enhance the drama. The natural step over which the body is carried contributes to the uneasy verticality of the design, a metaphor for the physical exertion of the clandestine action. Three heads are visible behind the main group, painted in more muted, monochromatic tones; the central figure wears a turban, as one might expect of Joseph of Arimathea, and appears to be a disguised portrait of someone related to the commission.

Original fragments of a compositional drawing are in the Uffizi, but more of the initial image is recorded in a copy in Chicago that reveals significant differences to the painting (fig. 3.12).[20] In the copy the figures are smaller and more integrated into the landscape, and are viewed from a higher angle. Narrative elements appear, like the three crosses on Golgotha and various secondary figures in the middle ground, as well as the cave at the right edge, but all were apparently eliminated in the end as Polidoro brought greater intensity and concentration to the design. The woman behind the Virgin's left shoulder gestures outwardly here, whereas in the painting she is notably self-possessed. Conversely, the bearer of Christ's lower body looks downward in the drawing, while in the painting he looks up at his companion to unify the action. In yet another major change, Polidoro shifted one of the female mourners from the right to the lower left, in order

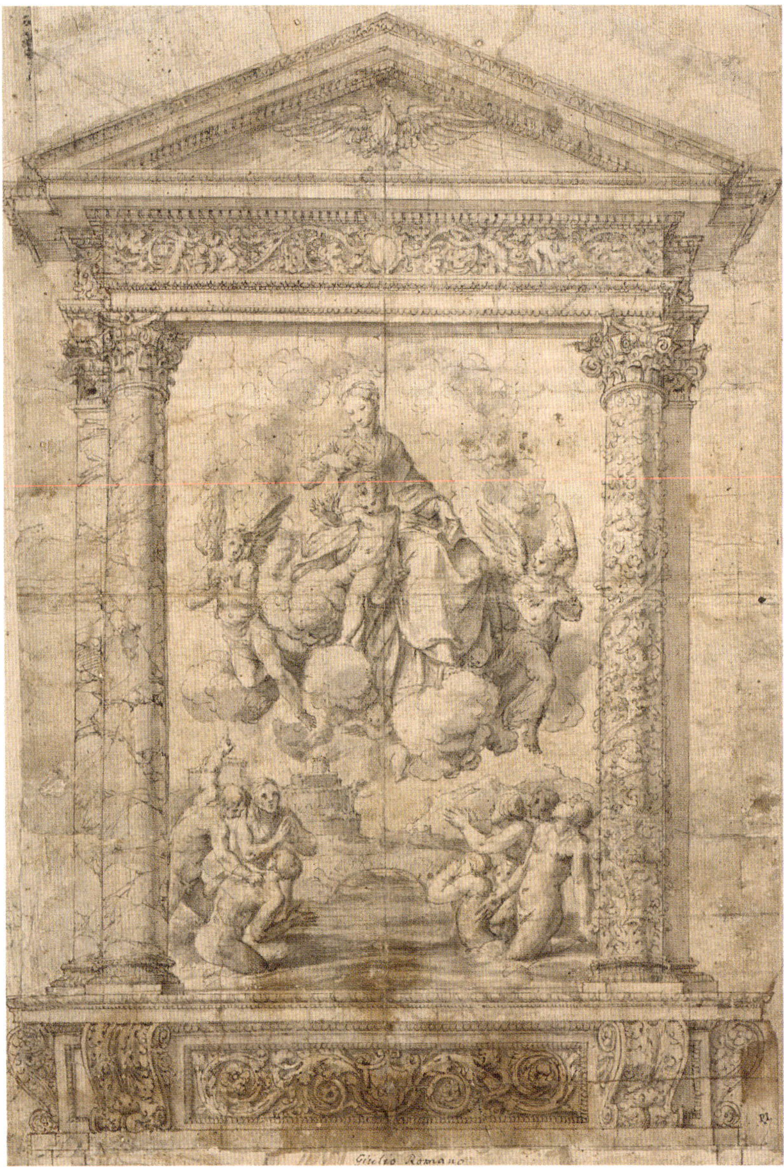

3.13 *Altarpiece Study*. Pen and brown ink, and brown and grey wash, on laid paper, 36.5 × 25.3 cm. Albertina, Vienna

to fill the empty corner beneath John. The design as finally executed is less anecdotal, more successfully concentrated.

In Naples Polidoro developed, through the larger Pescheria paintings, a less evolved facet of his art: religious themes with the intensity, and even tragedy or pathos, that he had previously introduced exclusively to secular subjects on Roman facades. Among other details, the *all'antica* treatment of the leggings of the Nicodemus figure supporting Christ from behind in the *Entombment* recalls the antique influence that had distinguished Polidoro's Roman art, as does the manner in which the Joseph of Arimathea character in the top centre holds

his cloak and, in a more sublimated way, the relief-like treatment of all the Pescheria designs. This hybrid interpretation, evoking the ancients but within the bounds of religious sincerity, parallels the contemporary religious poetry of Sannazzaro, who could write of Christ at the same moment: 'the exalted ruler of Olympus is dead'.[21] Other new aspects of Polidoro's approach to religious painting – the mellifluous, adrenalised technique and the resplendent, gem-like colour – would evaporate in his repertoire in Sicily, as he moved further away from Rome.

Vasari's account, cited earlier, indicates that Polidoro decorated a side altar in the Pescheria church with an

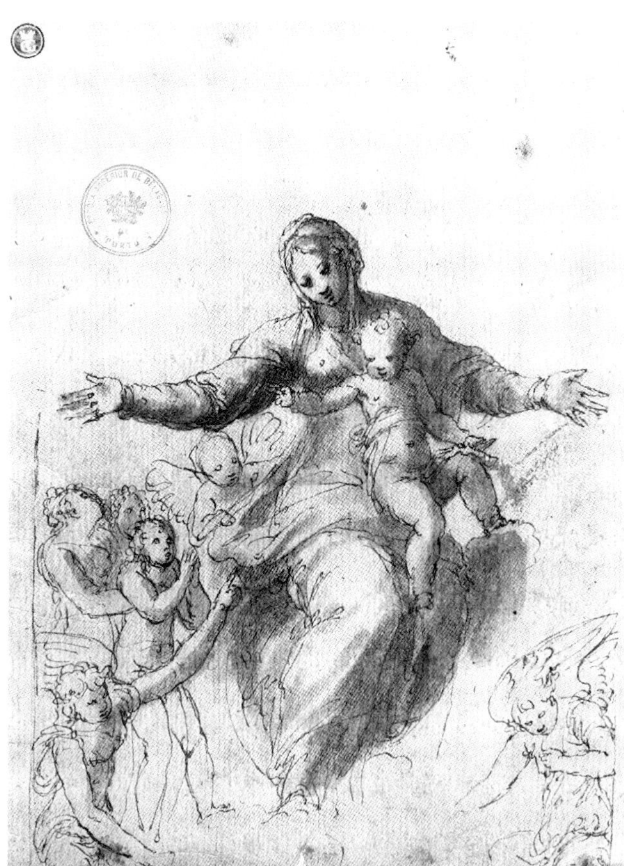

3.14 *Virgin and Child in Glory with Angels.* Pen and brown ink, and brown wash, over black chalk, with some stylus, on laid paper, 20.7 × 15.6 cm. Faculty of Arts, University of Oporto, Porto

image of the Virgin and Child and the addition of souls in Purgatory. This is likely the work in the palace of Giovan Simone Moccia featuring 'l'anime del Purgatorio', cited in 1634 by Giulio Cesare Capaccio, who traced it to Santa Maria delle Grazie.[22] Because the Virgin is not mentioned in his description, this was presumably by then a fragment or the account was simply casual. It is uncertain who ordered more work by Polidoro for the Pescheria, but possibly it was commissioned by an affluent family, or supported more generally by a collection of alms that flooded in during this period. There would have been no shortage of locals from all levels of society anxious to display their devotion to the miraculous image of the Virgin on the main altar, while the particularly terrible plague in Naples in 1526 renewed the cult of souls, if it had ever slackened.

The design for this other altarpiece may be recorded in another rich compositional drawing in the Albertina (fig. 3.13).[23] The arrangement and treatment of subject matter overlap so much with the Windsor study in the lower part that one wonders if Polidoro eliminated the imagery of the souls displayed in that sheet and transposed them instead to the design for this second smaller painting for the same church. The basic arrangement of the altarpiece, with the Virgin and Child in Glory group, is loosely derived from Raphael's *Madonna of Foligno*, now in the Vatican but at that date on the high altar of Santa Maria in Aracoeli in Rome. More specific to the Maria delle Grazie commission, with an exposed breast the Virgin sustains with her milk the tormented nude souls writhing, half-submerged, in the river below. In the distance appears a building resembling Castel Sant'Angelo, an explicit reference to the alternative dedication of the church to the Archangel Michael, and perhaps also a comment on the pope fleeing the Sack of Rome for that fortress, where he was held hostage for several months.[24] Michael is frequently portrayed weighing souls, including in representations of Purgatory. However, Vasari, in his description of Polidoro's work in the church, characterised the second work as a *tavolina*, a small panel, while the scale implied by the frame of the Vienna drawing is that of an ambitious large-scale altarpiece with lavish ornamentation of coloured marble or carved wood, handled with two different solutions on either side of the structure, as in a study to be shown to a patron for approval. Once again a suspicion remains that the Vienna sheet, like the Windsor example for the high altar, records a plan too expensive or stylistically progressive to be realised in the Pescheria church and was significantly reduced in the end. A more specific study from earlier in the design process, executed in the artist's characteristic wiry pen and ink, survives in Porto (fig. 3.14). Here, the Virgin and Child are accompanied by more angels, some of whom rehearse the grateful poses of the souls below.[25] The main difference is the Virgin's open-armed gesture, which is more extroverted and welcoming than in the more decorous finished drawing. In the end, Polidoro returned to the safer sanctity of Raphael's prototype.

In one part of Vasari's life of Polidoro, the author listed incompletely and disjointedly, without patrons, other works Polidoro produced in Naples of the more private, secular type for which he was often celebrated in Rome, including facades. As is often the case, therefore, what has

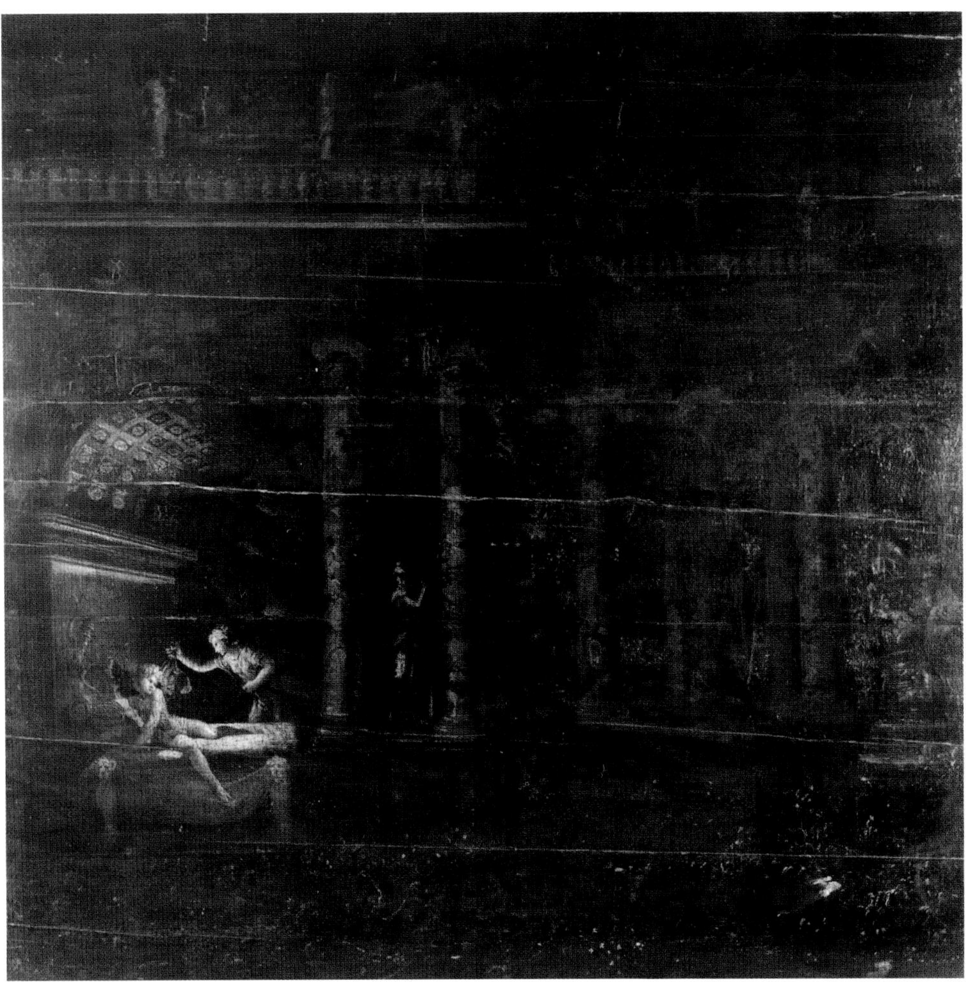

3.15 *Psyche Discovers Cupid.* Oil on panel, 157.8 × 162.9 cm. Royal Collection, Hampton Court

and has not survived distort our view: 'Ma pure essendo predicto le virtù sue, . . . fece al conte di . . . una volta dipinta a tempera, con alcune facciate; ch'è tenuta cosa bellissima. E così [. . .] fece il cortile di chiaro e scuro al signore . . ., ed [. . .] insieme alcune logge, le quali sono molto piene d'ornamento e di bellezza e ben lavorate.'[26] The lacunae, present in the 1550 edition and not corrected in the second edition, indicate again how Vasari did not retain strong contacts in Naples who might have provided him with this information. Some patrons, all clustered in Sannazzaro's circle around the Accademia Pontaniana, were rapidly attracted to the painter's ability to reproduce the art and subject matter of Roman antiquity in Naples, which had its own glorious collections of ancient sculpture and a strong sense of nostalgia for that past. Other sources attest to Polidoro having decorated at least the facades of Palazzo Montalto and Palazzo Rota in Naples, as well as two soffits in the latter palace.[27]

The only likely surviving candidates for any of these commissions are a group of eight panels at Hampton Court, together with one in the Louvre with the same provenance – some of Polidoro's last attempts at mythological painting. They are known to have been purchased in Naples (they were acquired by Charles I), and the palace near Santa Chiara of the precocious soldier-poet Bernardino Rota, who also had a notable collection of antiquities, emerges as the most likely original location. But as tempting as it is to relate them to the two commissions recorded in the written sources, nothing is conclusive. One cannot even be certain whether these paintings were produced during Polidoro's second and final visit to Naples, or during his first sojourn of the earlier 1520s, although a later date is supported by their close stylistic relation to the Pescheria decorations.[28] Six are decorative but three (figs 3.15–3.17) are narratives extracted from Apuleius' *Metamorphoses* (*The Golden Ass*),

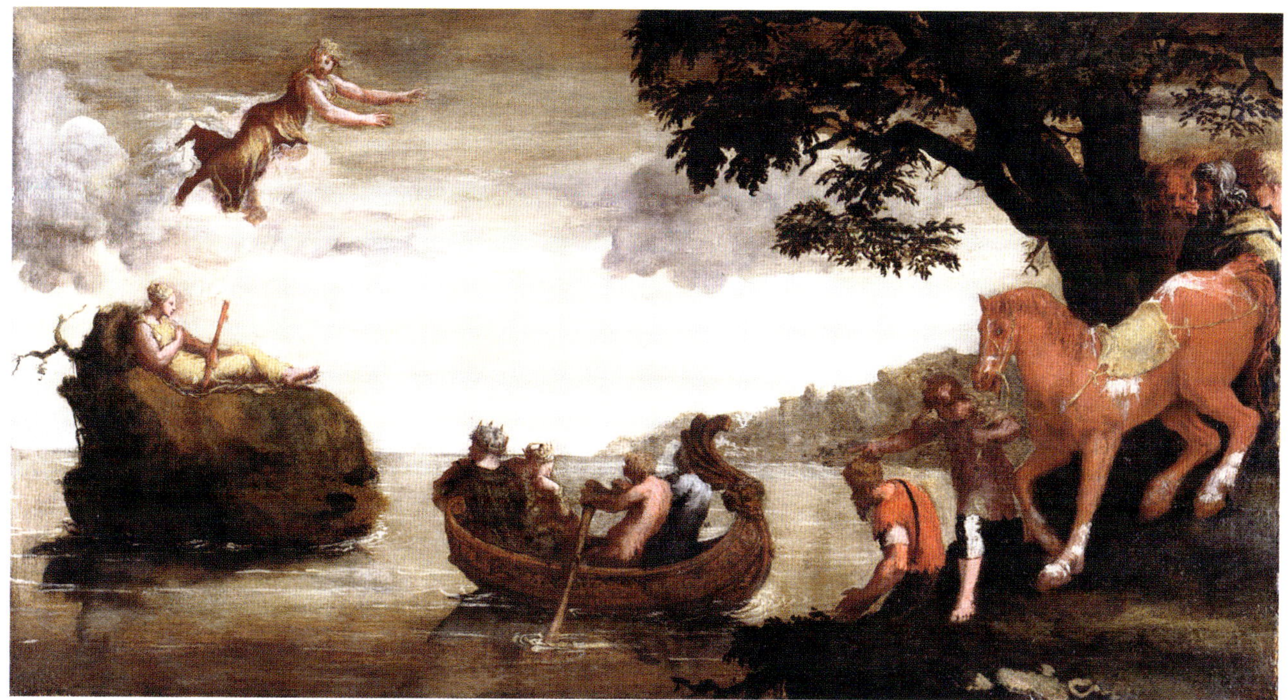

3.16 *Psyche Abandoned on a Rock*. Oil on panel, 86.4 × 161.6 cm. Royal Collection, Hampton Court

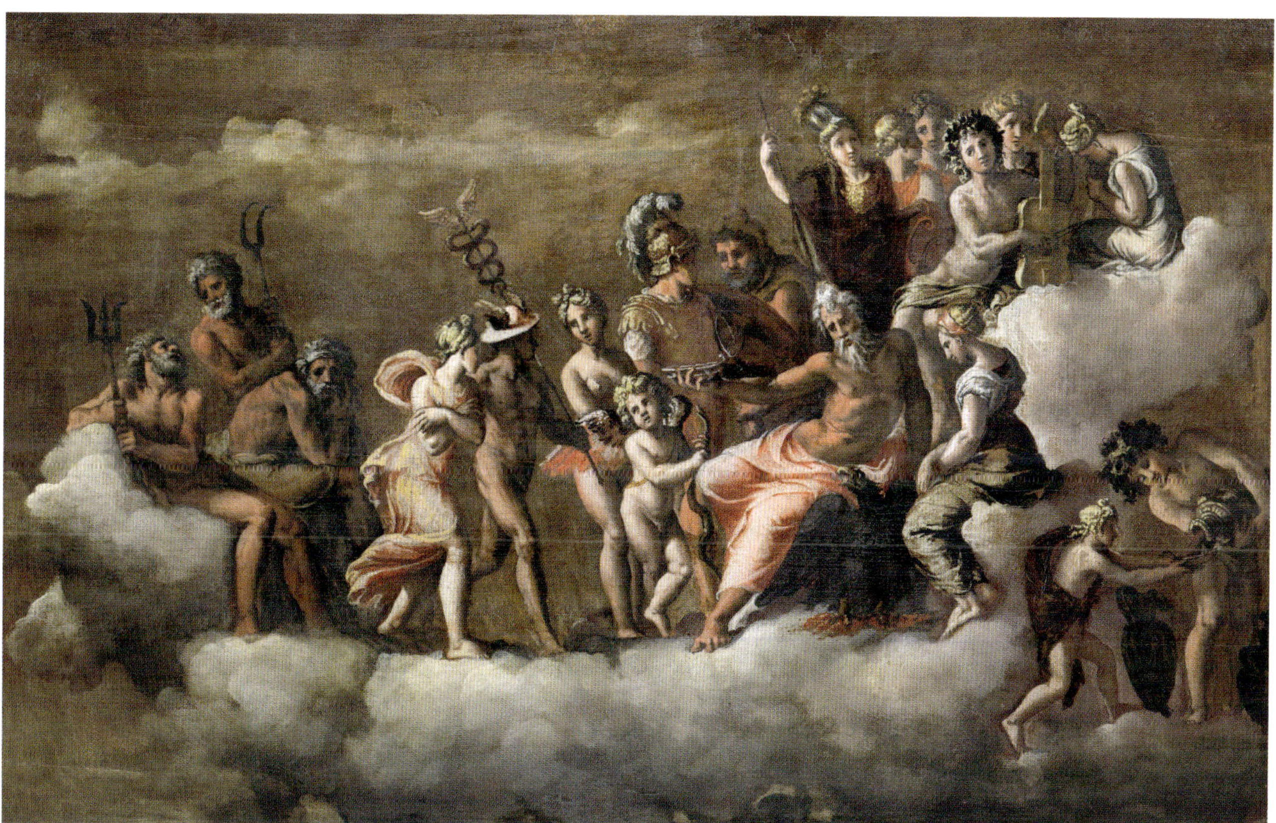

3.17 *Psyche Received on Olympus*. Oil on panel, 104.5 × 160.5 cm. Musée du Louvre, Paris, Département des Peintures

Books IV–VI, which was issued for the first time in an Italian translation in 1517 in Rome. Not only is it unclear for whom they were produced or where, it is not even known whether they were intended as parts of a piece of furniture, as wall panelling or for a ceiling, yet the fact that at least some were painted on a less expensive pinewood does suggest a relatively more functional installation – probably, given their subjects, in a bedroom setting. So broadly handled are these pictures that one is driven to defend the painter's technique by speculating that he was adjusting the finish for distant viewing on a ceiling rather than as part of a piece of furniture.

The *Psyche Discovers Cupid* painting is the largest of the three main narratives, among the eight surviving works (fig. 3.15). Considerably darkened, the surface now has a rough, corrugated aspect, anticipating the desperate condition of many of Polidoro's last Sicilian panels. It is represented as a night scene, with a restricted palette, and the dominant impression is of ruddy browns. Illustrating Book V of Apuleius' text, it depicts the moment when oil from Psyche's lamp falls on Cupid, waking the sleeping god of love, whose attribute, a bow, hangs on the wall behind. Both figures are depicted as open-mouthed and fully aware of one another. The daring internal light source that the artist introduced to direct a glow on the face of Cupid became an obsession in Rome during the 1520s for artists like Sebastiano del Piombo, Rosso and Parmigianino. Vasari attested that Gianfrancesco Penni painted a now lost *Saint Christopher* near a side door of Santa Maria dell'Anima in Rome with a hermit in a cave holding a lantern, although Raphael's *Liberation of Saint Peter* provided the ultimate model for members of the workshop like Polidoro.[29] As Joannides has identified, a figure drawing in the Louvre exists for the Cupid, a unique surviving preparatory sketch for this group, although almost identical to the finished pose and disappointingly unyielding of information about Polidoro's creative process.[30]

The design is innovative for its expanse of empty space, recalling the earlier San Silvestro al Quirinale frescoes. It is also the only image to feature architecture, and this is one of its most impressive aspects: it boasts an ambitious colonnaded portico, including variegated marble columns with Ionic capitals and statues surmounting the balustrade. The barrel vault with coffers bearing rosettes distinguishes a bedroom of a mythological god. A sliver of floral garden is revealed in the immediate right foreground, with an elaborate fountain that must have originally been dazzling but is sadly almost illegible now. Even more imperceptible are the tiny grisaille figures on the fountain, reminiscent of the artist's Roman facade decorations.

The *Psyche Abandoned on a Rock* (fig. 3.16) is smaller than the *Psyche Discovers Cupid*, closer in scale to the Louvre panel, which may be relevant to its original position. The low viewpoint is presumably further evidence for an adjustment related to the work's initial placement. The painting is brighter than *Psyche Discovers Cupid* but even following a recent cleaning it is muted in atmosphere, evocative of the subject's pathos. As in Book IV of Apuleius' text, Psyche is abandoned by her parents, respecting the wishes of Apollo, while above the West Wind carries her back to Cupid's palace. The composition is relaxed, almost extemporised, without a strong narrative direction. Psyche is abandoned on a solitary rock off the shore, trapped like a character on a parade float. Her cross-legged pose, with a staff, recalls the Calliope from Raphael's Stanza della Segnatura, itself inspired by the ancient sculpture of Ariadne in the Belvedere, also personally known to Polidoro. Ironically, compared to the Roman facades, in which he preferred to assimilate his source material, Polidoro quoted more obviously from ancient sculpture in a sophisticated private setting, presumably to flatter the taste of the patron. Psyche appears twice in the same panel as she drifts back to shore. Her parents, in their elegant *all'antica* boat, are rowed back towards the shore, the mother hiding her face in abject sorrow. Some soldiers greet them, one guiding a cinnamon-coloured horse walking cautiously down the slope. The group of male heads at the right margin is a typical Polidoro clustering, as are the sturdy figure types – a narrative related not by means of facial expression but rather the movement of bodies and broad gesture. Yet the artist also appreciated the value of sensitive understatement in narrative, in contrast to Giulio Romano for example. The work has a delightful fairy-tale quality and restrained delicacy of effect that soften the prevailing view of Polidoro as an interpreter predominantly of violent subjects, which had already been expressed in the sixteenth century and was based on his Roman output alone.

The one surviving painting from this group not at Hampton Court, the Louvre's panel *Psyche Received on Olympus*, represents the conclusion to the series with the reuniting of the couple (fig. 3.17). It also happens to be the only one with a direct precedent, a work by Raphael's workshop in Villa Farnesina in Rome. It has suffered, but overall the surface is as fresh as any single surviving Polidoro painting. It displays the technical freedom of one of the artist's pen and ink drawings: the use of white in a flickering impasto is precisely how the heightening was applied in his sketches. A spectacular freedom of touch is evident, particularly in these highlights applied almost with disdain. The handling is so loose, even coarse, that one is again driven to wonder how closely scrutinised the panel was intended to be. Neither polished nor controlled, the picture differs in finish to paintings by Giulio or the other members of Raphael's workshop, who preferred to emulate smooth materials like stone and precious jewels. The medium here was so oil-rich that the paint has coagulated in places, while some of the outlines are awkwardly reinforced in a black that appears to be original. The existence of these paintings discourages the notion that Polidoro played a major part in executing any designs of Giulio and Penni during his earlier years in Rome, given their different techniques and Polidoro's bold, almost improvised approach to colour, formed in the Louvre panel by olive green combined with red-orange or gold shades. Polidoro freely employed *cangianti* here, though with duller colours than were commonly used: a typical combination is light olive laid over brown. One exception to this vivid but unified scheme is the girl with the crossed arms, whose clothing is a riveting yellow over rose. Another unusually scintillating effect is achieved by the wholly pink cloak of Jupiter clashing with the red fire in the eagle's talons. It was desirable for Polidoro to emphasise Jupiter, a dominant figure in the story, through colour, rather than copy his counterpart on the Farnesina ceiling, who is dressed in a more dignified blue. While Polidoro respected Raphael's basic composition from the Farnesina fresco by depicting the characters seated on clouds in a horizontal, frieze-like arrangement, he preferred to arrange his 19 figures less uniformly, and in

clusters, isolating discrete narrative incidents. His design lacks the solemn processional clarity of Raphael's, even if it is rhythmically more vibrant and varied. The artist is never pedantic but exploits his knowledge to create surprising details such as the ochre and black vase in the corner – an exceptional inclusion of an ancient lekythos in a Renaissance painting, perhaps from the patron's own collection.

Unusual for their survival, six decorative panels can be associated with this commission, all in the Royal Collection at Hampton Court (figs 3.18–3.23). Vigorously painted, their action takes place on a strip-like piece of ground, surrounded by water, against a warm neutral backdrop. They reveal Polidoro's sophisticated and spirited evocation of a certain genre of ancient painting, with a mélange of direct quotes and witty, sometimes mocking invention. More than any other surviving picture they attest to his absorption of the Domus Aurea decorations and other ancient art available in Rome, especially coins, gems and cameos, mediated through Raphael's and Giovanni da Udine's decorations in several locations, including Villa Madama, Cardinal Bibbiena's bathroom in the Vatican, and the Vatican Loggia. Subjects are self-evident, such as putti playing a form of croquet (fig. 3.21) and the thrashing of a satyr with a freshly clipped branch (fig. 3.20), and complement the main narrative with a mild, humorous eroticism. Despite their infectious levity, Shearman points out that these additional ornamental panels were explicitly produced as faux-antique paintings and, as such, are as knowingly sophisticated as anything the artist produced.[31]

Vasari briefly worked in Naples in the mid-1540s and so was relatively well informed about art in the city compared to that of many other parts of Italy away from Florence and Rome. This would allow that the few paintings by Polidoro cited by Vasari were all the major public commissions he undertook during his relatively compressed time in Naples. And so we must be suspicious of any other works by Polidoro yielded by local Neapolitan sources, few of which seem credible. For example, one painting attributed to Polidoro is mentioned in earlier sources in the church of Santa Maria delle Grazie alla Zabatteria, again featuring the popular image of the Virgin of Grace offering divine intervention to reduce the time that souls would remain in Purgatory, but in this case with

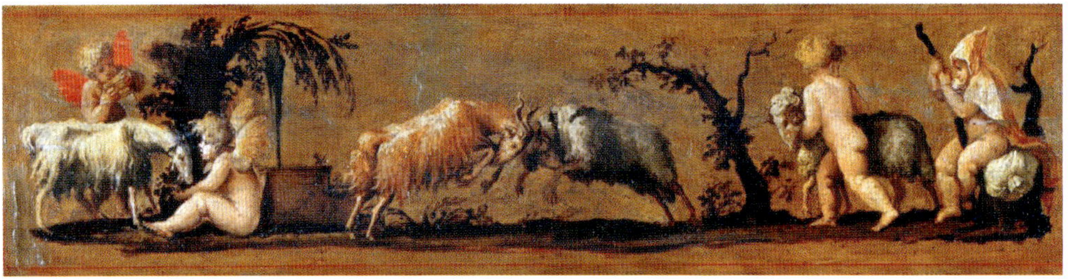

3.18 *Putti with Goats*. Oil on panel, 31 × 120 cm. Royal Collection, Hampton Court

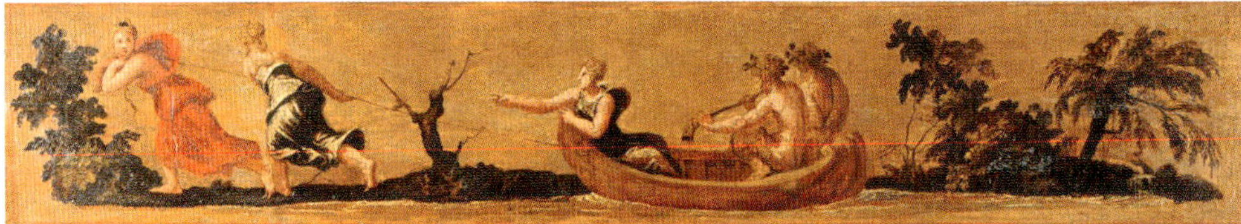

3.19 *A Boating Party*. Oil on panel, 29.5 × 151 cm. Royal Collection, Hampton Court

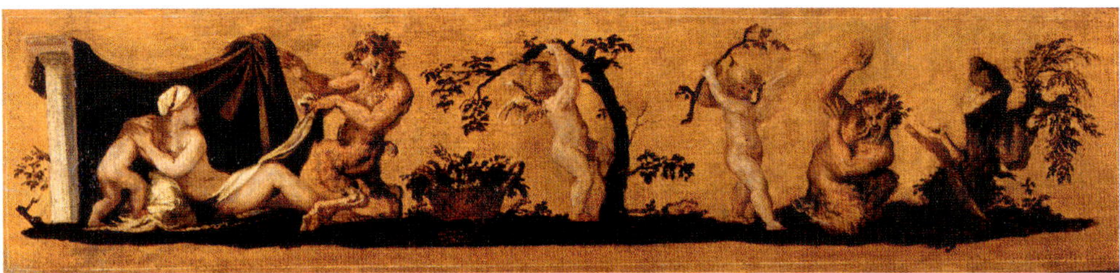

3.20 *Discovery of a Nymph, Satyrs and Putti*. Oil on panel, 30.2 × 120.3 cm. Royal Collection, Hampton Court

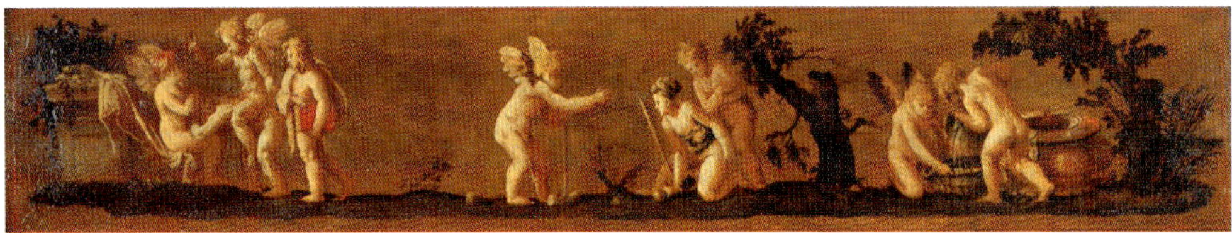

3.21 *Putti with Mallets and Balls*. Oil on panel, 30.3 × 150.3 cm. Royal Collection, Hampton Court

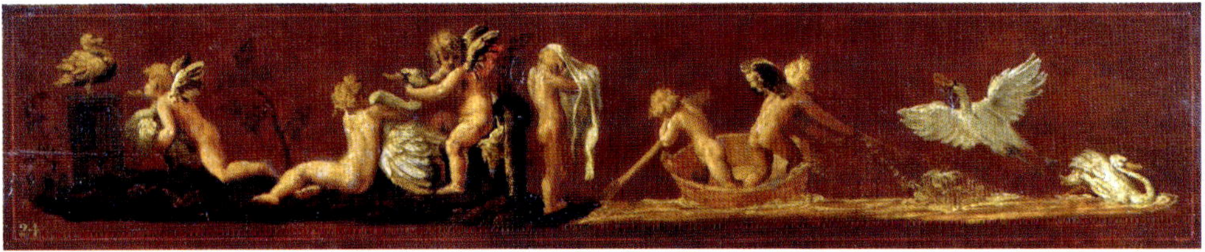

3.22 *Putti with Swans*. Oil on panel, 30.2 × 141.9 cm. Royal Collection, Hampton Court

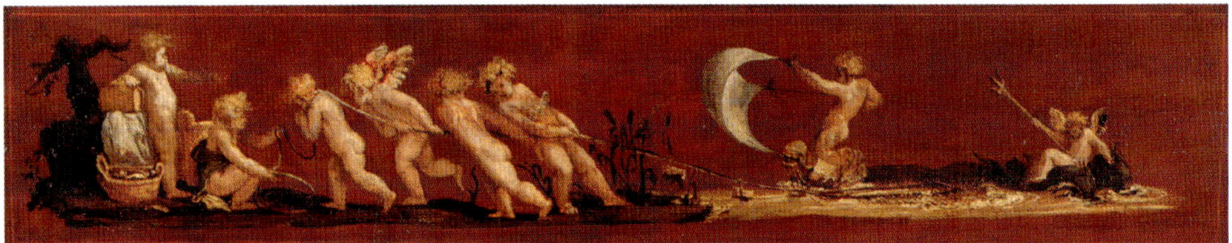

3.23 *Putti Pulling a Net*. Oil on panel, 29.8 × 141 cm. Royal Collection, Hampton Court

Saints Sebastian and Roch added. The picture is lost, and in first citing it D'Engenio suggests that it was not commissioned until 1566, so after Polidoro's death.[32] There is graphic evidence, however, from the verso of a drawing now in the Royal Collection, a sheet that also includes two earlier studies for the *Saint Andrew* in the Pescheria altarpiece, that while in Naples he designed a *Tobias and the Angel*.[33] This was presumably meant for an independent painting, to judge by the frame lines in the drawing, but the commission is not recorded and was perhaps never executed.

The brief but intense time Polidoro spent in Naples was naturally a transitional one between his more substantial periods in Rome and Messina. In Naples he felt free to explore publicly, for the first and final time in his career, some of the elegant facets of the style of painting developed in Rome more consistently by artists like Perino, Parmigianino and Rosso. Clearly it was Polidoro's memory of his Roman experience, rather than the explicit demands of Neapolitan taste, that encouraged these stylistic tendencies. Despite the complex circumstances of his career, he interpreted them with a refreshing liberty. There is a certain irony in Polidoro offering the most refined pictures he made after leaving Rome to patrons who would have had limited appreciation of the subtler aspects of his entirely up-to-date style, grounded in the Roman antique, especially in the case of those produced in the context of popular devotion around a miracle-working image. It also makes us contemplate what direction painting in Rome might have taken had the events of May 1527 been avoided and all those talented young artists remained in close proximity.

Informed viewers of art in Naples would have known that Polidoro had been a pupil of Raphael, and the one autograph altarpiece there by Raphael, the *Madonna of the Fish* (fig. 3.1; now in the Prado), provided a model from which people could have judged the master's style. Yet, ironically, despite the evanescent beauty of its angel, this was among the most austere and simplified of Raphael's altarpieces and cannot be said to have impressed Polidoro much in Naples, given his comprehensive knowledge of the master's work. The case of Rosso in Sansepolcro, where he also supplied a work of extreme sophistication following the Sack of Rome, provides a parallel for Polidoro's experience.[34] Afterwards, however, the two artists moved in diametrically opposed directions. Whereas contemporaries like Rosso and Parmigianino went on from these vicissitudes to create even more sophisticated and luxurious works, regardless of where they resided, Polidoro seems to have lost this inspiration with the increasing distance from Rome, and created in Sicily some of the most bewildering and brutal paintings of the entire Renaissance period by any artist.

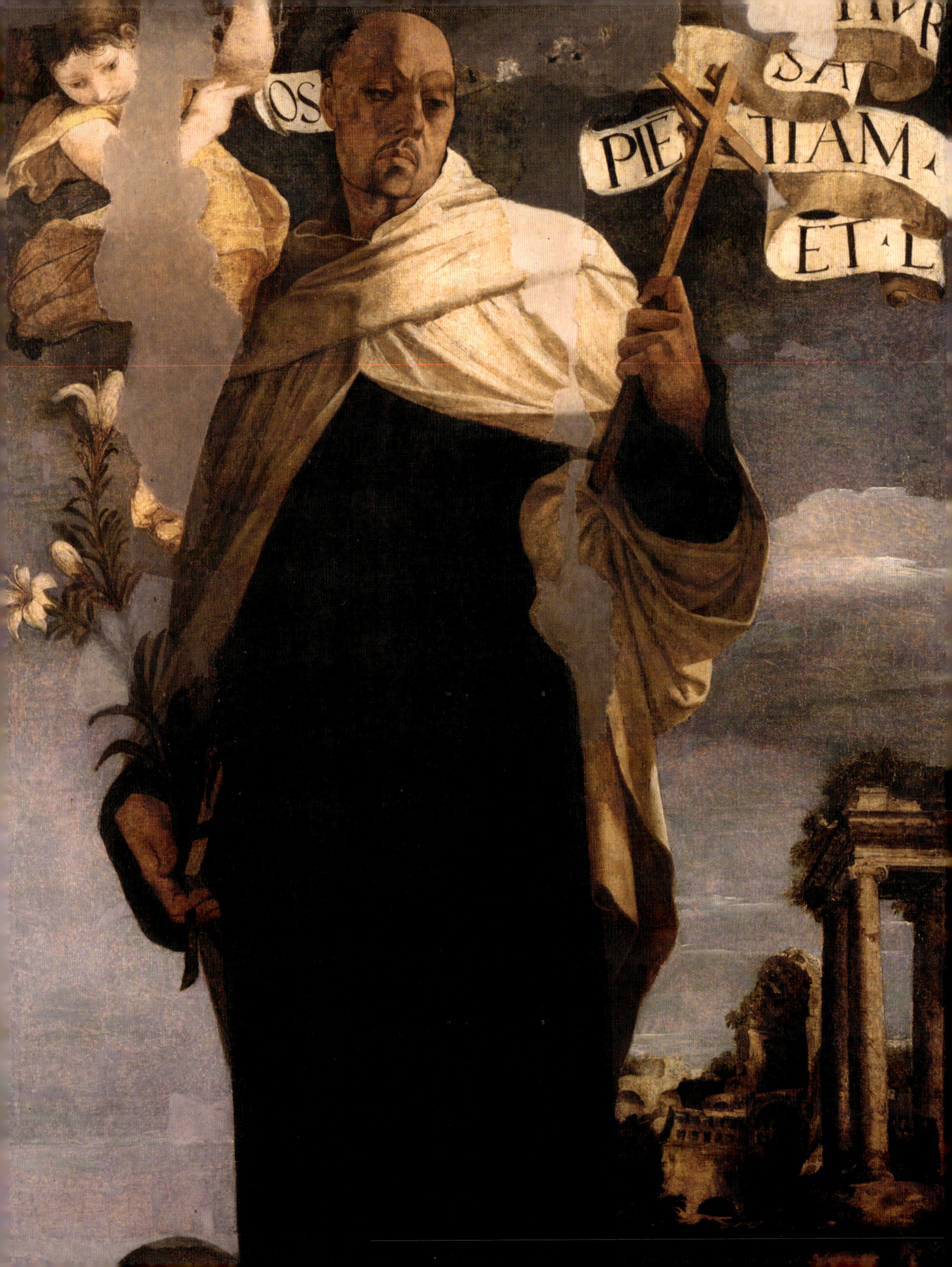
OS
PIE
TVR
SA
TIAM
ET L

4   In Messina

Vasari never visited Sicily, so his account of Polidoro's production there is much less detailed or trustworthy than for the Roman and Neapolitan periods. As a result, our knowledge of the entire last period of Polidoro's life must be reconstructed from a fragmented documentary and textual record. A reading of Vasari's life of Antonello da Messina, which cites only one work by that painter, a public altarpiece produced in Venice, is indicative of how few sources for art he had south of Naples. The Florentine sculptor and Servite friar Giovanni Angelo Montorsoli, who had been active extensively in Messina during the later 1540s and was known personally to Vasari, would have been an eyewitness but evidently he either gathered little information about Polidoro, even within just a few years of his death, or did not trouble to relate it.[1]

Polidoro had arrived in the maritime town of Messina in north-eastern Sicily from Naples by 7 October 1528, when he wrote a respectful letter to his former patron in Rome, Giovanni Antonio Milesi.[2] The phrasing implies that he had recently arrived. Why he went to distant Messina specifically is not known but the many links between Naples and Sicily must have been a factor. By far Polidoro's most important painting from this final stage of his life is the *Way to Calvary* executed for the church of the Catalan community by 1534 and discussed in the following chapter (fig. 5.1; the sole Messinese picture by Polidoro even mentioned by Vasari, it should be stressed). The only securely documented work is the *Nativity* for the church of Santa Maria dell'Altobasso, contracted in 1533 but executed largely by his workshop to judge on visual grounds, and not before 1535 it would seem (fig. 4.8). During his time on Sicily, Polidoro is just once documented outside Messina – in 1534, along the coast in Syracuse, Augusta and Milazzo, supplying drawings, probably for maps and fortifications, for the Viceroy of Sicily, Ettore Pignatelli, Duke of Monteleone.[3] The decorations for the triumphal entry of the Holy Roman Emperor Charles V in 1535 provide another definitive fixed date, although the evidence for this ephemeral production only survives in some brisk preparatory drawings (figs 4.13–4.17) and summary descriptions. Although Polidoro appears to have quickly dominated the art market in Messina – a city then under Spanish dominion – the nature of his output changed utterly, as he no longer frescoed facades with classical

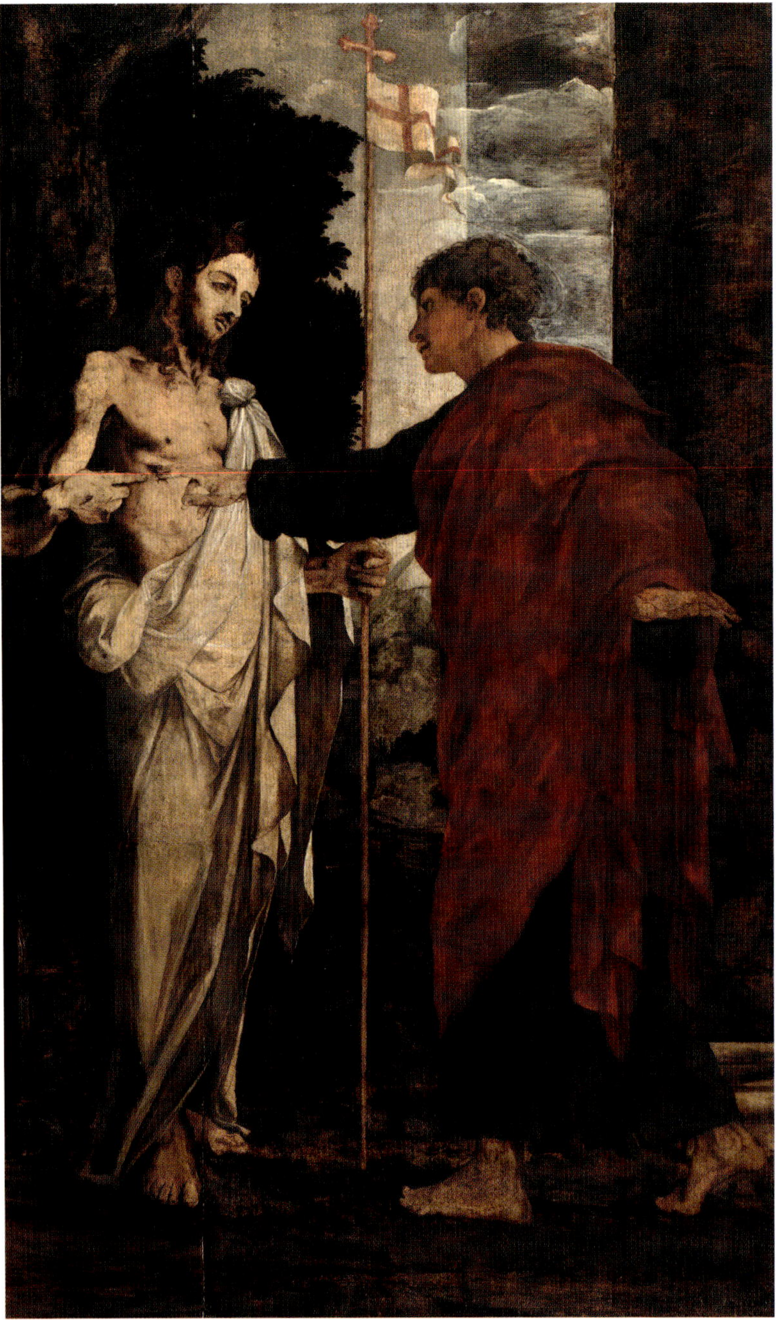

4.1 *Incredulity of Saint Thomas.* Oil on panel, 202.5 × 124.5 cm. The Samuel Courtauld Trust, Courtauld Institute of Art, London

subjects but became by necessity almost exclusively a supplier of religious images. Further south in Sicily the pull of ancient Rome was weaker than it had been in Naples, despite the presence of classical ruins on the island. Polidoro's reaction to this dramatic shift in culture and patronage is, sadly, not recorded, but even compared to Naples, Sicily would have been an unprecedented experience for a fresco specialist from Lombardy nurtured in the Vatican.

After his arrival in Messina and prior to 1534 and the defining commission of the monumental *Way to Calvary*, Polidoro executed a few paintings of higher quality than the documented Altobasso panel. They must be reconstituted through attributions and with the assistance of non-contemporary descriptions. Attributed to Polidoro by Pouncey and Gere when it re-emerged on the art market in 1958, the *Incredulity of Saint Thomas* (fig. 4.1) in the Courtauld Gallery is one of these works, among the first that Polidoro executed after his arrival in Messina in 1528, to judge by its relation to his Roman-period style.[4] It is not easily dated or documented but it was likely painted for the altar controlled by the Faraone family in the local church dedicated to Saint Thomas, itself completed in 1530. With the protagonists set towards the frontal plane, though with ample space around them to imply an expanse, the design is anchored by the compact shapes of these two monumental figures tilted away from the viewer. The thick column of coloured marble behind Thomas reinforces the full right margin of the panel, while behind Christ there is a corresponding stabilising tree, the fully verdant branches of which provide a convenient dark foil for his head. The flag of the Resurrection held by Christ at the centre of the panel defines the axis point of the composition. The exterior setting with mountainous landscape contradicts the story related in John 20: 24–29, in which, for symbolic reasons, Christ appeared indoors to the Apostles, who feared they might be persecuted for acknowledging him in public. The insistent presence of the natural world, familiar from the artist's Roman paintings, survives in this work.

Polidoro's choice of colours was conventional here, as Thomas wears his canonical red and a now rather coagulated green, and Christ appears in white, as dictated by the Gospel source. Open-mouthed, Thomas steps toward Christ, posed *all'antica*, his weight on his front foot and an arm stretched out behind him for equilibrium. The artist had painted many similarly balanced figures in the Roman facades, and of all the pictures he executed in Messina this example is most closely related to his earlier style. Thomas is the larger of the two figures, with a dominating physical presence. Christ steps sideways and towards the viewer, while guiding the fingers the saint is about to thrust into the wound on his chest. Christ is gaunt but muscular, with awkwardly long arms and a smallish torso – a common body type for Polidoro, again familiar from the Roman facades. He wears the white winding sheet like a toga, gathered in a knot at his shoulder. The drapery folds are predominantly broad, with crisp, swerving edges that also suggest the residual influence of free-standing antique sculpture. The interlocking poses and apodictic gestures lend the subject clarity and force. Christ's right hand, flattened to the picture plane, seems

deformed to maximise expressive impact. Remarkably, the shape of Christ's face could be construed as a diamond, on which is set a bulbous nose and a narrow, crooked mouth. In their angular toughness, areas of his body left naked appear to be hewn from a partially resistant substance like ivory. The panel has suffered (a section at the lower left is entirely lost), and while the restoration enhances the breadth of paint handling and dark overlay, both qualities doubtless characterised the original.

Raphael treated this subject once in Rome, in a bronze tondo likely designed around 1514–15 for the Chigi Chapel in Santa Maria della Pace, sometimes attributed to Lorenzetto and now at the Abbey of Chiaravalle in Lombardy.[5] There are significant differences between the two, however, and the composition of the tondo does not appear to have been Polidoro's source here. Instead, the Courtauld work evokes Raphael's tapestry cartoons in its general dependence on powerful gestures and tense, dramatic pathos. Yet Polidoro's picture has a severe beauty and liberated technique that differentiate it sharply from the style of Raphael and other later students of the master in Rome. The *Incredulity of Saint Thomas* more familiarly pays homage to Polidoro's facade frescoes in its monumental clarity, but his style of painting in Messina was to become much more uncompromising.

Polidoro's so-called Carmine altarpiece is another work produced relatively soon after his arrival in Messina. It was painted, as its shorthand title suggests, for the local church of the Carmelite Order. Polidoro executed several paintings in Sicily for this order of hermits devoted to Saint Albert, allegedly founded in the twelfth century on Mount Carmel in Palestine. He apparently resided in their monastery and was eventually buried there, indicating an almost familial relationship.[6] Sources record a polyptych with a *Transfiguration* as the centrepiece on the high altar.[7] Sadly, much of this altarpiece was destroyed in the earthquake of February 1783, as was a *Deposition* with over life-size figures, probably executed in fresco in the refectory, which appears to have been among the most locally esteemed of his later paintings.[8] The Marullo – one of the most deeply rooted aristocratic families in Messina, whose members numbered among them the counts of Condojanni – possessed burial rights around the high altar and they may have paid for all or part of the altarpiece, with the advice and approval of the Carmelite

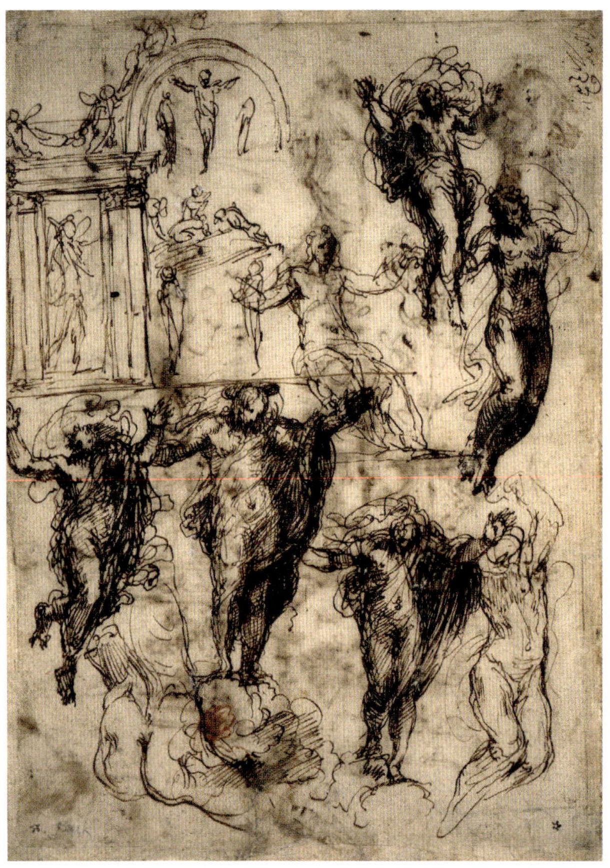

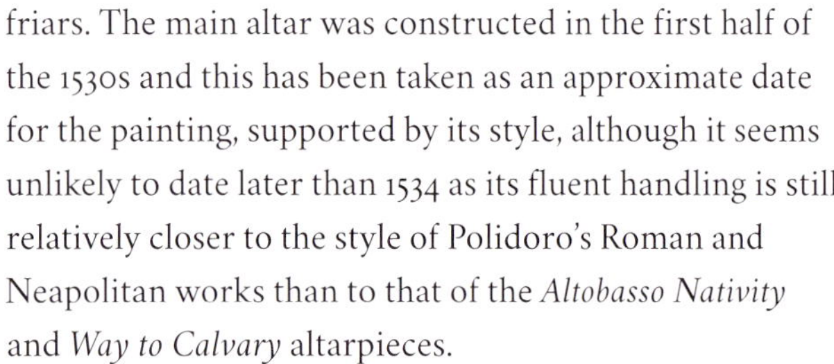

4.2 *Studies for the Transfiguration*. Pen and brown ink on laid paper, 21 × 15.5 cm. British Museum, London

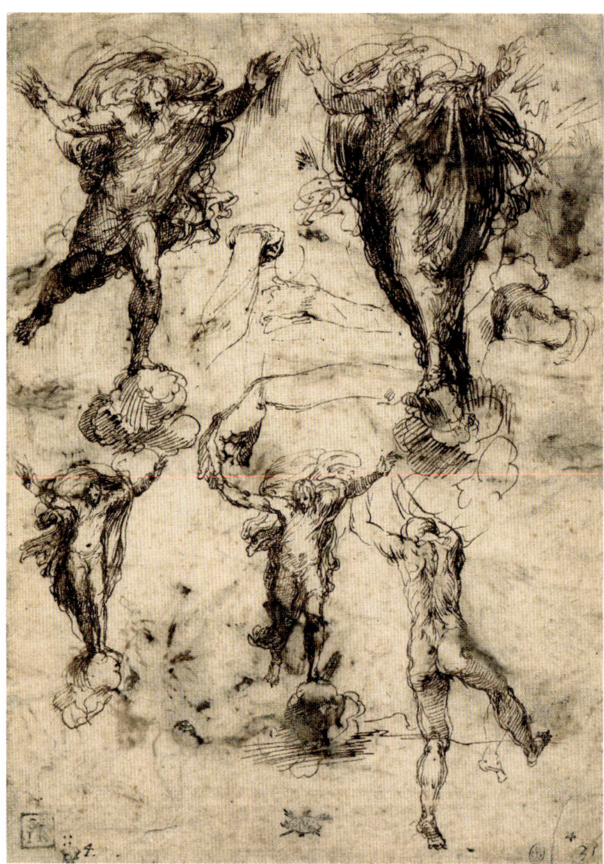

4.3 *Studies for the Transfiguration*. Pen and brown ink on laid paper, 21.9 × 15.9 cm. British Museum, London

friars. The main altar was constructed in the first half of the 1530s and this has been taken as an approximate date for the painting, supported by its style, although it seems unlikely to date later than 1534 as its fluent handling is still relatively closer to the style of Polidoro's Roman and Neapolitan works than to that of the *Altobasso Nativity* and *Way to Calvary* altarpieces.

Fortunately, several surviving drawings by Polidoro, and later copies, accurately record the appearance of the design of the high altarpiece, which had been removed from its original location by the early nineteenth century at the latest. Two sketches in the British Museum (figs 4.2 and 4.3), one double-sided, are related to this work. One (fig. 4.2) elaborates the triptych format with a Serlian-type arch, allowing for additional vertical figures on the side, as in the Pescheria altar (figs 3.3 and 3.4). Both drawings focus mainly on alternative ideas for the centralised figure of Christ, handled in Polidoro's pulsating graphic style in a wiry pen and ink elaborating buoyant and elongated bodies. Other, more resolved compositional drawings

survive – including one in Berlin (fig. 4.4), apparently a damaged original – that record the main narrative design at a late stage. This can be assumed because several painted derivations after this popular lost work reflect this image in most details. The design is predicated on two rows of monumental figures: the lower row with the three Apostles hunched over in the foreground and the upper row including Christ standing on clouds, all of whom are positioned towards the margins. The prophets Moses and Elijah are mirror images of one another, each gliding with a trailing foot elegantly suspended, as if captured in an aerial pirouette. The background setting of Mount Tabor seems unusually perfunctory for Polidoro, who accentuated the undistracted visionary potential of the subject. Variety is instead transmitted in the rhythms and curving lines of the individual bodies around which draperies swirl. Polidoro's increasing tendency to exaggerate and elongate his figures is pronounced in these drawings. Individual poses are stretched and contorted beyond the realm of the possible, and so if they were

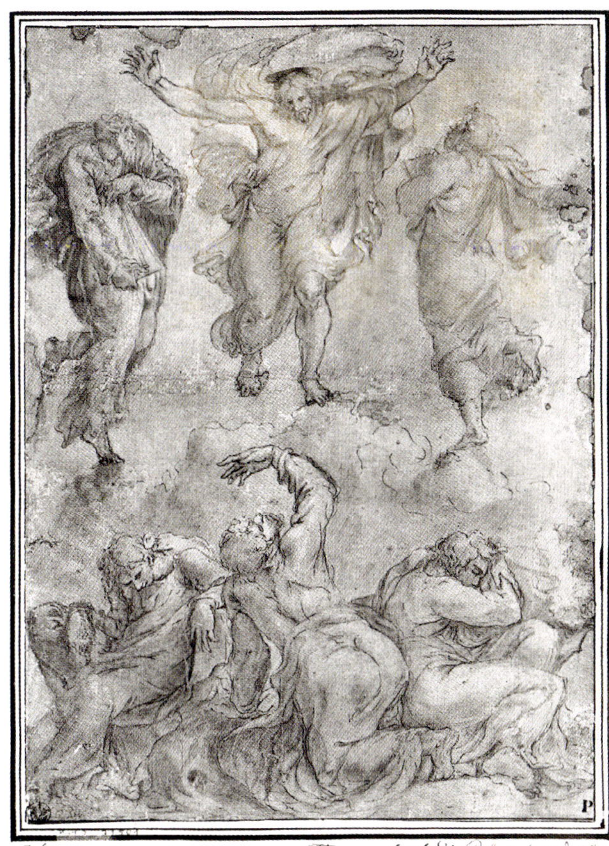

4.4 Copy after Polidoro (?), *Transfiguration*. Pen and brown ink, and brown wash, with white heightening (oxidised) over traces of black chalk on brown prepared paper, 35 × 24.6 cm. Staatliche Museen zu Berlin, Kupferstichkabinett

developed initially through studies after models in the workshop, any sense of this has disappeared. There remains an element of tender refinement related to the grisaille *Annunciation* tondi in Naples (figs 3.5 and 3.6), but there is also a greater urgency expressed in the powerful emotional tenor of the work. Polidoro desired here to create the maximum impact by means of the thick-limbed, onrushing Christ, in this unique miracle of the Gospels; such is the explosive way he must have recalled, or wished to reinterpret, the upper part of Raphael's late *Transfiguration* in Rome. In one significant amendment Polidoro attempted to reverse the scale of Christ and the prophets in Raphael's picture, making the Saviour smaller and so accentuating his dynamic forward movement towards the spectator. A memorial to the city Polidoro had left for the south in 1528, this vigorous composition was extremely influential, its imprint even felt back in Naples, in an altarpiece by Marco Pino.

The *Transfiguration* in the Courtauld Gallery (fig. 4.5) is too reduced in scale to be the original central panel from

the Carmine altarpiece.[9] It is probably either Polidoro's subsequent reprise of his own work, with numerous changes and for a quite different purpose, even a different patron, or a record of the original altarpiece, a format that will be explored in more detail in the final chapter. The unusual shape of the top cannot be original and the panel must have been trimmed at some point. There are also pentimenti, so it can never have been a direct copy; arguably it is more a creative reinterpretation in a format Polidoro revolutionised. In Messina Polidoro created numerous paintings with figures reduced in scale, for which Raphael provided precedents in Rome, such as the *Vision of Ezekiel*, now in Palazzo Pitti in Florence. But those prototypes have exquisite surfaces compared to Polidoro's bold, corrugated ones, nearly drained of local colour – among the first features of what would become his signature style towards the end of his life in Messina, as will be discussed. The authorship of this panel has been questioned: Sebastiano del Piombo, Pedro Ruviale and Deodato Guinaccia have all been proposed, although it was ascribed to Polidoro as early as 1806 and this attribution seems convincing enough, even if the date and purpose require further argument.[10] Importantly, the Courtauld picture traces its provenance to Messina and the Marchese di Montagano collection. The damaged and possibly corrupted Latin inscription identifying a patron on a tablet in the lower left corner has been transcribed as: 'Ex Gisulforum Familia/Ego Ian Paulus Gisulfis per/M. Ae Caroli V R.I/Cancel.Italica Pre/fectus Tabula hanc/Pro me et meis P.F./A.R.S. V. MDXVIII.' An imperial coat of arms is included nearby as a fictive object. The work also contains an unusual small, bust-length portrait in simulated ancient relief, on a stone placed almost casually in the lower left corner – a very rare case of Polidoro attempting portraiture and an entirely ingenious way to reduce the scale of the donor in relation to the sacred figures. This was a retrograde form evoking painted sculpture that he attempted on several panels executed in Messina. Presumably the portrait represents the patron as inscribed, Paolo Gisulfo. The inscribed date of 1518 is inaccurate (Charles V, also inscribed, became emperor in 1519), but the Sicilian Gisulfi traced their origins to Lombardy, which may account for their patronage of Polidoro. Assuming the reference to the Gisulfi is accurate, the Courtauld panel cannot have been

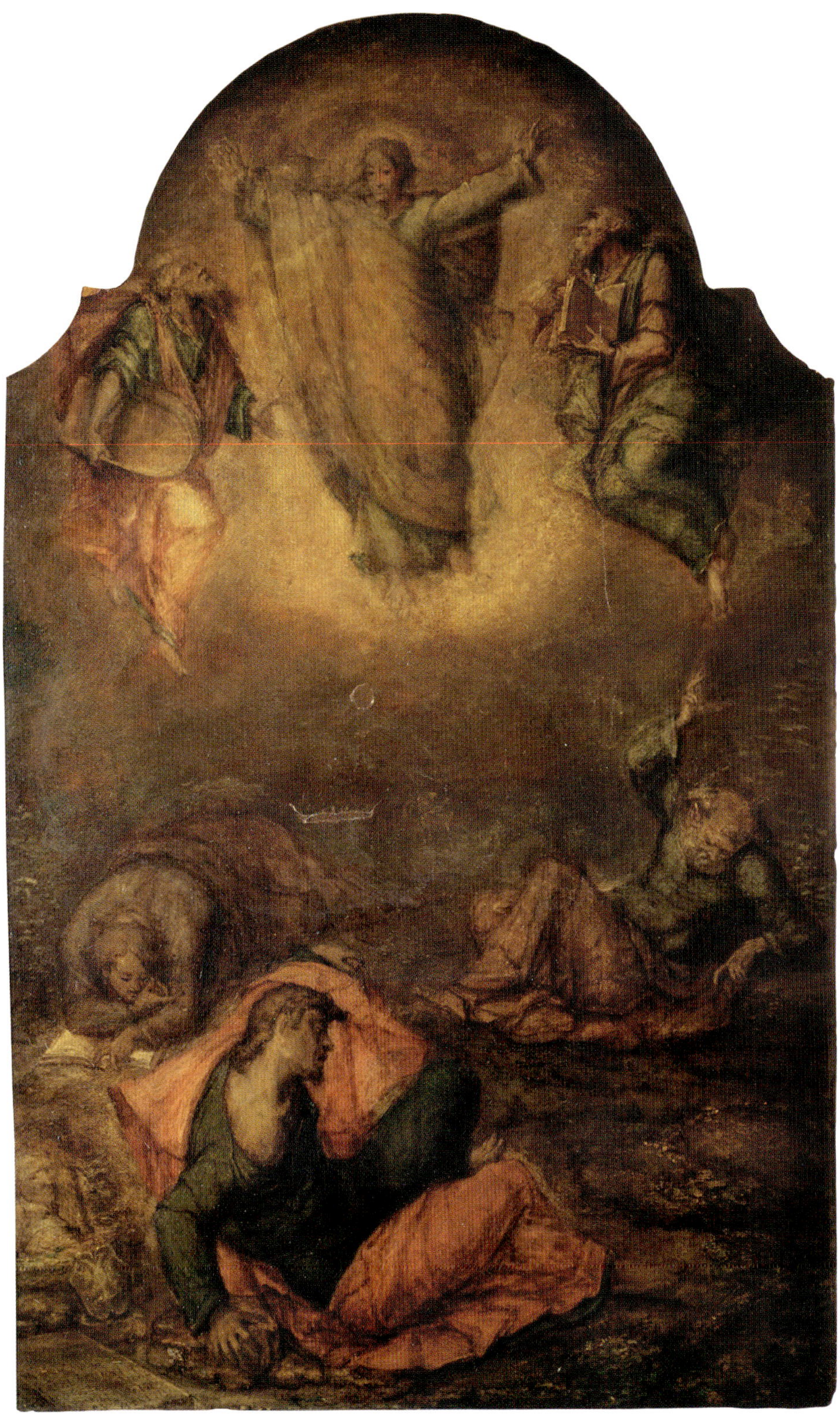

4.5 *Transfiguration*. Oil on panel, 65.2 × 42 cm. The Samuel Courtauld Trust, Courtauld Institute of Art, London

preparatory for the Carmine altarpiece, which was likely commissioned by the Marullo family. In fact, it dates closer to 1540, to judge the work on stylistic grounds (which will be addressed in the final chapter), and thus follows the larger work. It must be a variant of some kind.

Two side panels for Polidoro's Carmine polyptych, each containing a single Carmelite saint, are all that survives of the original.[11] They are both of high quality, if damaged. *Saint Albert*, depicting the Carmelite also known as Albert Siculus or Albert of Trapani, is in Turin (fig. 4.6). This work was transferred from panel to canvas after its acquisition by the gallery in 1957. Old attributions to Tanzio da Varallo and Lorenzo Lotto are instructive and attest to the uncanny power and decisive, portrait-like aspect of the image. A preparatory drawing in pen and ink at Chatsworth House (fig. 4.7), first identified by Pouncey as Polidoro's study for this work, features many of the panel's elements in reverse.[12] Executed in pen and ink, typically for the artist, the sketch is expressive and irregular, even nervous in the almost overwhelming shower of long lines establishing the centre, while grids of strokes define the dense shadows at the sides. Notably the drawing reverses the direction of the painting, as if the artist used this old-fashioned creative device to inspire his own creativity. The sketch also features a flaming censer, evoking an apocalyptic image from Revelation 8, the opening of the sixth seal, when an angel brought fire to the earth through an altar. Why this attribute was substituted in the finished painting is unclear, not least because earthquakes were prevalent in this part of Italy and so it was already highly appropriate.

The painting depicts the saint before a landscape, standing directly on his attribute, the devil, who has the upper body of a woman and a curving snake-like tail. Over his shoulder an angel appears with an unravelling scroll inscribed with a verse from Psalm 36: 30: '*Os eqit sapientia loquetur et iudicat*' (The mouth of the righteous speaketh wisdom, and his tongue talketh of judgement). Despite the atavism of this device, Polidoro made it appear convincingly immediate and urgent. The unabashedly stern and self-possessed saint gazes intensely at a crucifix and perhaps past it into the viewer's space; this is not a typical attribute, nor are the lilies, and so it seems clear the artist was recalling his Quirinale *Saint Catherine of Siena* (fig. 1.24) for this figure. His head is more expressive for

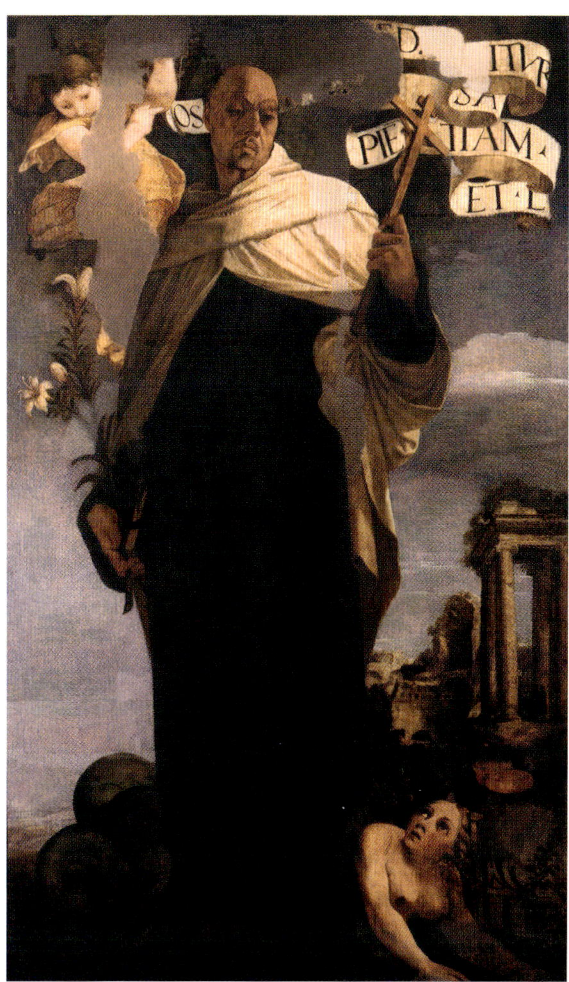

4.6 *Saint Albert*. Oil on canvas, 167 × 103 cm. Galleria Sabauda, Turin

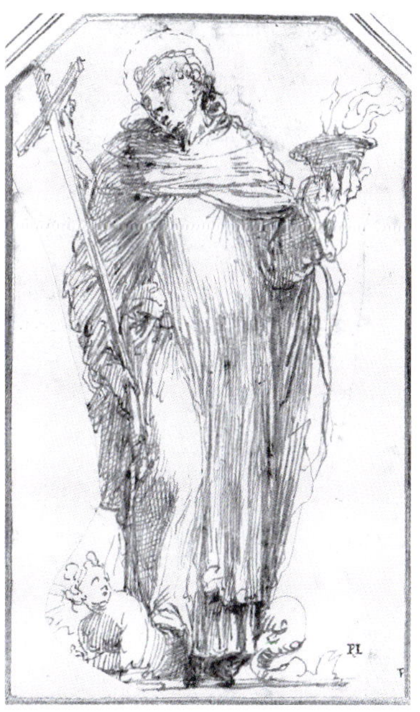

4.7 *Saint Albert*. Pen and brown ink on laid paper, 16.4 × 9.9 cm. Chatsworth House

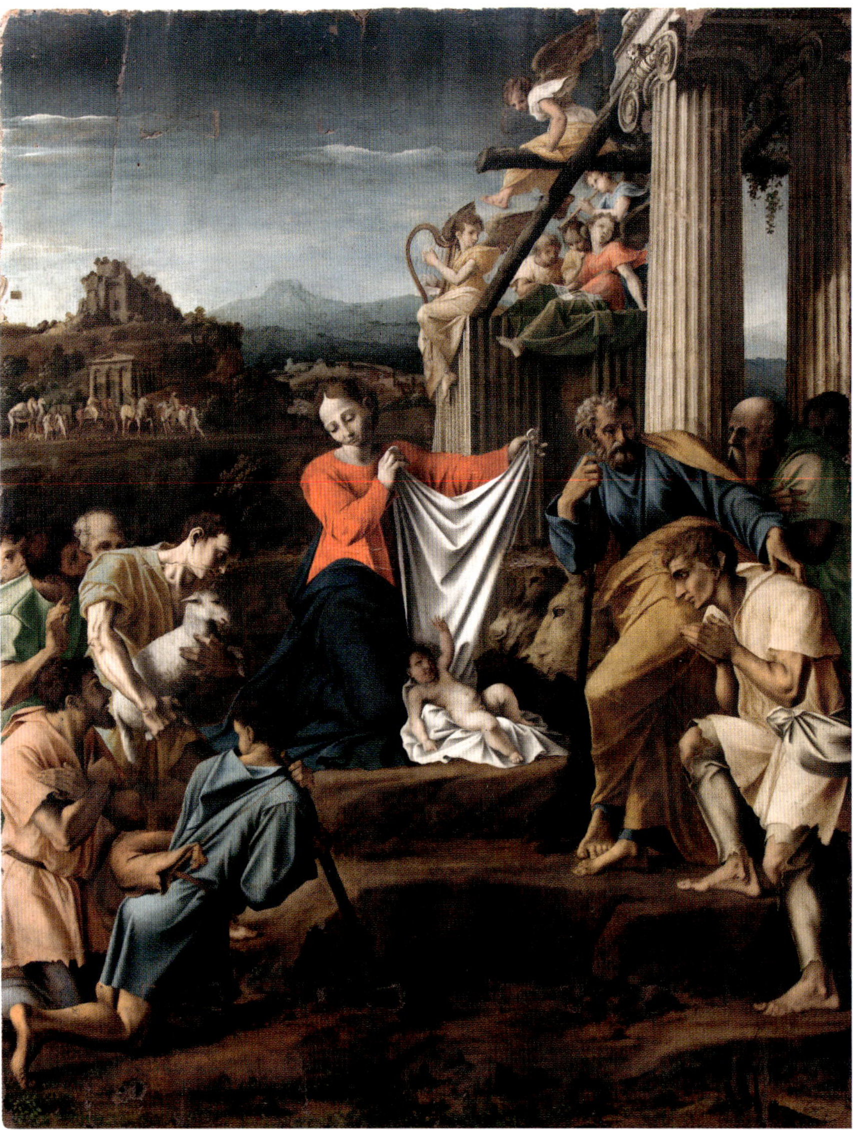

4.8 *Altobasso Nativity*. Oil on panel, 257 × 200 cm. Museo Regionale, Messina

being asymmetrical, and also elegantly reduced in scale compared to the massive, attenuated body. Because of the original placement of the work high on the chapel wall, Polidoro depicted him from a very low angle, but this added to his imposing majesty. A landscape with ancient ruins elevated in the design recalls the efforts of his late Roman period.

Born in Sicily in around 1250, Albert had been canonised as recently as 1476. His main cult was at his birthplace of Trapani on the west coast of Sicily. Polidoro commemorated him complete with a tonsure and traces of a beard, as an ascetic who emphatically triumphs over Satan. He fits generally into a type, explored by Raphael and his workshop in Rome, of single full-length saints

with a macabre attribute at their feet, such as the Louvre *Saint Michael* or the *Saint Margaret* now in the Kunsthistorisches Museum, Vienna. Polidoro retains the self-contained elegance of those images in the twist of the pose, but his image is notably more intense and urgent in its treatment. Even the devil seems to tremble with fear.

Another fragment of this altarpiece, showing the Carmelite saint Angelo, survives in a private collection in Rome.[13] This figure receives the light from the same direction as Albert, but to judge by his three-quarter length stance has been drastically cut down. The saint appears with knives in his chest and head, holds a martyr's palm while he is crowned, and gestures downwards to earth with his outstretched left hand. Also canonised

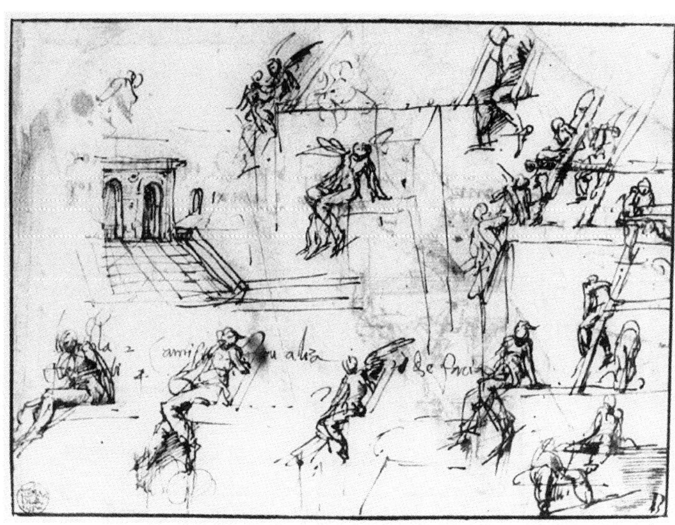

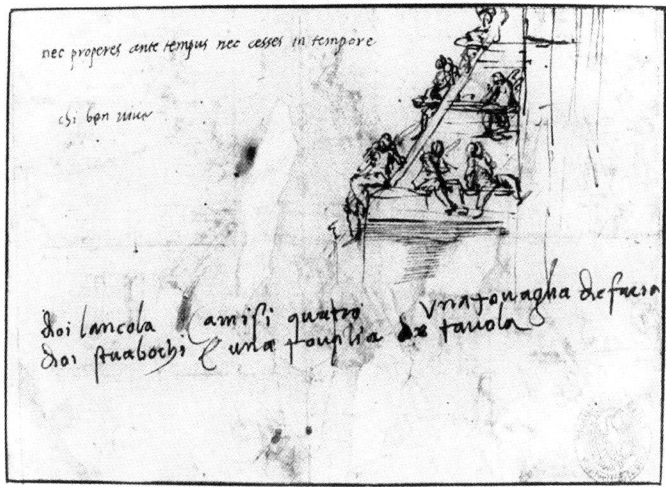

4.9–4.10 *Angels in Architecture and an Architectural Study* (recto) and *Angels in Architecture* (verso). Pen and brown ink on laid paper, 17.4 × 21 cm. Staatliche Museen zu Berlin, Kupferstichkabinett

recently, before 1464, and martyred in Sicily, Angelo is depicted as a young, beardless figure, viciously stabbed like a Carmelite Saint Peter Martyr. Of Jewish parentage, Angelo was sent by the Order to Sicily from Mount Carmel, where he had been a hermit. He converted many to Christianity, and performed miracles, but was murdered while preaching at Leocata, in Sicily, by a knight he denounced for incest. Represented in a landscape in profile, looking up towards the light source, Angelo makes a pleading gesture of intercession, recalling a deacon in the upper left of Raphael's *Transfiguration*. This figure is the less individualised of the two surviving Carmine fragments, but in relative terms these more portrait-like types are an evolution from those seen in the Naples

altarpiece towards an even greater particularity. The conception, too, is starker and more imposing than that of the saints on the earlier Pescheria altarpiece, pointing to the direction of the artist's development.

Except for the *Way to Calvary* altarpiece, completed in 1534, the only other major surviving painting by Polidoro in Messina to be supported by a contemporary document, in this case a legal contract drafted by a notary, is the *Altobasso Nativity* (fig. 4.8), now in Messina's Museo Regionale. This was commissioned from Polidoro by the confraternity attached to the church of Santa Maria dell'Altobasso, in the higher part of Messina, in the name of their treasurer, Alessandro Falcone, on 5 February 1533.[14] According to the contract, the artist was to execute a

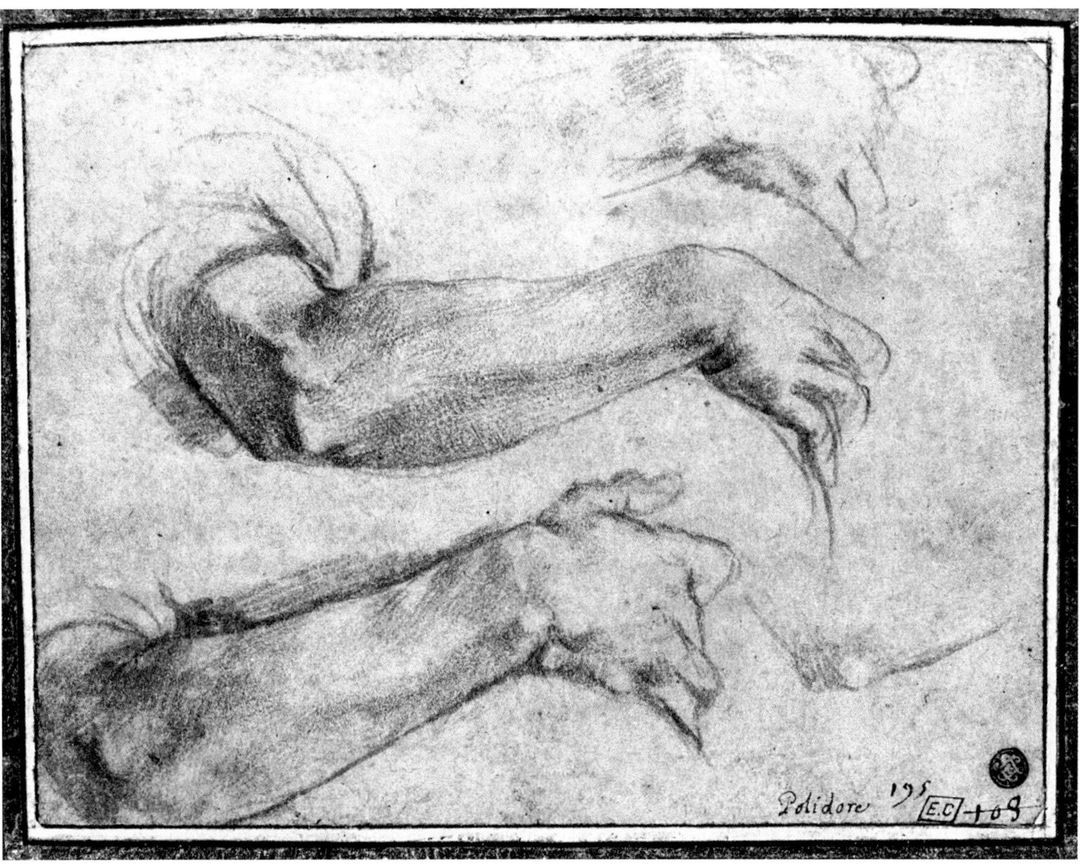

4.11 *Four Studies of a Right Arm*. Red chalk on laid paper, 10.3 × 13.7 cm. Musée du Louvre, Cabinet des Dessins, Paris

Nativity of Christ with the Magi in the background for the high altar. He was to be paid 94 ducats for the painting and given a generous amount of time, until the end of 1534, to execute it. There is graphic evidence in a double-sided drawing in Berlin (figs 4.9 and 4.10) that he was still designing the Altobasso altarpiece in 1535, at the time of the entry of Charles V into Messina, and so it appears that the execution was protracted due to a heavy workload and that it was completed following the *Way to Calvary*.[15] The artist may have been permitted to employ his assistant to finish it because of the new pressure to make designs for the events surrounding the emperor's appearance on the island, and to ensure it was ready for that special moment. There is no precise confirmation of the *Nativity*'s completion date, but an altarpiece of this subject in Messina by a Calabrese painter who emulated Polidoro's style, Pietro Negrone, signed and dated 1540, reflects it, and so provides a latest possible date for the painting.[16]

The Berlin drawing features various ideas for the poses and contours of the angels seated on the architectural planks that form a trellis over the ruined building at the top right of the painting. Individual figure studies also appear on this sheet – a variety of spontaneous creations in pen and ink that anticipate Piranesi in their furious energy – as well as studies showing groups of angels together. The smeared ink on the partially started figure at the upper left of the recto betrays the agitation of the artist's handling and reveals something of his spontaneous approach to the creative process.

Several leg and arm studies have been related to the preparation of the Altobasso altarpiece, but the one most convincingly connected to it is in the Louvre (fig. 4.11).[17] As Lanfranco Ravelli has pointed out, this drawing is significant for appearing to relate directly to the right arm of the shepherd kneeling near the left edge. Studied from two different angles, the bony limb is shown with a rolled-up sleeve and is supporting something against the figure's chest that will become the lamb in the painting, where the arm is positioned more vertically. Polidoro typically handled chalk in smoother lines than in pen, with more strongly reinforced contours, but the sheet still has the distinctive angularity of his touch.

Nonetheless, and despite the existence of a contract, the quality of execution of the Altobasso panel indicates that it was completed with the assistance of the artist's workshop, as it lacks the overall power and assurance of the Courtauld *Incredulity of Saint Thomas* and the surviving saints from the Carmine altarpiece. The visual evidence suggests that in Messina during the mid-1530s Polidoro came to depend more on assistants to execute his designs, one of whom is identifiable, on the basis of stylistic inference, as the minor local artist Stefano Giordano.[18] Whether or not Polidoro came to view himself in Messina as a new Raphael, content with designing rather than executing his public commissions (and, of course, this is the arrangement he had likely been most comfortable with in collaborating with Maturino in Rome before 1527), this reliance on assistants – something for which there is no evidence during his Naples sojourn after the Sack of Rome or the first part of the Messinese period, or indeed later on the island – may simply correspond to the sheer volume of commissions available there around 1535, including the triumphal entry of Charles V. How incentivised patrons in Messina were by having a work entirely in the master's hand, as opposed to a less costly production with assistance, is open to speculation in the absence of written sources. Some earlier writers, especially Francesco Susinno, already recognising the workshop element in the execution of the Altobasso picture, even considered it to be Polidoro's last effort, completed after his death, but this theory can be rejected in light of the appearance of a number of other paintings by Polidoro that must date yet later.

The Altobasso altarpiece features the Virgin unveiling the Christ Child for the shepherds, who have come to worship the newborn Saviour, as told in the first part of Luke's Gospel. Six shepherds appear on the left, while three arrive from the right, brought forward by Joseph. The composition is predicated on these groups entering from either side of the pictorial field, concentrating attention on the centre in an entirely conventional way. A gathering of six young angels sing and play instruments, perched in a charmingly spontaneous way above the main action upon classical ruins – symbolic of the fall of the old order that occurred with the birth of Christ. More modestly portrayed than one would find even in papal Rome, the Virgin is simply attired in her canonical red dress and blue cloak, without trimmings or even a veil to cover her head. She displays the child with humility bordering on shyness: her downcast expression seems prescient of Christ's death, reinforced by a white blanket resembling a winding sheet.

The composition forms a catenary curve, with the main protagonists posed near the very centre of the panel. Polidoro organised the design around self-contained sets of figures and overall it has a loose, staccato quality. The principal figures of Christ and the Virgin are raised and set back slightly on two natural steps of earth to create a powerful funnelling effect. Although one must take the participation of the workshop into account, the style represented here, compared to Polidoro's Neapolitan production, is certainly cruder. The palette is largely restricted but the most richly painted areas are the landscape with the procession of the Magi in the distance and the group of musician angels, while the main figures

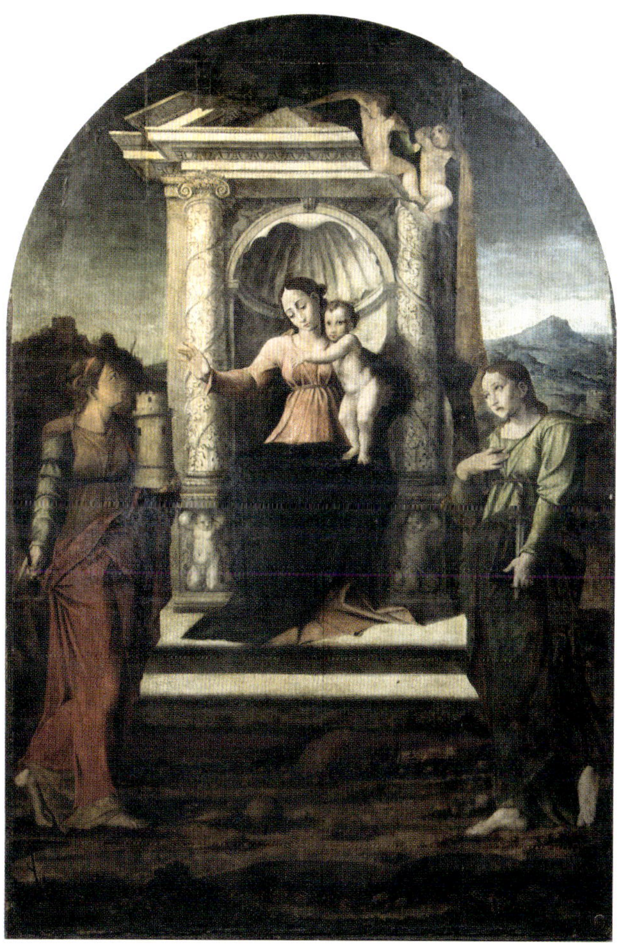

4.12 Stefano Giordano, *Saints Lucy and Barbara with the Virgin and Child Enthroned*. Oil on panel, 293 × 200 cm. Museo Regionale, Messina

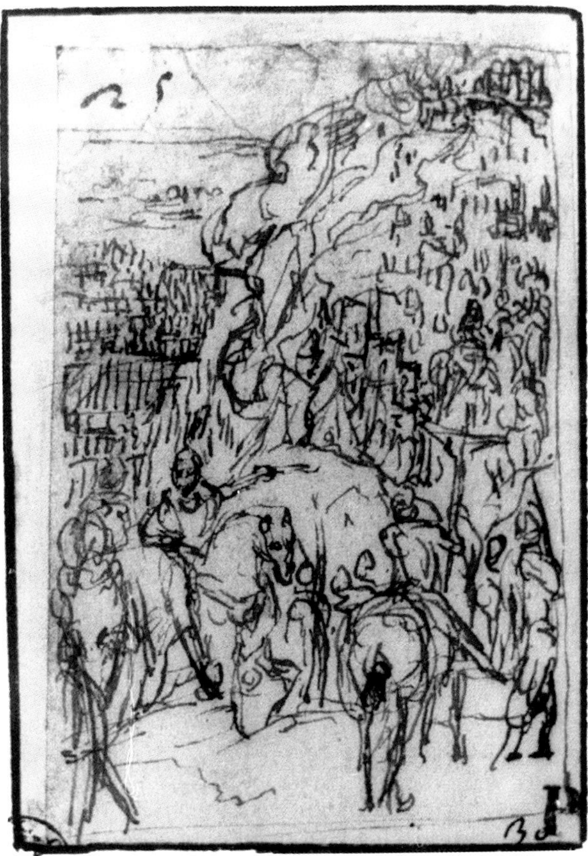

4.13 *Scene of an Entry into Battle from the Entry of Charles V.* Pen and brown ink on laid paper, 8.4 × 5.8 cm. Staatliche Museen zu Berlin, Kupferstichkabinett

are handled in a dry technique alien to Polidoro's own relatively liberated approach. One explanation is that the master himself started the upper part of the panel from a scaffold and subsequently left the rest to assistants. There are still, however, notable hints of formal sophistication in Joseph's cross-legged pose, derived from antique models, and especially in the ancient-inspired architecture of massive fluted columns and square piers, and the placement of the building on a powerful diagonal.

A number of other paintings in this period emanate from in and around the territory of Messina, and are related to Polidoro's style, such as one featuring *Saints Lucy and Barbara with the Virgin and Child Enthroned*, also in the Museo Regionale (fig. 4.12).[19] In the absence of documents or preliminary drawings attributable to Polidoro, it is impossible to know if he might have subcontracted these other commissions to local painters like Stefano Giordano, or whether they were independent works by other artists produced in the shadow of recently

sanctioned public taste. Certainly many of the religious paintings of this derivative, secondary-level quality include representations of fragmentary ancient sculpture and so reflect Polidoro's sensibility and experience. In Sicily he created a new formula for the altarpiece: a dominant, centrally placed saint before marble classical architecture, often depicted incomplete or in fragments, representing the fall of the old order in the face of steadfast Christian heroes, who usually stare directly at the viewer or intently at the Virgin and Christ.

One of the more unusual and involved projects of Polidoro's career was the design of the decorations for the triumphal entry of Charles V into Messina during the autumn of 1535, a major civic as well as artistic event.[20] His work as a public designer of those numerous Roman facades for once prepared him well for this unique project, and the rich complexity of the result can hardly have been surpassed anywhere else in Italy. The Holy Roman Emperor, by virtue of his inheritance of the crown of Aragon, was also ruler of Sicily and Naples, and this added to the special nature of his appearance. Charles V had led imperial troops to North Africa, where he defeated Barbarossa (who had made an alliance with the French) at La Goletta on 14 July and Tunis on 21 July, although with hindsight these triumphs had more significance as propaganda than as real strategic gains in the battle with the so-called infidel. By late August the emperor had reached Trapani on Sicily. The first important triumphal entry after his African victories was at Palermo on 12 September 1535. By 13 October he had arrived in Messina. The following month he went north to Naples, hoping then to enter Rome and to meet the Farnese pope, Paul III, which he eventually did in 1536.

Most of the graphic evidence related to the entry of Charles V into Messina is found in Polidoro's so-called Berlin sketchbook. This reconstituted sketchbook contains 22 drawings, although about half a dozen others, destroyed during the Second World War, are recorded in old photographs, from which we can finally appreciate the artist's astounding virtuosity as a designer. It is one of the most remarkable graphic survivals of the entire Renaissance period. Some drawings could originally have been part of sketchbooks, although how they relate to Polidoro's own practice remains unclear, not least because what survives was only made into an album at a later date,

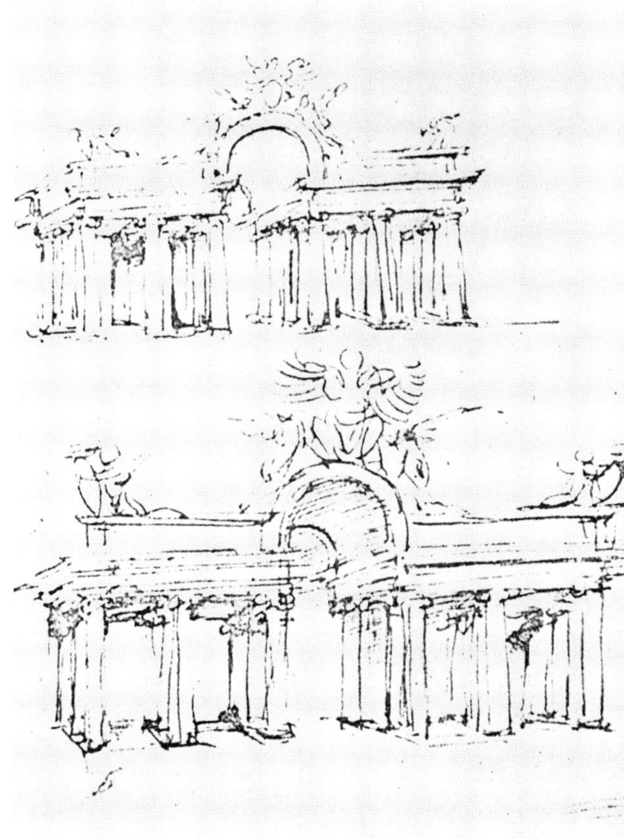

4.14 *Fame Arch*. Pen and brown ink on laid paper, dimensions unknown. Formerly Staatliche Museen zu Berlin, Kunstgewerbemuseum

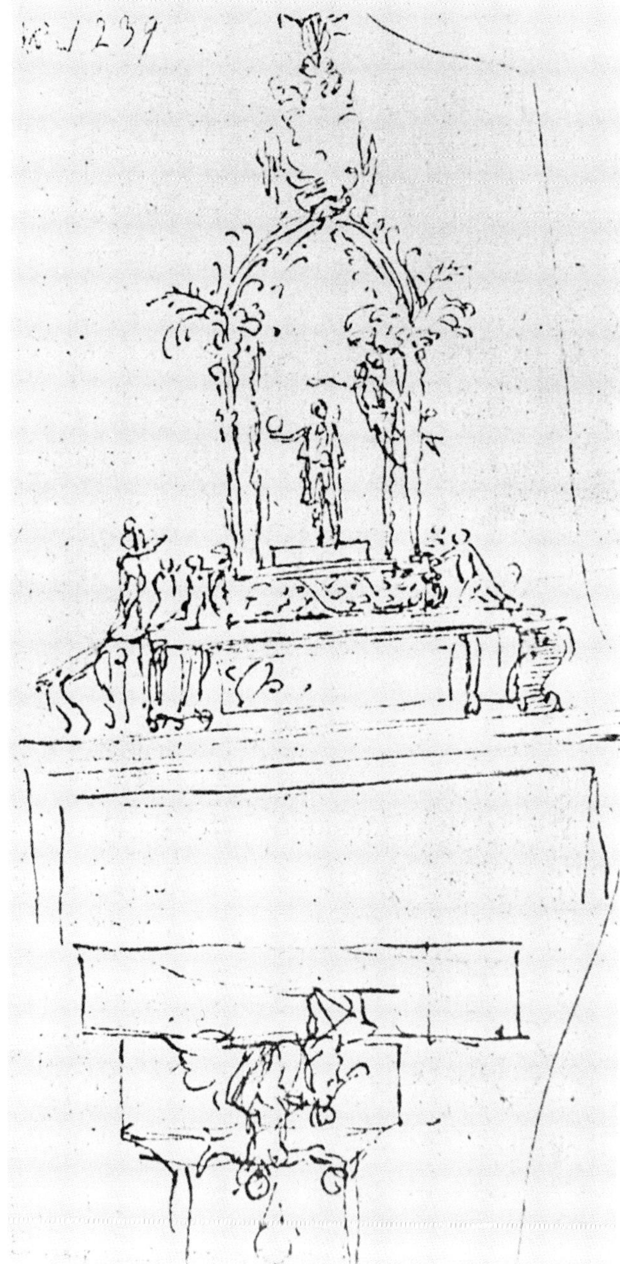

4.15 *Vara Arch*. Pen and brown ink on laid paper, 22.5 × 11.2 cm. Formerly Staatliche Museen zu Berlin, Kunstgewerbemuseum

probably compiled by the eighteenth-century Roman sculptor Bartolomeo Cavaceppi. Furthermore, the album shows no evidence of any binding and comprises different types of paper, and at least two contrasting watermarks (Briquet 10719 and 10736) have been identified. Drawings (see fig. 4.13) are distinguished by a confident, even casual, rapid handling of the pen, the ink flicked almost disdainfully onto the paper. Some sketches feature an unusual coiling of lines as the artist revealed a natural tendency, established in his Roman facade decorations, to create patterns on the page. So loosely drawn are some of the sketches that an attribution to a sixteenth-century artist, let alone Polidoro, would be difficult to sustain without knowledge of their survival in this sketchbook.

The formal entrance into Messina took place on 21 October 1535, the feast day of Saint Ursula. In addition to Vasari's text and Polidoro's drawings in Berlin, there are written eyewitness accounts of this dynamic occasion, the most definitive by a priest, Cola Giacomo d'Alibrando, who had his description published locally by Petruccio Spira within days of the conclusion of the events on 15 December 1535.[21] There is only one copy of the original book extant, in the civic library in Palermo. Alibrando explicitly attributed certain decorations to Polidoro in two passages, but other artists and architects also contributed to this massive project, which involved the whole of the citizenry in procession and religious ceremony. The resident Benedictine literary figure and mathematician,

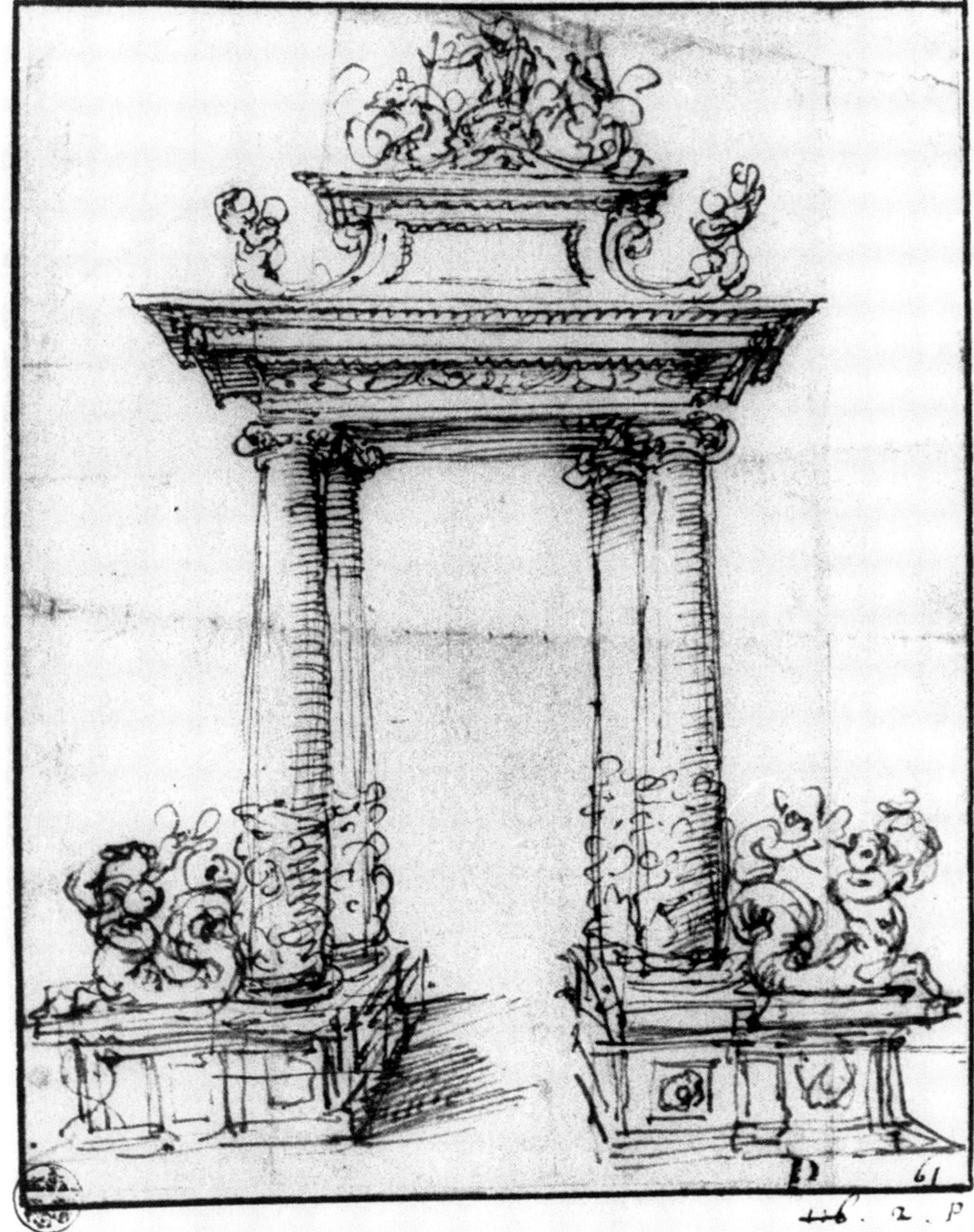

4.16 *Marine Arch*. Pen and brown ink on laid paper, 16.9 × 13.7 cm. Staatliche Museen zu Berlin, Kupferstichkabinett

Francesco Maurolico, who certainly had good reason to insinuate himself into the emperor's good graces, invented some of the Latin inscriptions for Polidoro's designs.

The emperor and his entourage entered the city through the Porta di Sant'Antonio and reached the first arch designed by Polidoro, which had 18 columns and was decorated with paintings and Victory figures with the arms of the emperor and the city. A sheet, once in Berlin (now destroyed), with two studies for this impressive structure features three groups of three columns supporting a central arch and shield (fig. 4.14). The procession subsequently passed through another arch decorated with four columns and a figure of Fame with two trumpets. Alibrando explicitly attributed these two structures to Polidoro. Nothing securely related to the latter structure appears to survive among the drawings.

Charles V was then presented with the spectacle of two decorated chariots, which continued on the route with him. The first was pulled by six captured soldiers and filled with war booty, while the second was larger and featured

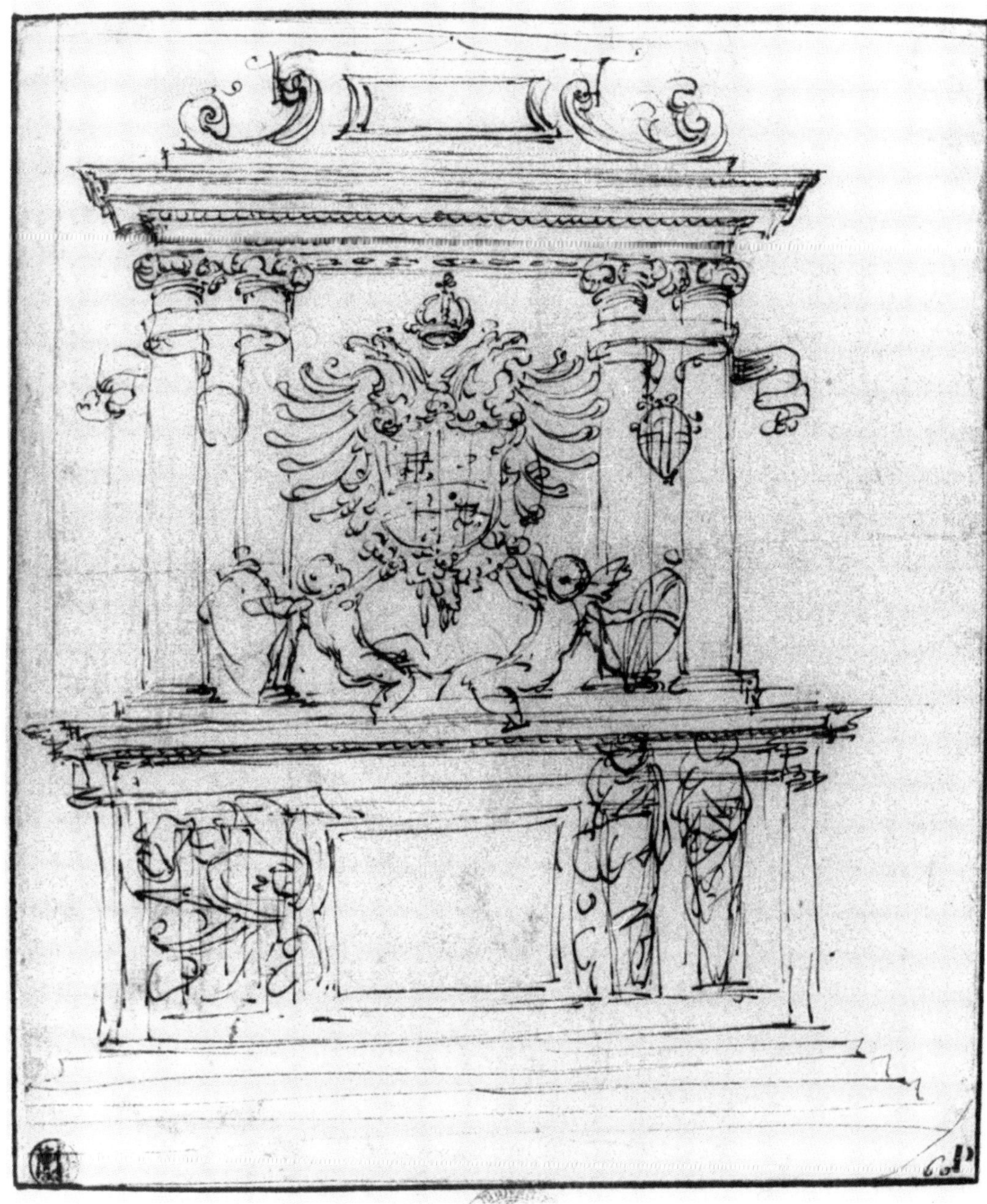

4.17 *Habsburg Arch*. Pen and brown ink on laid paper, 26 × 20.6 cm. Staatliche Museen zu Berlin, Kupferstichkabinett

youths dressed as the Cardinal Virtues and, at the summit, an image of Charles V himself standing on the earth, holding a small figure representing Victory. This spectacle is echoed in the parade of the *vara* triumphal cart ('bara' in Italian, meaning 'coffin') that still takes place in Messina today to celebrate the Feast of the Assumption.[22] The evidence of several drawings in Berlin, and another now destroyed, suggests Polidoro was directly involved as a designer with the second chariot at least. The *Vara Arch* drawing (fig. 4.15) appears to show the standing emperor

with an orb, being crowned by a figure emerging from an arboreal frame. A number of supplicants kneel before him on the main architectural form. On the verso of this sheet he is represented seated, with an allegory of Justice holding her scales portrayed in a billowing floral form at the summit. The entourage eventually reached the cathedral, where the facade was decorated with the emperor's heraldic design. A memorial service was held in the cathedral, sumptuously prepared for the event, after which Charles V retired to his residence. On 20 November 1535 he then

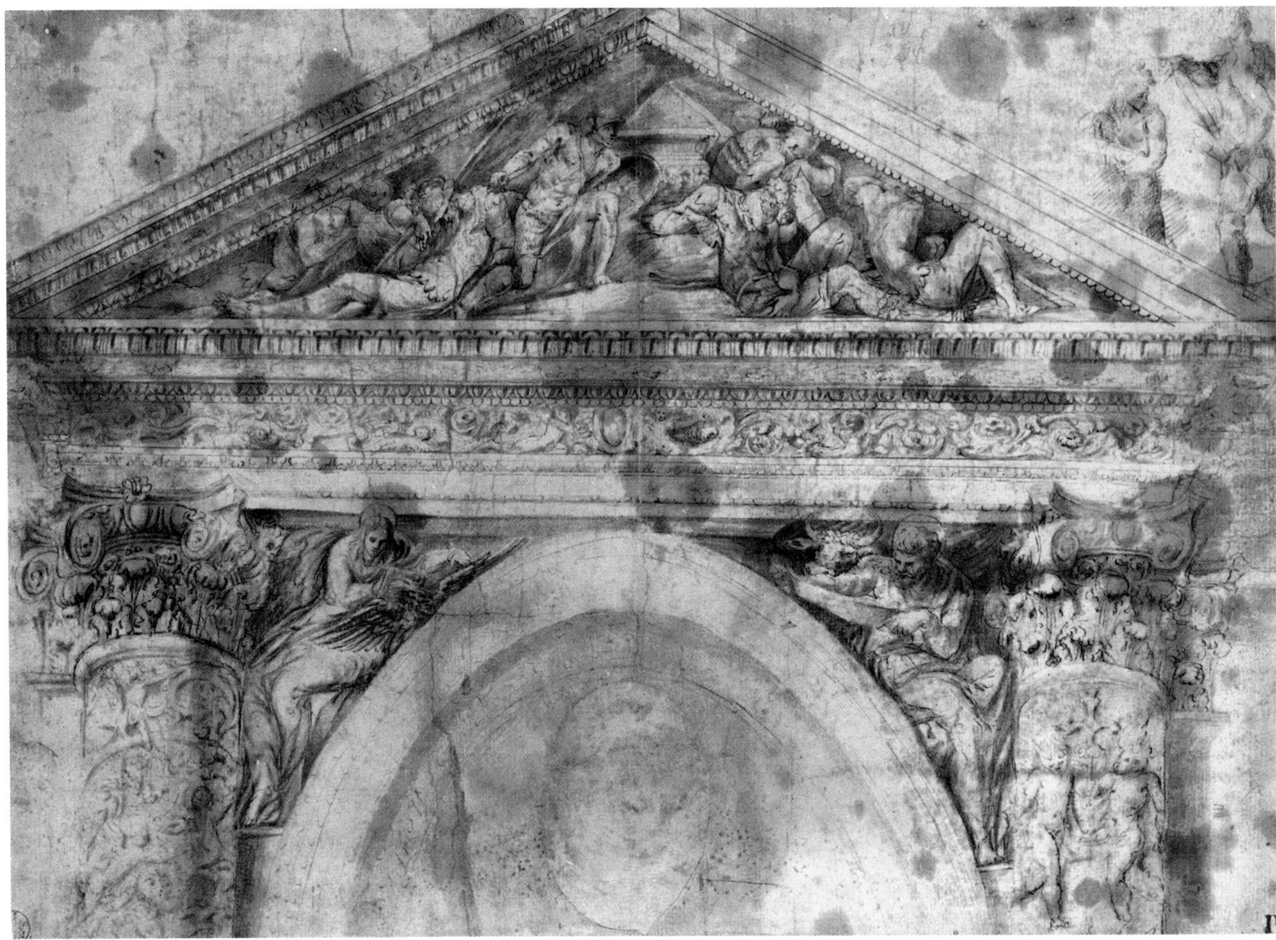

4.18 *Study for a Facade with the Resurrection of Christ and Two Evangelists*. Pen and brown ink, and grey wash, on laid paper, 27.9 × 40.4 cm. Staatliche Museen zu Berlin, Kupferstichkabinett

departed Messina and encountered the final arch, with four columns, at the Gate of Santa Maria del Pilerio 'alla Marina', also directly attributed to Polidoro by Alibrando. Not surprisingly, this arch featured maritime imagery. A sheet in Berlin (fig. 4.16) records Polidoro's design for this structure, with sea gods at the base and a Neptune who dramatically appears to ride straight out towards the public on a chariot surmounting the arch.

Another drawing in Berlin for the triumphal entry (fig. 4.17), featuring putti supporting the Habsburg arms and those of Messina, does not relate explicitly to any textual account, so we can assume Polidoro executed more work than Alibrando indicated. The verso also includes spontaneous sketches of landscape with clouds, two elaborate candelabra and a ground plan for a building, reflecting the diverse uses to which these pages were put. The so-called Berlin sketchbook is replete with Polidoro drawings for a variety of projects contemporary with but

not related to the entry, including liturgical objects and attempts at monumental architecture. There are various studies for religious subjects not otherwise recorded in the written sources, including a Saint Sebastian, a John the Baptist and a *pietà*, reminding us how little we have securely discovered about the breadth of Polidoro's activity in Sicily. The most resolved are solutions for a tympanum arch, and a study for the monumental *Resurrection of Christ* (fig. 4.18). The drawings appear too ambitious for temporary decorations surrounding the entry, so presumably were intended as designs for permanent alterations to the cathedral – rare firm evidence of Polidoro as an architect, for which documentation is otherwise lacking.[23] The organised commotion of the event is fortunately recorded in sketches related to the transportation of the Ark of the Covenant by David into Jerusalem, again probably connected to the entry, the most resolved of which survives in the British Museum (fig. 4.19).[24]

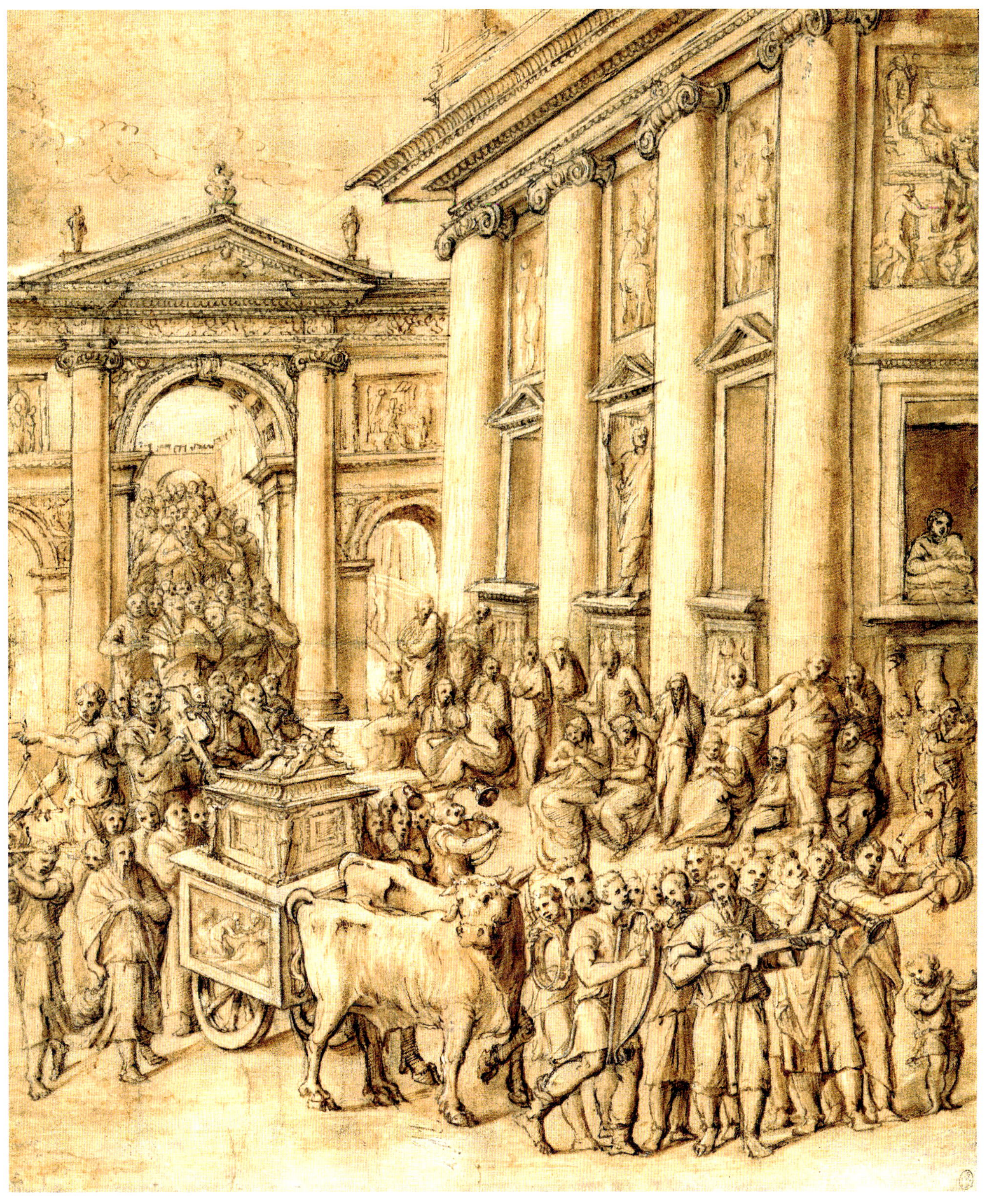

4.19 *Triumph of David*. Pen and brown ink, and brown wash, with white heightening on laid paper, 33.1 × 28.4 cm. British Museum, London

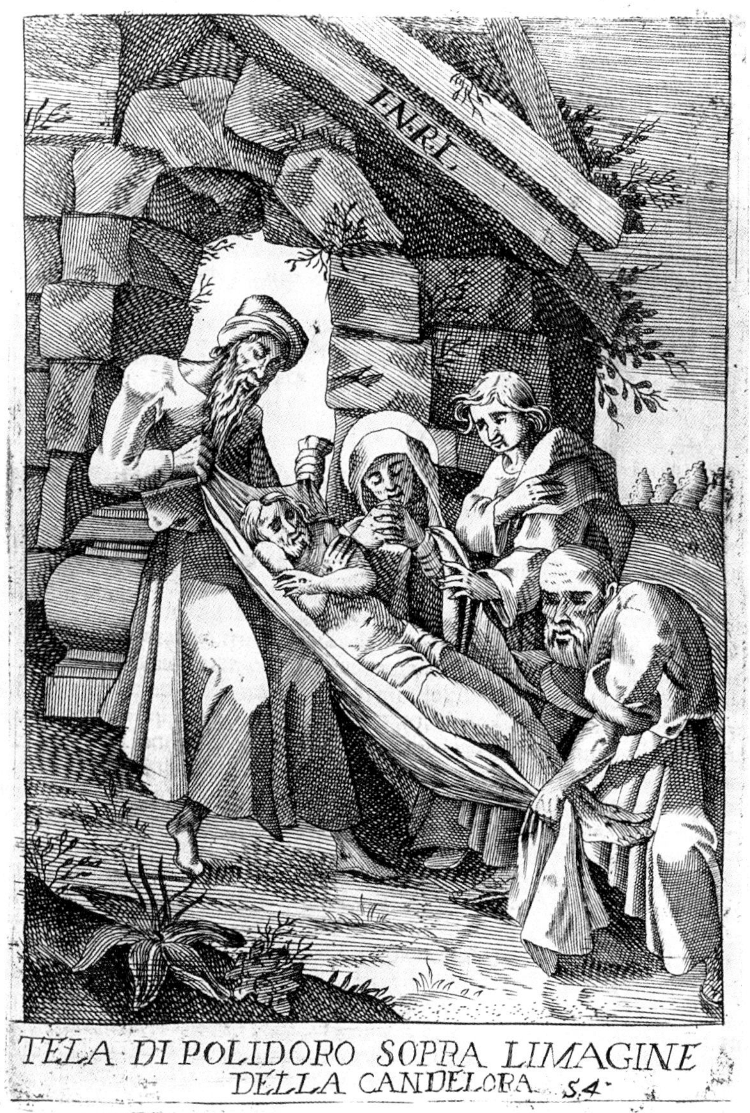

4.20 Placido Samperi, Print after Polidoro's Candelora *Deposition*. Inscribed: 'Canvas of Polidoro over the altarpiece in the Candelora church'

While the last decade of Polidoro's life in Messina is now somewhat mysterious, one nonetheless has the impression from sources that his work filled the churches of the earthquake-prone city, even if employing this written evidence is not always straightforward and the account is necessarily rather intermittent. For example, in 1644 the Jesuit priest and author Samperi records that Polidoro produced the canvas cover for an altarpiece in the church of the Candelora in Messina and published a print after the now lost work (fig. 4.20), but its stylistic crudity does not help confirm the assessment.[25] Drawings assist more in the reconstruction of different altarpieces recorded in the later written sources, which appear on stylistic grounds to have been executed during the first half of the 1530s, prior to the entry of Charles V. A complete drawing in the Uffizi of an *Annunciation* (fig. 4.21), following on from the studies for the Naples Pescheria altarpiece, with its elaborate frame, probably relates to the lost painting once in the oratory of Santa Maria dell'Alto in Messina.[26] Attributed by Bernice Davidson, and independently by Michael Hirst, it is exquisitely drawn, with thin spare lines and a notable economy of means, in a soft, luminous, almost reckless style that foreshadows sketches of the Baroque period. The damage to the paper does not detract from the quality of the study. The relatively more elegant style would place

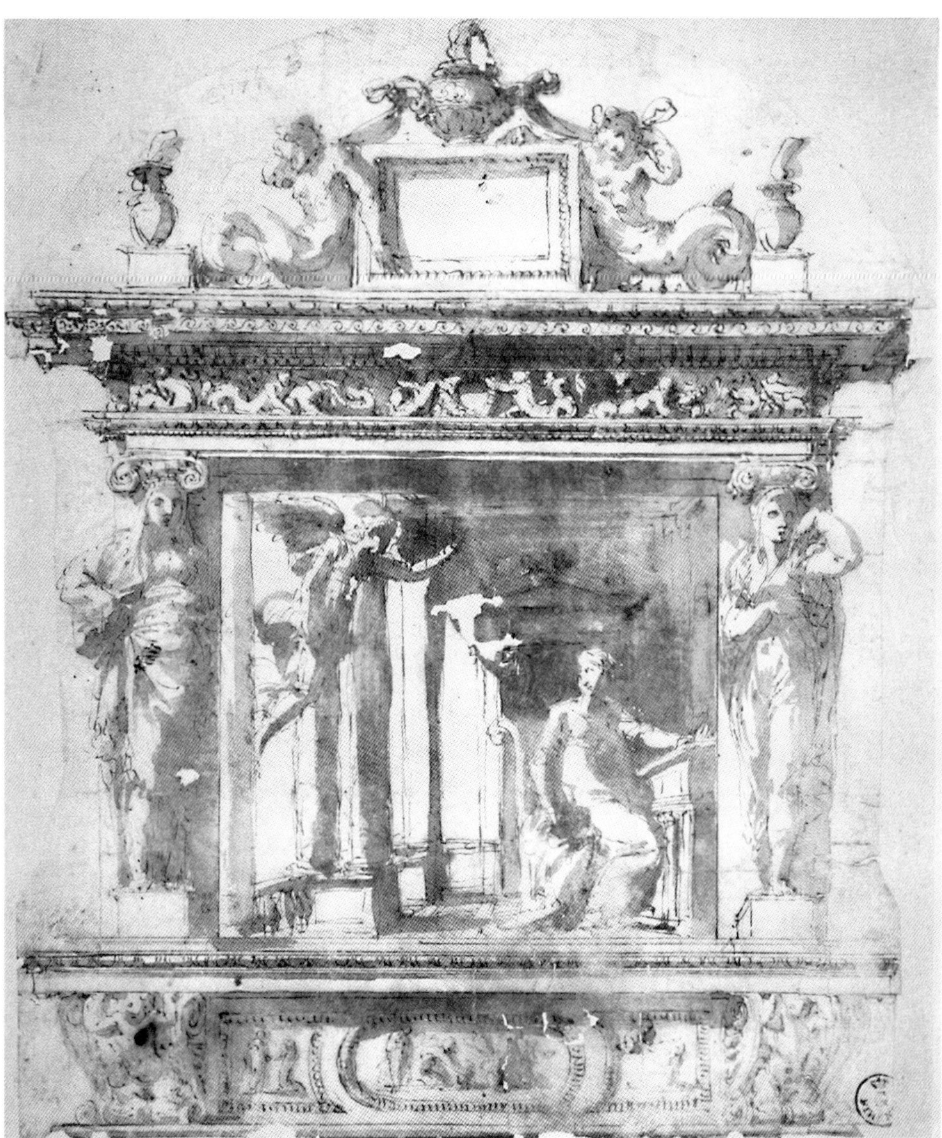

4.21 *Annunciation*. Pen and brown ink, and brown wash, ruled with stylus, on laid paper, 26.7 × 22.5 cm. Gabinetto Disegni e Stampe degli Uffizi, Florence

the work closer to the Naples period than to the end of the artist's life, approximately around 1530. The presence of marine imagery in the frame links it to Messina more broadly, while the massive caryatids standing on their square plinths recall the lower parts of the Vatican Stanze, in which Polidoro is not known to have participated but which he clearly observed and remembered.

Several related drawings, including a fairly resolved sheet in the Fogg Art Museum (fig. 4.23) and especially the recto of a double-sided preparatory study in the Metropolitan Museum of Art (fig. 4.22), relate to the most ambitious of these lost Messina paintings, once in the church of Saints Peter and Paul 'Pisani', presumably on

the high altar and commissioned by the Pisan maritime community in Messina, who traditionally had banking interests on Sicily.[27] The different studies correspond to reveal an altarpiece with a Virgin and Child placed in a niche, seated on an elevated throne decorated with lion's heads and attended by two putti holding a garland – a direct reminiscence of Raphael's fresco of Isaiah in Sant'Agostino in Rome, where Polidoro had himself worked on the Martelli altar. Two male saints flank the central figures in a traditional arrangement. Clearly Saints Peter and Paul are present but the two saints wearing mitres are more difficult to identify specifically. The saints enact a true *sacra conversazione*, agitated in dialogue as

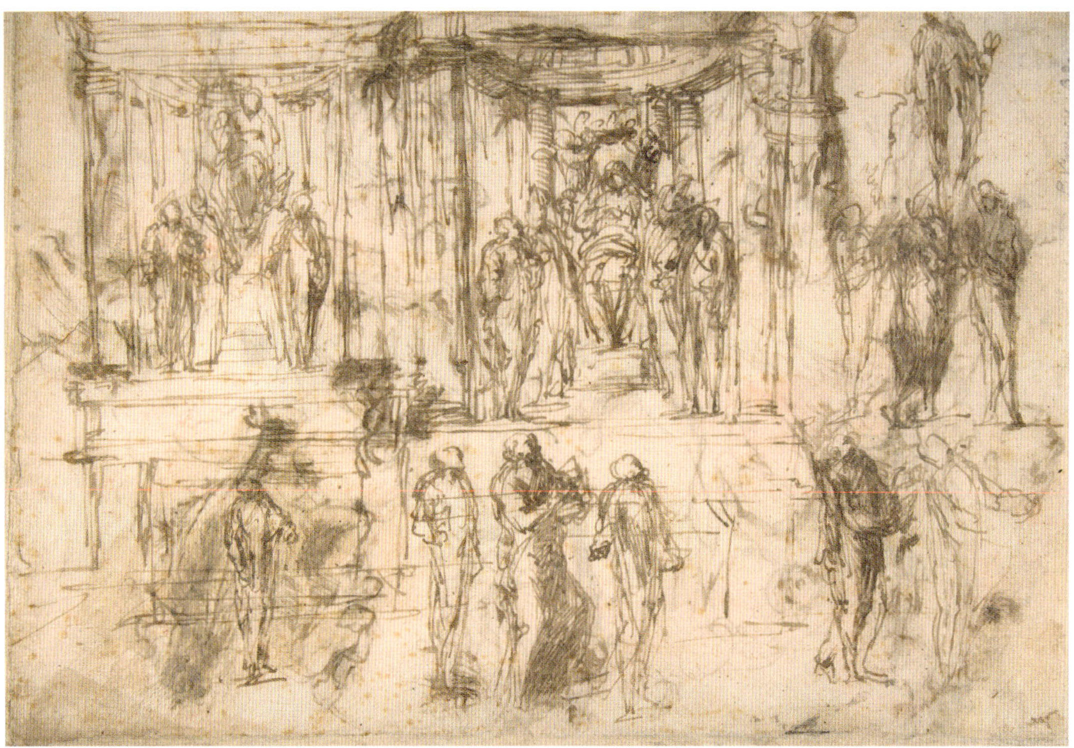

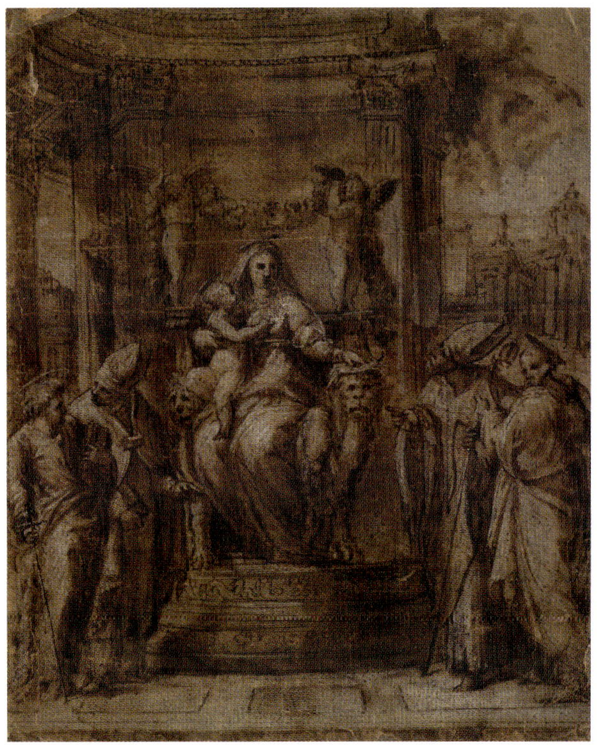

they engage with one another and the divine centre.
They stand in a colonnade that opens on to a deep landscape
filled with architecture, reminiscent of the San Silvestro
frescoes. One of the drawings (fig. 4.22) includes the altar
and reveals a strip for a predella, which is not filled in.
Fortunately, the verso of the sheet in New York contains
interspersed studies for the two prophets in the lost
Carmine *Transfiguration*, thus allowing us by inference
to date the 'Pisani' church painting to the earlier 1530s.

A damaged compositional drawing in the Uffizi of the
Presentation of the Christ Child in the Temple (fig. 4.24) was
likely executed for the painting by Polidoro recorded in
the Jesuit church of San Nicola Vecchio dei Gentiluomini
in Messina.[28] The lack of symmetry is notable in this
claustrophobic design weighted to the viewer's right,
while the reduction of figure scale in relation to the vast
architecture recalls the approach to the San Silvestro
frescoes. The general arrangement can be paralleled
with the design developed in the 'Pisani' drawings, again
indicating a date in the earlier 1530s.

Yet another finished drawing by Polidoro, for an
unidentified chapel and depicting the *Way to Calvary*,
is not related to any document but is a resonant image
because of the importance of the subject for the island
(fig. 4.25).[29] Unusually, this drawing, now in Stuttgart,

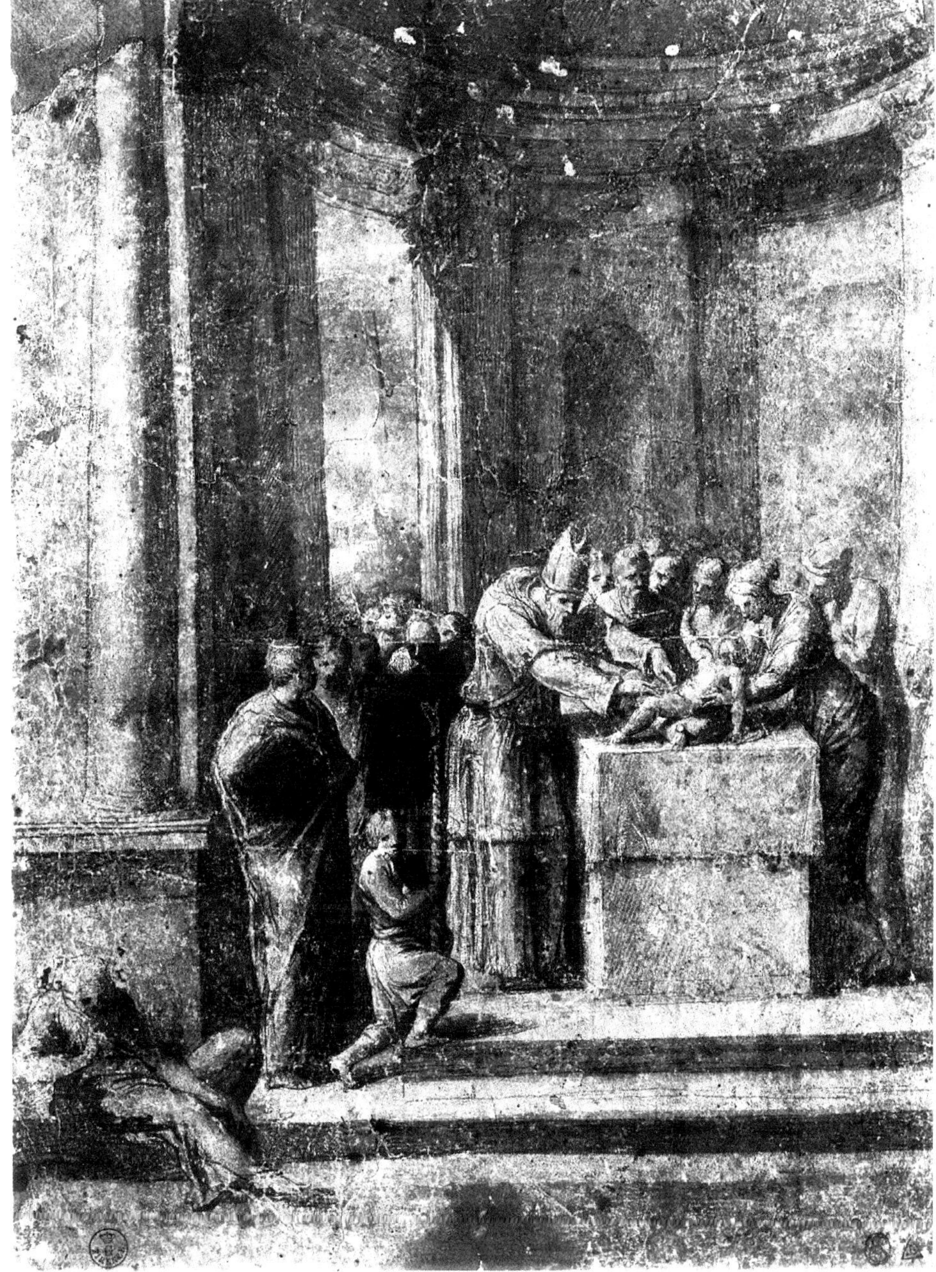

4.24 *Presentation of the Christ Child in the Temple*. Pen and brown ink, and brown wash, with white heightening over traces of black chalk on laid paper, 27.6 × 20.5 cm. Gabinetto Disegni e Stampe degli Uffizi, Florence

was reproduced in an engraving by the Master of the Die, who was active in Rome, dated, along with several others from different original sources, to 1532.[30] It is clearly meant for a fresco in a rounded niche chapel, and includes the architecture and altar with a prominent coat of arms containing a cardinal's hat, so the commission was significant but is nonetheless mysterious. Assuming the date of the print is near contemporary, the printmaker must have accessed the drawing in Rome while Polidoro

was in Sicily. The study was perhaps, then, intended for a Roman rather than Messinese chapel, and if so would be rare evidence for his continuing links to the papal city. There were two Roman cardinals of high nobility linked to Monreale in Sicily, not Messina, in this period – Pompeo Colonna and Ippolito de'Medici – but nothing connects them to Polidoro.[31] In stylistic terms this drawing also represents his first engagement with Raphael's altarpiece in Palermo – *Lo Spasimo di Sicilia* – a painting that would

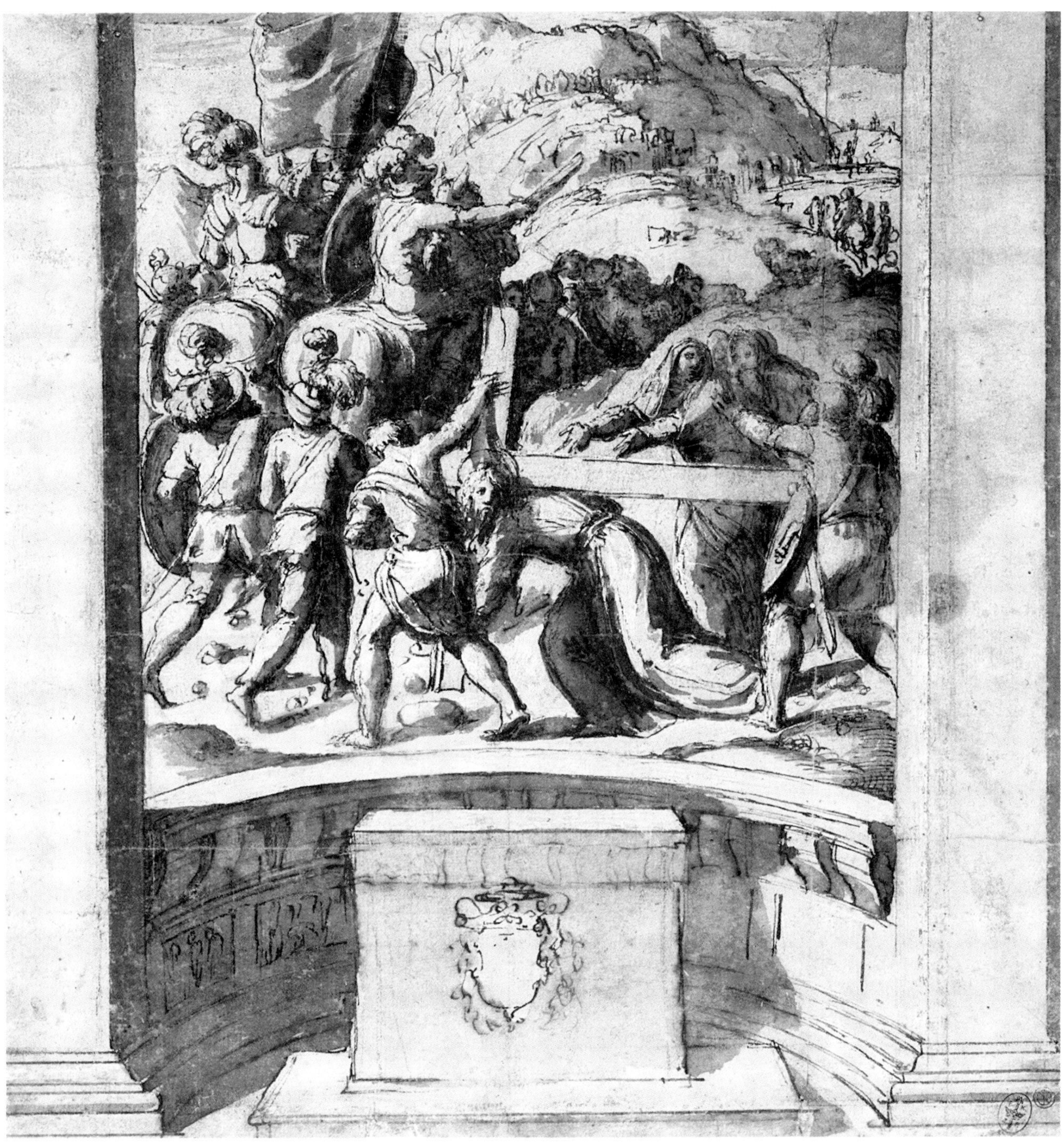

4.25 *Way to Calvary*. Pen and brown ink, and brown wash, on laid paper, 28 × 27 cm. Staatsgalerie, Stuttgart

preoccupy him in his remaining years. While he could have known Raphael's image from a print, it is more likely he was inspired, like his patron, by the original in Sicily and made an otherwise undocumented study trip to Palermo. In the absence of any evidence related to its patronage, it is hard to say more about this intriguingly ambitious sheet.

Polidoro was also involved in some rare mythological paintings in Messina, namely a cycle based on Ovid's telling of the Meleager myth in Book VIII of *Metamorphoses*. A preparatory drawing survives in Florence (fig. 4.26) and four panels were recorded in the collection of Cardinal Antonio Barberini by 1644 but remain otherwise untraced.[32] The inventory sources suggest a set of lost narrative panels recalling in format the Cupid and Psyche paintings produced in Naples, now found mainly in the Royal Collection at Hampton Court. A remarkable survival, a worksheet on poor-quality paper, apparently from early in the design process, it illustrates the vigorous drama of the myth's Calydonian boar hunt with an exhilarating graphic touch.[33] The frieze-like arrangement betrays a lingering nostalgia for the Roman facade frescoes. Coincidentally, this particular subject was one that preoccupied Raphael in his later years, as in a putative commission for Duke Alfonso d'Este in Ferrara, left incomplete at the artist's death and for which a drawing was certainly produced.[34] Polidoro may well have known the design as a youth in the workshop, but since it is lost it cannot be certain this was a model for his image, fascinating as the comparison is. The drawings for the Meleager paintings were definitely executed in Messina, but perhaps they were made directly for export back to Rome, given that they were already in the Roman Barberini collection by the seventeenth century at the latest – fleeting evidence again, perhaps, of a link to his former life or the promise of a future back in the city. A slight sketch of a *Venus and Cupid* survives from this later phase of Polidoro's career but as far as we know he would never represent a mythological story again.[35] The drawing of Meleager in the Uffizi, coupled with another with a mysterious narrative in the British Museum (fig. 4.27), are among his most spirited conceptions of any period. Their secular subject matter is a poignant reminder of what Polidoro had relinquished in Rome and Naples, as a study of the final period of his career makes abundantly clear.

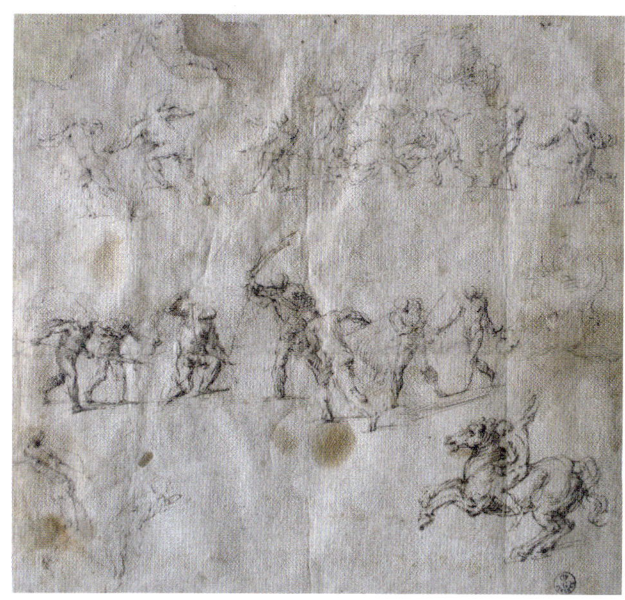

4.26 *Studies of Meleager*. Pen and brown ink with traces of metal stylus on laid paper, 21.8 × 23.2 cm. Gabinetto Disegni e Stampe degli Uffizi, Florence

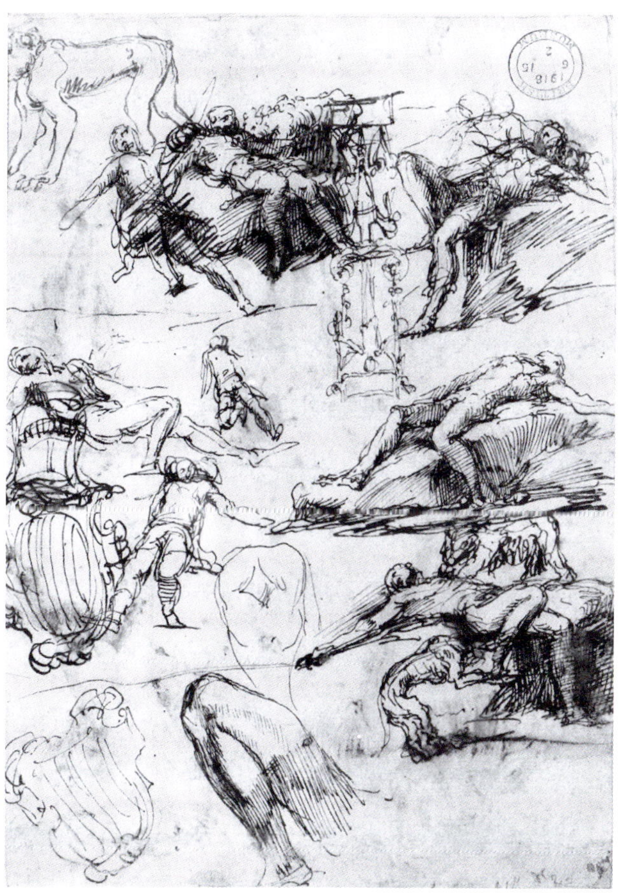

4.27 *Studies for the Transfiguration and a Man Attacked by Animals*. Pen and brown ink on laid paper, 21.9 × 15.9 cm. British Museum, London

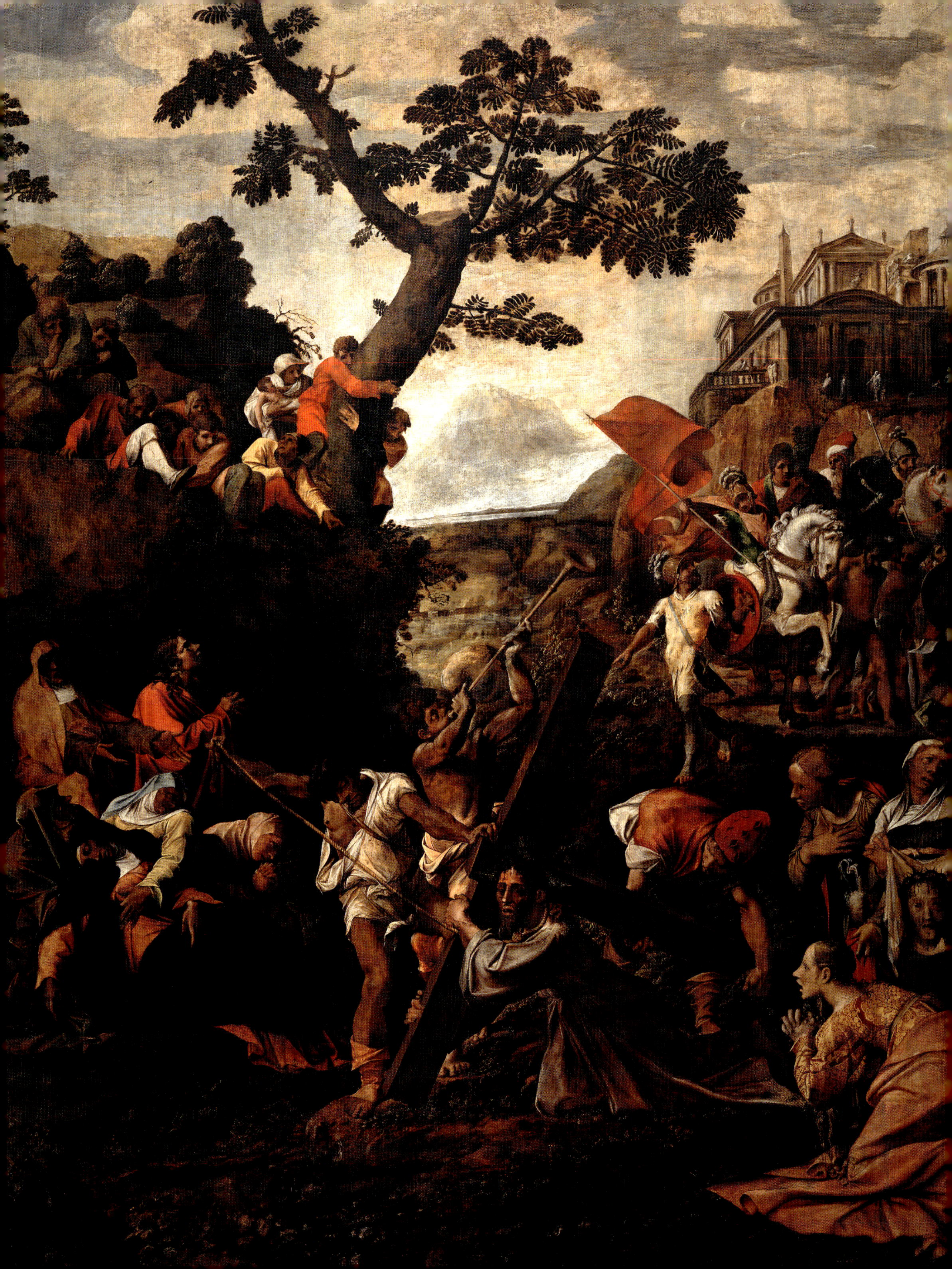

5   The *Spasmo* of 1534

On 1 September 1534 Cola Giacomo Alibrando, the priest from Messina, submitted to the local publishers Petruccio Spira and Joandominico Morabito a long religious poem entitled *Il Spasmo di Maria Vergine* (The Paroxysm of the Virgin Mary).[1] The text describes, following a public procession approved by the bishop Antonio de Lignamine, the installation in the church of Santissima Annunziata dei Catalani of Polidoro's recently completed altarpiece, the *Way to Calvary*, now in the Capodimonte (fig. 5.1). The book is dedicated to an indigenous patrician, Pietro Ansalone, who was the local consul of the Catalan neighbourhood in Messina and the original patron of Polidoro's painting, which was produced not for the high altar of the church but for the chapel of the attached oratory of the Catalan brotherhood. As in other foreign places, and like other expatriate groups, the Catalan community in Messina was close-knit, for linguistic, economic and devotional reasons. The altarpiece remained in the Norman-period church for which it was painted until the late eighteenth century, when

5.1 *Way to Calvary*. Oil on panel, 310 × 247 cm. Museo di Capodimonte, Naples

it was removed to Naples after the earthquake that damaged so much of Polidoro's work in Messina.[2]

Polidoro's surviving later paintings are, almost without exception, strikingly unusual in style and technique, and in some cases the very attribution of apparent originals will most likely remain a source of permanent controversy. But Alibrando's contemporary poem helps to provide a unique interpretative code for these works, and as such supports the attributions of these remarkably raw and sensate paintings to Polidoro himself. The text is of such significance that it merits treatment as a separate chapter.

The largest panel Polidoro may have ever produced, the *Way to Calvary* depicts the part of the Passion in which Christ carries his own cross to Golgotha, as related in most detail in John's Gospel. It is not known precisely when the *Way to Calvary* was originally ordered from Polidoro, but it was definitely executed prior to 1 September 1534, when it was reproduced as a woodcut and described in Alibrando's small book. Presumably the poem was not written simultaneously with the painting but in its wake, as a commemoration. The altarpiece does not depend on the text but is enlightened by it in a way

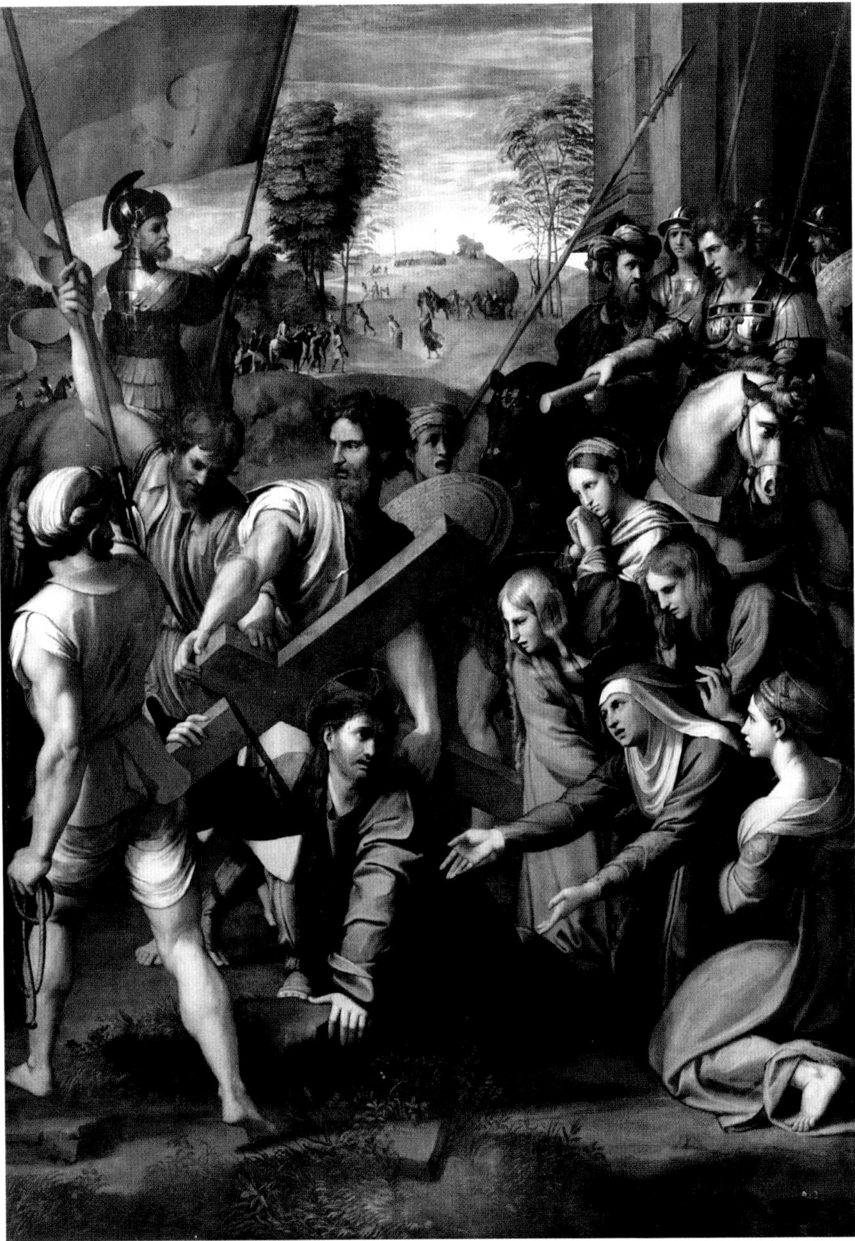

5.2 Raphael, *Spasimo di Sicilia*. Oil on canvas transferred from panel, 318 × 229 cm.
Museo del Prado, Madrid

that is tremendously rare for the period, and even seems provocatively contemporary.

It is significant that Pietro Ansalone, the confraternity's agent for this commission, had a family chapel in Santa Maria dello Spasimo in Palermo, the church in which Raphael's so-called *Spasimo di Sicilia* formed the high altarpiece (fig. 5.2).[3] He clearly desired a version of this image in Messina. Raphael's signed work was engraved by Agostino Veneziano in 1517, which provides an end date for the design at least. The painting has a remarkable

history. On its maiden journey from Rome, where it was painted, to Palermo, the picture was allegedly – and miraculously – the sole object to survive a shipwreck. The pope personally intervened to ensure the return of the work from the Genoese sailors who had recovered it to its original owners. The panel now had the status of a divine relic, prestige that is relevant to Alibrando's description of Polidoro's picture as itself a *'reliquia santa'*.

The fact that Raphael's was the most famous recent religious picture on the island is critical for deciphering

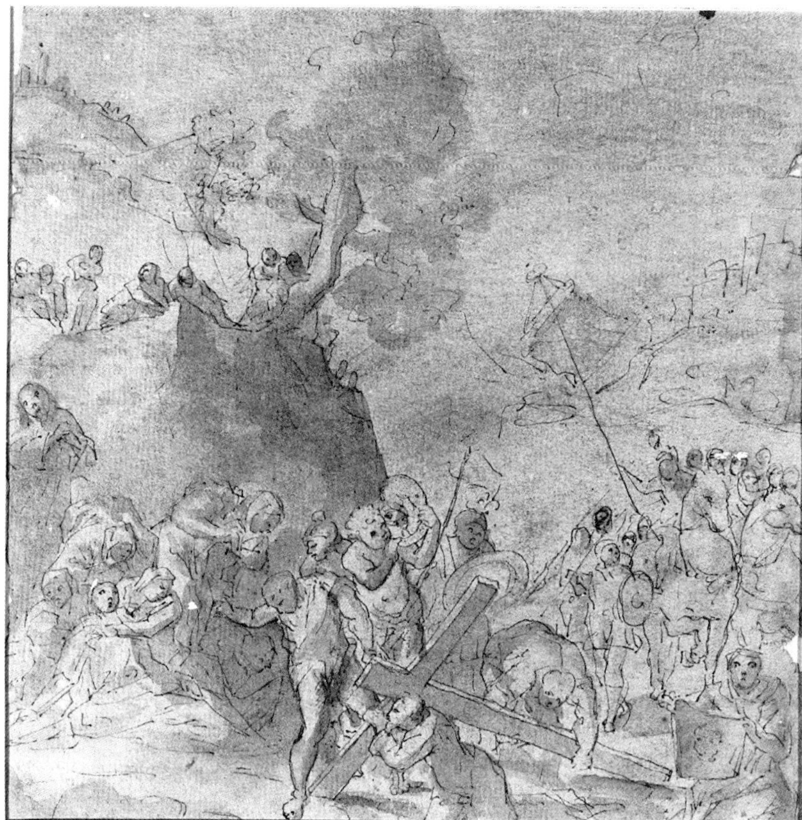

5.3 Copy after Polidoro, *Way to Calvary*. Pen and brown ink, and brown wash, on laid paper, 27.5 × 20.8 cm. Galleria Regionale della Sicilia, Palermo

Polidoro's last stylistic development, as the work provides a benchmark from which to establish his final progression. Because of his early exposure to Raphael's workshop, Polidoro was particularly well suited to creating paintings related to this altarpiece, and he may have been asked to execute stylistically related work on this and other occasions, while accepting that he lacked Raphael's technical facility as a painter to produce a close replica. His first response to the image is recorded in the drawing in Stuttgart, completed by 1532, discussed in Chapter 4 (see fig. 4.25). The presence of Raphael's miracle-working panel on the island could alone account for the choice of subject for Polidoro's Messinese altarpiece, but Polidoro's training and background certainly encouraged it as well. Whether he went in person to Palermo to revisit Raphael's picture is not documented but likely.

One compositional drawing related to Polidoro's monumental altarpiece survives in the Galleria Regionale della Sicilia in Palermo (fig. 5.3).[4] The drawing must be a copy of a lost Polidoro original, for the handling seems slacker and the line more broken than he usually tolerated.

There are some significant changes between the drawing and the painting. For example, Christ looks at the Virgin in the sketch rather than outwards; in the end Polidoro abandoned this rapport between mother and son. While still suffering, in the painting the Virgin seems also to be more conscious. The position of John the Evangelist was shifted slightly closer to the centre. The Veronica figure has a notably different pose and expression, while the kneeling Magdalen does not appear at all in the copy. The upper part of the design is emptier in the sketch – Polidoro would later move the middle-ground figures further upwards and separate them further from those in the foreground – and the strong diagonals and groupings of the painting are not yet apparent. There are also three smaller painted panels in London, Rome and Naples that are generally considered preparatory for the altarpiece (figs 6.7–6.9), but these will be discussed in Chapter 6.

If the proximity of Raphael's miracle-working panel, combined with Polidoro's artistic background, may account for the selection of the Way to Calvary theme for the altarpiece, or more specifically Christ Fallen under the

Cross, it seems likely that Polidoro was instructed by the patron to make direct reference to the Raphael in composition and quality ('*modo et forma*' is the formal clause that frequently appears in artistic contracts). The emphasis on the Virgin's paroxysm and direct absorption of Christ's suffering, it should be stressed, represents a relatively new, apocryphal subject matter in the history of art, and may in part account for Alibrando's need to write a textual account of Polidoro's prominent work. The author was boldly promoting the recent Marian cult around a novel theme, which had been established as a feast as recently as 1476 and was controversial in a manner comparable to the Immaculate Conception. Particularly among Dominicans, as opposed to the Franciscans and Servites, the belief that the Virgin could suffer in this vulnerable manner was formally rejected.[5] Although Polidoro did not follow Raphael's more extreme treatment of the Virgin, her position, virtually in Christ's path and held as if in a *pietà*, leaves little doubt as to the symbolic equivalence of mother and son.

Polidoro was not especially respectful in his treatment of the subject of Raphael's model. He produced a thoroughly original composition, in which the main narrative unfolds as a frieze of moderately scaled figures moving from right to left, recessed from the picture plane. The Virgin swoons as if unconscious on the left margin of the panel.[6] She is supported and comforted by two attendants, while two more women beside her pray and gesticulate past her in the direction of Christ. Behind this group of mourners John the Evangelist glances heavenward. In the opposite lower corner, a figure, presumably representing Mary Magdalen, kneels in prayer, staring directly at Christ with an open mouth and an anguished expression. Her richly brocaded gold and red damask dress and red drapery are fully consonant with previous representations of the Magdalen. Another female figure appears behind her, holding an ointment jar for embalming the body. Veronica, displaying the veil bearing Christ's image, appears in this second group of mourners too (curiously enough the image is much larger than the real face of Christ in the painting). Some onlookers appear on an outcrop at the left. On the opposite side a group of soldiers, a few on horses, follow with two more victims, representing the good and bad thieves.

In the lower centre of the picture Christ is seen with a radiant nimbus and wearing a dark robe, as is appropriate to his physical suffering. The gilt trim on his garment was old fashioned by this date. His face is so brutalised as to be almost unrecognisable as a traditional type, and he himself appears resigned to his torment. The gashes on his forehead from the crown of thorns he wears are prominent. Polidoro also emphasised Christ's physical suffering with the grotesque actions of the tormenters. This treatment seems particularly severe compared to the more idealised features of his counterpart in Raphael's altarpiece, and was presumably intended as an unusually direct appeal to the spectator. The artist's introduction of a less than ideally beautiful likeness of the Saviour was an aspect that Raphael would never have permitted. Polidoro alone pushed the boundaries of art of the period, confronting the viewer with difficult subject matter.

The trumpeter in the middle distance evokes the noise of the procession to the church when the altarpiece was installed, as recorded in Alibrando's poem. There is a central focus in the face of Christ, but attention is displaced overall to the various grouped incidents. Individual figures are distinctly stunted and doll-like, with over-large heads in proportion to their bodies, of the type sometimes seen on the palace facades. The actual morphologies are strangely distorted, with protruding features and large foreheads that seem almost animalistic. Gestures are forceful and unambiguous; the choreographed aggression is more like that of sculpted rather than painted bodies.

Among the rather stumpy figures there is a strange combination of deep, almost bruised colours, contrasted with more metallic, drained tones. These men and women appear to be modelled out of a malleable material such as clay, like the first humans created by Prometheus. By way of contrast, the background colours tend towards the rich, fertile browns familiar from Polidoro's earlier fresco paintings at San Silvestro al Quirinale in Rome. The sudden vista in the centre, with a softly rendered distant mountain range, is particularly glorious, as is the prominent architecture towards the top right margin, aspects that explicitly recall Polidoro's Roman work.

Compared to Raphael's *Spasimo di Sicilia*, Polidoro's painting has more figures, which are also smaller in scale, and there is more lateral movement in Polidoro's broader panel. Landscape is more prominent in Polidoro's altarpiece than in Raphael's. The new narrative focus is less the relationship of Christ and the Virgin than the Saviour's personal suffering in a tumultuous scene. In Polidoro's picture, the Virgin has fainted and the Magdalen takes her role from Raphael's painting more obliquely, through her fixed gaze towards Christ, unacknowledged by him. The viewer will search in vain among Polidoro's types for anything resembling the refinement seen in the features of the figures in Raphael's picture. Polidoro's ideal of beauty is much more rugged and genuinely strange – the icy clarity and empathy of Raphael's narrative have been sacrificed in preference for a concentrated, abrupt and cumulative effect. This expression by the disciple, who seems not to have been at all intimidated by his master's work, even a literally miraculous one, is more severe and unambiguous, and also more pessimistic. If both works are suitable models for contemplation, Raphael's message seems esoteric and Polidoro's visceral, perhaps even mystical, but certainly shockingly violent, accentuated now by the compromised state of preservation of the panel.

With this broad comparison of styles in mind, it is helpful to turn to Alibrando's poem to see how it might provide at least a partial explanation for these divergent interpretations of the same subject. For Polidoro scholars, the *Spasmo* of 1534 is, with the exception of Vasari's life of the painter, the single most valuable written document about the artist.[7] This is fortunate because the altarpiece to which it relates is, arguably, the most important surviving panel painting of the artist's entire career. But it is a rather unusual type of document for the period and its exceptional nature should be stressed. It does not simply make passing mention of a painter or an art object, as in Dante's *Purgatorio*, Boccaccio's *Amorosa visione* or Ariosto's *Orlando furioso*, to take some celebrated poetic examples; rather, prose examples aside, it is unique in being written exclusively about a contemporary painting, and almost certainly with the direct knowledge of the painter, and as such also functioned as a work of laudatory propaganda on his behalf. The uniqueness of Alibrando's poem is made further apparent when it is compared to another poem with a long section devoted to art, namely Giovanni Santi's rhymed chronicle, *La Vita e le gesta di Federico di Montefeltro Duca d'Urbino*, completed just prior

to Santi's death in 1494, which lists the most famous painters in Italy, but no specific works.[8] Instead, because of the theologising element in its characterisations, Alibrando's approach most closely parallels in tone the brief comments made in letters written in around 1500 by another ecclesiastic, the Carmelite Fra Pietro da Novellara in Florence, to Isabella d'Este in Mantua, as in this description of Leonardo's lost design for the *Madonna of the Yarnwinders*:

> The little picture which he is doing is of a Madonna seated as if she were about to spin yarn. The Child has placed his foot on the basket of yarns and has grasped the yarnwinder and gazes attentively at the four spokes that are in the form of a cross. As if desirous of the cross he smiles and holds it firm, and is unwilling to yield it to his mother who seems to want to take it away from him.[9]

Yet, because of its length and personalised emotion, Alibrando's poem is clearly richer and much more evocative than what is essentially erudite reportage.

The single known copy of the *Spasmo* is in the Biblioteca Regionale Universitaria in Messina, where it is bound with three other historical tracts, published in 1498, 1512 and 1536 respectively. The book is made up of 33 pages and, when opened, measures about 20 by 31 centimetres. Considering that only one copy of the book appears to exist in a public collection, this would imply that a very small number of copies were printed and that the book had a limited distribution, although the tone of the poem suggests that it was intended to be more than just private memorabilia for the patrons of the altarpiece. There can be no doubt, however, that it was created for an initiated and devout audience. The stress on the indulgences available through a visit to this church suggests that the book had an auxiliary mercantile purpose in promoting this fact.[10]

The book includes on the back cover a print with the inscription 'gran mirci a messina' over the coat of arms of the town. Of greater interest is the crude woodcut based on Polidoro's altarpiece, likely produced by a local craftsman, that appears as a frontispiece (fig. 5.4).[11] Curiously, a drawing by the artist in Berlin of the same date includes a trial printed image of a Virgin and Child

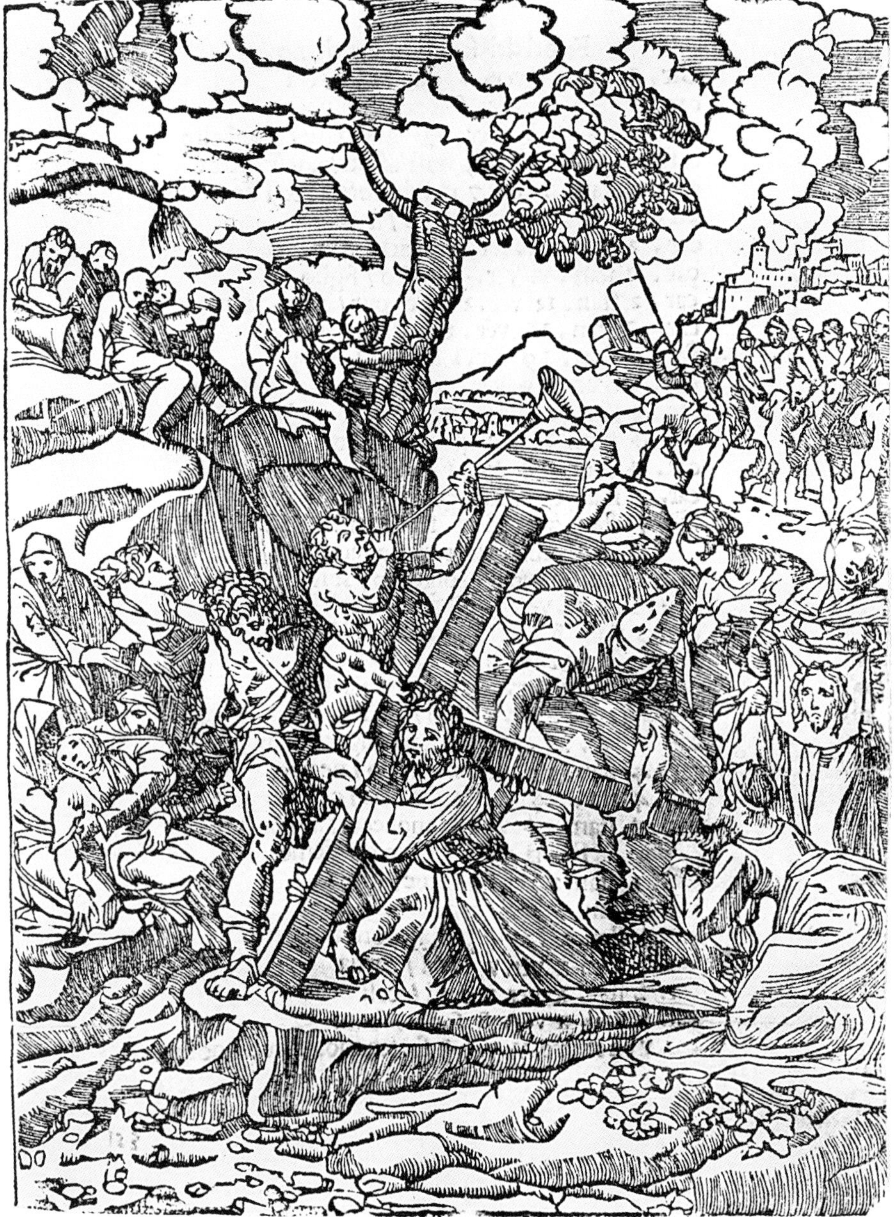

5.4 *Way to Calvary*. Woodcut. Frontispiece to Cola Giacomo di Alibrando's *Il Spasmo di Maria Vergine* (Messina, 1534)

(fig. 5.5), implying that Polidoro was experimenting with printmakers for the first time in his career at the same moment that the book was being produced, although whether he cut these prints himself is doubtful.

The paper on which the woodcut is printed has a watermark depicting an open hand, which also appears on at least five surviving drawings by Polidoro (two in Berlin, two in the Uffizi and one in the British Museum), including two from the so-called Berlin sketchbook, dated

to *c.*1535. One of these bears some inscriptions, informal notes, presumably in the artist's own hand and referencing his laundry, which on the recto are partially cut off by the drawing ('lancola et camisi 2 (?) [. . .] de facia'), while on the verso read 'doi lancola camisi quatro una tovaglia de facia/ doi stuabochi e una tovaglia de tavola'. The verso also has a fragment of a Latin text adapted from Seneca, Letter 22, Part 6, derived from Epicurus, on the negativity of a lack of commitment in life – 'nec properes ante tempus nec cesses

in tempore' – as well as a more commonplace fragment
in the vernacular: 'chi ben vive'. The latter two inscriptions
almost certainly relate to passages intended for the
triumphal arches that Polidoro designed for the entry
of Charles V into Messina in 1535, following the emperor's
African campaign. They provide rare literary evidence
of the cultural level to which Polidoro may have been
asked to aspire.

In terms of historiography, Alibrando's book has had
a sporadic reception until quite recently. Samperi, in a
volume published in Messina in 1644, was the first to
quote parts of the text, but only in a fragmentary way and
without much analysis. In fact, almost all scholars have
reviewed the text on the basis of excerpts such as those
published by Samperi and have not, apparently, consulted
the precious original, until its full publication in 1999.[12]
It is likely that the work was not reprinted sooner in part
because of the general neglect of Renaissance literature
produced in Messina, as well as the slow critical acceptance
of Polidoro's later style.

Alibrando's book is divided into four sections,
of which the first is the principal part. This is the poem,
or *historia* as it is referred to by the author himself,
dedicated to 'Il Spasmo della Vergine' and discussing
all aspects of Polidoro's painting of the *Way to Calvary*,
including its interpretation. The book also contains a
sonnet by Alibrando dedicated to the Virgin, as well as
two final components, short encomia by the local
polymath Francesco Maurolico, called Archimedes, and
by Don Thomaso Stagno of Messina, a Benedictine monk
of San Placido in Messina.

Of direct interest to art historians, therefore, is the
long main poem. The basic structure is that of an
ambitious quasi-epic narrative told in somewhat turgid

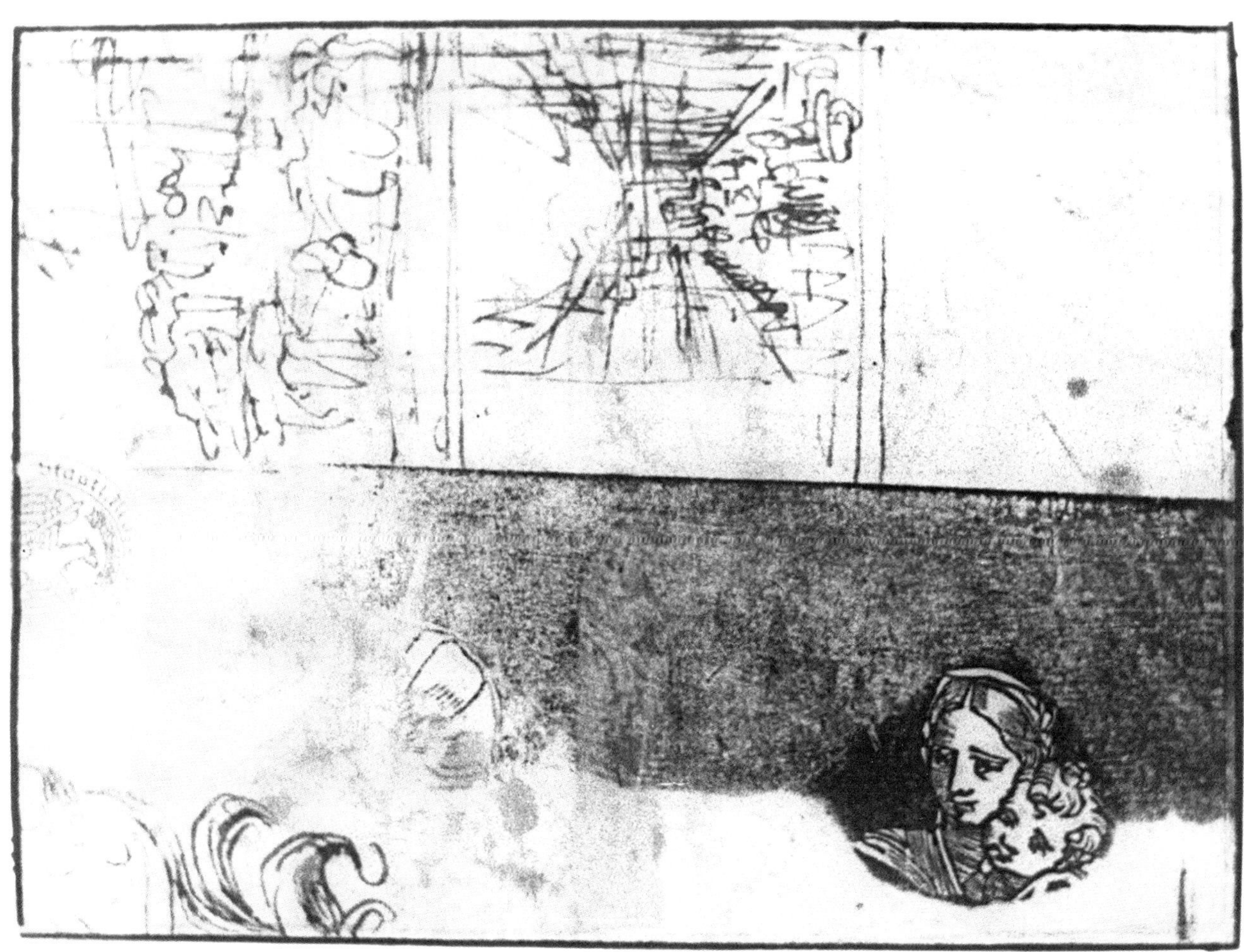

5.5 Various studies and Virgin and Child print. Pen and brown ink on laid paper, with engraving, 10 × 14.2 cm. Staatliche Museen zu Berlin,
Kupferstichkabinett

rather than lyrical prose, which concentrates on the picture's emotional appeal in an explicit way, while highlighting local and fraternal devotion. The main poem is composed of 76 stanze of eight lines each. These octaves are hendecasyllabic (of eleven syllables). The rhyme scheme is a standard one – ABABABCC – and fairly consistent, as found in the first stanza:

> L'interno spasmo, il grave e rio dolore
> di Maria sconsolata, e quel martire
> ch'ebbe il suo mesto figlio uscendo fuore
> de la città condotto per morire,
> la mia devozion con tristo core
> vuol ch'io debbia signor a voi ridire
> però ascoltar via piaccia e meco a canto
> vi preparate un largo mar di pianto.[13]

> (The inner spasm, the deep and bitter grief of disconsolate Mary,
> And the martyrdom of her son when he was led out of town to his death.
> My devotion calls me to recount it with a heart full of sorrow.
> So I ask you to listen to me and be ready to shed a river of tears with me.)

This first stanza respects a classic structure in which, after explaining his chosen title, the author adopts a personal tone in order to attract the reader, after which, in the second stanza, he invokes the Muses to assist him. This conventionality is typical of the text, which is not considered by scholars of Italian literature to be a great work in its own right. Alibrando relies in places on an unsophisticated, low style of rhyme (*campare* and *vivere* in stanza 27), and introduces common words (*mamelle* for breasts and *ventre* for belly in stanza 29). Overall, it is perhaps too unpolished a vernacular to have much formal literary merit, even if the author mostly resists falling back on local dialect and makes the conventional references to Dante, Petrarch and others. Yet whatever Alibrando's text lacks in literary importance is more than compensated for by its art historical significance.

The poem is significant for a number of reasons. First, it is narrowly important for what it relates about the history of this commission. It reveals details known from no other source, for example that it was Ansalone who approached Polidoro to complete the project. The Ansalone family also commissioned a painting from Polidoro for their chapel in the oratory of Santa Lucia in Messina and must have deeply admired him.[13] It is questionable, however, how much the poet was sincerely interested in such matters, and everything he relates must be considered critically (there are always problems in relating any text directly to a visual image and this instance, however tantalisingly close the writer was to the artist, is no exception). The poet claims, for example, that Polidoro painted this enormous panel for free, yet it seems unlikely this is true, thus immediately betraying that the poem might be misleading as a source of information.

Second, the work is important for expressing general attitudes towards a contemporary artist like Polidoro, although, again, the evidence must be weighed up rather cautiously. The poem offers the usual praise of the modern artist in relation to Apelles and Zeuxis, painters of ancient Greece, for example. Alibrando tells us, too, in a banal manner that Polidoro's talent was God-given; there is irony here for a painter who made his name in Rome almost exclusively producing *all'antica* subjects in style and subject matter. Neither does Alibrando provide enlightening descriptions of Polidoro's work practice. The painting is completed with a miraculous rhetorical swiftness in just one stanza – the rather comical stanza 15. This lack of involvement with technical practicalities is entirely typical of literary responses to works of art from earlier periods. Vasari's *Lives of the Artists*, first published only a decade and a half later, was partly written to make up for the absence of a more pragmatic understanding of technical artistic practice in published texts. On the whole, the poet's expressed attitudes about the painter and his work are disappointing. Even the adjectives do not directly concern the formal aspects of the painting but instead characterise objects described: we read of a 'viso almo e fiorito' (spiritual and blooming countenance) and a 'faccia vaga e bella' (attractive and beautiful face). Elements like colour, design and drawing are not considered. Alibrando does tell us in the ninth stanza, however, that Polidoro was equal to all the moderns, and was as good, specifically, as Michelangelo and Raphael (a combination again worth highlighting for the elevated reputation of the painter among contemporaries).

Third, the poem is useful for describing in some detail
the installation of the work in its original location, and it
is here that the poet finally comes into his own, treating
the image and the whole event of its creation as if they
were part of a popular *sacra rappresentazione*, a genre still
common in the Renaissance period. The account is useful
for reminding us that the patronage of public altarpieces
had a broader civic component as well as the narrower
rapport between client and artist. There are very few
extant accounts of installation in the history of art, while
those that do survive usually come from record books
and are consequently relatively brief and descriptive.[14]
Alibrando is, in contrast to other aspects of his writing,
highly skilled at evoking the event, down to such details as
the painter tearing off the curtain from the painting at the
last moment, to the astonishment of the assembled throng.
Colourful passages about the groups of flagellants and
clerics, vividly recreating the event, are of value to a social
historian. They reflect laterally, too, on some of Polidoro's

most unusual drawings: a considerable number from
the 1530s are of genre-type subjects, as in the examples
illustrating scenes of daily religious life in Messina,
including a spectacular sheet depicting a Mass, now in
the Louvre (fig. 5.6). So elaborately and carefully conceived
is this drawing that one might imagine it is a preparatory
work for a subject painting in a predella, featuring a saint
presiding over Mass, although the figures appear to be in
contemporary dress. Rougher, more spontaneous sheets
exist and are more vivid in this respect, as we are able
literally to see through Polidoro's eyes, scanning across
public scenes and yet applying a compositional rigour
and rhythm, recalling certain of the ancient narratives
from the Roman facades. Polidoro's curiosity to record
the world around him finds few precedents among his
contemporaries, but also suggests that the intensity of
religious devotion in Sicily struck him as more lively and
intense than in papal Rome. These drawings can be
compared to Raphael's *Mass at Bolsena* fresco in the

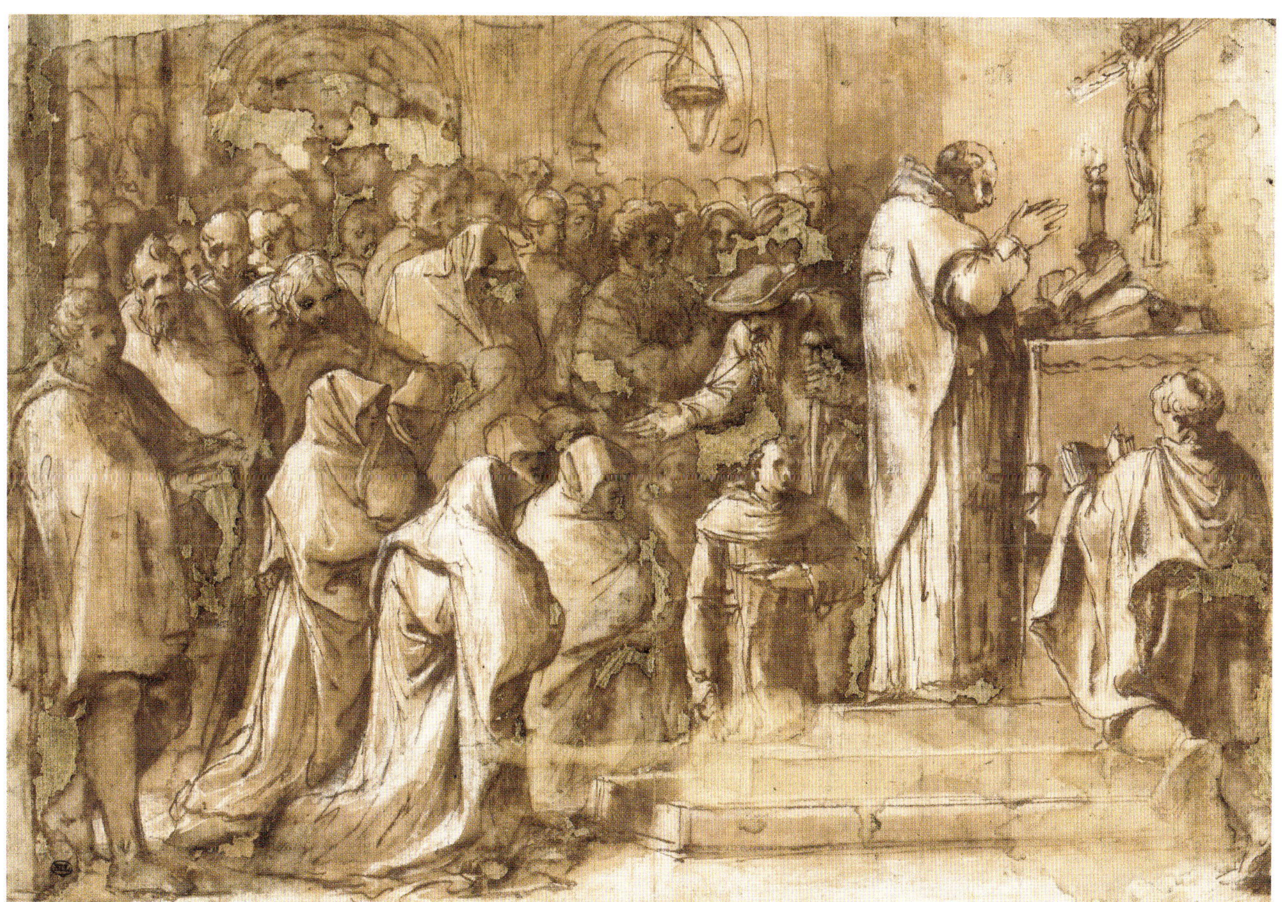

5.6 *Celebration of Mass*. Pen and brown ink, and brown wash, with white heightening over traces of black chalk on brown washed paper, 20.8 × 30.4
cm. Musée du Louvre, Paris, Cabinet des Dessins

Vatican, but the juxtaposition only further stresses how less exalted Polidoro was in his reportage.

Most significantly and intriguingly, the poem is important above all for a fourth aspect: what it reveals about attitudes towards religious art in this period and how works of art could be described and so understood by contemporaries. This is a nuanced issue, especially for Polidoro given the idiosyncratic nature of his later style, for which there is little primary evidence. Artists' contracts are, of course, frustratingly pragmatic, being more concerned with payment and completion than subject matter, except at a basic descriptive level. Unusually, Alibrando's poem provides a very close and complete description of Polidoro's painting, which is itself remarkable, but it goes far beyond this to provide narrative and emotional justification for each character, both good and evil. To take an example of the directness and vividness of his language in relation to the image, it is worth comparing stanza 30 to the central image of the suffering Christ:

> Now the ruthless executioner sees the Good Jesus fall on the ground.
> And the sight makes him yet more rabid as he fears that Jesus will not make it to Calvary.
> So he grabs him with one hand and pushes him forth.
> And with the other he hits him and pulls him along by a rope.

Alibrando's tone is basically empathetic, but above all it is a flexible mode. To bring his subject to life he uses various devices that can be catalogued. For example, he puts words into the mouths of the characters, as in stanzas 21 and 22, when Christ speaks directly to his mother (or to John in stanza 26). He also uses frightening auditory images, as in stanza 46, when mentioning the trumpet sounded by an executioner in Christ's ear. He might speak to and admonish himself, as at the end of stanza 39, where he asks what he is doing as a participant in this drama to assist Christ. He also often prompts the reader's response, as in stanza 24: 'the Maries supporting the Virgin are thoughtful in sorrow [. . .] and whosoever sees them could not help crying. They do not know how to help her for they are barely alive, and each struggles to hold her.' Or he might go further to appeal directly to the reader's

conscience, as in stanza 39: 'I told myself the soul cries out at that spectacle. What are you waiting for?' In stanza 40, the reader is even asked to assist Christ by removing the cross from his back. In passages like these, the author seems to be in a sort of trance, and as if before the real event; the physical painting dissolves. This mystical perspective on a work of art is especially intriguing, as it seems to produce a manner of looking at Polidoro's late brown-toned paintings, discussed in Chapter 6, with their tactile, yet rather unfixed surfaces. It is familiar from the devotional exercises of the Franciscan saint Bonaventure, based on the evocation of Christ's suffering. But, just to stress the point again, in the *Spasmo* the recollection of the Passion is not imagined in the mind's eye but filtered through an actual image, available in the book as a print for those readers who might not have seen the original.

In addition to commemorating a specific work of art, the poem can also be approached in a more mundane fashion as an animated sermon, which, importantly, does not presuppose that a reader knows the painting in person, because of the completeness and message of the account, and has a genuine feel for the work under examination. In the context of its physicality, it is significant that near the end, in stanza 67, the poet urges anyone who can visit the church to leave a donation at the altar in order to gain pardon. The painting is itself described in stanza 71 as having the status of a 'reliquia santa rara et eccellente'. Here the relevance of the almost certainly false statement that Polidoro painted the work free of charge is fully revealed, as the painting is also described as being like a pious donation, and so the artist's piety must naturally be unquestioned.[15] Given these notions of deeply serious religious devotion, it is impressive to recall that these works – the painting and the poem – were created in a powerfully devout style prior to the creation of the Council of Trent, which led to the Counter-Reformation in Italy.

The example of Polidoro filtered through Alibrando's pen reveals how the desire to represent powerful narrative and sincere pathos remained a central concern for the generation of artists following Raphael (and Leonardo), and how this could be intensely deepened and amplified in the hands of the most sensitive. Such a view diverges from the more traditional stylistic interpretation of artists of Polidoro's generation.[16] In the end, Polidoro was certainly not overwhelmed by his master's work but developed it through a quite different – perhaps less intellectually exclusive and dignified but no less complex – interpretation, one that addressed the viewer more through the heart than the mind. That his image of the *Way to Calvary* was more influential in Sicily than Raphael's own is a tribute not just to the fact that Polidoro inspired a group of close followers, but also to the attractive intensity and inclusiveness of his vision. How far he and Alibrando might have discussed their forceful, vivid mode of expression will remain debatable, but their approaches, although cast in different genres, do so much to enlighten each other, and might even provide evidence for some form of collaboration, in which the painter was not subservient to the writer but participated in a mutually beneficial exchange. It must be more than a coincidence that the profound intensity of the paintings of Polidoro's Sicilian period was part of a wider cultural climate in Messina, as revealed by Alibrando's unique text. And so, paradoxically, it is not in papal Rome that an inspiring cultural context for the art of Polidoro is documented, but rather in a more isolated location on the island of Sicily. With Alibrando's poem in mind, an examination of the final paintings he produced in Messina can be attempted with conviction.

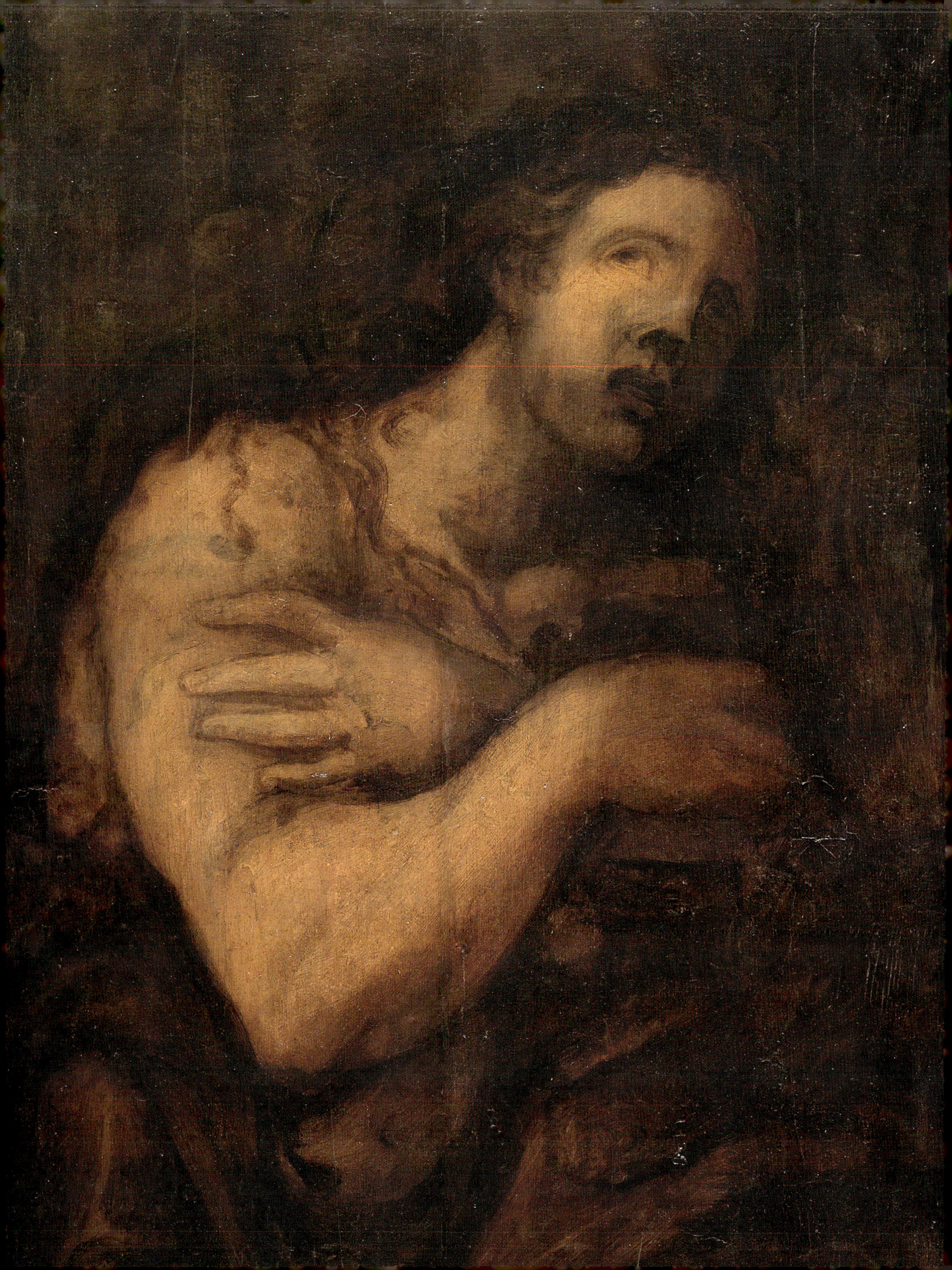

6 Messina: The Last Paintings

If all the documented altarpieces executed by Polidoro in Messina are dated to the period up to 1535, the artist's activity between the triumphal entry of Charles V into Messina on 21 October 1535 and his death in 1543 is, at first glance, completely enigmatic. This gap is so wide that some critics, starting with Giuseppe La Farina in the nineteenth century, suggested that Polidoro must instead have died around 1535.[1] Vasari indirectly supported the notion of an earlier death date when he wrote that the altarpiece of the *Way to Calvary* was Polidoro's final effort. While it is true that there are no documents or dated works for Polidoro from the last eight years of his life, it now seems over-cautious to question the later death date, pronounced by Vasari himself, because a large body of nearly 30 paintings, all distinguished by their dark brown appearance, may be assigned to this last period, if not without some likely permanent controversy. Vasari, whose sources could tell him almost nothing about art in Sicily of any period, is of no assistance in contending with these final years of Polidoro's career.

Although credit must be given to venerable scholars like Luigi Lanzi, who attributed works of this type to Polidoro without hesitation, it is fair to observe that the paintings from this late stage of his life have been validated only relatively recently, grouped in museums in Messina, Palermo and Naples, with a few isolated examples in English and private collections. These unusual panels, which collectively seem to erode the boundary between the finished and unfinished, beg questions, however, given that their attribution, patronage and function all require speculation. A few can be linked to different inventories and published references, at least placing them securely in Messina. Two may be signed: the *Pentecost* in Palermo (fig. 6.1) and the *Agony in the Garden* in Messina (fig. 6.2) both appear to carry the same initials, 'P.CA.C.P.', as first proposed by Raffaello Delogu in 1963. This can be plausibly expanded as 'Polidorus Caldara Caravagiensis pinxit', but it must be admitted this is not a form that Polidoro is otherwise known to have used, and the letters are not entirely legible. The suspicion must remain as to whether or not these annotations are later additions. Even if these signatures are specious, however, this would still suggest an attribution to Polidoro, as in

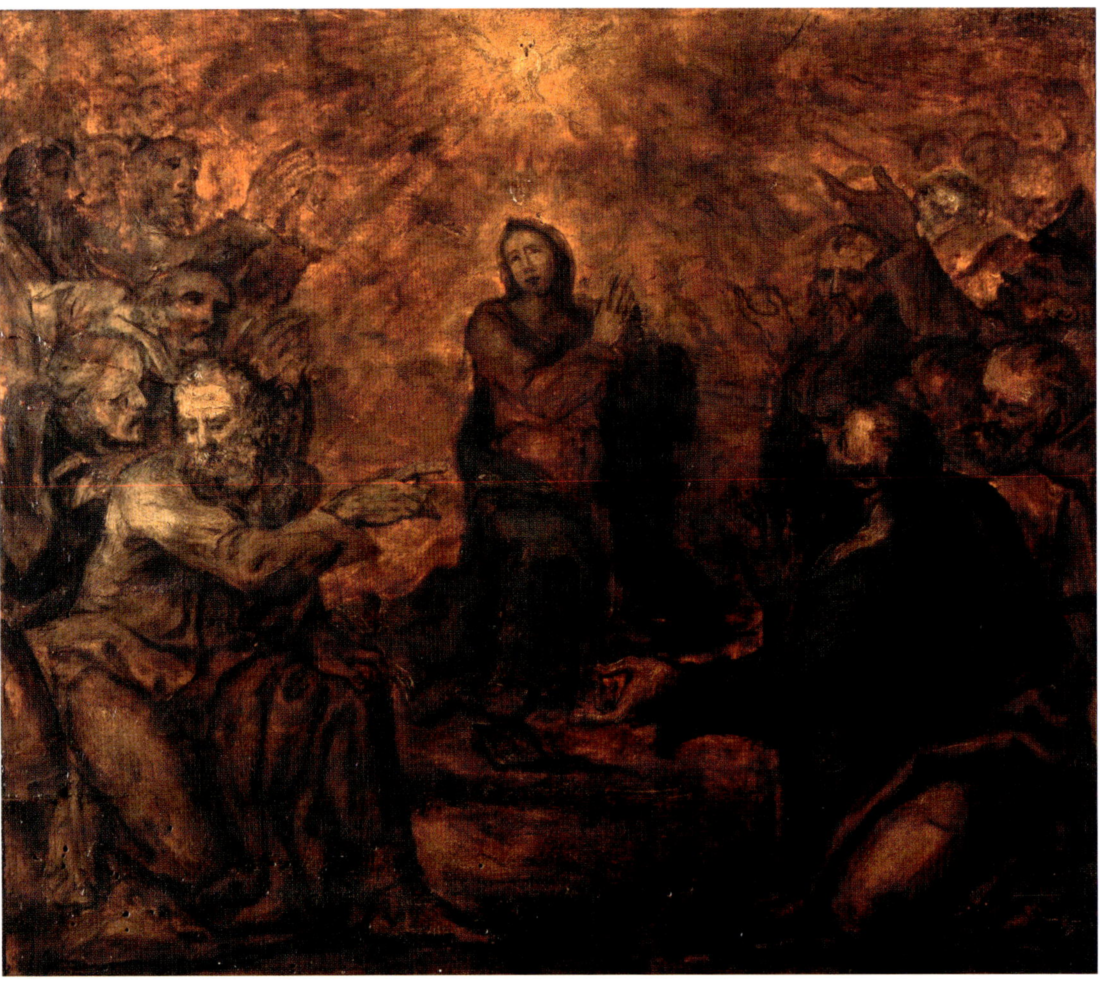

6.1 *Pentecost*. Oil on panel, 42 × 49 cm. Galleria Regionale della Sicilia, Palermo

terms of the art market late Polidoro would hardly be the first choice of any restorer or forger. With one exception, no drawings or documents securely relate to any of the paintings in this group either (although there are works on paper by Polidoro that can certainly be stylistically dated to near the end of his life) and this is another problem for those who advocate attributions to Polidoro. It is, therefore, not surprising that some of the more crudely executed examples have also been ascribed to artists in Polidoro's circle rather than to the master, most consistently to a minor artist born in Naples but active locally during the second half of the sixteenth century, Deodato Guinaccia, even though the work of these secondary artists is not easily definable either.[2] Yet the assumption that the majority of these paintings are Polidoro's final efforts, produced within his last decade, while not supported by direct documentary or graphic evidence, seems plausible, even if it must be defended

largely on stylistic grounds. The definitive exhibition organised by Leone de Castris in Naples in 1988 seems to have resolved the main group of attributions to Polidoro's name. The recent publication of extensive underdrawing in some of the smaller Capodimonte panels is crucial in defending the attributions as only the master could have worked so spontaneously.[3] Further examinations of this nature should help resolve all the attributions. Under the circumstances, these paintings are best first approached as a group, despite the fact that they would have been executed across a considerable time span, possibly as broad as 1535–43.

Various references in the secondary sources to Polidoro paintings can, in some cases, be linked to specific examples, which is significant, even if these notices are later in date and many textual attributions need to be excluded. Francesco Susinno's text of 1724, the mid-seventeenth-century inventory of the Don Antonio Ruffo

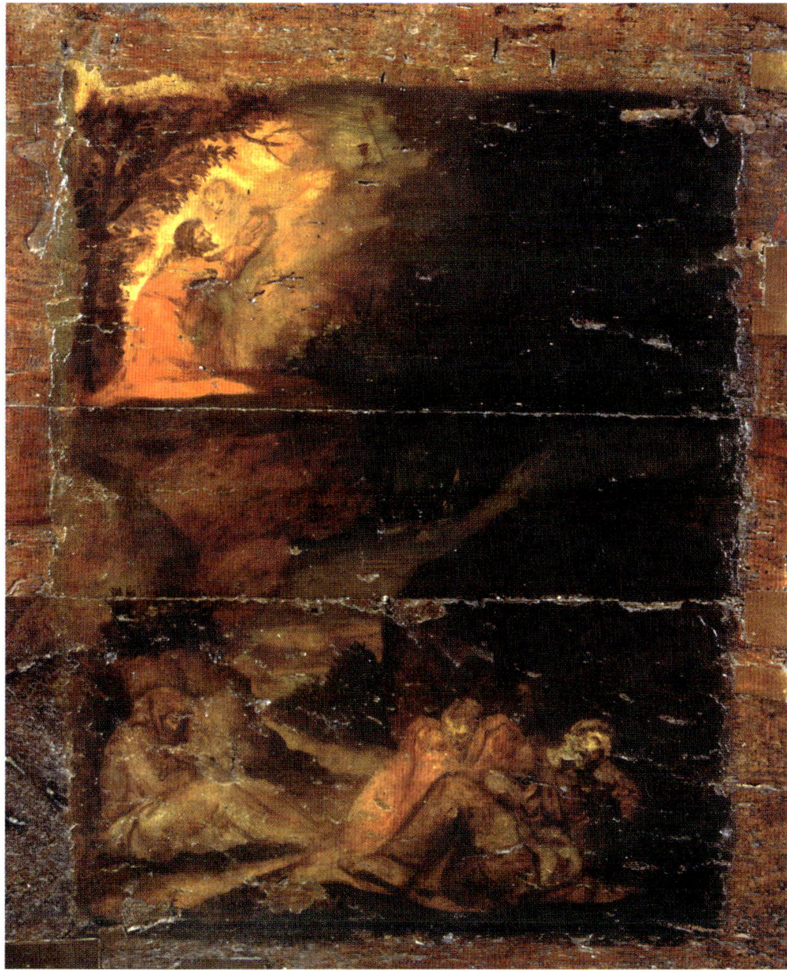

6.2 *Agony in the Garden*. Oil on panel, 68 × 83 cm. Museo Regionale, Messina

Collection, and the Marchese di Montagano inventory of 1783 are the principal sources of written information in this regard, and they show no hesitation in ascribing paintings of this tenebrous nature directly to Polidoro. Given Ruffo's interest in major painters like Rembrandt and Ribera, his collecting of later Polidoro is especially telling. One group, including the six larger paintings in the Capodimonte featuring three Franciscan saints (figs 6.16–6.18), a *Saint Mary Magdalen* (fig. 6.19), a *Calling of Saint Matthew* (fig. 6.22) and a fragment of an *Assumption of the Virgin* (fig. 6.21), and perhaps also the *Christ Among the Apostles* formerly on the art market in London (fig. 6.20), as proposed by Leone de Castris, may have once formed part of an elaborate altarpiece. Our earliest published source, Susinno, the first biographer of artists in Messina, writing nearly two centuries later, describes one by Polidoro's hand: 'Virgin with angels, Saint Francis with the stigmata and other saints'. This work was painted for the Capuchin church of the Friars Minor, Santa Maria degli Angeli, outside the old Porta Imperiale of Messina.[4] The presence of Saint Francis of Paola, one of the founders of that reformed order of Franciscans, only in existence since 1520, makes this written link to Polidoro's paintings more certain. According to Susinno, the Capuchins also owned a small Nativity scene, which may be another painting now in the Capodimonte.[5] Two other, probably very late paintings in the Capodimonte, one featuring the *Adoration of the Shepherds* (fig. 6.11) and the other a later version of the allegedly signed *Pentecost* (fig. 6.12), seem to be for a different commission. Polidoro may have produced the *Salome with the Head of John the Baptist and Executioner* (fig. 6.24), now in the Capodimonte and stylistically tightly linked to this late group in Messina, as an autonomous work for an individual patron. The four fragments of a large *Crucifixion* or *Deposition from the Cross* – in the collection of the Subba brothers in Messina

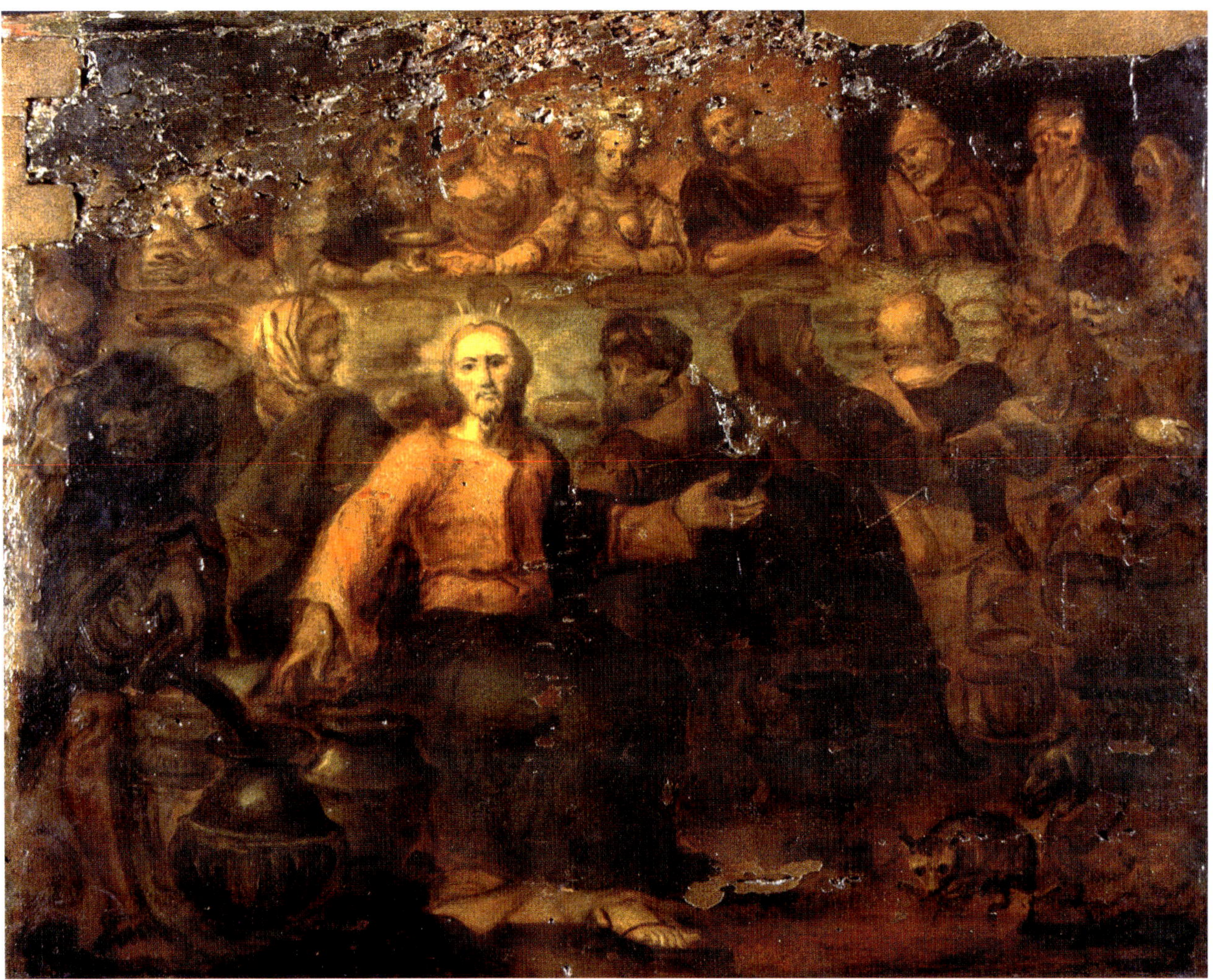

6.3 *Wedding at Cana*. Oil on panel, 48 × 60.5 cm. Museo Regionale, Messina

in the eighteenth century, presumably damaged by the particularly devastating earthquake that struck Messina in 1783, and now in a Neapolitan private collection – are likely all that remains of a Deposition from the Clarisse church of Santa Maria di Montevergine.[6] The mention by Susinno of various unidentified small panels attributed to Polidoro in Messinese private collections can account for the other paintings, including the *Healing of the Blind* (fig. 6.10) and *Pentecost* (fig. 6.1), both now in Palermo, as well as the *Wedding at Cana* (fig. 6.3) and *Agony in the Garden* (fig. 6.2), still in Messina, and one or more of the *Way to Calvary* panels (figs 6.7–6.9).[7] Other paintings trace a specific provenance to local collections in Messina, such as the Capodimonte *Pentecost* and a *Decollation of the Baptist* in private hands in Bergamo. The especially damaged panels featuring the *Martyrdom of Saint Placidus and His Companions* (figs 6.4 and 6.5), a haunting pair, may

well have been executed for the confraternity of that dedication, attached to the Benedictine Cassinese church of San Giovanni di Malta in Messina, but this seductive hypothesis is symptomatic of the difficulty of making secure connections between these works and original patrons in Sicily. As a popular saint on the island, Placidus could justifiably have appeared in almost any location. Certainly the sixth-century martyrdom of saints at the hands of an Arab leader was topical in sixteenth-century Messina. To take a comparable example, as Messina had a priory of the order of the Knights of Malta, one wonders if some of the late John the Baptist paintings and drawings might have been commissioned by them in honour of their patron saint. To add to the mystery, the possibility should be considered that even the smaller paintings may have been intended for public locations, perhaps as parts of ambitious polypytchs, a format that was less prevalent

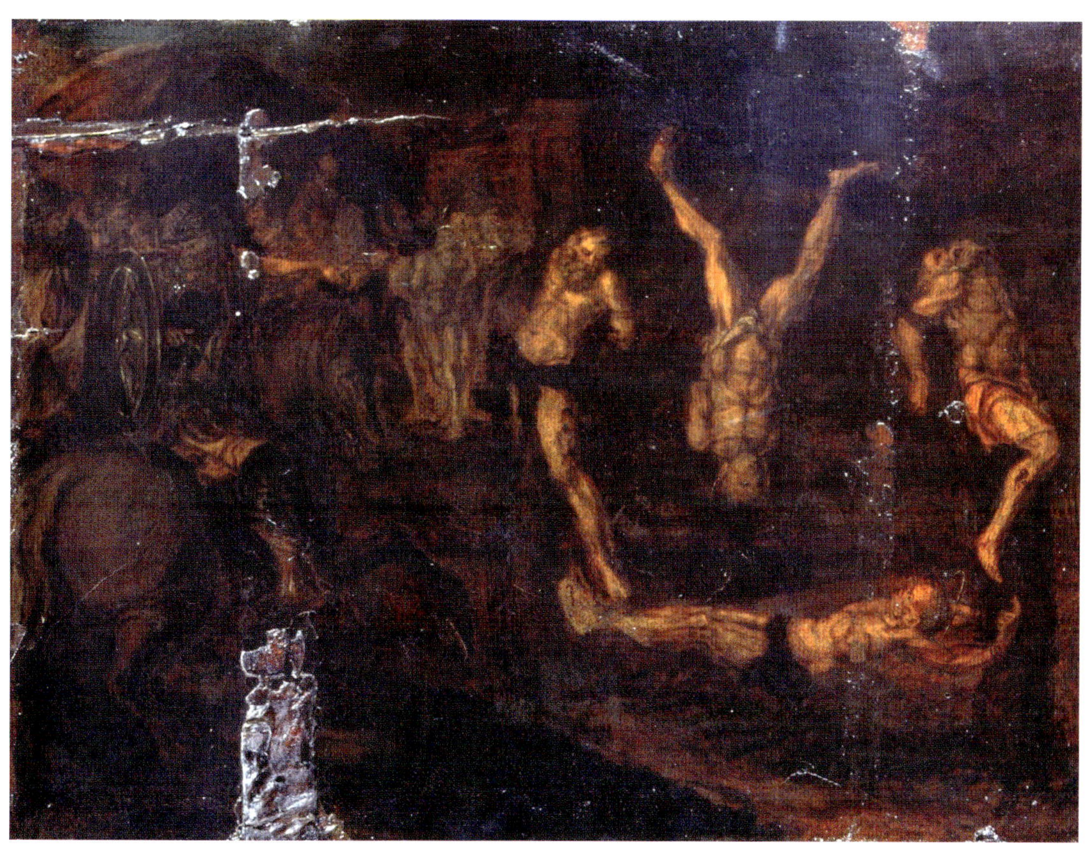

TOP AND ABOVE: 6.4–6.5 *The Martyrdom of Saint Placidus and His Companions*. Oil on panel, 57.5 × 80.5 cm and 58 × 77.5 cm. Museo Regionale, Messina

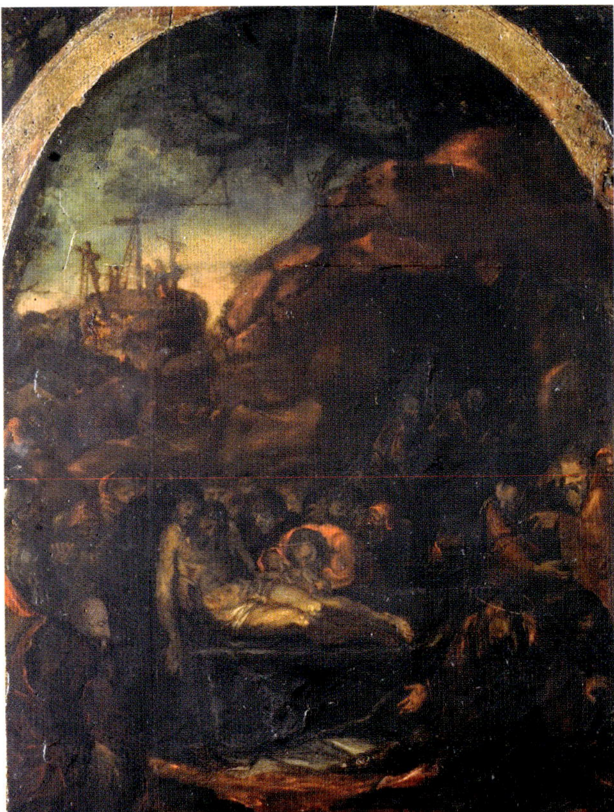

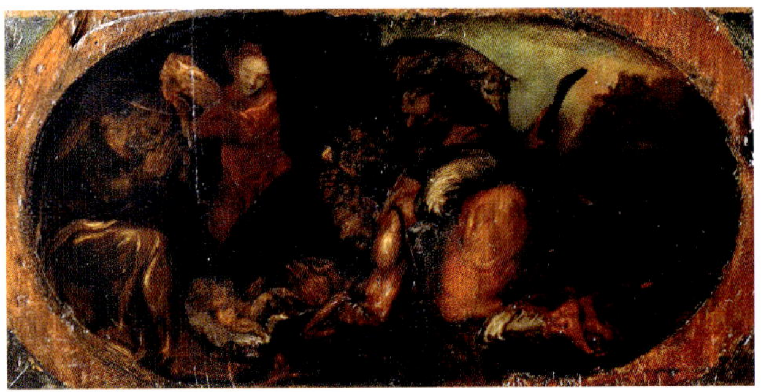

6.6 *Deposition* and *Adoration of the Shepherds* in oval predella. Oil on panel, overall 103 × 58 cm. Galleria Regionale della Sicilia, Palermo

So strange is the visual appearance of this body of paintings attributed to Polidoro, it is best to summarise the works as a consistent whole. From an examination of the different panels, it is certain that Polidoro was unusually restricted in his choice of wood supports and consistently relied on recycled furniture. Several different types of wood were used, although walnut is the most common. Whether he was handicapped in this regard by the limited financial resources or commitments of his patrons, or the availability of high-quality new material, is uncertain, but the paintings were also executed with a comparable technical swagger. Each appears to have been painted over the most perfunctory and loose underdrawing in black chalk (but sometimes directly in paint), over a roughly applied brownish priming layer that is apparent in all parts of the panel, and this establishes the harmonising incandescent quality of the whole. The relatively sombre colouring of this priming layer reduced the reflective property of the white gesso, and provided a middle tone and an impression of atmospheric depth in the finished paintings, while creating the brown shadows. The ground for Roman facade frescoes was not pure white, so Polidoro would have been used to a tinted base layer from his earliest and most frequent experiences as a painter. He exploited and developed his practical knowledge in his late panel pictures to quite different effect. On top of the priming layer, the black underdrawing is sometimes left visible as the only indication of form, which attests to some premeditation on the painter's part. A dark colour was generally also introduced to bolster the contours, but clarity and legibility of outline were not the painter's main intentions.

Given the absence of preliminary drawings, it seems likely that the paintings were conceived directly on the panel with only the most casual preparation. The *Agony in the Garden* in Messina (fig. 6.2) provides explicit evidence for a remarkably spontaneous approach – the divine patch of yellow light around Christ has been painted wet into wet, as if the artist was impatient to complete the panel. Occasionally in these later paintings there are splashes of local colour, especially red and green, which leap out of the pictures like traffic signals. These images are even stranger when it is recalled that Polidoro's drawing style never suffered the same dramatic reduction in line and form, as far as can be gathered from the works on paper

in contemporary Rome. Yet more confusingly, panels that seem to be grouped by subject matter are often of different dimensions and cannot easily be matched. With regard to attribution several individual paintings have, not unreasonably, been doubted by different scholars, all of whom have shared anxieties in ascribing such rebarbative works to an artist trained in Raphael's workshop. Even for the paintings on the crude outer limits of this group, however, like the small altarpiece in Palermo featuring a *Deposition* and an *Adoration of the Shepherds* (fig. 6.6), it seems difficult to imagine a different author.

stylistically dated to this last period. There is no evidence
that he simply forgot how to draw, and no explicit
correlation between this style of painting and his drawing.[8]
It seems likely that he altered his approach to design and
did not make as many preparatory studies for these works
as he might have done previously, developing a style of
painting not reliant on drawing. This would also help to
account for their more collapsed appearance. It is pertinent
here to recall Vasari's comment that Polidoro and Maturino
in Rome were feeble artists on the rare occasion they
introduced colour, and that he regarded one of their early
(lost) paintings in the church of Sant'Agostino as the effort
of 'idioti'.[9] The late work cannot be said to represent a decline
because even in Rome Polidoro was more an expedient
painter than a fluent one.

The paintings are not true monochrome, although
there is an insistent impression of brown – the viscous
light of Purgatory. In the context of a relatively
conservative Sicily under Spanish domination it might
be plausible to think of these plangent backgrounds as
the equivalent of gold grounds in earlier painting of the
region. To this extent, they may reveal an awareness and
veneration of earlier traditions, although even in this
period gold grounds were still occasionally seen in
provincial painting south of Rome. The general proximity
of the figures to the picture plane might also reflect an
awareness of fourteenth-century altarpieces. Sadly, none
of these works attributed to Polidoro survive *in situ*. The
surfaces are rough and discontinuous, not enamel smooth
as one would expect in a conventional grisaille painting
seeking to create an illusion of sculpture – the type
Polidoro painted as a young artist in Rome. Nonetheless,
while the Roman facade frescoes were grasped as much
by the intellect as the eye, these last panel paintings are
almost completely *felt* rather than deciphered for content.
Their resinous palette is consciously restricted, and
although there are always broad additions of wash-like
local colour at the final stage of painting, relieving the
ruddy, tenebrous tonalities established especially by the
priming layer, any superficial beauty of unadulterated
pigment is purposely subdued. The layers of paint are
roughly applied in thick, fluid brush strokes and create
a lambent coppery effect over the brownish ground.
The works have a glassy finish, with the pigmented areas
raised well above the support in a particularly oil-rich

medium that presumably facilitated the free application
of paint. Polidoro also manipulated the paint into
sculptural ridges, producing a surface that might best be
described as cartographic. Individual brush strokes are
thick but so porous that there are often gaps left in which
the priming layer shows through and disrupts the surface.
With such crude, confident handling, the forms appear to
melt and the light – such as it is – remains murky, lending
the paintings a mysterious, even spectral quality. Few details
are introduced, and the effect is instead a generalised one
of stilted movement and a ghostly, rather suffocating
Cimmerian atmosphere. The main impression is of a
fracturing, brumous complexion.

In these final works, Polidoro, who was not a confident
colourist as Vasari never hesitated to mention, developed
a manner of tonal painting completely foreign in appearance
to that favoured by Venetian artists of the sixteenth
century, such as Titian and Tintoretto. Given Antonello da
Messina's apocryphally pioneering role in the development
of oil painting in the previous century, there is some irony
in Polidoro creating these exploratory late works in Messina.
Even accepting that Polidoro could not approach Raphael's
technical proficiency, they are the mysterious last will and
testament of an artist who had passed through the master's
studio but who seems to have neglected to recall the
methodical technique he must have learned there, a curious
resolution of the promise of an artist celebrated for his
depiction of serene, graceful beauty. Polidoro's late paintings
are a further reminder that he was not able to absorb the
full range of Raphael's achievements, but examined the
master in an oblique, personal way that seems to fulfil
Rainer Maria Rilke's prophesy, in an entry in his Florentine
Diary, that decline would necessarily follow Raphael's
greatness. Polidoro's late style would have only a few rather
insubstantial followers in Sicily, although for a reason that
is still not easy to explain, Michelangelo Biondo, the Venetian
doctor active in Rome at the court of Paul III, in 1549 placed
Polidoro with Leonardo da Vinci in his schools of artists,
as if linking together the dark, rather lacerated style of
the two painters.[10]

It seems generally accepted that these late paintings
by Polidoro are among the first oil sketches in the history
of art, coinciding roughly chronologically with the
advancements of Domenico Beccafumi in Siena. Both
anticipated the practice of Rubens.[11] An oil sketch is most

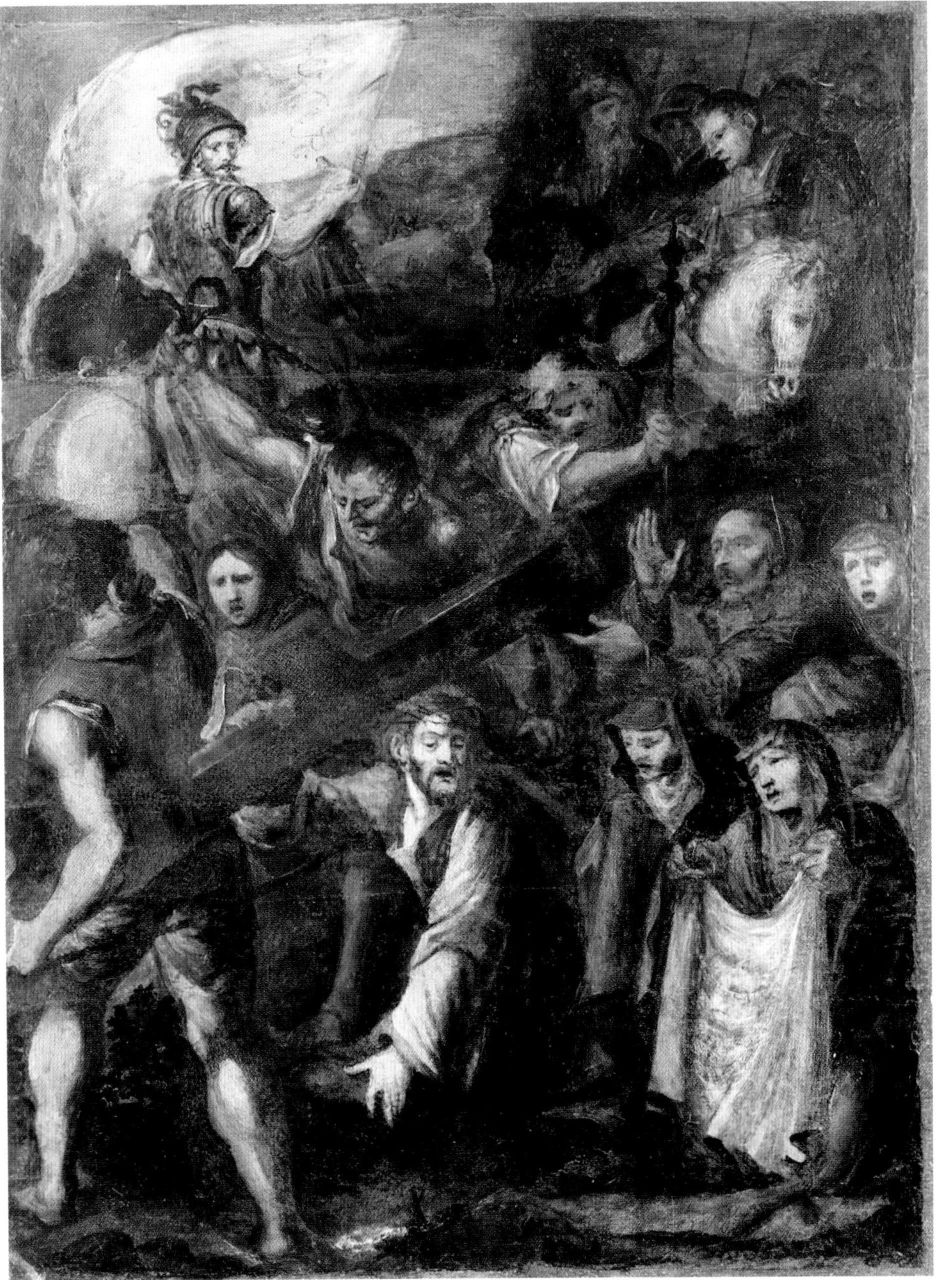

6.7 *Way to Calvary*. Oil on panel, 60 × 45 cm. Musei Vaticani, Pinacoteca

succinctly defined as a work of art that is preparatory for another; it is typically on a smaller scale, and is often shown to a patron prior to signing a contract. Rubens, for example, employed the medium for presentation pieces for patrons, in order to show them a version of the projected work, or as spontaneous preparation and process, sometimes for the benefit of the workshop, but only very rarely for its own sake.[12] Rubens's practice was, however, to be the antithesis of Polidoro's, an artist who arguably created

autonomous sketches as ends in themselves. Many of these paintings by Polidoro were exhibited in churches as completed works and cannot, therefore, be considered preparatory. (The effect of these panels grouped on an altar for public display must have been even more overwhelming than if they had been presented in a private setting.) Furthermore, except in the case of the group depicting the *Way to Calvary*, not even the smaller panels can be definitely related to surviving larger-scale works and so, to stress the

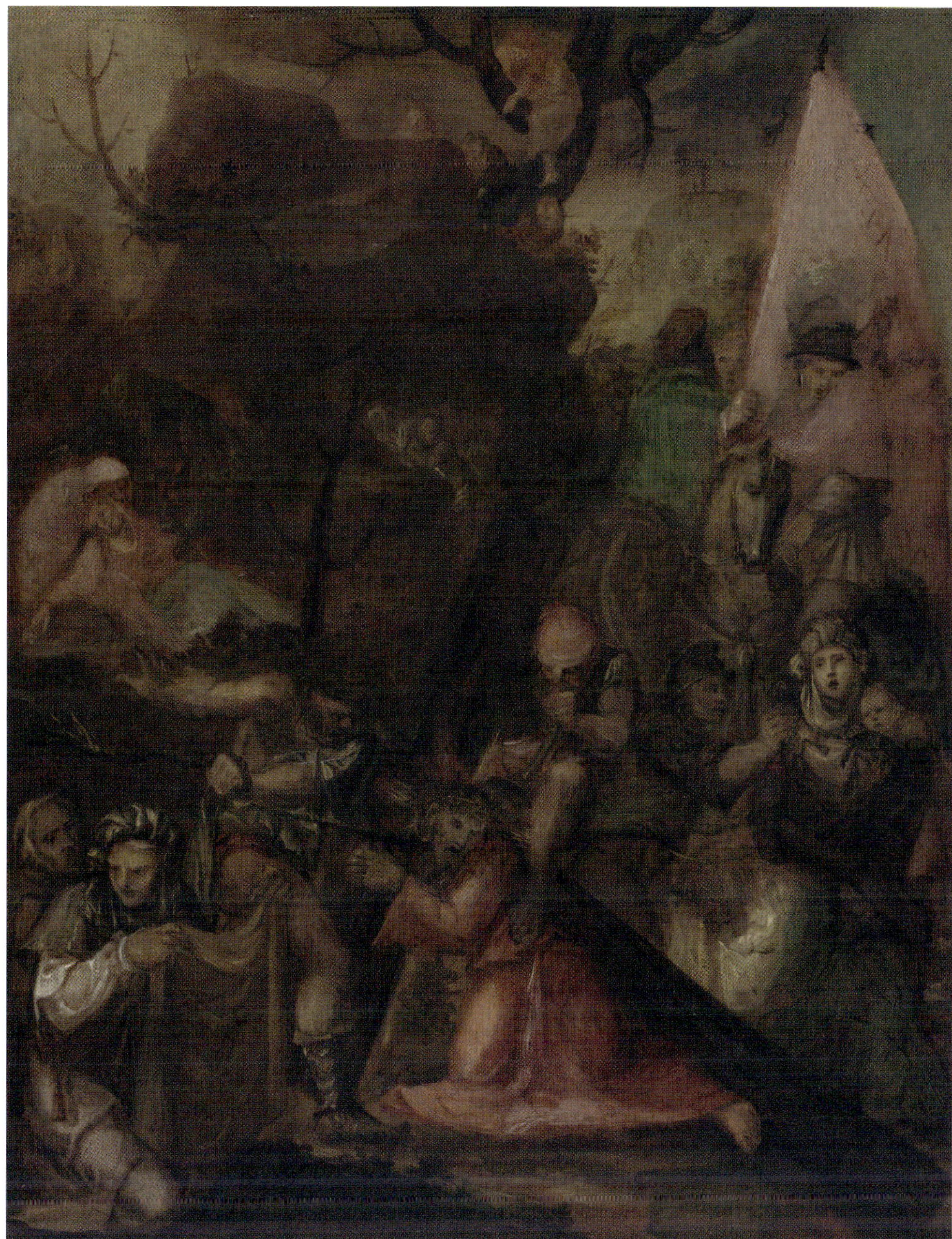

6.8 *Way to Calvary*. Oil on panel, 75.3 × 59 cm. National Gallery, London. Bought with a grant from the Art Fund (with a contribution from the Wolfson Foundation) and donation from the George Beaumont Group, 2003

point again, they were apparently ends in themselves and not part of a creative process leading to a more finished result.

With these observations in mind, it must also be questioned whether even the three better-known panels illustrating the *Way to Calvary* were preparatory for the larger altarpiece painted for Messina (fig. 5.1), as has also been suggested – a theory undermined, in any case, by the stylistic dating of the artist's 'brown' paintings to after 1535. When looked at in the context of the entire group, it is

more likely that these smaller panels were produced as independent works, as Polidoro's own later derivations of his famous altarpiece in Messina, and as his record of a celebrated composition by Raphael (fig. 5.2), each executed at a different point in the artist's final years and for several patrons. As autograph reductions they belong to a category as distinct and rare as the oil sketch.

The Vatican *Way to Calvary* (fig. 6.7) was discovered and published by Alessandro Marabottini.[13] It has been

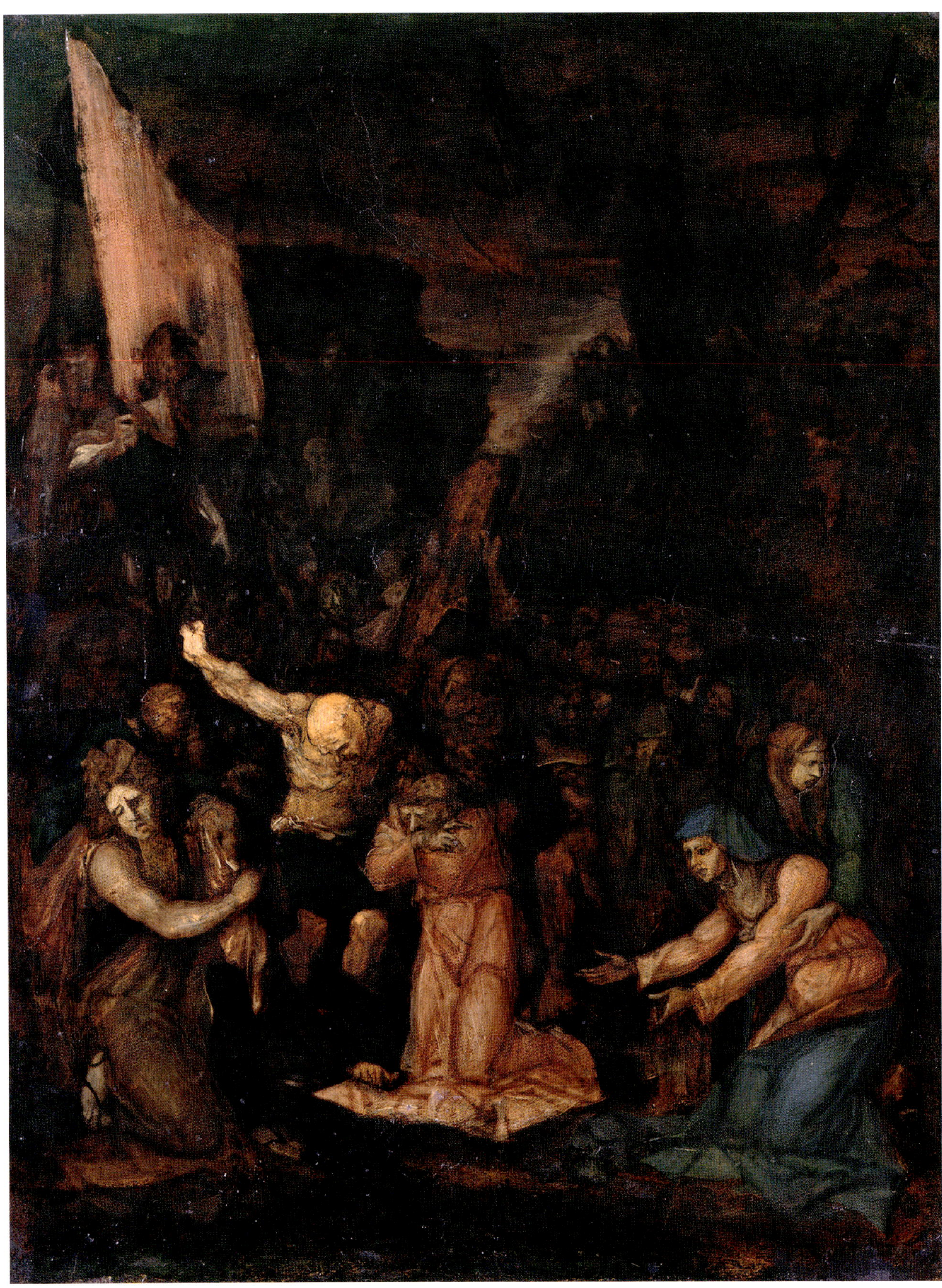

6.9 *Way to Calvary*. Oil on panel, 71 × 54 cm. Museo di Capodimonte, Naples

called a *bozzetto*, or sketch, for the Catalani altarpiece and certainly appears to be the first in the sequence of three works with this subject. Rather than a preparatory sketch, however, this is presumably Polidoro's record of Raphael's miraculous altarpiece, then in the church of Santa Maria dello Spasimo in Palermo. Indeed, the originality of Polidoro's effort needs to be stressed, as in these vivid, excoriated paintings, he appears to invent the oil sketch on panel although, as discussed, 'sketch' is not the best term given that they were not preparatory. The Vatican panel is so crude compared to the prototype that one wonders if it was even painted by Polidoro from memory. There are many similarities between the two paintings, including the basic design and certain poses, but there are also many inspired changes in Polidoro's example, such as the addition of a figure supporting the Cross, perhaps Simon of Cyrene. Polidoro transformed the group around the Virgin in the Raphael to a group with Veronica and possibly the Virgin. The only character who could represent the Virgin is the woman beside Veronica, who is somewhat overshadowed by the prominent veil on which Christ's face is visible. John the Evangelist was eliminated by Polidoro, although it is inconceivable that he would have planned his large public altarpiece without the presence of John and the Virgin. In more formal terms, Raphael's research into feminine beauty and purified refinement is entirely annulled. Almost no colours correspond to the prototype, and to this degree the Vatican picture cannot be considered a direct copy either. The open mouths and heightened emotions of the characters are developed from Raphael's example, but in Polidoro's painting they seem more extreme. Certainly the smaller format encouraged Polidoro to treat the subject more intensely and from a closer viewpoint, but the elimination of any tenderness is typical of his later work and of his own personal contribution to this new subject matter, as explored in the previous chapter.

The London National Gallery panel (fig. 6.8) has no long-term recorded provenance, but it was discovered and attributed to Polidoro by its previous owner Philip Pouncey.[14] Of the three reduced panels by Polidoro of this subject, it is the closest to the Catalani altarpiece and has been considered to be the final element in the sequence before the production of the large-scale painting. This claim would require giving the work a date prior to the completion of the main altarpiece by 1535, a hypothesis that seems questionable. It is the largest of the three smaller versions and this immediately opens up the possibility that it was produced at some date after the altarpiece, as a variant replica of Polidoro's own famous original. The painter has introduced ideas in the National Gallery panel that are more radical than those found in the larger altarpiece, such as the bird-like form of John the Evangelist sweeping in above the distraught Virgin. There are other conspicuous differences between the two works: the powerful anecdotal detail of the mother and child pushed away by a soldier at the right was added, along with a haunting group of onlookers in the upper centre, while the group with the Virgin is also located deeper in space. All the clothing is different in colour. Christ is even given a radiating nimbus in the small panel. Consonant with the rougher handling and smaller scale, the narrative is told in an emotional torrent of action kept close to the picture plane, which contrasts with the grim pace of the altarpiece. Any fluid rhythms are halted in the smaller work, which has the quality of a stained-glass window or mosaic, its pieces apparently slotted together. The freedom from pictorial tradition that Polidoro felt is especially evident in the collapsing, ectoplasmic form of the Magdalen, dressed in white and green in the right corner. Only the positioning of Christ and some of the soldiers recalls Raphael's altarpiece. It is, therefore, difficult to follow how the National Gallery panel could logically lead to the Catalani painting, and more plausible to view it as a later variant with new ideas introduced.

The Capodimonte version (fig. 6.9) is slightly smaller than the National Gallery painting but similar in its figural proportions. The major difference is the compression of the figures into the lower part of the panel and a corresponding greater density in the middle ground. The Virgin in the lower right corner, with outstretched arms and supported from behind, is closer to Raphael's *Spasimo di Sicilia* altarpiece than either of the other two sketches of this subject by Polidoro. Otherwise, it recalls little of Raphael's altarpiece once in Palermo. Chronologically, this, rather than the National Gallery panel, must be the last of the three versions of this subject, as it is the least composed and has the uncontrolled, disjunctive rhythms and nightmarish quality of the other

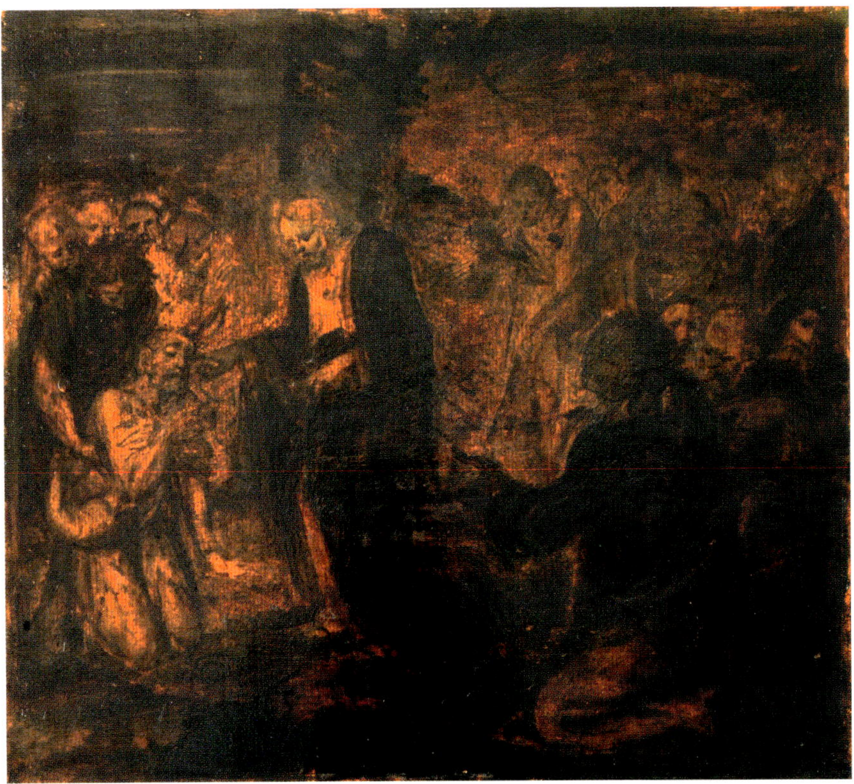

6.10 *Healing of the Blind*. Oil on panel, 35.5 × 40.5 cm. Galleria Regionale della Sicilia, Palermo

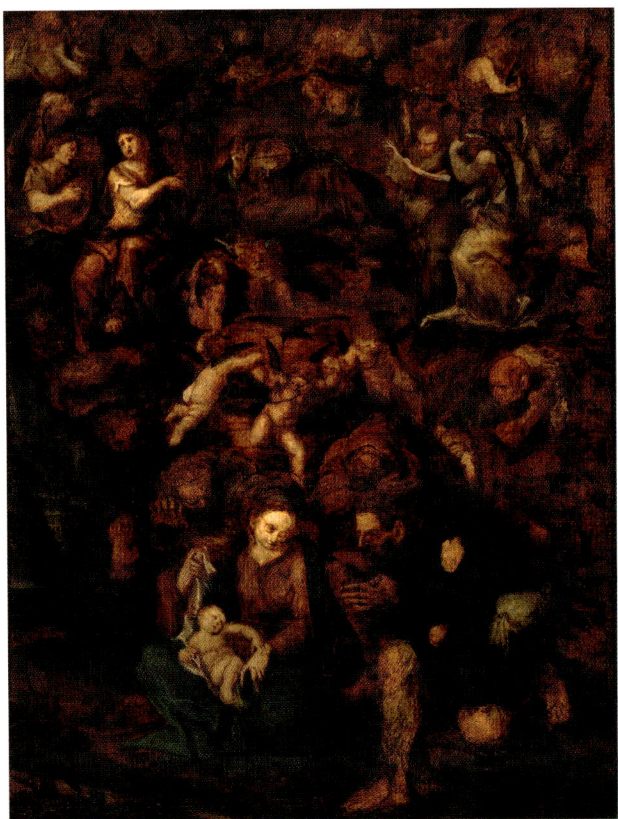

6.11 *Adoration of the Shepherds*. Oil on panel, 71 × 53 cm. Museo di Capodimonte, Naples

final works. It even appears to represent a different moment in the story, as Christ has halted, at which point Simon of Cyrene, a passerby, was commandeered by the Romans to carry the Cross for him. Christ makes a very specific gesture, his arms crossed in piety. The ghoulish torturer who steps on Christ's cloak also adds a narrative touch not found in the other paintings.

It would be equally misleading to describe Polidoro's final efforts as crude solely because of their direct execution, itself very unusual for paintings on such large panels. What we are witnessing here is a painter well-versed in the direct and expedient handling of large-scale fresco choosing to use this approach for panel painting, often on a significant scale – a medium of which he had only intermittent previous experience. His tendency to emphasise the contours of faces and bodies is present in both genres. This rapid and daring technique can also be detected in works whose medium encouraged a broader handling, as demonstrated by tapestry cartoons such as those designed by Raphael for the Sistine Chapel. The artists in Raphael's workshop were certainly capable of this breadth of technique when required, but only Polidoro dared to apply it to panel paintings intended to be seen from a closer viewpoint, in this specific context in provincial Messina, away from the scrutiny of rival artists and, one assumes, in an environment with a less inflexible set of patrons compared to Rome. Although it is difficult to sustain this point too far because of the lack of surviving examples, ephemeral works like the arches that Polidoro designed for the triumphal entry of Charles V in 1535 presumably also featured a comparable breadth of handling, open and unembellished, for the sake of expediency and because of the long viewing distances anticipated. This ephemeral genre provided another precedent for this technique, not by coincidence it would seem, at the very start of the period in which these late Polidoro paintings appear.

While these are some of the most original works of the sixteenth century in any media, they are also some of the least superficially appealing. Polidoro's late paintings are remorselessly serious and introspective, and yet engaging in their explicit acknowledgement of a viewer's emotional reaction, compared to the preoccupation with superficial elegance, suavity and polish found in the painting of artists like Parmigianino and Perino del Vaga, or even in Polidoro's own pictures of his second period in Naples. Formally, they abnegate the gentler, more graceful naturalism of these contemporary artists, not to mention Raphael, embracing a different standard of beauty, one that no longer aimed to provide pure visual or cerebral pleasure. In some the treatment of the subject matter seems improvised during the course of execution, while the compositions generally owe little to pictorial precedents and the saintly types are non-canonical. Although they do not appear to be deliberately primitive, the results can seem simplified and unsophisticated. It is often difficult even to initiate a discussion of composition or narrative field in any usual, rational sense. The designs are, typically, compressed to the frame and based on bulky and cumbersome figures – overlapping rather than formally interrelating – and there is also an awkward juxtaposition of scales. There are no described backgrounds, proper settings or architectural demarcations. The introduction of a high viewpoint seems more a formal shortcut than one required for illusionistic purposes. Similarly, in a work like the *Healing of the Blind* in Palermo (fig. 6.10), while the composition is weighted to the left for a reason presumably relating to its original installation

in a narrative sequence, damage overwhelms almost any analysis of its design. There is some architecture in this case but it hardly features in the spatial demarcation.

Emotionally, these sensate late panels by Polidoro are harsh and uncompromising; they have an austere spirituality in which meaning is felt as much as described, something entirely alien to Roman art of the previous decade. The closest parallel for their sense of earnest, at times even torpid or grotesque, pathos would be Sebastiano del Piombo's later devotional paintings, several of which were executed for the Spanish market, but by comparison Polidoro's seem far more intuitive and raw. It says much about their singularity that, unlike Sebastiano's, there is no evidence Polidoro's paintings were dispatched to Spain, even though Sicily was then under Spanish dominion. There is also no direct evidence that Polidoro returned to Rome after May 1527, and certainly any possible influence from Michelangelo's *Last Judgement* in the Sistine Chapel can be disregarded following its recent cleaning to reveal a smooth, crystalline finish. Looking at these final works by Polidoro, for whose appreciation we have to adjust our very perceptions of Renaissance painting, one is driven to wonder what he even remembered of Raphael's art.

And yet there is no evidence that this type of painting was anything but admired by the earliest local commentators. In 1724, nearly two centuries following their presumed creation, Susinno wrote of Polidoro's 'beautiful narratives', which probably included the *Healing of the Blind*.[15] He also described another picture, possibly the Capodimonte *Adoration of the Shepherds* (fig. 6.11) as 'copious with little full-length figures, a thing so delightful and dreamlike'.[16] Whether he was correct or not, Susinno was generously prepared to believe that the deteriorating condition of certain works had reduced their original beauty. Such comments remind us that notions of beauty are always relative, that to condemn Polidoro's last style as ugly or controversial is perilous, and even that all attributions are suspect. The late *Adoration of the Shepherds* in Naples is a clear example of Polidoro seeking to create a positive emotional tone because it can be contrasted with the stylistically earlier *Adoration* in Palermo (fig. 6.6). The composition is almost illegible at first glance. The Virgin and Child are shifted down to the front lower

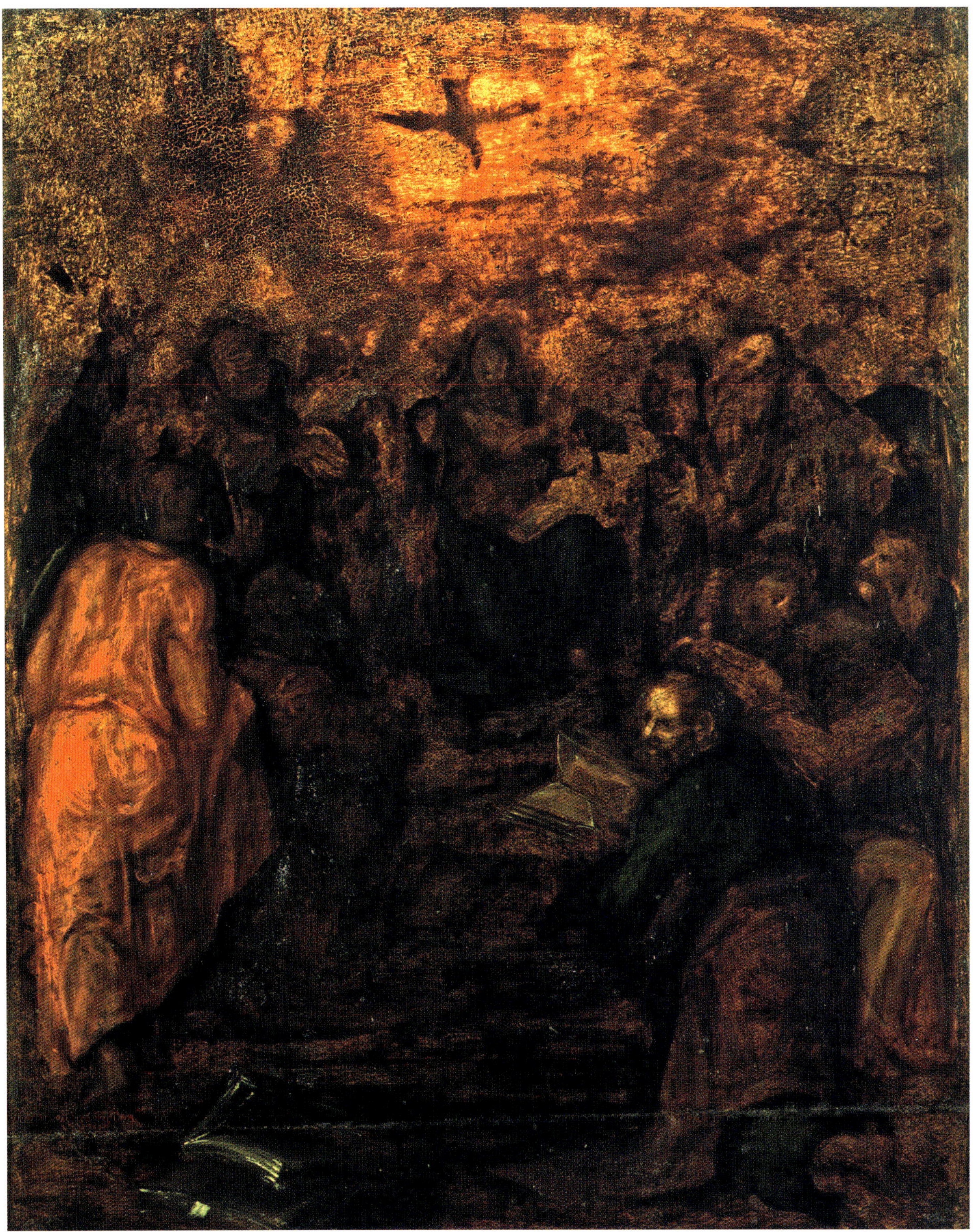

6.12 *Pentecost*. Oil on panel, 72 × 57 cm. Museo di Capodimonte, Naples

centre of the picture, with Joseph placed behind and hunched over. The shepherds are reduced in number to three and are much older and less physically attractive. The supernatural element becomes more insistent, with a full host of angels and God the Father with a triangular halo. Indeed, more than half of the picture surface is filled with the divine support group. The joyous element is submerged in the strange complexion of the panel. This

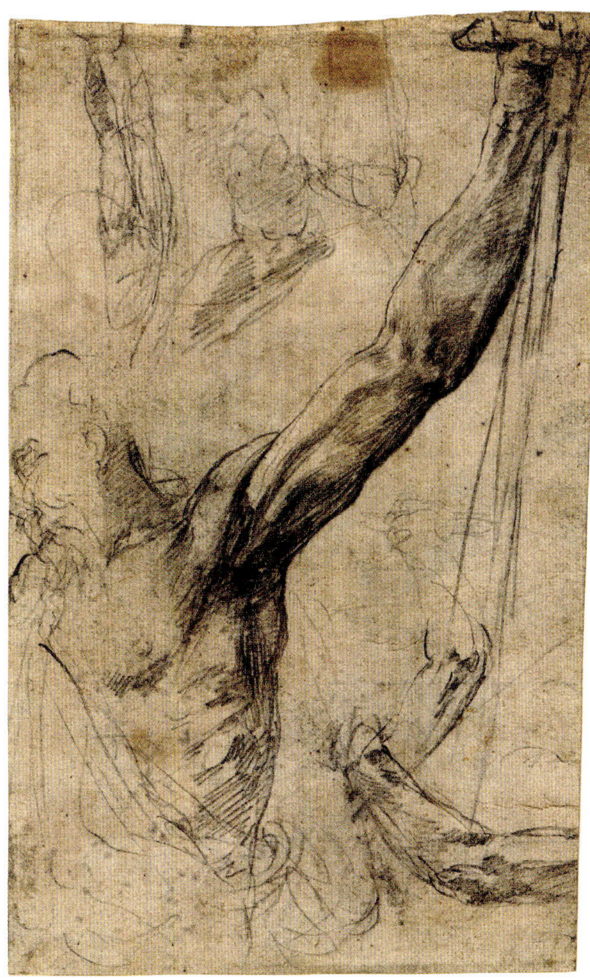

6.13 *Study of a Man with His Left Arm Raised and Various Arm Studies.* Black chalk on laid paper, 20.3 × 13.2 cm. British Museum, London

method suited subjects that occurred in darkness much better, such as the *Agony in the Garden*. The Naples panel has comparable dimensions to the even more ragged *Pentecost* (fig. 6.12), in the same museum, and is perhaps related to the same original commission. These paintings almost seem to chart memories of a half-recalled composition rather than any immediately recognisable religious themes.

There are no exceptions to Polidoro's approach in the last years of his life. He even produced large public altarpieces with this nocturnal technique and grim, ponderous figure style, as for example in the four fragments from a *Crucifixion* now in a private collection.[17] A print discovered by Achim Gnann records the entire design.[18] The panels share stylistic qualities with all the later paintings, including the scoured, bruised surfaces, and there is little need to analyse them here. The work

is unique, however, as the only one of the late group to which secure preparatory drawings relate, in this instance two powerful studies in the British Museum for the figure of Christ, one of which is illustrated here (fig. 6.13). This is a worksheet including five attempts at representing an arm and several studies of a bearded model with a sash of drapery and a staff to support his upraised arm for the purpose of life drawing. It is almost a *notomia secca*, or dried anatomy, as the man seems too withered and old to portray Christ. Black chalk was used to create the drama of the lighting, to three-dimensional effect. Surprisingly analytical compared to the final painting, in which form seems to have collapsed, it is treated in a controlled range of black chalk, from greasy and sharp to smudged.

Two of the most resolved but equally enigmatic of the late works, formerly attributed to the Genoese artist Luca Cambiaso, are to be found in the Christ Church Picture Gallery, University of Oxford (figs 6.14 and 6.15). In the *David and Goliath*, the panel is original. It is possibly walnut, or at least a harder wood than the traditional poplar used in the majority of Italian panel paintings. The construction of the support has an improvised quality to it. The work further establishes Polidoro's apparently frequent need to repurpose old doors and furniture for his later paintings in Messina.[19] It is formed of two planks vertically joined, with apparently original extensions at the top and bottom. Few pentimenti are visible, although there are signs of some in the stomach area of Goliath, attesting to the difficulty the painter had in fixing the daring foreshortening of this figure. It is likely that the two Christ Church panel works were originally paired, as both are claustrophobic, dominated by foreground giants, with the addition of smaller figures in contorted, acrobatic poses in the upper part. However, they would have formed a rare pairing of Old Testament and hagiographical subjects. Whether they were true pendants or produced as part of a larger complex cannot be established. In the *Saint Christopher* the main figure appears hunched over, his right hand on a rock and his staff held in the other, providing support. There is certainly a residual classicism, unusual in Polidoro's later efforts, in the powerfully depicted head of Christopher, with its massive scale and curly hair. The unusual portrait on the rock appears to be original, as is the coat of arms. While indicating that these are commissioned works, both features have defied

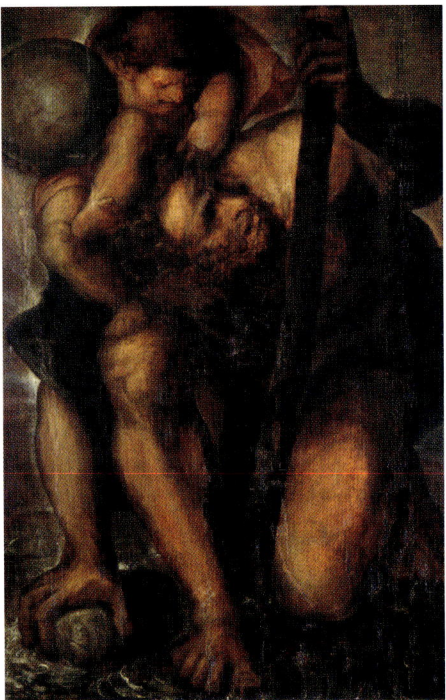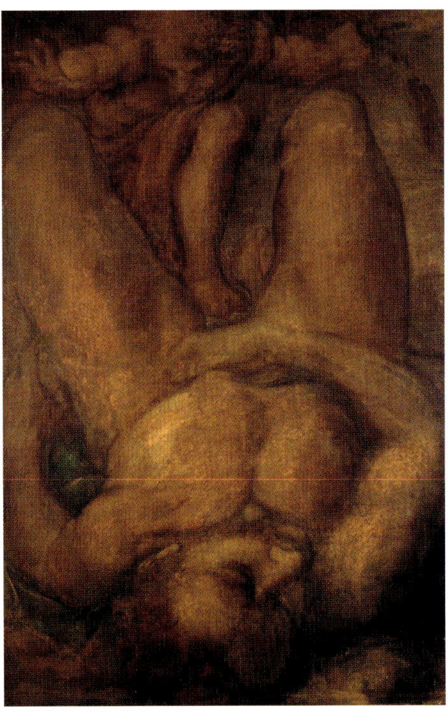

6.14 *Saint Christopher*. Oil on panel, 145 × 103 cm. Christ Church Picture Gallery, University of Oxford

6.15 *David and Goliath*. Oil on panel, 145 × 99 cm. Christ Church Picture Gallery, University of Oxford

elucidation thus far. Christopher took his name from the Greek for 'Christ-bearer'. According to *The Golden Legend*, compiled by Jacobus de Voragine in the thirteenth century, Christopher was carrying the Christ Child across a river when the water became turbulent and the body of Christ became heavier. Polidoro captures this well by demonstrating his struggle and surprise. The metaphor of Christopher bearing the world on his shoulders is stressed by the inclusion of a symbolic globe, although this is also an attribute of Christ as Salvator Mundi. Christopher used an uprooted palm tree as a staff, later planted by order of Christ, after which it miraculously bore fruit.

The giant in the *David and Goliath* is represented in a supine position with his arm across his stomach and his body almost teetering towards the viewer's space, demonstrating Polidoro's consummate skill at foreshortening. David adopts an expressive, ungainly pose that ultimately derives from Michelangelo's *Haman* fresco on the Sistine Chapel ceiling. He holds the sling and sword together in one hand, away from Goliath's corpse, while brutally stepping on his groin. The stone that has just wounded the wretched giant in the forehead is visible in the lower right corner, and his head is about to be cut off

– a particularly dramatic moment in the story. Goliath appears to be lying on some blue-green drapery, which must have been part of his military uniform. True to the biblical text, the shepherd boy David has no armour or weapons. A fresco by Polidoro of Saint Christopher is recorded in the Messina sources at the Capuchin church of Santa Maria degli Angeli, but no example on panel, not to mention a David and Goliath, and so the Christ Church panels must be considered undocumented examples of the artist's later style in Messina, and two of the most formally outstanding.[20]

Four fragments in Naples featuring three Franciscan saints and the Magdalen were almost certainly once part of an altarpiece in Santa Maria degli Angeli (figs 6.16–6.19). Executed on individual panels, two kneeling saints face to their left and two full-length figures face to their right, with a symmetry that suggests they were originally part of a polyptych. They share a similar intensity, with agitated poses, bulky bodies with large heads and hands, and tormented, furtive looks. Unusually, they seem to be peasant types. The life-scale figures from the murky backgrounds of earlier works are here transposed to the foreground as massive individual saints. With their dark habits dominating against the monochromatic brown

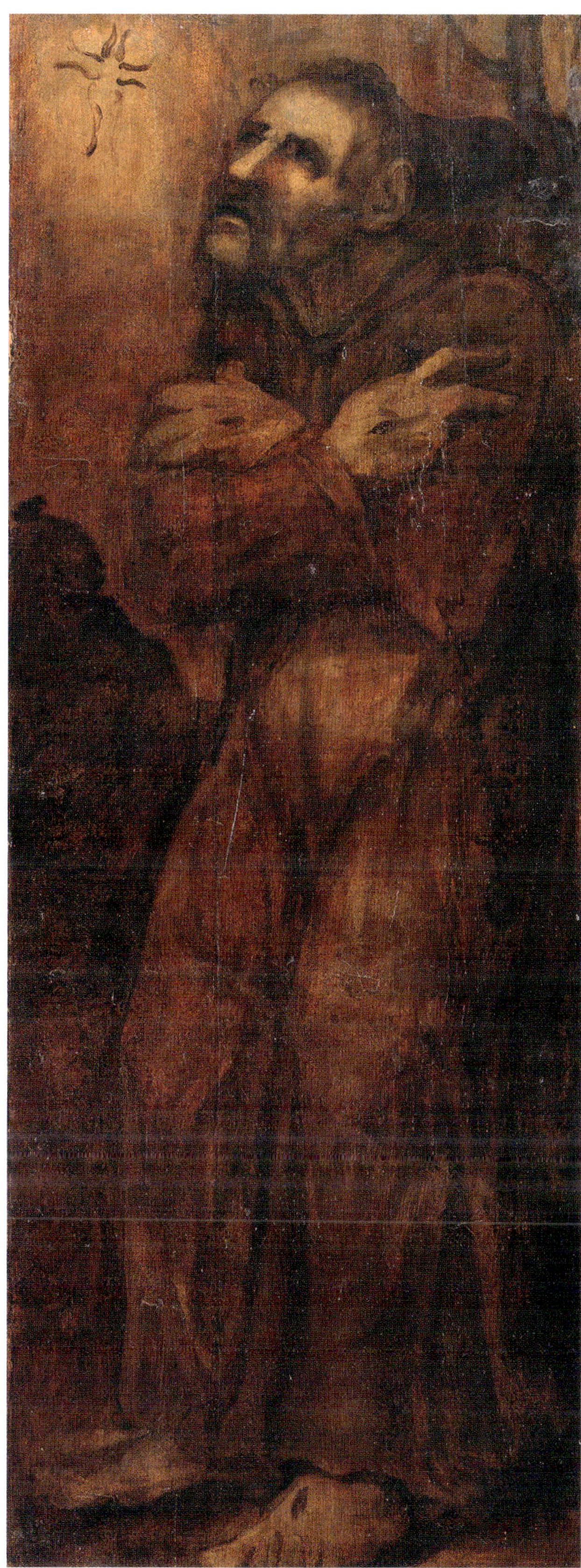

6.16 *Saint Francis*. Oil on panel, 160 × 70 cm. Museo di Capodimonte, Naples

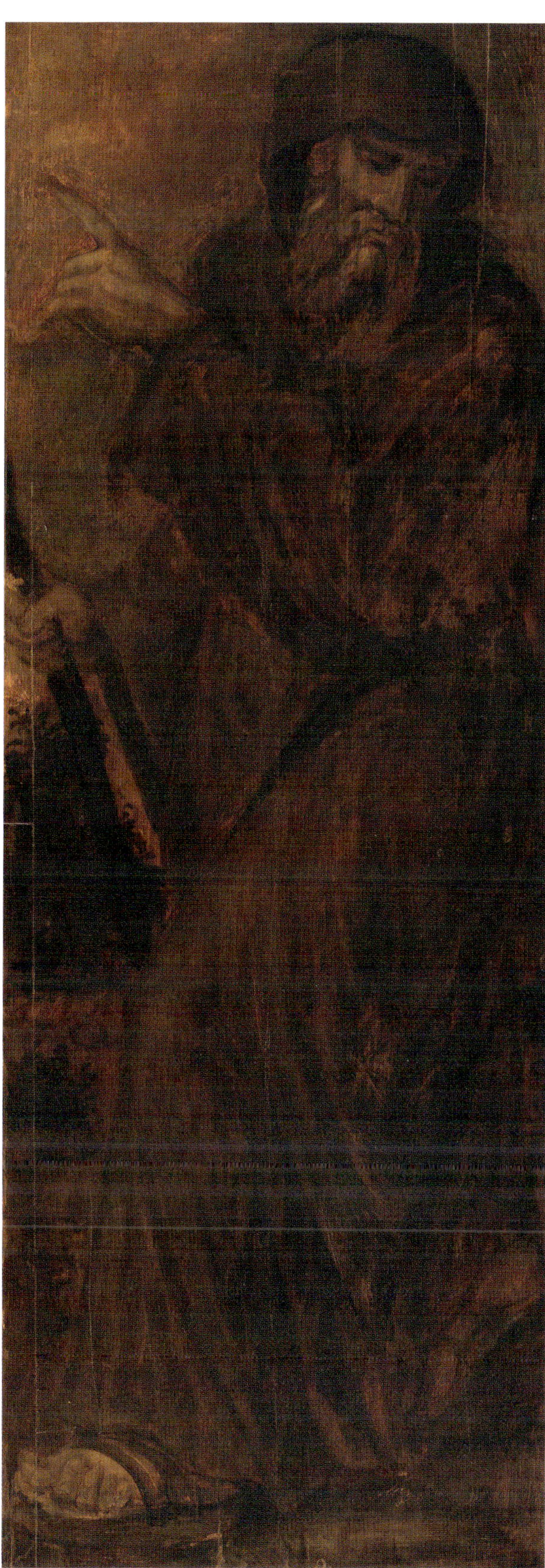

6.17 *Saint Francis of Paola*. Oil on panel, 161 × 69 cm. Museo di Capodimonte, Naples

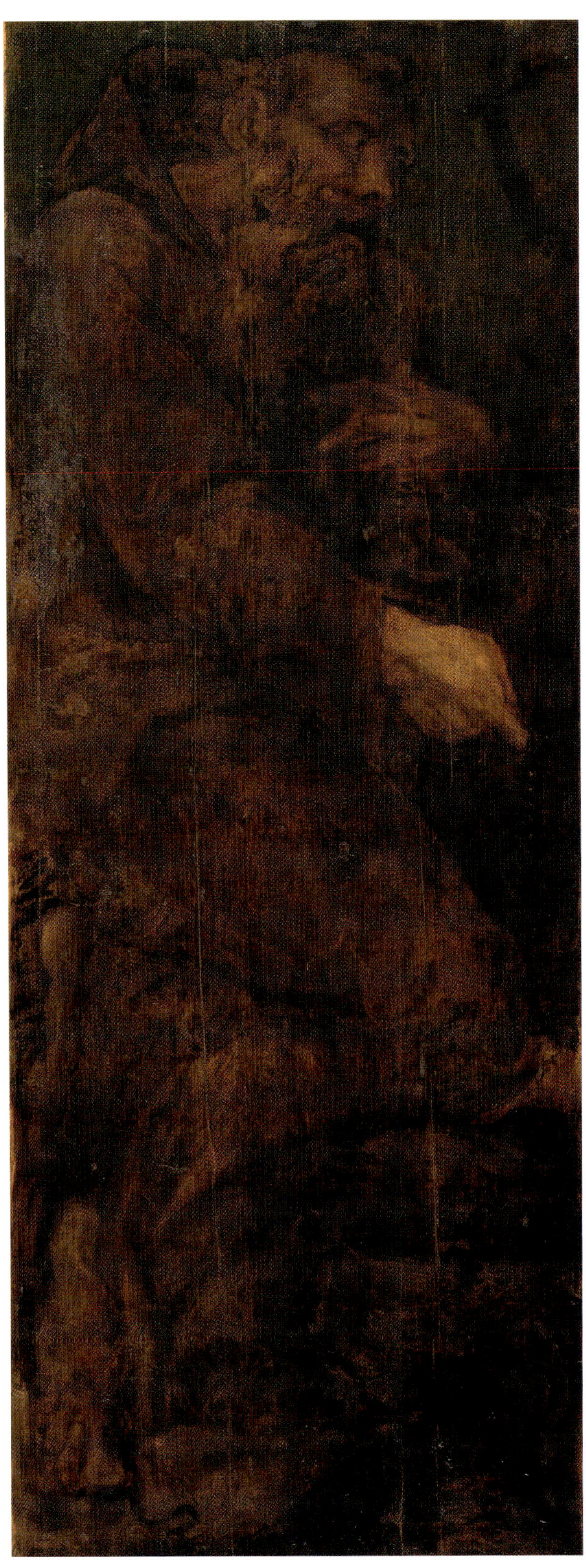

6.18 *Franciscan Saint*, or *Saint Anthony Abbot*? Oil on panel, 161 × 70 cm. Museo di Capodimonte, Naples

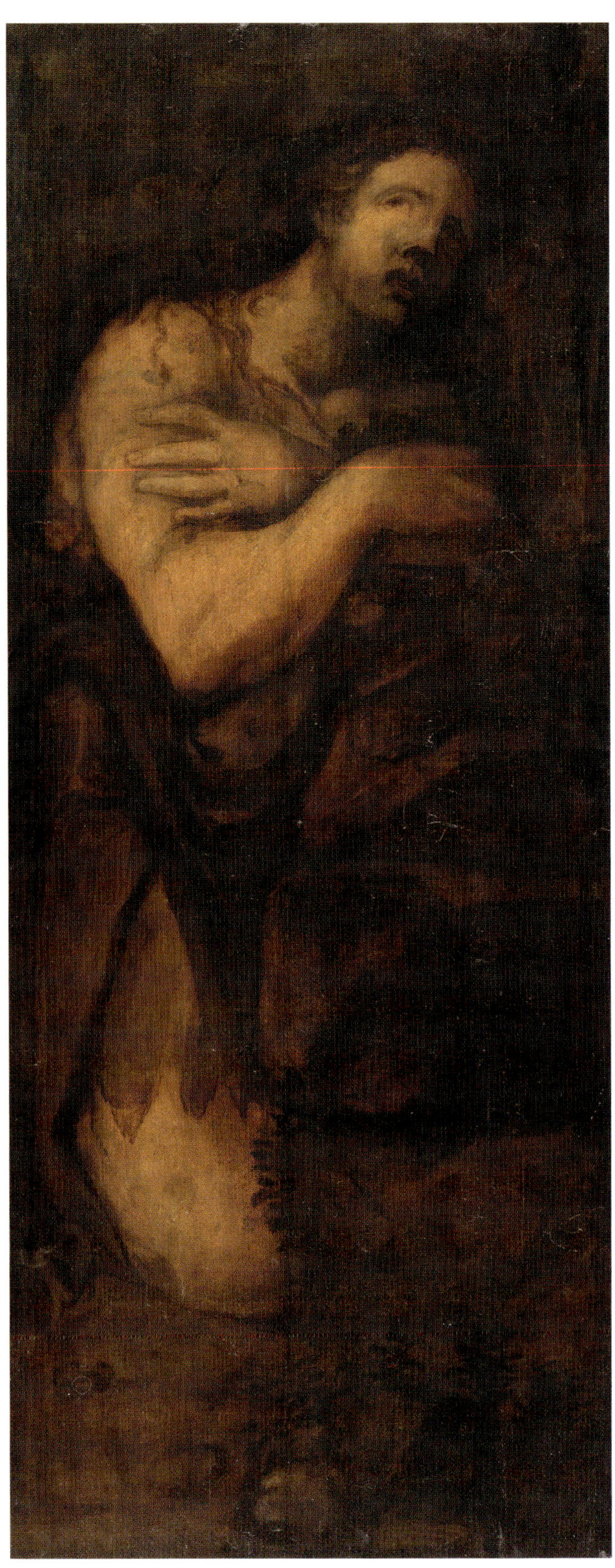

6.19 *Saint Mary Magdalen*. Oil on panel, 159 × 68 cm. Museo di Capodimonte, Naples

grounds, the mood is claustrophobic. The paint is thick
and coagulated but seems to move as if in emotional
rapport with the characters. The saints are all surprisingly
communicative, while seeming introspective and almost
blinded by emotional fervour. The development from
the San Silvestro al Quirinale Magdalen frescoes to this
Magdalen, within 20 years, is barely fathomable.

Given the relatively recent identification of this related
group of late works, it would not be surprising for more
examples to emerge from storage vaults in museums
and private collections. One imposing newer addition
to the group is a badly damaged *Immaculate Conception*,
discovered in the deposit of the regional museum in
Messina and attributed to Polidoro by Leone de Castris,
overturning a previous attribution to Marco Pino, who
admittedly did admire the older artist's style.[21] It was
certainly an altarpiece, and the suggestion has been made
that the four Naples saints flanked it on their separate
panels. While the work has no provenance, the Virgin's
exemption from Original Sin was a subject especially
promoted by the Franciscans, starting in the second half
of the fifteenth century, and so the proposal has merit.

These late paintings not only feature unusual
treatments of conventional themes but also some rare
subjects. The *Christ Among the Apostles*, once in the
Walpole Gallery in London, belongs to this group
(fig. 6.20). It is painted on a single piece of badly cracked
poplar. Like the others, it is not precisely monochrome,
even if this is the general impression. There are earthy
brown-red mixtures, some white highlights with black
outlines and perhaps some yellow, but except for the
black underdrawing there are no other pigments.
The brushwork is visibly free and forceful, even haphazard,
thickly applied in only a few layers. Individual figures
are blocky in form and strangely muted, as inexpressive
as somnambulists, improvising their own movements.
Yet the rugged elegance of the picture is undeniably
moving. Despite the slow monumentality of the image,
the impossibly crowded juxtaposition of enormous heads
and truncated busts, some almost totally occluded, creates
urgency. The speaking Christ is placed in the centre and
although not the largest figure, he is the only one who
extends to the full height of the support. There appear to
be 12 apostles, plus one extra figure in a black hood by
Christ's right ear, who must be either Judas or, conversely,

a Capuchin friar. Peter is the only other identifiable figure
because of his attribute of the crossed keys. The hands
of Christ and Peter are paralleled in pose; the painter
barely attempted to vary their arrangement in stressing
their shared fate of extreme suffering in death. The panel
appears to show a rarely depicted subject following the
Crucifixion, told in all the Gospels, as in Matthew 28: 16–20:

> Now the eleven disciples went to Galilee, to the
> mountain to which Jesus had directed them. And when
> they saw him they worshipped him; but some doubted.
> And Jesus came and said to them, 'All authority in
> heaven and on earth has been given to me. Go there-
> fore and make disciples of all nations, baptising them
> in the name of the Father and of the Son and of the
> Holy Spirit, teaching them to observe all that I have
> commanded you; and lo, I am with you always, to the
> close of the age.' The moment when they first visited
> him, he breathed on them and spoke: 'Receive the Holy
> Spirit. If you forgive the sins of any, they are forgiven;
> if you retain the sins of any, they are retained.'

This interpretation, however, is potentially in doubt as
Christ does not display the stigmata in Polidoro's painting.
Perhaps it is simply a representation of the apostles
together, in which Christ acts as a figural attribute.

Closely related is an *Assumption of the Virgin* in Naples,
also part of the Santa Maria degli Angeli group (fig. 6.21).
The *Assumption* features a dense stacking of bust-length
apostles similar to the ex-Walpole panel, although here
the scene is divided into two. The apostles seem grimly
locked in debate, more preoccupied among themselves
than with the miracle happening above their heads, in
contrast to their more alert counterparts in the Monteluce
altarpiece by Raphael's workshop, now in the Vatican.
A disembodied arm even touches the tomb. The attire
of these figures, like that of the hooded man who appears
in the ex-Walpole painting, recalls the Capuchin habit.
The spectral feet of the Virgin, painted as translucent
red contours on a yellow ground, are a particularly
remarkable conception, whose eccentricity verges on the
anti-decorous. Given the similar dimensions to the *Christ
Among the Apostles* painting, one is left to wonder if this
panel was always intended to remain this shape, as part
of a cycle perhaps dedicated to the twelve apostles.

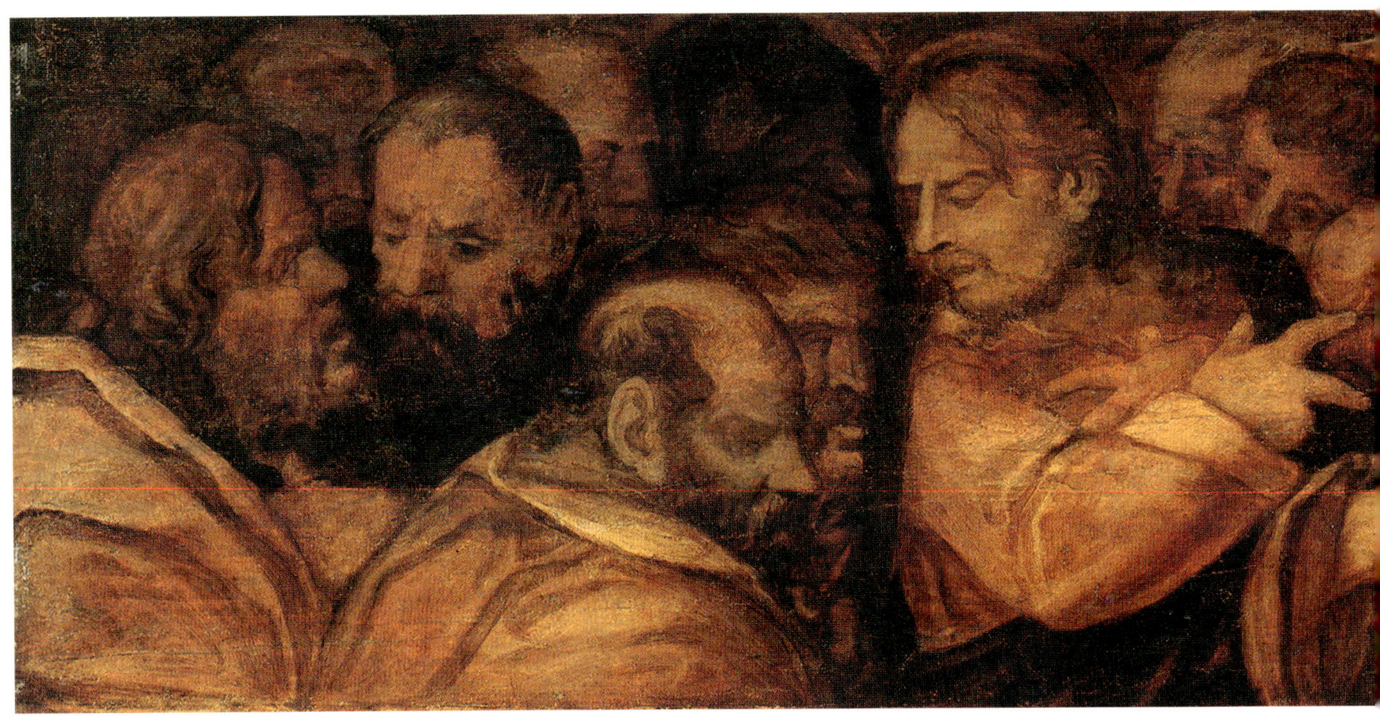

6.20 *Christ Among the Apostles*. Oil on panel, 59.9 × 151.5 cm. Formerly Walpole Gallery, London

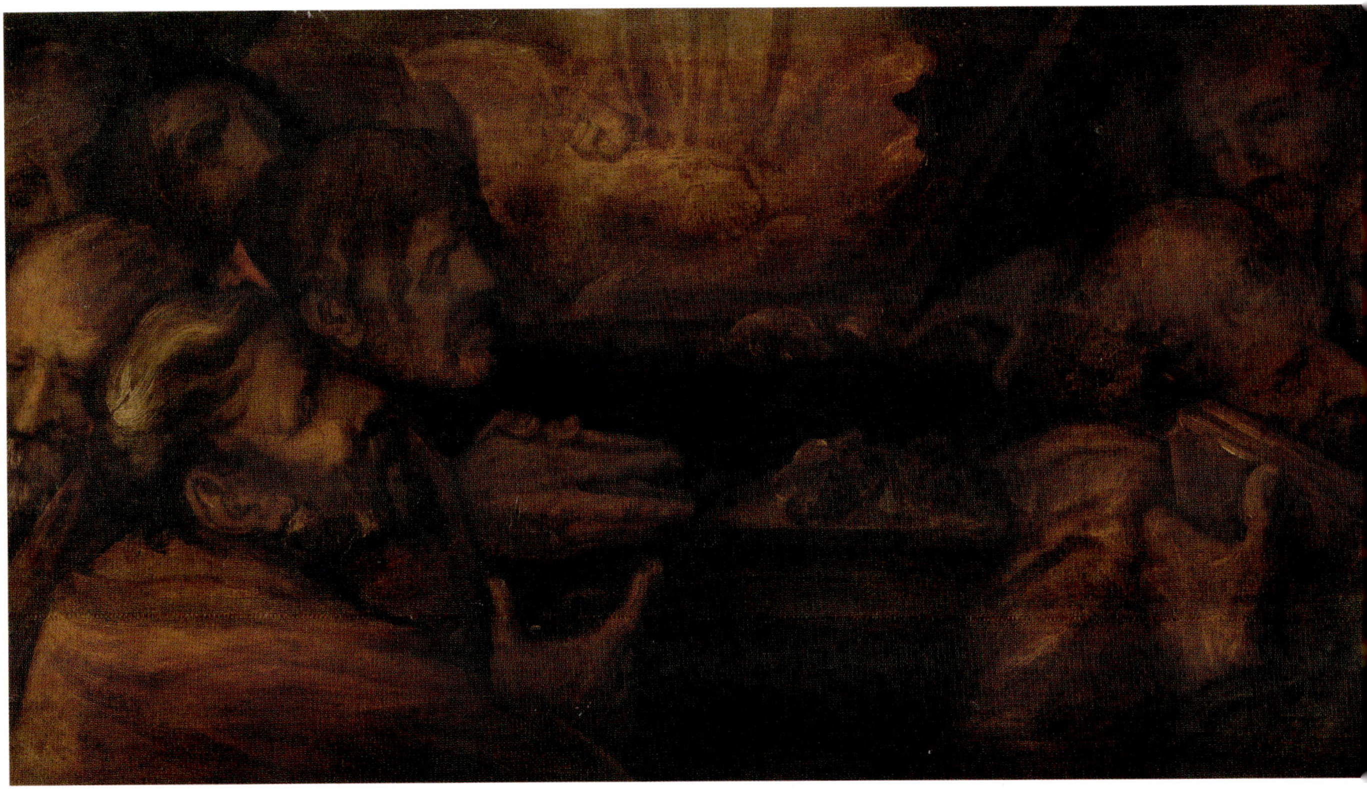

6.21 *Assumption of the Virgin*. Oil on panel, 69 × 155 cm. Museo di Capodimonte, Naples

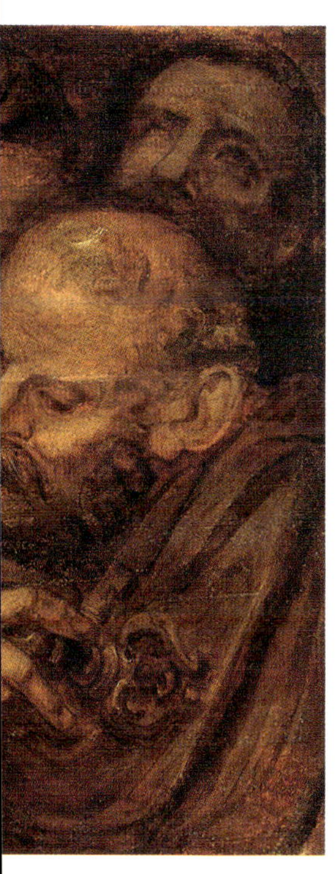

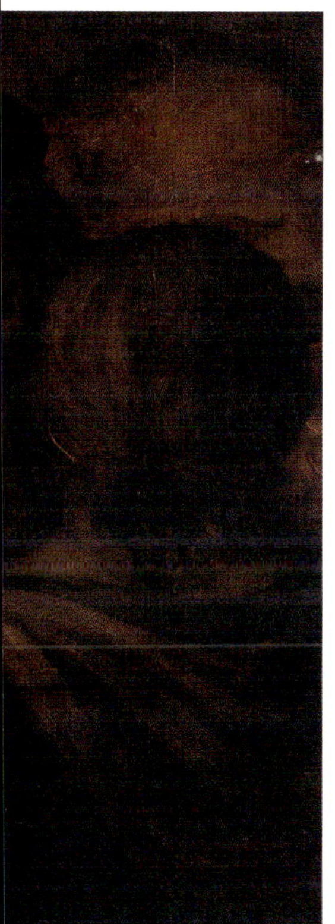

The *Calling of Saint Matthew*, also in Naples, relates to these pictures in its compressed horizontal format (fig. 6.22). The same stylistic analysis can be applied to the agitated, claustrophobic design, in which the massive heads practically collide in a stilted telling of the narrative. Christ appears in profile and vigorously gestures to Matthew, who accepts his fate by making a prayer gesture, while apparently keeping his eyes pressed shut and so internalising the sentiment. Another disembodied hand even skewers its way from the background into the dramatic centre to reinforce the message of the painting.

One other relatively recent discovery to add to this body of work is a *Pietà with a Donor*, once exhibited at the Matthiesen Gallery in London (fig. 6.23).[22] It is related in its monumental claustrophobia to the Christ Church Picture Gallery paintings (figs 6.14 and 6.15). This pine panel made from a reused door is uniquely important in Polidoro's work for including a traditional donor portrait on the same scale as the religious characters. Deciphering a fragmentary inscription, Leone de Castris identified the individual as possibly the Bishop of Messina, Antonio de Lignamine. A coat of arms is visible in the upper right corner of the panel. His bishop's crosier appears balanced on the man's shoulder, although it must also be recognised that the individual appears younger than De Lignamine, who died in 1537, suggesting this must be an idealised posthumous likeness. The empathetic gesture of the distraught Virgin Mary to acknowledge and honour the donor is atypical and reveals the artist's willingness to take liberties with artistic convention in Messina. The awkward turn of her body to allow her to gain space on the panel is remarkable, as if Polidoro began painting with a figure scale in mind and refused to compromise. As seen in other late paintings, but especially evident here, is the depiction of the figures as ghostly apparitions with eyes closed, as if to encourage even the viewer not to look at the image but to internalise the terrible event and articulate their own interpretation of a ubiquitous narrative. The donor is the exception as the only contemporary figure depicted. This is a unique survival of portrait painting to scale in Polidoro's corpus.[23]

The *Salome with the Head of John the Baptist and Executioner* panel (fig. 6.24; now in the Capodimonte) is not, like many of these other works, from the Montagano bequest but from a different source, the Museo Borbonico

in Naples, acquired in 1850 from the collection of a ship's
captain, Onofrio Spasiano, already with a prescient
attribution to Polidoro.[24] It is yet another large painting
in a horizontal format, with three-quarter length figures,
and is possibly an independent picture rather than part
of a more elaborate altarpiece. The panel is most notable
because Salome appears in profile with an elegant coiffure
– a rare attempt at superficial beauty in these late
productions. With the frontal placement of the severed
head and awkward but reverberating emotional content,
the painting inevitably brings to mind the other
Caravaggio's late work, as he approached the year of his
death in 1610. He certainly saw the work of his predecessor
during his own time in Messina, and it was doubtless
an influence.

In the end, it is irresistible to speculate on the motives
and thought processes behind Polidoro's final pictures.
The direct expression, emotional and physical, might
indicate that he was satisfying a more entrenched and
reactionary market for religious art in Sicily than that
found in Rome or Naples. The principal theory, that he
was inspired by sympathetic contact with the penitent
Franciscans, namely the relatively new order of the
Capuchins, who desired to return explicitly to the
rigorous devotion of Saint Francis himself, deserves
consideration. His work was, after all, present in one
of their churches in Messina, and perhaps they pushed
the artist towards a more austere, despondent style of
painting challenging convention.[25] Although they were
not Franciscans, it is certain that Polidoro was also
sympathetic to members of the local Carmelite Order,
who provided him with space for his living quarters and
eventual burial.[26] There is no question that controversial
Reformist preachers of the Capuchin Order, like
Bernardino Ochino, were present in Sicily during some of
this period, insisting on salvation through Christ alone.[27]
Yet these pictures are so unconventional as to go beyond
even this proposal, which gives credit to a patron's
instruction rather than the artist's creativity. It is difficult
to believe that Polidoro was appeasing the taste of any
patron or group, especially one without a traditional
or meaningful experience of the visual arts, let alone
swerving dangerously towards anti-papal, Lutheran
heresy in images on panel that could not be disguised as
easily as words, leaving them legible to potential critics,

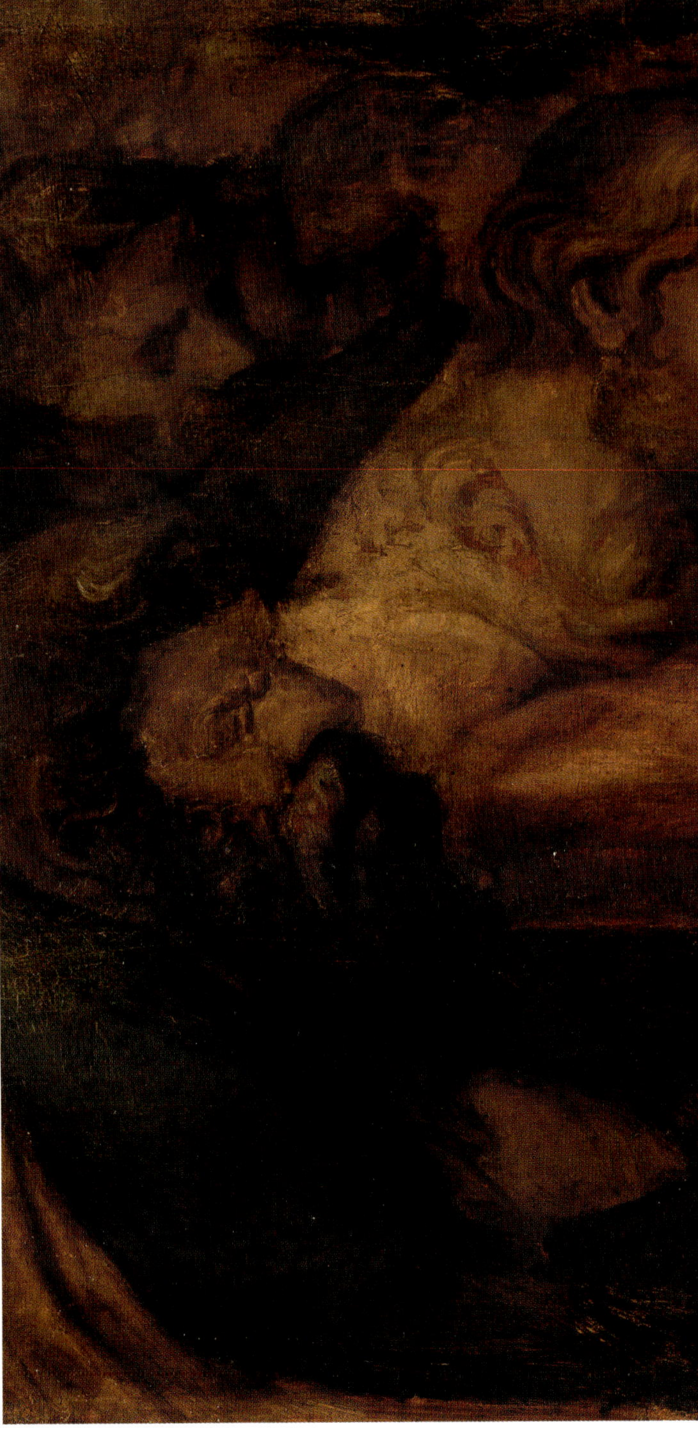

6.22 *Calling of Saint Matthew*. Oil on panel, 85 × 132 cm. Museo di Capodimonte, N

of which there were many. It is a typical interpretative
reflex among art historians to look for impiety where
there is visual mystery. How far these often literally
elusive reform groups, who occupied a fluid, inconsistent
place in religious life of the period, were even specifically
interested in the arts also requires exploration but it seems

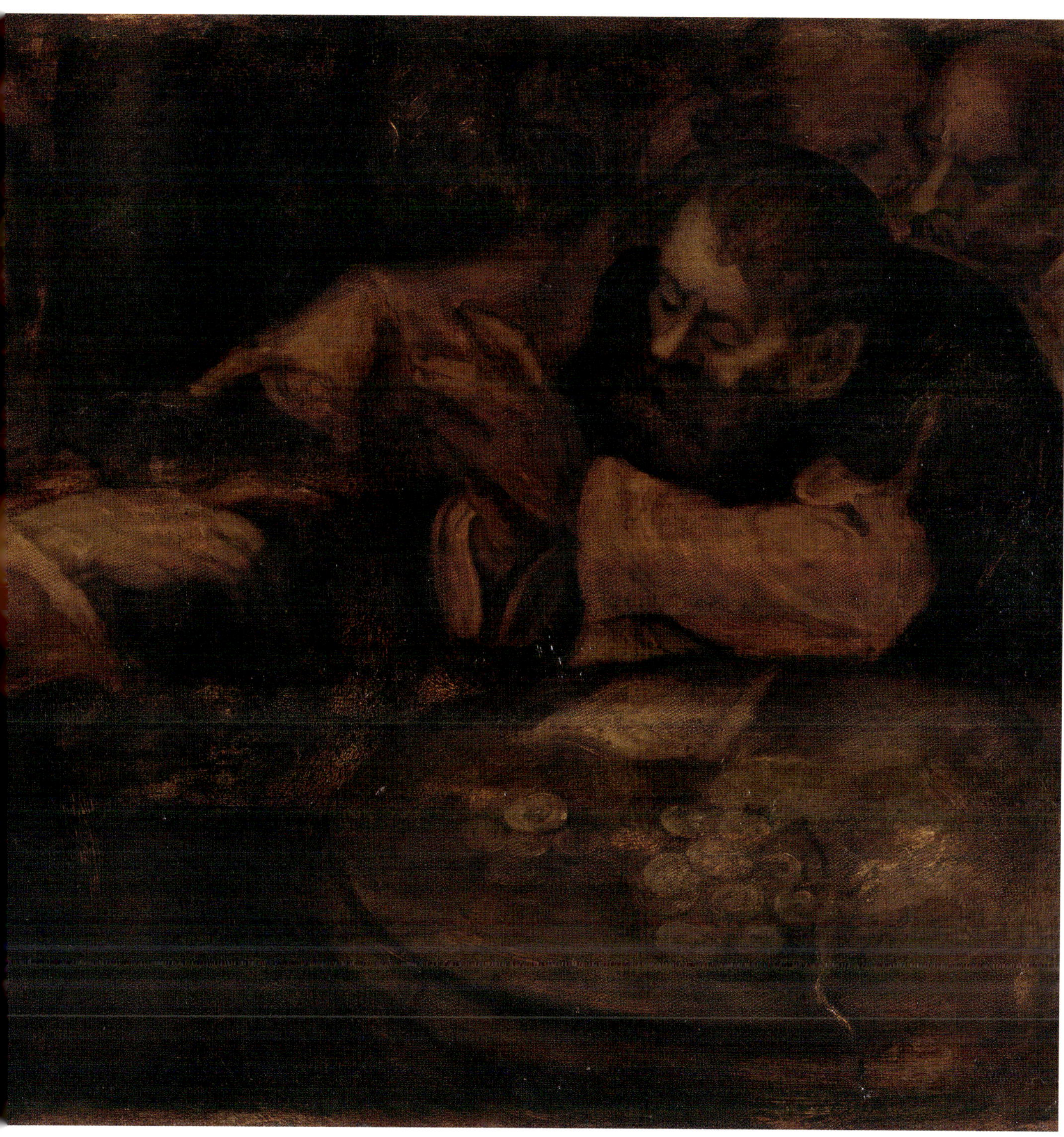

far-fetched to believe they expected the conventional altarpiece format to be a vehicle for their ideas. For its sensate emotional qualities this work, which asks the viewer to feel mystically as much as to see rationally, could just as easily be described as anticipating the Counter-Reformation in its orthodoxy, keeping in mind that

Polidoro died prior to the formation of the Council of Trent in 1545.[28] The most explicit evidence we have is the earlier text by Alibrando related to the artist's *Way to Calvary* altarpiece for the Catalans, which supports viewing the paintings through the more traditional lens of a vivid spiritual exercise devoted to emulating the

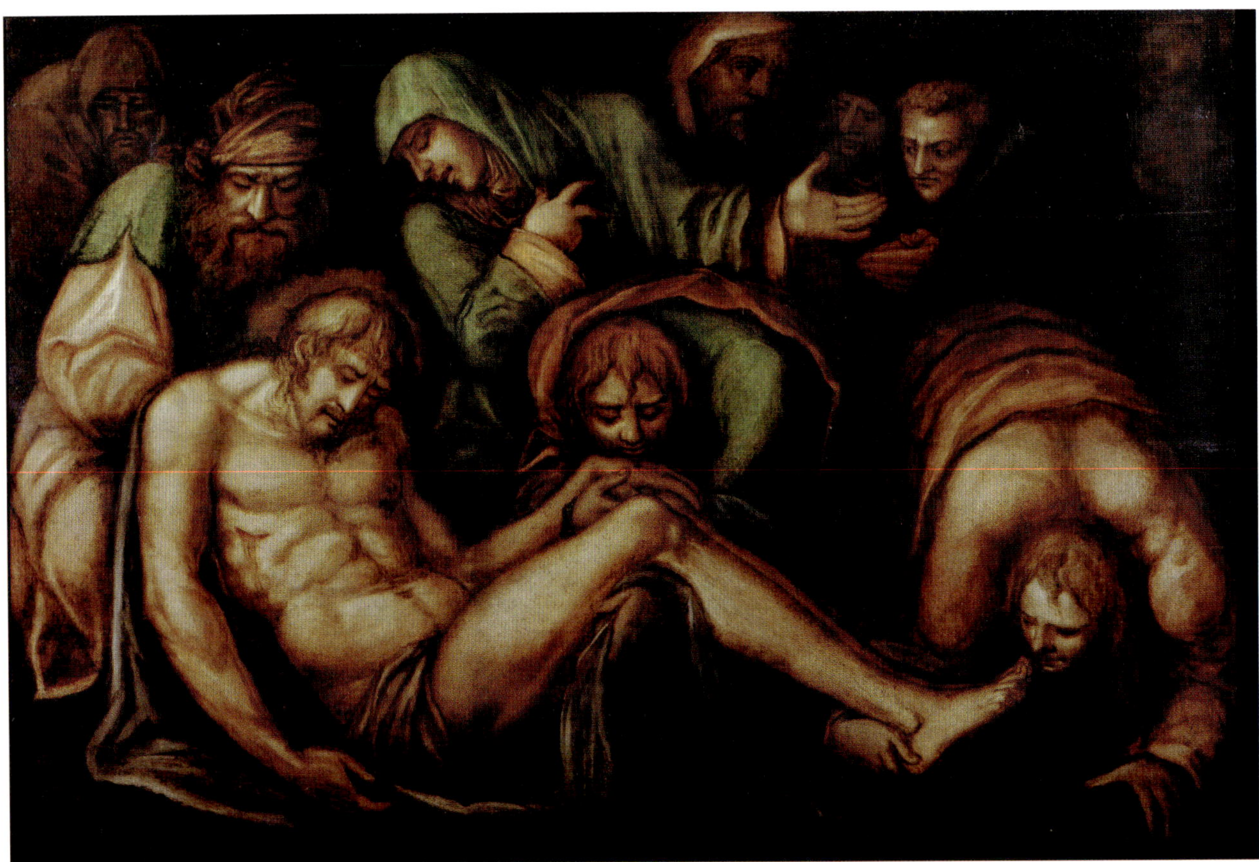

6.23 *Pietà with a Donor*. Oil on panel, 127.7 × 193.5 cm. Formerly Matthiesen Gallery, London

Passion of Christ, as promoted by the Franciscan saint Bonaventure. This theology was preoccupied with storytelling and strong pathos, as opposed to radical, mutable religious sentiments formulated under stressful conditions. It may be that in this period Polidoro exploited in his art the same chaotic and confusing religious liberty and diversity that permitted reformers like Ochino to develop heterodox views, prior to the strict conformity that would abruptly emerge in 1545, just after the painter's death.

A suspicion lingers, too, that Polidoro was so dominant an artist in Sicily during his lifetime that no patron would have considered challenging his approach or the final result. There was no alternative artist of his stature, given his distinguished background in Raphael's circle in the Vatican. It is also relevant to this argument that these pictures are not temporary aberrations in Polidoro's stylistic development, supplied for only one commission, because there is no other late work from his hand that is more conventional in appearance. Despite the overall consistency, in other ways it is a large and disparate group,

produced over an approximately eight-year period from around 1535 to 1543, and for a number of different patrons in Messina. Definite conclusions may well never be reached on this matter, but it seems most plausible to approach these final works in terms of the artist's single-minded creative process and desire to move the spectator, made possible by more liberty from any external criticism than he had previously experienced in Rome or Naples. Perhaps Polidoro, who seems always to have found inspiration easily, developed late in life a more direct and subjective, sensory and sonorous mode of painting, in which he displayed his raw genius both in public and in prominent private collections in Messina. The dissolving, trance-like state described by Alibrando in his account of the *Way to Calvary* altarpiece comes to mind. Polidoro's style was clearly still widely in demand in Messina. Despite the apparent crudity and breadth of the late work, it should be recalled that this style also represents a progressive notion of facility and freedom from the past. As such these pictures are the supreme expressions of an original, individual talent operating against the notion of

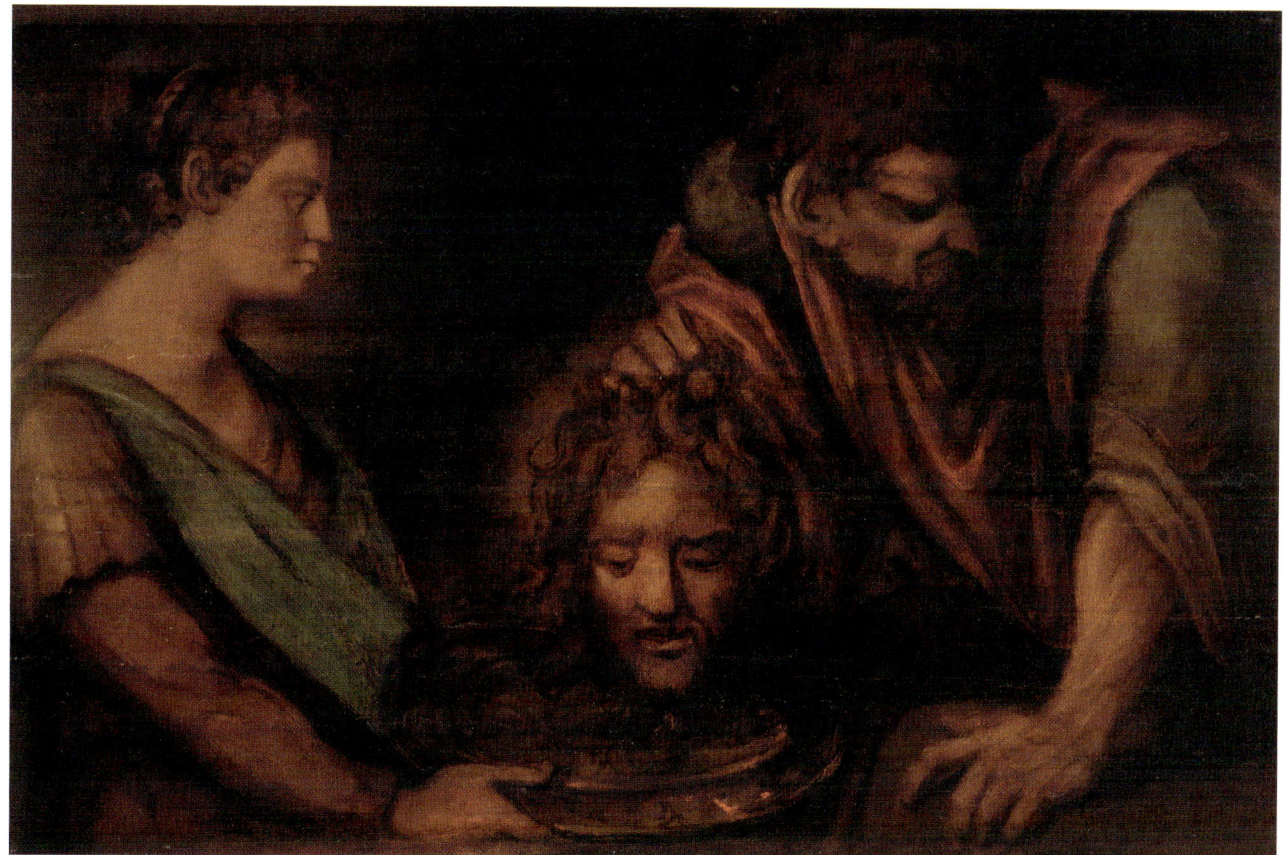

6.24 *Salome with the Head of John the Baptist and Executioner.* Oil on panel, 70 × 109 cm. Museo di Capodimonte, Naples

a craftsman in an environment that can have expected or
required little else. Susinno's memorable characterisation
of one of these late paintings as 'un gran pensierone' is
useful for reminding us of their cerebral quality as well
as emotional foundation.[29] Certainly, unless we appreciate
how expressive and disturbing is Polidoro's entire body
of work, even if the formal appearance varies, the artist is
denied what was doubtless most important to him, namely
his personal distinctiveness compared to Raphael's model
of elegance and refinement, in an age when recognisable
styles were necessary for success.[30]

The final mystery of Polidoro's life is his death. Vasari's
vivid account of his murder at the hand of a servant who
stole his money on the eve of the artist's return to Rome
has not been independently corroborated. The fact that he
excised from the 1568 edition of the artist's biography an
epitaph published in the first edition of 1550 suggests that
Vasari himself had developed significant doubts about the
account.[31] The destruction of so many archives in Sicily
will doubtless leave Polidoro's death, as well as the many
questions surrounding his last works, as mysteries forever.

Documented Chronology

1490 Birthdate of Polidoro according to G. Biffi in unpublished MS. Vite of Cremonese artists, written *c.*1750. Vasari (1550, pp. 765–6) has the artist working as a labourer in the Vatican Loggia at age 18, which puts his birthdate more plausibly to *c.*1498–1500.

1517 A Polidoro da Caravaggio lived in Rome near Santa Lucia alle Botteghe Oscure in 1517 (Gnoli 1936–8, p. 96, no source), who may or may not be our artist.

1521, 31 MARCH Completion of Jacopo Sansovino's sculpture for the Martelli altarpiece in Sant'Agostino in Rome, with subsidiary frescoes by Polidoro.

C.1523-4 In Naples according to a letter from Pietro Summonte to Marcantonio Michiel (Nicolini 1925, p. 164), frescoing a palace in chiaroscuro, with imagery derived from the Column of Trajan ('cavate dall'esempio della Colonna di Traiano').

1526, 20 JANUARY Payment for the erection of the scaffolding in Fra Mariano's chapel in San Silvestro al Quirinale, Rome, presumed to be for the fresco decorations of Polidoro (unpublished).

1527, 6 MAY Caught up in the Sack of Rome.

1527, 19 NOVEMBER Contract for an altarpiece for the church of Sant'Agostino in Naples (Zezza 1994, p. 136).

1528, 7 OCTOBER Letter from Polidoro in Messina to G. A. Milesi in Rome (Amati 1867, p. 12, no source). The artist had been in Naples just prior to this date.

1533, 5 FEBRUARY Contract for the *Altobasso Nativity* in Messina (published in Mauceri 1928, pp. 3–5).

1534, 4 MAY Documented in Syracuse, Augusta and Milazzo making drawings, probably military in nature, for the Viceroy of Sicily, Ettore Pignatelli (Leone de Castris 2001, p. 398, n. 33).

1534, BEFORE SEPTEMBER Installation of the *Way to Calvary* in Santissima Annunziata dei Catalani in Messina, as described in Alibrando 1534.

1535 Entry of Charles V into Messina with designs by Polidoro, as first described in Alibrando 1535.

1537 Polidoro and Maturino praised in the fourth book of Serlio's treatise, *Regoli generali di Architettura*, as painters of facades in Rome.

1543 Death date, according to Vasari (1550, p. 774).

Notes

1 ROME

1. On Biffi see Leone de Castris 2001, p. 9.
2. Vasari 1550, p. 765.
3. For the Loggia in general, the reader might start with Dacos 2008.
4. Nicolini 1925, pp. 164–5.
5. Franklin 2000, pp. 12–21. See also Deswarte-Rosa 1984, pp. 170–72, and 2004, pp. 247–90. Deswarte-Rosa was first responsible for discovering De Hollanda's ownership of Polidoro drawings. See Franklin 1997, pp. 78–80, for Vasari's use of a Polidoro drawing of a comparable type for the woodcut portrait of the so-called Morto da Feltre in the 1568 *Lives*, further supporting a Roman dating of the Lugt Foundation and Louvre drawings.
6. See Passavant 1839, I, p. 384 and note 1; and Lomazzo 1584.
7. Pliny 1952, xxxvii, 37.
8. This is argued most strenuously by Wolk-Simon in New York 2004, pp. 101–2.
9. Gnoli 1936–8, p. 96: 'Suo padre di cui ignoriamo il nome, era forse uno di quei tanti muratori che nei primi del Cinquecento da Caravaggio vennero stabilirsi a Roma, e Polidoro lo troviamo nel 1517 abitare a Santa Lucia alle Botteghe Oscure una casa presa a fitto da quella chiesa.'
10. Cruciani 1983, p. 472, as pointed out to me by Michael Hirst.
11. Dacos 2008, p. 330, note 1: 'una loggia dipinta; e lavorata de stucchi alla anticha: opra di raphaello'. A drawing commonly attributed to Polidoro and considered a reference point to this period is the copy from the lower part of one bay in the Vatican Loggia in the Wallace Collection, London, but I do not believe this to be by his hand (Leone de Castris 2001, p. 480, no. 148); nor is a comparable sheet in the Rust Collection (p. 492, no. 284).

12. Shearman 2003, pp. 807–11.
13. Vasari 1550–68, V, p. 448.
14. Dacos and Furlan 1987, p. 35, noted a graffito with the word 'CARAVAGIO', possibly Polidoro, in the cryptoporticus of the Domus Aurea.
15. Hirst 1981, p. 62, and Shearman 2003, p. 607.
16. For example, the lower part of the Sala di Costantino has been attributed to Polidoro but this is not convincing, as pointed out by Quednau 1986, p. 248. The artist was already independent by 1524, assuming these were executed last in sequence, and so cannot have been involved with this project. These frescoes were repainted by Giovanni Guerra at the end of the sixteenth century and cannot be easily judged (see the document published in Bertolotti 1883, pp. 44–5). Damaged frescoes of the Passion cycle in the Svizzeri chapel in the church of Santa Maria del Campo Santo Teutonico have often been attributed to Polidoro on stylistic grounds but the poor quality of the work does not recommend this view. It must have been Perino's commission, to judge from a drawing at the J. Paul Getty Museum recording his complete idea for the project. The patron was a captain of the Swiss Guard, Kaspar Röist, who had served Adrian VI, and the commission was possibly allocated during his pontificate, c.1522, and finished by a different painter from Perino's design, recalling too that Polidoro absented himself from Rome during that pontificate. Mancini had already rejected the Polidoro attribution in his treatise of painting of c.1621 (I, p. 269) and considered the frescoes to be by the hand of a German artist. See Wolk-Simon in Gouwens and Reiss 2005, pp. 263–5, which also, importantly,

addresses the subject of collaboration in general in Raphael's workshop after 1520. For a recent attribution to Polidoro, also unconvincing, of some decorative frescoes in the sacristy of San Pietro in Vincoli, see Castrovinci 2007, pp. 9–30.
17. The Louvre drawing was attributed to Polidoro by Voss 1920, I, p. 82. Shearman (1965, p. 35) cautioned on the attributional difficulties in his review of Pouncey and Gere 1962. The essays in Steinby 1996 review the literature on the villa. On the subject see Bull 2005, p. 143. For a debt to Raphael's Prado *Visitation* for the '*dextrarum iunctio*' handshake, see Gardner von Teuffel in Falomir Faus 2013, p. 65.
18. For the palace in general see Montini and Averini 1957 and Cogotti-Gigli 1995. See also Ravelli 1988 and Wolk-Simon 2002, pp. 11–15.
19. Vasari 1550, p. 769: 'nella casa di Baldassino, da Sant'Agostino, fecero graffiti e storie, e nel cortile alcune teste di imperatori sopra le finestre.' See also Vasari 1550, pp. 855–6, for mention of Perino's work in Palazzo Baldassini.
20. Frommel 1973, II, p. 23.
21. Cogotti-Gigli 1995, p. 7.
22. Ottawa 2009, pp. 146–8, entry by L. Wolk-Simon, as in the following two notes. See also Wolk-Simon 2002, pp. 11–21.
23. Ottawa 2009, pp. 146–8.
24. Ottawa 2009, pp. 146–8, no. 27.
25. Leone de Castris 2001, p. 488, no. 244. See also Paris 2005, p. 84, no. 47, entry by D. Cordellier.
26. The identification proposed by Cola is cited in Cogotti-Gigli 1995, pp. 69–70.
27. Hirst 1972, p. 162. Boucher 1991, p. 67.
28. Vasari 1550, p. 770. See Leone de Castris

2001, p. 428, no. 127. The attribution is due to Popham but Kultzen (1961a, p. 27) was apparently the first to relate it to Vasari's citation of the Martelli chapel in Sant'Agostino in Rome.

29. Leone de Castris 2001, p. 474, no. 76.

30. Pietro Summonte letter to Marcantonio Michiel (Nicolini 1925, pp. 164–5), *c*.1523–4: '[Maestro] Polidoro da Caravaggio, famoso in opere di chiaro e obscuro, benché iovene assai, dipinge oggi le quattro mura del cortiglio e una loggia nella casa del signor Ludovico di Montalto, dove sono di vaghe cose, per la maior parte cavate dall'esempio della Colonna di Traiano.'

31. For the Belli work see Vatican 1984–5, p. 378, no. 149a–c, and Vicenza 2000, pp. 114–15, 287, no. 1. Incidentally, Belli owned a '*quadro di Maturino*' according to his inventory of 1556.

32. For the Windsor drawing see Clayton 1999–2001, pp. 202–3, no. 61. Leone de Castris 2001, p. 493, no. 287; and Ottawa 2009, pp. 160–61, no. 32, entry by D. Franklin. Vasari 1550–68, IV, p. 625.

33. Vasari 1550, p. 768. Wolk-Simon in Gouwens and Reiss 2005, p. 265, recalls that both Perino del Vaga and Pellegrino da Modena also produced now lost works in this same church, a fresco of Saint Peter and other undefined figures. See also Wolk-Simon's account of Pellegrino da Modena specifically in the same church in Falomir Faus 2013, p. 109.

34. For the patron and chapel see especially Assonitis 2003, pp. 205–88, and Shearman 2003, pp. 247–50. See also Ravelli 1987 and Gnann 1991, pp. 134–9, especially for a reconstruction of the lower section. I reject the widely accepted notion that a compositional drawing in Chantilly is preparatory for this chapel. While by Polidoro's hand, the subject matter links it to a different as yet unidentified chapel. See also the doubts expressed by B. Peronnet in Chantilly 1997, p. 107. Similarly, a light and smoothly handled pen drawing in the Staatliche Museen zu Berlin related to the lower left part of the scene with the Noli Me Tangere and the narrative above must be a copy, as Kultzen and Gere long ago recognised (but see Mantua 1999, p. 343, no. 251, where the attribution is maintained).

35. Florence, Archivio di Stato, Corporazioni Religiose Soppresse dal Governo Francese, 102, Santa Maria Novella, vol. 327, Entrata e Uscita di Papa Clemente VII, 1523–7, fol. 43 left: E addì XX decto [Ianuarii MDXXVI] ducati sessantaquattro d'oro di camera pagati a Frate Mariano per fornire il palcho di Monte Cavallo ducati 64. Fol. 50 left: E adì XX detto [Aprilis MDXXVI] ducati dieci d'oro pagati a ser Pietropolo Marzi per dare a Pulidoro ducati 10. Fol. 53 left: E addì XXV di Maggio [MDXXVI] ducati dodici pagati a Polidoro per ordine di ser Pietro Polo Marzi ducati 12. Fol. 56 left: [XXX Exitus Iunii MDXXXVI] E ducati venticinque d'oro di camera pagati a ser Pietro Polo Marzi per dare a Polidoro ducati 25.

36. Vasari 1550, p. 769.

37. Stollhans 1992, pp. 506–25, provides a full account of the patron and his patronage at the church.

38. On a previous restoration see Rome 1970, p. 14, no. 9, entry by L. Mortari.

39. Sickel 2004, pp. 497–508, especially p. 506 for the dedication.

40. Ravelli 1987, p. 25.

41. Ravelli 1987, p. 135.

42. Vasari 1550, p. 590.

43. See Mantua 1999, p. 344, no. 252, entry by A. Gnann. Leone de Castris 2001, pp. 489–90, no. 260. This figure is almost interchangeable with the ancient Clelia on the Chiavica facade at Corte Savella.

44. Two of the three subjects were depicted by Giulio Romano and Penni in the chapel of Santissima Trinità dei Monti (now destroyed), known through copies and a Marcantonio Raimondi print, but there is no formal relation to Polidoro's work. For the chapel and its subject matter see Witcombe 2002, pp. 273–92, and Vannugli 2005, pp. 59–96. A Polidoro drawing of the *Feast in the House of Simon*, likely from his Roman period but related neither to the Quirinale fresco, nor stylistically to Giulio's and Penni's chapel, is reassembled by Joannides 2013, pp. 159–64.

45. Raymond of Capua 2003, pp. 304–5.

46. Turner 1961, pp. 275–87.

47. On the possible influence of Northern European art on Polidoro's depiction of landscape see the measured account in Meijer 1974, pp. 62–8. On this subject Gombrich 1966, pp. 107–21, remains fundamental.

48. Leone de Castris 2001, pp. 477–8, no. 124.

49. Castiglione 1910, p. 127.

50. Moro's attribution (1990, p. 55) of a double-sided drawing of a '*girotondo*' of children in the Ambrosiana (Leone de Castris 2001, p. 481, no. 167) to Boccaccino merits respect and would have implications for other attributions. The tentative attribution to Maturino in Mantua 1999, p. 372, no. 278, cannot itself be correct but further weakens belief in Polidoro's authorship. Presumably, the other genre drawing in the Ambrosiana is by the same hand (Leone de Castris 2001, p. 481, no. 168). A well-known drawing in the Louvre featuring five figures (Leone de Castris 2001, p. 484, no. 201), which might not be a genre study, seems not to be by Polidoro even if the attribution remains elusive (see McTavish 2008, p. 391). A drawing of a seated boy writing in the Ashmolean (Leone de Castris 2001, p. 483, no. 185) cannot be by Polidoro in my view either.

51. Franklin 2000, pp. 14–17. See also Gnann and Plomp 2012–13, p. 228, no. 88.

52. Leone de Castris 2001, p. 487, no. 227. This scene is traditionally called the 'card players' but, as Hugo Chapman pointed out to me, the figures are holding pieces of paper.

2 'A PARTICULAR GENIUS FOR FREEZES': THE FACADES

1. The title of this chapter is from Dufresnoy 1695 in Dryden's translation (p. 217).

2. Vasari 1996, p. 895 (Vasari 1550, p. 771). The first mention and praise in print of their collective achievement was in the fourth book of Serlio's treatise on architecture in 1537, fol. 191 verso. Kultzen should be given major credit for the most exacting research to date on the facades. In addition to his numerous articles, see his important review of Marabottini 1969 in the *Art Bulletin* in 1973, pp. 637–9. The most recent complete catalogue is found in Leone de Castris 2001. Gnann has attempted more than any scholar to establish a chronology for the facades. The most evolved attempt to separate the hands of Polidoro and Maturino is Dacos 1982, pp. 9–28.

3. Gere 1985–6, p. 63.

4. Alberti and Zuccaro 1604, p. 8. For the importance of Polidoro for the Zuccari see Brooks 2007, pp. 71–7, Strinati 1974, pp. 85–117, and Acidini Luchinat 1998–9, I, p. 12. Even earlier, in a letter of 1544 written by the doctor Papera to a colleague, Michelangelo and Polidoro are praised together in the context of their thorough absorption of ancient art (Bottari and Ticozzi 1822, V, p. 264).

5. Shearman 1967, pp. 61–2.

6. Lomazzo 1584, p. 481. In a later treatise Bisagno (1642, p. 232) distinguishes Polidoro among major artists by his 'martial' approach to the human body.

7. Brooks 2007, pp. 36 and 38.

8. On the Branconio palace see Frommel 1973, pp. 13–22, and Madrid 2012, p. 118.

9. Vasari 1550, p. 664.

10. Vasari 1550, p. 994.

11. Vasari 1550, p. 854. For a quotation from Polidoro in a drawing attributed to Perino see Hirst 1965, pp. 569–71. L. Wolk-Simon (written communication) ascribes this sheet to Guglielmo della Porta.

12. On Peruzzi see Pericoli Ridolfini 1982, pp. 653–78, and Macioce 1987, pp. 647–68.

13. Kultzen 1968, pp. 263–8. Leone de Castris 2001, p. 494, no. 4. For an attribution to Polidoro and Tamagni of some frescoes datable to the mid-1520s in the sacristy of the church see Castrovinci 2007, pp. 9–16.

14. Harb 2015, p. 157, nos 18–19.

15. Chiarini 1963, p. 554; Herrmann-Fiore 1983–4, pp. 268–72; Leone de Castris 2001, p. 495, no. 7. Herrmann-Fiore 1990, pp. 277–83, provides an extended exegesis of this commission. See also Herrmann-Fiore 2011, pp. 42–51.

16. Vasari 1550, p. 767. Kultzen 1975, pp. 296–301.

17. Leone de Castris 2001, pp. 502–3, no. 38. Crucial here is Kultzen 1977, p. 348.

18. Leone de Castris 2001, p. 496, no. 13.

19. Vasari 1907, Chapter XXV, p. 240, translation by L. S. Maclehose.

20. Vasari 1550, p. 767. See also Vasari 1907, p. 299.

21. Pliny 1952, pp. 271 and 283.

22. Alberti 1966, p. 82.

23. Leonardo 1989, p. 15, translation by M. Kemp.

24. This facade near San Silvestro cannot be that mentioned by Vasari as having been done in a similar location in collaboration with Pellegrino da Modena, who died in 1523, so it was a relatively early work (Vasari 1550, p. 766). See Wolk-Simon in Falomir Faus 2013, pp. 107–8. For Bernini's borrowings see Grassi 1964, pp. 174–7.

25. Vasari 1550, p. 772. See Kultzen 1967, pp. 409–11. Leone de Castris 2001, p. 497, no. 18. Bull 2005, pp. 268–9.

26. Leone de Castris 2001, pp. 498–9, no. 19. See Frommel 1973, pp. 198–206, for the other Palazzo Gaddi.

27. Leone de Castris 2001, pp. 500–01, no. 29.

28. See Vasari 1550, V, p. 769. Kultzen 1961b, pp. 207–12, and Leone de Castris 2001, p. 502, no. 35.

29. Leone de Castris 2001, pp. 473–4, no. 75.

30. P. L. Casella, *De Primis Italiae Colonis* (1606). Translation from Gombrich 1987, p. 226.

31. Leone de Castris 2001, p. 495, no. 6. For the restoration see Masini, Miracola, Colucci 2013. For Taddeo Zuccari's coloured frescoes in the same location see Gere 1969, pp. 101–2, and Brooks 2007, p. 54. For a nuanced discussion of a drawn copy attributed to Perino after one of the frescoes see Cieri Via 2012, pp. 63–74.

32. For the Bufalo family see Wren Christian 2010, pp. 280–86, no. 8.

33. As elucidated by Kultzen 1959–60, pp. 99–120.

34. Kultzen (1973, p. 637) writes of the 'objectivity' of the facade style.

35. Most authoritative to date on the technique of the frescoes is Masini, Miracola, Colucci 2013, pp. 105–12, essay by A. M. Marinelli.

36. Vasari 1550, p. 771.

37. Agosti and Farinella 1984, pp. 353–4. The authors reject, however, one of Kultzen's proposed quotations in note 5. Indicative of this absorption is the example properly cited by Ravelli 1996, pp. 67–8, of the so-called Muse sarcophagus in the Louvre, which influenced Polidoro's fresco of the Muses and Poets at Casino del Bufalo, but there are no explicit quotations. More compelling are the relationships proposed for the same frescoes by Kultzen 1959–60, pp. 109–14. See also Haskell and Penny 1982, p. 195 and note 17, for a quotation from the so-called Borghese Dancers on Palazzo Milesi.

38. For a discussion of this dichotomy in Ligorio, for example, see H. Burns in Gaston 1988, pp. 19–92.

39. Vasari 1550–68, IV, p. 307.

40. Castelvetro 1571, pp. 103–4.

41. Leone de Castris 2001, p. 484, no. 196. The drawing compares stylistically to one in Stockholm once owned by De Hollanda and so likely a Roman period drawing, featuring a red chalk figure study of a Triton. This might tentatively be linked to the lost facade mentioned by Vasari featuring *mostri marini* in San Rocco a Ripetta (Franklin 2001, p. 16).

42. Ottawa 2009, pp. 156–7, no. 30, entry by R. Eitel-Porter. For the significant later dating of the commission see Bilancia 2014, p. 264.

43. Leone de Castris 2001, p. 467, no. 3. For the former attribution see Amsterdam 1981, cat. 135. The subject of this drawing, Caio Murno, a Roman general, was forced to flee the city by the dictator Sulla, taking refuge in the swamps of Minturno, where he was to have been assassinated but escaped.

44. The Weimar drawing was first attributed to Polidoro by Oberhuber. See also Leone de Castris 2001, p. 492, no. 286, and Demele 2010, pp. 53–4, no. 27.

45. Herrmann-Fiore 1983–4, p. 210, and Herrmann-Fiore 1990, p. 276.

46. Ottawa 2009, no. 31, pp. 158–9, entry by D. McTavish.

47. It appeared at Christie's, London, on 8 July 2003, lot 2. The attribution was not then widely accepted. It was published by Leone de Castris 2004, p. 40, dated to the early Roman period.

48. Winner 1967, pp. 115–16, no. 72. Gere (1971, p. 66) supported the attribution with the most vigour. See also Mantua 1999, p. 367, no. 275. Monbeig Goguel attributed the drawing to Francesco Salviati. Kultzen (1990, pp. 124–31) refers the ancient sculpture of a lion hunt in the Capitoline to a field on Palazzo Ricci by Polidoro, but as an inspiration not a direct quotation. A double-sided drawing in the V&A with copies after the antique (Leone de Castris 2001, p. 480, no. 145) usually attributed to Polidoro is too weak to be considered autograph and may have more than one hand.

49. As pointed out by Canedy 1976, p. 20, note 53. Leone de Castris 2001, p. 478, no. 131.

50. Leone de Castris 2001, p. 480, no. 143. The two studies of male figures have been described as studies after the antique but given the presence of books they may equally be prophets or saints.

51. Canedy 1976, p. 20, note 53, points to a sarcophagus later copied by Girolamo da Carpi thought to be in the church of Sant'Angelo in Pescheria during the sixteenth century, now at Wilton House, Wiltshire.

52. Franklin 2000, p. 18, and Turner 2000, pp. 26–7, no. 5. Leone de Castris has doubted the attribution.

53. Spencer 1960, pp. 176–8.

54. Leone de Castris 2001, p. 472, no. 56. Another splendid example, formerly attributed perfectly reasonably to Giovanni da Udine, is in the Louvre (Leone de Castris 2001, p. 485, no. 206). To judge on stylistic grounds, the drawing appears to be after 1527 and so provides, on the verso, rare evidence of a later interest in ancient motifs (published in Paris 2007, p. 75, no. 32).

55. P. P. Bober in Gaston 1988, p. 287, writes that by his mid-30s Ligorio 'was already a respected antiquary, having relinquished his earlier occupations as a facade painter of grottesche for topographical and archaeological investigations'.

3 FLIGHT TO NAPLES

1. Vasari 1550, p. 772.

2. Vincenzo Borghini expanded on this episode involving Vasari in Naples in his *Selva di notizie* (Barocchi, I, 1971, p. 630). Vasari's attitude towards Naples was criticised by De Dominici in his 'Life of Lama', II, 1742–5, p. 196. On this subject see Rubin 1995, pp. 142–3, and Loconte 2008, pp. 438–59.

3. Stumpel 1990, pp. 37–9. Shearman 2003, pp. 379–80. Madrid 2012, pp. 88–93, no. 1.

4. Fritz 1997. Madrid 2012, pp. 275–8, no. 76.

5. Vasari 1550, pp. 694–5. For Penni's biography and death see Madrid 2012, p. 174.

6. Zezza 1994, p. 136. For a more cautious view of Polidoro's potential involvement in this commission see Leone de Castris 2001, p. 287. See also Naldi 2009.

7. De Pietri 1634, p. 203.

8. Vasari 1550, p. 772: 'Onde egli lavorando a opere per alcuni pittori, fece in Santa Maria della Grazia un San Pietro nella maggior cappella; e così aiutò in molte cose que'pittori, più per campare la vita che per altro.' The work is mentioned by D'Engenio 1624, p. 205. For a more specific location to the left of the high altar see Sarnelli 1685, p. 152.

9. De Dominici 1742, II, pp. 41–2. See also Leone de Castris 2001, p. 17, note 54, who suggests the account may be invented. On Sabatini in general see Padula 1986, pp. 210–15.

10. For Saint Peter in Naples see Villano 1526, pp. 19–24, and Capaccio 1634, p. 81: 'il quale nel viaggio d'Antiochia in Roma passò per Napoli, e in presenza sua fè cader tutti gli idoli, e trà gli altri Pastore e Polluce che sopra gli angoli di detto timpano eran collocati. E già si veggono in quel rimanente due busti tronchi di quei fratelli che per gloria di Napoli non mai di là devono rimoversi.'

11. Vasari 1996, p. 896: The original Italian is given in Vasari 1550, p. 772: 'fece ancora in Sant'Angelo, allato alla Pescheria di Napoli, una tavolina a olio, nella quale è una Nostra Donna ed alcuni ignudi d'anime cruciate; la quale di disegno più che di colorito è tenuta bellissima: similmente alcuni quadri in quella dell'altar maggiore di figure intere sole, nel medesimo modo lavorate'. For the closest example of another major painter of this period having to work on framing an icon see Perino del Vaga at San Marcello al Corso in Rome (Parma Armani 1986,

pp. 257–8). See also the more local example by Severo Ierace, a follower of Andrea Sabatini, for a commission in Campania published by Leone de Castris in Palermo 1995–6, p. 140, no. 27. See also the survey in Naldi 2001, pp. 15–30.

12. Villano 1526, p. 15.

13. Leone de Castris 2001, p. 492, no. 288.

14. D'Engenio 1623, p. 450. He also lamented their dispersal. Carletti (1776, p. 63) mentioned that of the many different paintings by Polidoro once in this church only those on the high altar remained.

15. Celano 1692, IV, p. 249.

16. Leone de Castris 2001, p. 480, no. D151. See also Scrase 2011, pp. 527–8, no. 547.

17. Celano 1792, IV, pp. 99–100.

18. See the example in Casanova Uccella 1976, no. 28.

19. Hirst 1989, pp. 238–40.

20. Folds McCullagh and Giles 1997, p. 368, no. 599. Leone de Castris 2001, fig. 358, illustrates a crude painted copy in a private collection after the entire first design, for which see also Pugliatti 1990, pp. 5–6. There is also a partial copy at Chatsworth House (1070).

21. Sannazzaro 2009, p. 95.

22. Capaccio 1634, p. 858: 'e con diligenze, e spese, conservò quella bellissima tavola di Polidoro, dove sono dipinte l'anime del Purgatorio, che con tante fatiche si hebbe dalla chiesa di Santa Maria delle Grazie nella pietra del pesce, cosa di molto valore'. Capaccio's text was completed by 1630 but not published until 1634.

23. Leone de Castris 2001, p. 490, no. 262. Gnann and Plomp 2012–13, p. 231, no. 90. Other drawings held in the Albertina have been related to this altarpiece but the relationship is not entirely convincing (Leone de Castris 2001, nos 264, 268).

24. See Steen Hansen 2014, pp. 337–40, for a more extended interpretation suggesting that Polidoro was portraying a desecrated Rome as a counter to a more divinely saved Naples. Polidoro included Castel Sant'Angelo in a genre drawing now in the Musée Atger, Montpellier.

25. Turner 2000, no. 6; Leone de Castris 2001, p. 488, no. 245. Conversely, an autograph drawing in Haarlem cannot relate to this painting as the Virgin's breasts are covered (Gnann and Plomp 2012–13, p. 233, no. 91). On the subject in Naples see Strazzullo 1954, pp. 107–26.

26. Vasari 1550, p. 772. Alessandro Nova pointed out to me one other instance, in the second edition of the life of Leonardo da Vinci, in which a name is left out. In the life of Andrea del Sarto, Vasari (1550, p. 725) mentions that a version of the *Sacrifice of Isaac* was sent to Naples, but he was unable to discover the location and left it blank.

27. Capaccio 1634, p. 857, for Rota, and p. 859 for Revertera. See Giusti and Leone de Castris 1985, pp. 44–6. For the history of Palazzo Rota see Pane 2014, pp. 100–18. For a recent discovery of a decorative fresco in a Neopolitan palace, perhaps distantly related to Polidoro, see Zezza 2016, pp. 17–22.

28. For these paintings in general see Whittaker and Clayton 2007, pp. 56–64. Despite Dacos's attribution to Maturino, if we accept they were painted in Naples in *c*.1527–8 they must be by Polidoro alone. Most scholars placed them earlier, to *c*.1523–5, until Gnann (1997, pp. 198–214) proposed the later dating of *c*.1527–8, which is convincing on stylistic grounds. Marabottini attempted to identify them with the set from Palazzo Rota in Naples (1969, p. 254) but this is problematic as those were painted in grisaille, as Shearman pointed out in 1983, p. 199. Leone de Castris (2001, pp. 268–9), however, defended the connection to Palazzo Rota and draws attention to the fact that Celano referenced two different rooms in the palace in which Polidoro worked. On the principal subject see the classic study by Vertova 1979, pp. 104–21.

29. Vasari 1550, p. 694.

30. Joannides 1983, p. 48. See also Gnann 1997, p. 205.

31. Shearman 1983, p. 199.

32. D'Engenio 1623, p. 446. Later descriptions and inventories attribute several religious works, facade frescoes and even portraits in Neapolitan collections to Polidoro but again, these references do not inspire confidence. Capaccio 1634, p. 858, is the earliest with a painting of Saint Cecilia in the palace of Don Antonio Carmignano. See also Ruotolo 1973, pp. 149–50, for three more paintings attributed to Polidoro in the Antinori palace; and Romanelli 1815, III, pp. 91, 97, 112 and 117, for others in different locations.

33. Whittaker and Clayton 2007, p. 92, no. 17.

34. Franklin 1994, Chapter 6.

4 IN MESSINA

1. Laschke 1993, p. 9. Vasari's account of Polidoro in Messina is 1550, pp. 772–4.

2. Leone de Castris 2001, p. 323, based on Amati 1867, p. 12.

3. Leone de Castris 2001, pp. 381 and 398, no. 33, based on Viscuso in Palermo 1999, pp. 28, 479, n. L.

4. Leone de Castris 2001, p. 323. An impressive autograph head study in red chalk at Windsor Castle, sometimes related to the Saint Thomas, does not seem sufficiently close to justify the connection (Leone de Castris 2001, p. 493, no. 292).

5. For the bronze see Shearman in Vicenza 2000, pp. 290–92, no. 4.

6. Buonfiglio e Costanzo 1606, fol. 32 verso. Hackert and Brano 1792, p. 17.

7. See Leone de Castris 2001, p. 330. For the destruction of the original see Di Marzo 1858–62, p. 229.

8. Susinno 1724, p. 60. See also Hackert and Brano 1792, p. 17, for praise of these frescoes.

9. Leone de Castris 2001, p. 363.

10. Arguments pertaining to the Deodato Guinaccia attribution are reviewed by Chelazzi Dini 1989, p. 95.

11. Gabrielli 1971, pp. 207–8. La Farina 1840, p. 37, records the two paintings in the church of the Maddalena in Messina, suggesting they were removed there after the earthquake of 1783.

12. Cambridge 1985, no. 46. Leone de Castris 2001, p. 473, no. 65. Closer to the Chatsworth drawing than the finished painting is a damaged study in the Rijksmuseum, Amsterdam, for the same figure but with an angel above his shoulder (Leone de Castris 2001, p. 467, no. 2).

13. Naples 1988–9, p. 108, no. IX.2.

14. See Mauceri 1928, p. 503, for the contract and restoration.

15. Marabottini points out that there was an apparatus of angels for the entry of Charles V (1969, p. 215, note 231) and proposes the study could be for that design. However, the angels are treated from the same angle, which suggests they were intended for a painting and not a three-dimensional object.

16. Jaffe 1985, pp. 157–9, is crucial for this artist.

17. Ravelli 1978, p. 181, no. 75. See also Leone de Castris 2001, p. 488, no. 243.

18. On Stefano Giordano in general see Pugliatti 1993, pp. 141–52. See also Leone de Castris in Naples 1988–9, pp. 141–5. Whether other paintings in Messina were designed by Polidoro and executed by Giordano there is rarely secure proof, but Leone de Castris (2001) is right to consider works like his plate 88 (p. 318) as a possible collaboration, or at least works based directly on Polidoro drawings. A magnificent Polidoro head study in the Uffizi has been plausibly associated with the preparation of this work (Leone de Castris 2001, p. 474, no. 82), overturning a proposed change of attribution to Peter de Kempeneer (Dacos 1999, pp. 112–17). The San Giacomo in Camaro outside Messina (Leone de Castris 2001, p. 423, fig. 539) appears to be yet another example of a Stefano Giordano painting after Polidoro's design. Susinno associates no less than three paintings of Saint James with Polidoro, two with predellas: the example at Camaro, plus those at Messina and Catania. The Malta *Crucifix* would seem to be another of these collaborative paintings (see Hirst 1989, p. 239). Note that the large drawing by Polidoro of a crucifix with a landscape, formerly on the art market in London (Leone de Castris 2001, p. 481, no. 155), is now in the Metropolitan Museum of Art, New York, inv. 2003.372.

19. Zeri and Campagna Cicala 1992, p. 94, no. 64.

20. The bibliography on the entry of Charles V is vast but Leone de Castris 2001, Chapter 16, is the best place to start.

21. Alibrando 1535.

22. Scorza 2012, p. 125.

23. One proposal for Polidoro as architect is presented by Di Giacomo 2005, pp. 85–8.

24. Leone de Castris 2001, p. 479, no. 139.

25. Samperi 1644, p. 466. See also Pugliatti 1990, pp. 6–10, which attempts, unconvincingly in my view, to relate the drawings related to the Naples *Entombment* to the lost Candelora curtain cover.

26. Buonfiglio e Costanzo 1606, fol. 26 verso. For the drawing see Leone de Castris 2001, p. 476, no. 105. Hirst's citation of Davidson's attribution is in 1989, p. 239.

27. Gallo 1756–8, p. 233.

28. Buonfiglio e Costanzo 1606, fol. 25 verso. For the drawing see Leone de Castris 2001, pp. 334–5 and p. 476, no. 110.

29. Leone de Castris 2001, p. 489, no. 251.

30. Bartsch 1982, 29, p. 159.

31. I owe this information to Rick Scorza.

32. Lavin 1975, p. 174.

33. Leone de Castris 2001, p. 475, no. 93.

34. Shearman 2003, pp. 460, 586 and 592. Jones and Penny 1983, p. 175.

35. Franklin 2010, pp. 160–62.

5 THE *SPASMO* OF 1534

1. For the text see Alibrando 1999. The copy is found in the Biblioteca Regionale Universitaria in Messina (segn. inv. B1/3). See also Lorenzini 2002, pp. 359–70, and Genovese 2011, pp. 447–51.

2. For the painting see Leone de Castris 2001, X.8.

3. Madrid 2012, pp. 94–102, no. 4. See also Vatican 1984–5, pp. 272–6, no. 102.

4. Leone de Castris 2001, p. 484, no. 193. I find it difficult to sustain the attribution to Polidoro of a red chalk drawing of trumpeters in the National Gallery of Scotland, Edinburgh.

5. For a general discussion of the subject in this period see Hamburgh 1981, pp. 45–70.

6. In a preparatory drawing presumably for this painting in a private collection, the Virgin is partly conscious but still more vulnerable than in Raphael's painting, indicating that Polidoro was more than fully aware of the degrees available to him in her treatment (Leone de Castris 2001, pp. 467–8, no. 10).

7. Vasari does not appear to have known Alibrando's book (1550, pp. 772–3). His text in the 1568 edition is essentially unchanged.

8. Baxandall 1972, pp. 113–14.

9. Kemp 1992, p. 11 (his translation).

10. Alibrando 1999, p. 39.

11. Leone de Castris (2001, pp. 388–9) argues that Polidoro was extensively involved with printmaking in Messina.

12. Samperi 1644, V, Chapter XXIII, pp. 607–19.

13. As pointed out by S. Ginzburg in Alibrando 1999, p. 42.

14. I am aware of a vivid account of 1518 involving a lost altarpiece by Gerino da Pistoia featuring Saints Barbara and Mary Magdalen. It describes how this painting was carried from the artist's house to the church of Santissima Annunziata in Pistoia accompanied by monks singing, music, candles and '*molto popolo*'. Archivio Storico di Pistoia, P.E., no. 86, Cronache dei convento dei Servi, fol. 169 (cited in Pistoia 1996, p. 156).

15. But see Genovese 2011, pp. 451–5, for a different interpretation accepting the artist's generosity in donating his painting without cost.

16. Franklin 2001, Chapter 12, stresses this point in relation to Vasari's art.

6 MESSINA: THE LAST PAINTINGS

1. La Farina 1835, pp. 17–29.
2. See Leone de Castris 2004, pp. 22–3, for a review of attributions other than to Polidoro for this group of paintings. See also Previtali 1978, p. 28; Chelazzi Dini 1980, p. 102; Campagna Cicala 1988, pp. 109–23; Chelazzi Dini 1989, p. 95; and Campagna Cicala 1996. See also Giusti in Naples 1988–9, pp. 193–5, and Keith, Moore Ede, Plazzotta 2004, pp. 36–47, for valuable technical analysis of the late paintings.
3. Cerasuolo 2009, p. 255 and figs 2, 4–6. See also Cerasuolo 2017.
4. Susinno 1724, p. 61.
5. Susinno 1724, p. 61.
6. Gnann 1993, pp. 159–71. The painting was first recorded in Gallo 1756–8, p. 215.
7. Susinno 1724, p. 61. An *Agony in the Garden* by Polidoro is mentioned in the Ruffo Collection (Ruffo 1916, p. 30).
8. For a proposal for a 'late' drawing by Polidoro see Franklin 2010, pp. 155–8.
9. Vasari 1550, p. 770.
10. Biondo 1549, pp. 19–20.
11. Ferrari (1990, pp. 8–9), like most scholars, addresses the paintings in the sequence Vatican, Capodimonte, Pouncey Collection, and as preparatory *bozzetti*. See, most recently, Cerasuolo 2009, pp. 253–65. My proposal that none of these sketches is preparatory was hinted at by De Marchi 2014, pp. 128–9, note 19.
12. See Held 1980, pp. 6–8, for a summary. On the oil sketch in general see Ferrari 1990. But see also Freeman Bauer (1978, p. 45), who cautions that the earlier history of the oil sketch is complex.
13. Marabottini 1967, pp. 170–85. Bonn 1999, pp. 556–7, no. 332, entry by A. Nesselrath.
14. Keith, Moore Ede, Plazzotta 2004, pp. 36–47.
15. Susinno 1724, pp. 58–9.
16. Susinno 1724, p. 61.
17. Leone de Castris (Naples 1988–9, p. 180) rightly questions linking the work with the description in Susinno 1724, p. 60, because that work in the refectory of the Carmine was probably a fresco and not a panel painting. He proposes (2001, p. 482, no. 174) a drawing in the Pushkin Museum, Moscow, as a preparatory work for that refectory painting.
18. Gnann 1993, pp. 159–71.
19. Leone de Castris 2001, p. 458.
20. Leone de Castris 2001, p. 458.
21. Leone de Castris 2001, pp. 452–4. See first Campagna Cicala 1988, pp. 109–21.
22. For this painting see Leone de Castris 2004.
23. A portrait in the National Gallery, London, attributed by Leone de Castris to Polidoro, is by Rosso following Zeri, I would maintain, as recently supported with force by Natali (Florence 2014, pp. 264–5, no. VII.5).
24. Leone de Castris 2001, p. 446.
25. Leone de Castris 2001, p. 21.
26. For the Carmelites see the discussion in Chapter 4.
27. Caponetto 1999, pp. 73–4.
28. Contrary to a veiled Lutheranism, D'Agostino (1989) finds instead the seeds of the Counter-Reformation in the unpretentious devotional quality of Polidoro's late paintings.
29. Susinno 1724, p. 60.
30. Steen Hansen (2014, pp. 340–53) credits the artist's suffering and reaction in religious terms to the Sack of Rome as the source of this apparent pessimism in the later work.
31. As pointed out to me by David Ekserdjian. Vasari 1550–68, IV, p. 470.

Selected Bibliography

ABBATE 1980
V. Abbate, 'Un trittico di Stefano Giordano', *Prospettiva*, 27 (1980), pp. 72–9

ABBATE AND PREVITALI 1972
F. Abbate and G. Previtali, *La Pittura napoletana del '500, in storia di Napoli*, 2 vols (Naples and Cava dei Tirreni, 1972)

ACIDINI LUCHINAT 1998–9
C. Acidini Luchinat, *Taddeo e Federico Zuccari, fratelli pittori del Cinquecento*, 2 vols (Milan and Rome, 1998–9)

AGOSTI AND FARINELLA 1984
G. Agosti and V. Farinella, 'Calore del marmo. Practica e tipologia delle deduzioni iconografiche', in *Memoria dell'antico nell'arte italiana*, I, ed. S. Settis (Turin, 1984), pp. 373–440

ALBERTI 1966
L. B. Alberti, *Leon Battista Alberti on Painting*, ed. J. Spencer (New Haven and London, 1966)

ALBERTI AND ZUCCARO 1604
R. Alberti and F. Zuccaro, *Origine e progresso dell'Accademia del disegno de' pittori, scultori e architetti di Roma* (Pavia, 1604)

ALIBRANDO 1534
N. J. Alibrando, *Il Spasmo di Maria Vergine* (Messina, 1534)

ALIBRANDO 1535
N. J. Alibrando, *Il Triompho, il qual fece Messina nella Intrata del Imperator Carlo* (Messina, 1535), ed. B. Agosti, G. Alfano and I. di Majo (Naples, 1999)

ALIBRANDO 1999
C. G. Alibrando, 'Il Spasmo di Maria Vergine' (1534), in *Ottave per un dipinto di Polidoro da Caravaggio a Messina*, ed. B. Agosti, G. Alfano and I. di Majo (Naples, 1999)

AMATI 1867
G. Amati, 'Interno ad una lettera inedita di Polidoro da Caravaggio', in *Il Buonarroti*, II (1867), pp. 4–12

AMSTERDAM 1981
Italiaanse Tekeningen II de XVde eu XVIde eeuw, ed. L. C. Frerichs (Amsterdam, 1981)

ARETINO 1548
P. Aretino, *Lettere sull'arte di Pietro Aretino* (1548), ed. E. Camesasca (Milan, 1957)

ARMENINI 1586
G. B. Armenini, *De'veri precetti della pittura* (Ravenna, 1586)

ASSONITIS 2003
A. Assonitis, 'Art and Savonarolian Reform at San Silvestro al Quirinale', *Archivium Fratrum Praedictorum*, 80 (2003), pp. 205–88

BACOU 1981
R. Bacou, *Italian Drawings from the Mariette Collection at the Louvre* (Milan, 1981)

BAGLIONE 1642
G. Baglione, *Le Vite de'Pittori, Scultori et Architetti* (Rome, 1642)

BARBERA 1987
G. Barbera, 'Il Libro illustrato a Messina dal Quattrocento all'Ottocento', in *Cinque secoli di stampa a Messina*, ed. G. Molonia (Messina, 1987), pp. 389–497

BAROCCHI 1971
Scritti d'arte del Cinquecento, ed. P. Barocchi, 3 vols (Milan and Naples, 1971–7)

BARRICELLI 1984
A. Barricelli, 'La Pittura in Sicilia dalla fine del Quattrocento alla controriforma', in *Storia dell'arte in Sicilia*, II (Naples, Palermo, 1984)

BARTSCH 1982
A. Bartsch, *The Illustrated Bartsch*, ed. W. L. Strauss, vol. 29 (Norwalk, CT, 1982)

BAUMGART 1931
F. Baumgart, 'Beitrage zu Raphael und seiner Werkstatt', *Munchner Jahrbuch der Bildenden Kunst*, 8 (1931), pp. 49–68

BAUMGARTEN 1908
P. M. Baumgarten, 'Cartularium vetus Campi Sancti Teutonicorum de Urbe', *Römische Quartalsschrift*, XLI, suppl. (1908), p. 90

BAXANDALL 1972
M. Baxandall, *Painting and Experience in Fifteenth-century Italy* (Oxford, 1972)

BEAN 1982
J. Bean, *15th and 16th-century Italian Drawings in the Metropolitan Museum of Art*, eds J. Bean and L. Turcic (New York, 1982)

BELOTTI 1956
B. Belotti, *Gli Eccellenti bergamaschi* (Bergamo, 1956)

BELTRAMELLI 1795
G. Beltramelli, *Pittori Bergamaschi, Postille alle Vite del Tassi, ms. 1795*, ed. F. Mazzini (Milan, 1970)

BERTOLOTTI 1881
A. Bertolotti, *Artisti Lombardi a Roma nei secoli XV, XVI e XVII* (Milan, 1881)

BERTOLOTTI 1883
A. Bertolotti, *Artisti Modenesi, Parmensi e della Lunigiana in Roma* (Modena, 1883)

BILANCIA 2014
F. Bilancia, 'L'Immagine di ponte e il palazzo di Alberto Serra in Via dei Coronari a Roma', in *La Festa delle arti*, eds V. Cazzato, S. Roberto, M. Bevilacqua (Rome, 2014)

BILARDO 1972–4
A. Bilardo, 'Dipinti inediti in territorio messinese', *Archivio storico messinese* (1972–4), pp. 167–86

BIONDO 1549
M. Biondo, *Della Nobilissima Pittura* (Venice, 1549)

BIRKE AND KERTÉSZ 1992
V. Birke and J. Kertész, *Die Italienischen Zeichnungen der Albertina. Generalverzeichnis, Band I, Inv.1–1200* (Vienna, Cologne and Weimar, 1992)

BISAGNO 1642
F. Bisagno, *Trattato della Pittura* (Venice, 1642)

BOLAFFIO 1890
L. F. Bolaffio, *Guida di Napoli e suoi contorni* (Milan, 1890)

BOLOGNA 1959
R. Bologna, *Roviale Spagnolo e la pittura napoletana del Cinquecento* (Naples, 1959)

BOLTEN 1969
J. Bolten, 'Messer Ulisse Severino da Cingoli', *Master Drawings*, VII (1969), pp. 123–46

BONIFACIO 1977
A. Bonifacio, *Gli Annuali dei tipografi messinesi del Cinquecento* (Vibo Valentia, 1977)

BONN 1999
'Hoch Renaissance im Vatikan 1503–1534', in *Kunst und Kultur im Rom der Papste I*, ed. P. Kruse (Bonn, 1999)

BORA 1979
G. Bora, *I Disegni lombardi e genovesi del Cinquecento* (Treviso, 1979)

BOREA 1961
E. Borea, 'Vicenda di Polidoro da Caravaggio', *Arte antica e moderna*, 13–16 (1961), pp. 209–27

BOREA 1962
E. Borea, 'Grazia e furia in Marco Pino', *Paragone*, 151 (1962), pp. 24–52

BORGHINI 1584
R. Borghini, *Il Riposo* (Florence, 1584)

BOTTARI 1929
S. Bottari, *Il Duomo di Messina* (Messina, 1929)

BOTTARI 1954
S. Bottari, *La Cultura figurativa in Sicilia* (Messina/Florence, 1954)

BOTTARI AND TICOZZI 1822
G. Bottari and S. Ticozzi, *Raccolta di lettere sulla pittura, scultura ed architettura*, V (Milan, 1822)

BOUCHER 1991
B. Boucher, *Jacopo Sansovino* (London and New Haven, 1991)

BRAHAM 1981
H. Braham, *The Princes Gate Collection* (London, 1981)

BROOKS 2007
J. Brooks, *Taddeo and Federico Zuccaro: Artist-Brothers in Renaissance Rome* (Los Angeles, 2007)

BULL 2005
M. Bull, *The Mirror of the Gods* (Oxford, 2005)

BUONFIGLIO E COSTANZO 1606
G. Buonfiglio e Costanzo, *Messina città nobilissima* (Venice, 1606; Messina, 1738)

BUSACCA 1873
A. Busacca, *Guida di Messina* (Messina, 1873)

BYAM SHAW 1976
J. Byam Shaw, *Drawings by Old Masters at Christ Church, Oxford* (Oxford, 1976)

BYAM SHAW 1982
J. Byam Shaw, *The Italian Drawings of the Frits Lugt Collection* (Paris, 1982)

CAMBRIDGE 1985
P. Pouncey, 'The Achievement of a Connoisseur', in *Italian Old Master Drawings*, eds J. Stock and D. Scrase (Cambridge, 1985)

CAMPAGNA CICALA 1985
F. Campagna Cicala, 'Una Copia da Polidoro da Caravaggio di Stefano Giordano', in *Scritti in onore di Vittorio di Paola* (Messina, 1985), pp. 63–72

CAMPAGNA CICALA 1988
F. Campagna Cicala, 'Riflessi di Marco Pino e Pedro Campaña sull'attività di Deodato Guinaccia. Confronti e ipotesi', in *La Cultura degli arazzi fiamminghi di Marsala tra Fiandre, Spagna e Italia: Atti del convegno* (Palermo, 1988), pp. 109–23

CAMPAGNA CICALA 1996
F. Campagna Cicala, *Aspetti della pittura a Messina nel Cinquecento* (Messina, 1996)

CAMPAGNA CICALA 1997
F. Campagna Cicala, 'Una Scheda per il periodo estremo di Polidoro', in *Scritti in onore di Alessandro Marabottini* (Rome, 1997), pp. 135–8

CAMPORI 1870
G. Campori, *Raccolta di cataloghi ed inventari inediti* (Modena, 1870)

CANEDY 1976
N. Canedy, *The Roman Sketchbook of Girolamo da Carpi* (London and Leiden, 1976)

CAPACCIO 1634
G. C. Capaccio, *Il Forastiero dialogi* (Naples, 1634)

CAPONETTO 1999
S. Caponetto, *The Protestant Reformation in Sixteenth-century Italy* (Kirksville, MO, 1999)

CAPUANI 1973
P. Capuani, 'Polidoro Caldara pittore eccellente e architetto d'elezione', *La Rivista di Bergamo* (1973), pp. 5–12

CARLETTI 1776
N. Carletti, *Topografia universale della città di Napoli* (Naples, 1776)

CASANOVA UCCELLA 1976
Arte a Gaeta. Dipinti dal XII al XVIII secolo, ed. M. L. Casanova Uccella (Gaeta, 1976)

CASSIRER 1920
K. Cassirer, 'Zeichnungen Polidoro da Caravaggios in den Berliner Museen', *Jahrbuch der Preussischen Kunstsammlungen*, XLI (1920), pp. 344–58

CASTELVETRO 1571
L. Castelvetro, *Castelvetro on the Art of Poetry* (1571), ed. A. Bongiorno (Binghamton, 1984)

CASTIGLIONE 1910
B. Castiglione, *Il Cortegiano*, ed. V. Cian, 2nd ed. (Florence, 1910)

CASTROVINCI 2007
R. Castrovinci, 'La Sacrestia di S. Pietro in Vincoli', *Storia dell'arte*, N.S., 18, 118 (2007), pp. 9–30

CAVALCASELLE AND CROWE 1882–5
G. B. Cavalcaselle and J. A. Crowe, *Raphael*, 2 vols (London, 1882–5)

CELANO 1692
C. Celano, *Notizie del bello dell'antico e del curioso della città di Napoli* (Naples, 1692)

CELANO 1792
C. Celano, *Notizie del bello dell'antico e del curioso della città di Napoli*, ed. S. Palermo (Naples, 1792)

CELIO 1638
G. Celio, *Memoria delli nomi dell'Artefici delle pitture, che sono in alcune Chiese, Facciate e Palazzi di Roma* (Naples, 1638)

CERASUOLO 2009
A. Cerasuolo, '"per questa confusion di segni…": La Genesi dei piccolo dipinti di Polidoro da Caravaggio', in *Arte e memoria dell'arte*, eds M. I. Catalano and P. Mania (Viterbo, 2009), pp. 253–65

CERASUOLO 2017
A. Cerasuolo, *Literature and Artistic Practice in Sixteenth-century Italy* (Leiden, 2017)

CHANTILLY 1997
Dessins Italiens du musée Condé à Chantilly. II Raphael et son cercle, ed. B. Peronnet (Chantilly, 1997)

CHATELET 1954
A. Chatelet, 'Two Landscape Drawings by Polidoro da Caravaggio', *Burlington Magazine*, XCVI (1954), pp. 181–2

CHELAZZI DINI 1980
G. Chelazzi Dini, review of Ravelli 1978, *Prospettiva*, 23 (1980), pp. 101–2

CHELAZZI DINI 1989
G. Chelazzi Dini, review of Naples 1988–9 exhibition, *Prospettiva*, 52 (1989), pp. 94–6

CHIARINI 1856–60
C. Celano, *Notizie del bello dell'antico e del curioso della città di Napoli*, ed. G. B. Chiarini, 5 vols (Naples, 1856–60)

CHIARINI 1963
M. Chiarini, 'Two Contributions: Polidoro and Salviati', *Burlington Magazine*, CV (1963), pp. 554–7

CIARDI DUPRÉ AND CHELAZZI DINI 1976
M. G. Ciardi Dupré and G. Chelazzi Dini, 'Polidoro Caldara da Caravaggio', *I Pittori bergamaschi dal XIII al XIX secolo. Il Cinquecento*, II (Bergamo, 1976), pp. 257–75

CIERI VIA 2012
C. Cieri Via, 'Polidoro da Caravaggio e Perin del Vaga. Un competizione sull'antico fra invenzione, copia e variazioni', in *Mosaico, Temi e metodi e critica per Gianni Carlo Sciolla* (Naples, 2012), pp. 63–74

CLAYTON 1999–2001
M. Clayton, *Raphael and His Circle. Drawings from Windsor Castle* (Windsor, 1999–2001)

COGOTTI AND GIGLI 1995
M. Cogotti and L. Gigli, *Palazzo Baldassini* (Rome, 1995)

COLLOBI RAGGHIANTI 1975
L. Collobi Ragghianti, 'Michele da Lucca, Polidoro e Rubens', *La Critica d'arte*, 139 (1975), pp. 11–20

CONSOLI 1970
Opere d'arte restaurate 1965–1969, XIII settimana dei musei Italiani, ed. G. Consoli (Messina, 1970)

COSTA 1900
F. Costa, 'A proposito della natività di Polidoro da Caravaggio', *Gazzetta di Messina e della Calabria*, 353 (1900)

CRUCIANI 1983
F. Cruciani, *Teatro nel Rinascimento, Rome 1450–1550* (Rome, 1983)

DACOS 1969
N. Dacos, *La Decouverte de la Domus Aurea et la formation des grotesques à la Renaissance* (London and Leyden, 1969)

DACOS 1977
N. Dacos, *Le Logge di Raffaello, maestro e bottega di fronte all'antico* (Rome, 1977)

DACOS 1980
N. Dacos, 'Pedro Campaña dopo Sviglia: Arazzi e altri inediti', *Bollettino d'arte*, 65, 8 (1980), pp. 1–44

DACOS 1982
N. Dacos, 'Ni Polidoro ni Peruzzi: Maturino', *Revue de l'art*, 57 (1982), pp. 9–28

DACOS 1999
N. Dacos, 'De Polidoro a Campaña: Deux dessins', *Dialoghi di storia dell'arte*, 8–9 (1999), pp. 112–17

DACOS 2008
N. Dacos, *The Loggia of Raphael: A Vatican Art Treasure* (New York, 2008)

DACOS AND FURLAN 1987
N. Dacos and C. Furlan, *Giovanni da Udine 1487–1561* (Udine, 1987)

D'AGOSTINO 1989
I. d'Agostino, 'Polidoro da Caravaggio e la diffusione della "Maniera Grande" nell'Italia meridionale', *Brutium*, LXVIII, 1 (1989), pp. 7–10

D'ALOE 1853
S. d'Aloe, *Naples, ses monuments et ses curiosités avec un catalogue detaillé du Musée Royal Bourbon* (Naples, 1853)

D'AMBRA AND DE LAUZIÈRES 1855
R. d'Ambra and A. de Lauzières, *Descrizione della città di Napoli e delle sue vicinanze* (Naples, 1855)

DE ANGELIS D'OSSAT 1947
G. de Angelis d'Ossat, 'La Casa grafita in Via della Maschera d'Oro', *Bollettino del centro studi storia dell'architettura* (1947), N.5, pp. 5–12

DE ANGELIS D'OSSAT 1957
G. de Angelis d'Ossat, 'Una Facciata di battaglie', *Strenna dei Romanisti* (1957), pp. 30–2

DE DOMINICI 1742–5
B. de Dominici, *Vite de'Pittori, scultori ed Architetti Napoletani* (Naples, 1742–5)

DE HOLLANDA 1548
F. de Hollanda, *De pintura antiga* (Lisbon, 1548)

DE MARCHI 2014
A. de Marchi, 'Raffaello, Polidoro e *Lo Spasimo di Sicilia*: Un Caso di scuola', in *L'Officina dello sguardo. Scritti in onore di Maria Andaloro* (Rome, 2014), pp. 123–9

DE PIETRI 1634
F. de Pietri, *Historia Napoletana* (Naples, 1634)

DE STEFANO 1560
P. de Stefano, *Descrizione dei luoghi sacri della città di Napoli* (Naples, 1560)

DELOGU 1963
R. Delogu, 'Polidoro ritrovato', *Cronache di archeologia e di storia dell'arte*, 2 (1963), pp. 123–8

DEMELE 2010
C. Demele, *Die italienischen Zeichnungen, Band 2. Bestandskatalog. Zeichnungen aus Goethes Besitz* (Cologne, Weimar and Vienna, 2010)

D'ENGENIO 1624
C. d'Engenio Caracciolo, *Napoli Sacra* (Naples, 1624)

DESWARTE-ROSA 1984
S. Deswarte-Rosa, 'Francisco de Holanda collectionneur (1514 ou 1518 – 1572)', *La Revue du Louvre*, XXXIV (1984), pp. 169–75

DESWARTE-ROSA 2004
S. Deswarte-Rosa, '"Tudo o Que Se Faz Em Este Mundo E Desenhar", Francisco de Holanda entre theorie et collection', in *El Modelo Italiano en las artes plasticas de la peninsula Iberica durante el Renacimento* (Valladolid, 2004), pp. 247–90

DE WAAL 1896
R. de Waal, *Der Campo Santo der Deutschen zu Rom* (Freiburg, 1896)

DI BELLA 1885
G. di Bella, *Illustrazione e critica su la porta di fianco della cattedrale di Messina* (Messina, 1885)

DI GIACOMO 2005
C. di Giacomo, 'I Restaurati portali di Polidoro Caldara di Caravaggio nel duomo di Messina: Appunti dal cantiere', *Interventi sulla 'questione meridionale'*, ed. F. Abbate (Rome, 2005), pp. 85–8

DI MARZO 1858–62
G. di Marzo, *Delle belle arti in Sicilia* (Palermo, 1858–62)

DOLCE 1557
L. Dolce, *Dialogo della pittura intitolata l'Aretino* (Venice, 1557)

DOLLMAYR 1895
H. Dollmayr, 'Raffaels Werkstätte', *Jahrbuch der Kunstsammlungen in Wien*, XVI (1895), pp. 232–63

DREYER 1979
P. Dreyer, *Kupferstichkabinett Berlin Italienische Zeichnungen* (Stuttgart and Zurich, 1979)

DUFRESNOY 1695
C. A. Dufresnoy, *De arte graphica. The Art of Painting*, trans. J. Dryden (London, 1695)

DURRER 1927
R. Durrer, *Die Schweizergarde in Rom und die Schweiz in päpstilichen Diesten* (Munich, 1927)

FALOMIR FAUS 2013
Late Raphael. Prado Conference Papers, ed. M. Falomir Faus (Madrid, 2013)

FERRARI 1990
O. Ferrari, *Bozzetti Italiani dal Manierismo al Barocco* (Naples, 1990)

FFOLLIOTT 1983
S. Ffolliott, *Civic Sculpture in the Renaissance: Montorsoli's Fountains at Messina* (Ann Arbor, 1983)

FILANGIERI 1883–91
G. Filangieri, *Documenti per la storia le arti e le industrie delle provincie napoletane*, 6 vols (Naples, 1883–91)

FILANGIERI 1902
A. Filangieri di Candida, 'La Galleria Nazionale di Napoli (documenti e ricerche)', *Le Gallerie nazionali Italiane*, V (1902), pp. 208–354

FISCHER PACE 1988
U. V. Fischer Pace, 'Santa Maria della Pietà. Die Kirche des Campo Santo Teutonico in Rom', in *Der Campo Santo Teutonico in Rom*, ed. E. Gatz, Supplement to *Römischen Quartalschrift*, 43, II (Rome, Freiburg and Vienna, 1988), pp. 79–86

FLORENCE 2014
Pontormo and Rosso Fiorentino: Diverging Paths of Mannerism, eds C. Falciani, A. Natali (Florence, 2014)

FOLDS MCCULLAGH AND GILES 1997
S. Folds McCullagh and L. Giles, *Italian Drawings before 1600 in the Art Institute of Chicago* (Chicago and Princeton, 1997)

FRANKLIN 1994
D. Franklin, *Rosso in Italy* (New Haven and London, 1994)

FRANKLIN 1997
D. Franklin, 'The Source for Vasari's Portrait of Morto da Feltre', *Print Quarterly*, XIV, no. 1 (1997), pp. 78–80

FRANKLIN 2000
D. Franklin, 'Francisco de Holanda's Collection of Drawings by Polidoro da Caravaggio', *Apollo*, CLI (2000), pp. 12–21

FRANKLIN 2001
D. Franklin, *Painting in Renaissance Florence, 1500–1550* (New Haven and London, 2001)

FRANKLIN 2010
D. Franklin, 'New Drawings by Polidoro da Caravaggio', *Master Drawings*, XLVIII (2010), pp. 155–62

FREEDBERG 1971
S. J. Freedberg, *Painting in Italy 1500 to 1600* (Harmondsworth, 1971)

FREEMAN BAUER 1978
L. Freeman Bauer, '"Quanto si disegna, si dipinge ancora": Some Observations on the Development of the Oil Sketch', *Storia dell'arte*, XXXII (1978), pp. 45–57

FRITZ 1997
M. Fritz, *Giulio Romano et Raphael: La Vice-reine de Naples* (Paris, 1997)

FROMMEL 1973
C. L. Frommel, *Der Römische Palastbau der Hochrenaissance* (Tubingen, 1973)

GABRIELLI 1971
N. Gabrielli, *Galleria Sabauda. Maestri Italiani* (Turin, 1971)

GALANTE 1873
G. A. Galante, *Guida sacra della città di Napoli* (Naples, 1873)

GALLO 1756–8
G. D. Gallo, *Annali della Città di Messina*, 3 vols (Messina, 1756–8)

GASTON 1988
Pirro Ligorio: Artist and Antiquarian, ed. R. W. Gaston (Milan, 1988)

GENOVESE 2011
V. E. Genovese, 'Postille messinesi: Il Golgotha di Gualteri Sicamino e il dono per Polidoro da Caravaggio', *Annali della Scuola Normale Superiore di Pisa; Classe di Lettere e Filosofia*, 5th Ser., 3, no. 2 (2011), pp. 435–63

GERE 1963
J. A. Gere, 'A Landscape Drawing by Polidoro da Caravaggio', *Master Drawings*, I (1963), pp. 43–5

GERE 1968
J. A. Gere, 'Two Copies after Polidoro da Caravaggio', *Master Drawings*, VI (1968), pp. 249–51

GERE 1969
J. A. Gere, *Taddeo Zuccaro: His Development in Drawings* (London, 1969)

GERE 1971
J. A. Gere, *Il Manierismo a Roma* (Milan, 1971)

GERE 1985–6
J. A. Gere, review of Ravelli's *Master Drawings*, XXIII–IV (1985–6), pp. 61–74

GERE AND POUNCEY 1983
J. A. Gere and P. Pouncey, *Italian Drawings in the Department of Prints and Drawings in the British Museum: Artists Working in Rome c.1550–c.1640* (London, 1983)

GIANNONE 1941
O. Giannone, *Guinte sulle vite de' pittori Napoletani*, ed. O. Morisani (Naples, 1941)

GIUCCI 1874
G. Giucci, *Dei graffiti e delle pitture che decorano le pareti esterne di alcuni edifici di Roma*, IX (Rome, 1874)

GIUSTI AND LEONE DE CASTRIS 1985
P. Giusti and P. Leone de Castris, *Forastieri e regnicoli. La Pittura moderna a Napoli nel primo Cinquecento* (Naples, 1985)

GNANN 1991
A. Gnann, 'Polidoro da Caravaggio in S. Silvestro al Quirinale in Rom: Die Ausmalung der Kapelle Fra Mariano del Piombos', *Arte Lombarda*, 98–9 (1991), pp. 134–9

GNANN 1993
A. Gnann, 'Zwei Kompositionen Polidoro da Caravaggios und deren Kopien', in *Musis et Litteris: Festschrift fur Bernhard Rupprecht zum 65. Geburstag* (Munich, 1993), pp. 159–71

GNANN 1997
A. Gnann, *Polidoro da Caravaggio (un 1499–1543). Die romischen Innendekorationen* (Munich, 1997)

GNANN AND PLOMP 2012–13
Raphael and His School, eds A. Gnann and M. C. Plomp (Amsterdam, 2012–13)

GNOLI 1891
D. Gnoli, 'La Cappella di Fra'Mariano del Piombo in Roma', *Archivio storico dell'arte*, IV (1891), pp. 117–26

GNOLI 1936–8
U. Gnoli, 'Facciate graffite e dipinte in Roma', *Il Vasari* (1936–8), pp. 89–123

GOLZIO 1936
V. Golzio, *Raffaello nei documenti* (Rome, 1936)

GOMBRICH 1966
E. Gombrich, *Norm and Form* (Oxford, 1966)

GOMBRICH 1987
E. Gombrich, 'An Early Seventeenth-century Canon of Artistic Excellence: Pierleone Casella's Elogio Illustrium Artificium of 1606', *Journal of the Warburg and Courtauld Institutes*, 52 (1987), pp. 224–32

GOUWENS AND REISS 2005
The Pontificate of Clement VII: History, Politics, Culture, eds K. Gouwens and S. Reiss (London, 2005)

GRASSI 1964
L. Grassi, 'Bernini: Two Unpublished Drawings and Related Problems', *Burlington Magazine*, CVI (1964), pp. 170–78

GRASSI 1966
L. Grassi, *Il Manierismo nella pittura del Cinquecento* (Rome, 1966)

GRASSI 1972
L. Grassi, 'Due disegni di Polidoro da Caravaggio', *Festschrift Luitpold Dussler* (Munich, 1972), pp. 252–62

GRILLI 1905
G. Grilli, 'Le Pitture a graffito e chiaroscuro di Polidoro e Maturino sulle facciate delle case di Roma', *Rassegna d'arte*, V (1905), pp. 97–102

GROSSO CACOPARDO 1821
G. Grosso Cacopardo, *Memorie di pittori messinesi e degli esteri che in Messina fiorirono dal sec. XII al XIX* (Messina, 1821)

GROSSO CACOPARDO 1826
G. Grosso Cacopardo, *Guida per la città di Messina* (Syracuse, 1826)

HAARLEM 1969
Drawings from the Teylers Museum, eds J. Q. van Regteren Altena and F. W. Ward Jackson (Haarlem, 1969)

HACKERT AND BRANO 1792
F. Hackert and G. Brano, *Memorie dei Pittori Messinese* (1792), ed. S. Bottari (Messina, 1932)

HALL 1999
M. Hall, *After Raphael: Painting in Central Italy in the Sixteenth Century* (Cambridge, 1999)

HAMBURGH 1981
H. Hamburgh, 'The Problem of Lo Spasimo of the Virgin in Cinquecento Paintings of the Descent from the Cross', *The Sixteenth-century Journal*, 12 (1981), pp. 45–75

HARB 2015
F. Harb, *The Drawings of Giorgio Vasari (1511–1574)* (Rome, 2015)

HASKELL AND PENNY 1982
F. Haskell and N. Penny, *Taste and the Antique* (1981) (New Haven and London, revised ed., 1982)

HAUSSLER 1974
B. Haussler, *Campo Santo Teutonico Rom* (Zurich and Munich, 1974)

HELD 1980
J. Held, *The Oil Sketches of Peter Paul Rubens, a Critical Catalogue* (Princeton, 1980)

HERMANIN 1950
F. Hermanin, 'Due bozzetti di Polidoro da Caravaggio', *Strenna dei romanisti*, 11 (1950), pp. 132–4

HERRMANN-FIORE 1983–4
K. Herrmann-Fiore, *Disegni degli Alberti* (Rome, 1983–4)

HERRMANN-FIORE 1990
K. Herrmann-Fiore, 'La Retorica romana delle facciate dipinte da Polidoro', in *Raffaello e l'Europa*, eds M. Fagiolo and M. L. Madonna (Rome, 1990), pp. 267–87

HERRMANN-FIORE 2011
K. Herrmann-Fiore, 'Roma trionfante: Riverbi del tema di Flavio Biondo sulle facciate romane del Cinquecento; il caso del Collegio Capranica decorato da Polidoro', in *Il Rinascimento a Roma*, eds M. G. Bernardini and M. Bussagli (Milan, 2011), pp. 42–51

HIRSCHFELD 1911
W. Hirschfeld, *Quellenstudien zur Geschichte der Fassadenmalerei in Rom in XVI und XVII Jahrhundert*, Hallenser Diss., Halle, 1911

HIRST 1965
M. Hirst, 'Tibaldi around Perino', *Burlington Magazine*, CVII (1965), pp. 569–71

HIRST 1972
M. Hirst, 'Addenda Sansoviniana', *Burlington Magazine*, CXIV (1972), pp. 162–3

HIRST 1981
M. Hirst, *Sebastiano del Piombo* (Oxford, 1981)

HIRST 1989
M. Hirst, review of Naples 1988–9, *Burlington Magazine*, CXXXI (1989), pp. 238 40

HIRST 2011
M. Hirst, *Michelangelo: The Achievement of Fame* (New Haven and London, 2011)

HYERACE 1986
L. Hyerace, 'Su Mariano Riccio e intorno alla pittura messinese della prima metà del Cinquecento', *Nuovi annali della facoltà di magistero dell'università di Messina*, 4 (1986), pp. 395–411

IEZZI 1975
E. Iezzi, *S. Silvestro al Quirinale* (Rome, 1975)

JAFFE 1985
D. Jaffe, 'Pietro Negroni as a Draughtsman', *Burlington Magazine*, CXXVII (1985), pp. 157–9

JOANNIDES 1983
P. Joannides, review of Shearman 1983, *Art Book Review*, 6 (1983), p. 48

JOANNIDES 2013
P. Joannides, 'A Composition by Polidoro da Caravaggio Re-composed', *Master Drawings*, 51 (2013), pp. 159–64

JONES AND PENNY 1983
R. Jones and N. Penny, *Raphael* (New Haven and London, 1983)

KEITH, MOORE EDE, PLAZZOTTA 2004
L. Keith, M. Moore Ede and C. Plazzotta, 'Polidoro da Caravaggio's Way to Calvary: Technique, Style and Function', *National Gallery Technical Bulletin*, 25 (2004), pp. 36–47

KEMP 1992
M. Kemp, *Leonardo da Vinci: The Mystery of the Madonna of the Yarnwinder* (Edinburgh, 1992)

KOERTE 1935
W. Koerte, *Der Palast Zuccari in Rom* (Leipzig, 1935)

KONECNY 1979
L. Konecny, 'A Note on Polidoro da Caravaggio's Way to Calvary', *Paragone*, 357 (1979), pp. 89–93

KULTZEN 1958
R. Kultzen, 'Over een verloren portret van Polidoro da Caravaggio in hat Palazzo Zuccari te Rom', *Bulletin Museum Boymans*, 9 (1958), pp. 97–103

KULTZEN 1959–60
R. Kultzen, 'Die Malereien Polidoros da Caravaggio im Giardino del Bufalo in Rom', *Mitteilungen des Kunsthistorischen Institutes in Florenz*, IX (1959–60), pp. 97–120

KULTZEN 1961A
R. Kultzen, 'Der Freskenzyklus in der ehemaligen Kapelle der Schweizergarde in Rom', *Zeitschrift fur Schweizerische Archaeologie und Kunstgeschichte*, XXI (1961), pp. 19–30

KULTZEN 1961B
R. Kultzen, 'Bemerkungen zu einer Fassadenmalerei Polidoros da Caravaggio an der Piazza Madama in Rom', *Miscellanea Bibliothecae Hertzianae*, XX (1961), pp. 207–12

KULTZEN 1961C
R. Kultzen, review of Pericoli Ridolfini's *Le Case Romane* (1960), *Kunstchronik*, XIV (1961), pp. 61–71

KULTZEN 1963
R. Kultzen, 'La Serie dei Dodici Cesari dipinta da Baldassare Peruzzi', *Bollettino d'arte*, 48 (1963), pp. 50–53

KULTZEN 1967
R. Kultzen, 'Eine Anmerkung zur Vermittlung figurlicher Kompositionstypen durch die italienische Buchillustration des spaten 15. Jahrhunderts', *Pantheon*, 25 (1967), pp. 407–17

KULTZEN 1968
R. Kultzen, 'Die Malereien Polidoros an der Fassade von S. Pietro in Vincoli', *Festschrift Ulrich Middeldorf* (Berlin, 1968), pp. 263–8

KULTZEN 1972
R. Kultzen, 'Bemerkungen zum Thema Fassadenmalerei in Rom', *Festschrift Luitpold Dussler* (Munich, 1972), pp. 263–79

KULTZEN 1973
R. Kultzen, review of Marabottini 1969, *Art Bulletin*, 55 (1973), pp. 637–9

KULTZEN 1975
R. Kultzen, 'Polidoros Tod der Tarpeia an der Casa degli Spinoli in Rom', *Wandlungen. Studien zur antiken und neueren Kunst* (Munich, 1975), pp. 296–301

KULTZEN 1977
R. Kultzen, 'Zur graphischen Uberlieferung der Facciata dei buoni auguri Polidoros in Rom', *Scritti di storia dell'arte in onore di Ugo Procacci*, II (Milan, 1977), pp. 347–55

KULTZEN 1990
R. Kultzen, 'Auf den Spuren einer verschollenen Tierkampfdarstellung von Polidoro da Caravaggio', in *Studien zur Kunstlerzeichnung: Klaus Schwager zum 65. Geburtstag*, eds S. Kummer and G. Satzinger (Stuttgart, 1990), pp. 124–31

KULTZEN 1998
R. Kultzen, review of Gnann 1997, *Kunstchronik*, 51 (1998), pp. 623–5

LA FARINA 1835
G. La Farina, *Intorno alle belle arti ed agli artisti fioriti in varie epoche a Messina* (Messina, 1835)

LA FARINA 1840
G. La Farina, *Messina e i suoi monumenti* (Messina, 1840)

LANZI 1795–6
L. Lanzi, *Storia pittorica della Italia* (Bassano, 1795–6)

LASCHKE 1993
B. Laschke, *Fra Giovan Angelo da Montorsoli* (Berlin, 1993)

LAVIN 1975
M. Lavin, *Seventeenth-century Barberini Documents and Inventories of Art* (New York, 1975)

LEONARDO 1989
Leonardo on Painting, ed. M. Kemp, trans. M. Kemp and M. Walker (New Haven and London, 1989)

LEONE DE CASTRIS 1983
P. Leone de Castris, 'Polidoro alla Pietra del pesce', *Ricerche di storia dell'arte*, 21 (1983), pp. 21–52

LEONE DE CASTRIS 1997
P. Leone de Castris, 'Due dipinti di Polidoro al tempo del Sacco', *Bolletino d'arte*, 99 (1997), pp. 61–6

LEONE DE CASTRIS 2001
P. Leone de Castris, *Polidoro da Caravaggio: L'Opera completa* (Naples, 2001)

LEONE DE CASTRIS 2004
P. Leone de Castris, *Polidoro and La Lignamine's Messina Lamentation* (London, 2004)

LEONE DE CASTRIS 2011
P. Leone de Castris, 'Due nuovi "numeri", e qualche considerazione, per Polidoro disegnatore', *Scritti in onore di Marina Causa Picone*, eds C. Vargas, A. Migliaccio and S. Causa (Naples, 2011), pp. 179–88

LILIUS 1981
H. Lilius, *Villa Lante al Gianicola. L'Architettura e la decorazione pittorica, in Acta Instituti Romani Finaldiae* (Rome, 1981)

LOCATELLI 1867
P. Locatelli, *Illustri Bergamaschi*, I (Bergamo, 1867)

LOCONTE 2008
A. Loconte, 'The North Looks South: Giorgio Vasari and Early Modern Visual Culture in the Kingdom of Naples', *Art History*, 31 (2008), pp. 438–59

LOMAZZO 1584
G. P. Lomazzo, *Trattato dell'Arte della Pittura* (Milan, 1584)

LOMAZZO 1590
G. P. Lomazzo, *Idea del Tempio della Pittura* (Milan, 1590)

LONGHI 1970
R. Longhi, 'Un Apice di Polidoro da Caravaggio', *Paragone*, 245 (1970), pp. 3–7

LORENZINI 2002
L. Lorenzini, 'Polidoro da Caravaggio e Nicola Alibrando: La bottega dell'artista e il trionfo della lirica', *La Parola del testo*, 6 (2002), pp. 359–70

LUGT 1921
F. Lugt, *Les Marques des collections de dessins et d'estampes* (1921), suppl. (Paris, 1956)

MCTAVISH 2008
D. McTavish, review of Paris 2007 exhibition, *Master Drawings*, 46 (2008), pp. 386–92

MACCARI 1885
E. Maccari, *Graffiti e chiaroscuri esistenti nell'esterno delle case di Roma* (Rome, 1885)

MACIOCE 1987
S. Macioce, 'In margine all'attivita di Polidoro pittore di facciate', in Baldassare Peruzzi, *Pittura scena e architettura nel Cinquecento* (Rome, 1987), pp. 647–68

MADRID 2012
Late Raphael, eds T. Henry and P. Joannides (Madrid, 2012)

MALIGNANI 1981
D. Malignani, *La Pittura in Sicilia fra maniera e controriforma* (Palermo, 1981)

MANCINI 1621
G. Mancini, *Considerazioni appartenenti alla Pittura* (c.1621), eds A. Marucchi and L. Salerno (Rome, 1956)

MANTUA 1999
Roma e lo stile classic di Raffaello, eds K. Oberhuber and A. Gnann (Mantua, 1999)

MARABOTTINI 1966
A. Marabottini, 'Intorno a Polidoro da Caravaggio', *Commentari*, XVII (1966), pp. 129–45

MARABOTTINI 1967
A. Marabottini, 'Genesi di un dipinto (l'Andata al Calvario di Polidoro a Capodimonte)', *Commentari*, XVIII (1967), pp. 170–85

MARABOTTINI 1969
A. Marabottini, *Polidoro da Caravaggio* (Rome, 1969)

MARABOTTINI 1972
A. Marabottini, 'Postilla a Polidoro', *Commentari*, XXIII (1972), pp. 366–75

MARABOTTINI 1976
A. Marabottini, 'Una Croce dipinta di Polidoro da Caravaggio a Malta', *Quaderni dell'istituto di storia dell'arte medievale e moderna*, Facoltà di Lettere e Filosofia, Università di Messina, 2 (1976), pp. 31–3

MARINI 2005
M. Marini, *Polidoro Caldara da Caravaggio. L'Invidia ela fortuna* (Venice, 2005)

MASINI, MIRACOLA, COLUCCI 2013
P. Masini, P. Miracola and I. Colucci, *Dal Giardino al museo. Polidoro da Caravaggio nel casino del Bufalo. Studi e restauro* (Rome, 2013)

MAUCERI 1922
E. Mauceri, 'Restauri e dipinti del Museo Nazionale di Messina', *Bollettino d'arte*, II (1922), pp. 581–6

MAUCERI 1923
E. Mauceri, 'Raffaello e la pittura messinese del '500', *Atti della R. Accademia Peloritana* (1923), pp. 212-16

MAUCERI 1928
E. Mauceri, 'Polidoro a Messina', *Sicilia*, January 1928, pp. 3–5

MAUCERI 1929
E. Mauceri, *Il Museo Nazionale di Messina* (Messina, 1929)

MAZZA 1938
E. Mazza, 'Polidoro da Caravaggio', *Rivista di Bergamo*, January 1938, pp. 2–6

MEIJER 1974
B. W. Meijer, 'An Unknown Landscape Drawing by Polidoro da Caravaggio and a Note on Jan van Scorel's in Italy', *Paragone*, 291 (1974), pp. 62–73

MESSINA 1979
Opere d'arte restaurate nel Messinese, ed. F. Campagna Cicala (Messina, 1979)

MONGITORE 1977
A. Mongitore, *Memorie dei pittori, scultori, architetti, artefici in cera siciliani*, ed. E. Natoli (Palermo, 1977)

MONTINI AND AVERINI 1957
U. Montini and R. Averini, *Palazzo Baldassini e l'arte di Giovanni da Udine* (Rome, 1957)

MORANDI 1874
G. Morandi, *L'Arte nella decorazione italiana: I graffiti ed i chiaroscuri* (Milan, 1874)

MORISANI 1958
O. Morisani, *Letteratura artistica a Napoli tra il '400 ed il '600* (Naples, 1958)

MORO 1990
F. Moro, 'Tra Polidoro e Boccaccino', *Osservatorio delle arti*, 5 (1990), pp. 51–5

MUNICH 1977
Stiftung Ratjen, Italienische Zeichnungen des 16.–18 Jahr., ed. H. List (Munich, 1977)

NALDI 2001
R. Naldi, 'Culto di Sant'Anna ed icone miracolose a Napoli nel primo cinquecento: Una Cornice per l'epigramma *IN PICTURAM* di Iacopo Sannazaro', *Napoli nobilissima*, V, II (2001), pp. 15–30

NALDI 2009
Marco Cardisco, Giorgio Vasari. Pittura, umanesimo religioso, immagini di culto, ed. R. Naldi (Naples, 2009)

NAPLES 1985
I Dipinti di Polidoro da Caravaggio per la chiesa della Pescheria a Napoli, ed. P. Leone de Castris (Naples, 1985)

NAPLES 1988–9
P. Leone De Castris, *Polidoro da Caravaggio fra Napoli e Messina* (Naples, 1988–9)

NEUMEYER 1928
A. Neumeyer, 'Einige italienische Handzeichnungen aus dem Hamburger Kupferstich-Kabinett', *Zeitschrift für Bildende Kunst*, 63 (1928), pp. 43–8

NEW YORK 1987
Drawings by Raphael and His Circle from British and North American Collections, ed. J. Gere (New York, 1987)

NEW YORK 2004
Painters of Reality, ed. A. Bayer (Cremona and New York, 2004)

NICOLINI 1925
F. Nicolini, *L'Arte Napoletana del Rinascimento* (Naples, 1925)

NOTRE DAME 1985
Renaissance Drawings from the Ambrosiana, ed. R. R. Coleman (Notre Dame, IN, 1985)

OBERHUBER 1963
K. Oberhuber, review of Pouncey and Gere 1962, in *Master Drawings*, I (1963), pp. 44–54

OTTAWA 2009
The Art of Papal Rome, ed. D. Franklin (Ottawa, 2009)

PACCHIOTTI 1927
C. Pacchiotti, 'Nuove attribuzioni a Polidoro da Caravaggio in Roma', *L'Arte*, XXX (1927), pp. 189–221

PADULA 1986
Andrea dal Salerno nel rinascimento meridionale, ed. G. Previtali (Padula, 1986)

PALERMO 1995–6
Maestri del disegno nelle collezioni di Palazzo Abatellis, ed. V. Abbate (Palermo, 1995–6)

PALERMO 1999
Vincenzo degli Azani da Pavia e la cultura figurativa in Sicilia nell'eta di Carlo V, ed. T. Viscuso (Palermo, 1999)

PANE 2014
A. Pane, 'Rinascimento perduto: Il Palazzo di Bernardino Rota in Napoli tra origini, trasformazioni e restauri', *Napoli nobilissima*, sesta series, 5 (2014), pp. 100–18

PARIS 1983
Autour de Raphael: Dessins et peintures du Musée du Louvre, eds R. Bacou and S. Béguin (Paris, 1983)

PARIS 2005
De la Renaissance à l'Age baroque. Une Collection de dessins italiens pour les musées de France, ed. D. Cordellier (Paris, 2005)

PARIS 2007
Polidoro da Caravaggio, ed. D. Cordellier (Paris, 2007)

PARKER 1956
K. T. Parker, *Catalogue of the Collection of Drawings in the Ashmolean Museum, II, Italian Schools* (1956) (new ed. Oxford, 1972)

PARMA ARMANI 1986
E. Parma Armani, *Perin del Vaga: L'Anello mancante* (Genoa, 1986)

PARRINO 1700
D. A. Parrino, *Napoli, Citta Nobilissima, Antica, e Fedelissima* (Naples, 1700)

PARRINO 1725
D. A. Parrino, *Nuova guida de' forastieri* (Naples, 1725)

PARRINO 1751
D. A. Parrino, *Nuova guida de' forastieri* (Naples, 1751)

PASSAVANT 1839
J. D. Passavant, *Raffael von Urbino und sein Vater G. Santi* (Leipzig, 1839)

PERICOLI RIDOLFINI 1960A
Le Case Romane con facciate graffite e dipinte, ed. C. Pericoli Ridolfini (Rome, 1960)

PERICOLI RIDOLFINI 1960B
C. Pericoli Ridolfini, 'La Mostra delle Case Romane con facciate graffite e dipinte', *Bollettino dei Musei Comunali di Roma*, 7 (Rome, 1960), pp. 1–8

PERICOLI RIDOLFINI 1962
C. Pericoli Ridolfini, 'Di un disegno dato a Polidoro da Caravaggio', *Bollettino della Unione di Storia e Arte* (1962), pp. 4–5

PERICOLI RIDOLFINI 1966
C. Pericoli Ridolfini, 'Un Disegno di Polidoro da Caravaggio nel Museo di Roma', *Bollettino dei Musei Comunali di Roma*, 13 (1966), pp. 30–39

PERICOLI RIDOLFINI 1982
C. Pericoli Ridolfini, 'Il Mondo classic nelle facciate dipinte o graffite romane nel Cinquecento', in *Il Lazio nell'antichita romana*, ed. R. Lefevre, Lunario Romano (Rome, 1982), pp. 653–78

PERRINO 1830
M. Perrino, *Dettaglio di quanto è relativo alla città di Napoli dalla sua origine al presente* (Naples, 1830)

PETRELLI 1982
F. Petrelli, 'Pietro Negrone', *Paragone*, 389 (1982), pp. 62–70

PETRUCCI 1956
A. Petrucci, *Il Caravaggio acquafortista e il mondo calcografico romano* (Rome, 1956)

PIDATELLA 2009
C. Pidatella, *Polidoro da Caravaggio* (Bergamo, 2009)

PISTOIA 1996
Fra Paolino e la pittura a pistoia nel primo '500, eds C. D'Afflitto, F. Falletti and A. Muzzi (Venice, 1996)

PLINY 1952
Pliny, *Natural History in Ten Volumes*, trans. H. Rackham, IX (Cambridge, MA, and London, 1952)

POPHAM AND WILDE 1949
A. E. Popham and J. Wilde, *The Italian Drawings at Windsor Castle* (London, 1949)

POUNCEY 1954
P. Pouncey, 'An Entombment by Rubens', *Burlington Magazine*, XCVI (1954), pp. 23–5

POUNCEY AND GERE 1962
P. Pouncey and J. A. Gere, *Italian Drawings in the Department of Prints and Drawings in the British Museum: Raphael and His Circle* (London, 1962)

PREVITALI 1978
G. Previtali, *La Pittura del Cinquecento a Napoli e nel vicereame* (Turin, 1978)

PUGLIATTI 1990
T. Pugliatti, 'Un'Immagine recuperata. Il Telone Polidoriano della Chiesa Messinese della Candelora ed una tavoletta di collezione privata', *Quaderni dell'Istituto di Storia dell'Arte Medievale e Moderna, Facoltà di Lettere e Filosofia, Università di Messina*, 14 (1990), pp. 5–11

PUGLIATTI 1993
T. Pugliatti, *Pittura del Cinquecento in Sicilia* (Naples, 1993)

QUEDNAU 1986
R. Quednau, 'Aspects of Raphael's "Ultima Maniera"', in *Raffaello a Roma*, ed. G. C. Argan (Rome, 1986), pp. 245–57

RAVELLI 1972
L. Ravelli, 'Gli Affreschi della Cappella della Passione in S. Maria della Pietà in Camposanto a Roma', *Bergamo arte*, XII (1972), pp. 23–8

RAVELLI 1978
L. Ravelli, *Polidoro Caldara da Caravaggio* (Bergamo, 1978)

RAVELLI 1982
L. Ravelli, 'Il Trasporto di Cristo al sepolcro di Polidoro Caldara da Caravaggio', *La Rivista di Bergamo*, 5 (1982), pp. 10–13

RAVELLI 1987
L. Ravelli, *Polidoro a San Silvestro al Quirinale* (Bergamo, 1987)

RAVELLI 1988
L. Ravelli, *Un Fregio di Polidoro a Palazzo Baldassini in Roma* (Bergamo, 1988)

RAVELLI 1996
L. Ravelli, 'Aggiornamenti su Polidoro da Caravaggio', *Arte documento*, 9 (1996), pp. 67–72

RAYMOND OF CAPUA 2003
Blessed Raymond of Capua, *The Life of Saint Catherine of Siena*, trans. G. Lamb (Rockford, IL, 2003)

ROHEN 1974
A. Rohen, 'Storie de'fatti de'Romani, Cristofano Gherardi e Polidoro da Caravaggio', *Storia dell'arte*, XX (1974), pp. 5–17

ROLFS 1910
W. Rolfs, *Geschichte der Malerei Neapels* (Leipzig, 1910)

ROMANELLI 1815
D. Romanelli, *Napoli antica e moderna*, 3 vols (Naples, 1815)

ROME 1970
Mostra dei restauri, 1969. XIII settimana dei musei (Rome, 1970)

ROME 1972
Il Paesaggio nel disegno del Cinquecento Europeo, eds F. Viatte, R. Bacou and G. Delle Piane (Rome, 1972)

ROME 1984
Aspetti dell'arte a Roma prima e dopo Raffaello (Rome, 1984)

ROSCI 1995
M. Rosci, 'L'Adorazione dei Pastori di Polidoro da Caravaggio', in *Napoli, l'Europa. Ricerche di storia dell'arte in onore di Ferdinando Bologna*, eds F. Abbate and F. Sricchia Santoro (Catanzaro, 1995), pp. 141–3

ROTILI 1972
M. Rotili, *L'Arte del Cinquecento nel regno di Napoli* (Naples, 1972)

RUBIN 1995
P. Rubin, *Giorgio Vasari: Art and History* (New Haven and London, 1995)

RUFFO 1916
V. Ruffo, 'La Galleria Ruffo in Messina nel sec. XVII', *Bollettino d'arte* (1916), pp. 21–64, 95–128, 165–92, 237–56, 284–320, 369–88

RUOTOLO 1973
R. Ruotolo, 'Collezioni e mecenati Napoletani del XVII secolo', *Napoli nobilissima*, XII (1973), pp. 145–53

SAMPERI 1644
P. Samperi, *Iconologia della gloriosa Vergine Madre di dio protrettrice di Messina* (Messina, 1644)

SAMPERI 1742
P. Samperi, *Messana illustrata* (Messina, 1742)

SANNAZZARO 2009
Jacopo Sannazzaro, Latin Poetry, trans. M. C. J. Putnam (Cambridge and London, 2009)

SARNELLI 1685
P. Sarnelli, *Guida de'Forestieri per la città di Napoli* (Naples, 1685)

SCANNELLI 1657
F. Scannelli, *Il microcosmo della Pittura* (Cesena, 1657)

SCARAMUCCIA 1674
L. Scaramuccia, *Le Finezze dei pennelli italiani* (Pavia, 1674)

SCORZA 2012
R. Scorza, 'Messina 1535 to Lepanto 1571. Vasari, Borghini and the Imagery of the Moors, Barbarians and Turks', in *The Slave in European Art*, eds E. McGrath and J. M. Massing (London and Turin, 2012), pp. 121–64

SCRASE 2011
D. Scrase, *Italian Drawings at The Fitzwilliam Museum, Cambridge* (Cambridge, 2011)

SEILERN 1969
A. Seilern, *Paintings and Drawings at 56 Princes Gate London SW7* (London, 1969)

SERLIO 1537
S. Serlio, *Regole generali di Architettura, Tutte le opere d'architettura e prospettiva* (Venice, 1537)

SHEARMAN 1965
J. Shearman, review of Pouncey and Gere 1962, *Burlington Magazine*, CVII (1965), pp. 34–6

SHEARMAN 1967
J. Shearman, *Mannerism* (Harmondsworth, 1967)

SHEARMAN 1983
J. Shearman, *The Pictures in the Collection of Her Majesty the Queen: The Early Italian Pictures* (Cambridge, 1983)

SHEARMAN 2003
J. Shearman, *Raphael in Early Modern Sources (1483–1602)* (New Haven and London, 2003)

SICKEL 2004
L. Sickel, 'Die Testamente des F. Mariano Fetti', *Quellen und Forschungen aus Italienischen Archiven und Bibliotheken*, 84 (2004), pp. 497–508

SIGISMONDO 1788–9
G. Sigismondo, *Descrizione della città di Napoli e suoi borghi* (Naples, 1788–9)

SPENCER 1960
J. B. Spencer, 'The Imperfect Parallel Betwixt Painting and Poetry', *Greece and Rome*, second ser., VII, 2 (1960), pp. 173–86

SRICCHIA SANTORO 1966
F. Sricchia Santoro, *Classicismo e manierismo nell'Italia centrale* (Milan, 1966)

SRICCHIA SANTORO 1982
F. Sricchia Santoro, 'Una Traccia per Polidoro', *Prospettiva*, 28 (1982), pp. 77–9

STEEN HANSEN 2014
M. Steen Hansen, 'After the Veronica: Crisis and the *Ars Sacra* of Polidoro da Caravaggio and Pontormo', *I Tatti Studies*, 17, 2 (2014), pp. 325–67

STEINBY 1996
Ianiculum – Gianicolo, ed. E. M. Steinby (Rome, 1996)

STOLLHANS 1988
C. J. Stollhans, 'Baldassare Peruzzi and His Patrons: Religious Paintings in Rome, 1503–1527', Northwestern University, Ph.D. thesis, 1988

STOLLHANS 1992
C. J. Stollhans, 'Fra Mariano, Peruzzi and Polidoro da Caravaggio: A New Look at Religious Landscapes in Renaissance Rome', *The Sixteenth-century Journal*, XXIII, 3 (1992), pp. 506–25

STOLLHANS 2014
C. J. Stollhans, *St Catherine of Alexandria in Renaissance Roman Art: Case Studies in Patronage* (Farnham, 2014)

STRAZZULLO 1954
F. Strazzullo, 'Per l'iconografia di Maria SS. Delle Grazie (dal Sec. XV al XVII)', *Arte Cristiana*, XLII (1954), pp. 107–26

STRINATI 1974
C. Strinati, 'Gli Anni difficili di Federico Zuccaro', *Storia dell'arte*, 21 (1974), pp. 85–117

STUMPEL 1990
J. Stumpel, *The Province of Painting: Theories of Italian Renaissance Art* (Utrecht, 1990)

SUMMONTE 1524
P. Summonte, 'Lettera al Magnifico Signor Marco Antonio Michiel', in F. Nicolini, *L'Arte Napoletana del Rinascimento e la lettera di Pietro Summonte a Marcantonio Michiel* (1524) (Naples, 1925)

SUSINNO 1724
F. Susinno, *Le vite de'Pittori Messinesi, c.1724*, ed. V. Martinelli (Florence, 1960)

TASSI 1793
F. M. Tassi, *Vite de'Pittori, Scultori e Architetti bergamaschi* (Bergamo, 1793), ed. F. Mazzini (Milan, 1970)

TICOZZI 1830–33
S. Ticozzi, *Dizionario degli architetti, scultori, pittori* (Milan, 1830–33)

TITI 1675
F. Titi, *Studio di Pittura, Scultura e Architettura nelle chiese di Roma* (Rome, 1675)

TITI 1763
F. Titi, *Descrizione delle pitture in Roma*, new ed. (Rome, 1763)

TOTTI 1638
P. Totti, *Ritratto di Roma Moderna* (Rome, 1638)

TURNER 1961
A. R. Turner, 'Two Landscapes in Renaissance Rome', *Art Bulletin*, XLIII (1961), pp. 275–87

TURNER 1966
A. R. Turner, *The Vision of Landscape* (Princeton, 1966)

TURNER 2000
N. Turner, *European Drawings from Portuguese Collections* (Lisbon, 2000)

VAN REGTEREN ALTENA 1966
J. Q. van Regteren Altena, *Les Dessins italiens de la reine Christine de Suède* (Stockholm, 1966)

VANNUGLI 2005
A. Vannugli, 'Un'altra "Lettera rubata": La Decorazione della Cappella di S. Maria Maddaelena nella SS. Trinita dei Monti e il vero *Noli Me Tangere* di Giulio Romano and Giovan Francesco Penni', *Storia dell'arte*, 111 (2005), pp. 59–96

VASARI 1550
G. Vasari, *Le Vite de' più eccellenti architetti, pittori, et scultori italiani, da Cimabue insino a' tempi moderni* (1550), ed. G. Previtali (Turin, 1986)

VASARI 1550–68
G. Vasari, *Le Vite de' più eccellenti Pittori, Scultori ed Architetti* (1550–68), ed. R. Bettarini, commentary P. Barocchi (Florence, 1976)

VASARI 1550 AND 1568
G. Vasari, *Les Vies des Plus Eccelentes Peintres, sculpteurs et architects: Polidoro da Caravaggio et Maturino Fiorentino* (1550, 1568), French translation, eds L. Frank and S. Tullio Cataldo (Milan, 2007)

VASARI 1568
G. Vasari, *Le Opere di Giorgio Vasari con nuove annotazioni e commenti di G. Milanesi* (1568), 8 vols (Florence, 1878–85)

VASARI 1907
G. Vasari, *Vasari on Technique* (1550), trans. L. S. Maclehose (New York, 1907)

VASARI 1996
G. Vasari, *Lives of the Painters, Sculptors and Architects* (1568), ed. D. Ekserdjian, trans. G. du C. de Vere, 2 vols (New York and Toronto, 1996)

VATICAN 1984–5
Raffaello in Vaticano (Vatican, 1984–5)

VENTURI 1898
A. Venturi, 'Un Quadro a Castroreale attribuito a Polidoro da Caravaggio', *L'Arte*, I (1898), pp. 373–4

VERTOVA 1979
L. Vertova, 'Cupid and Psyche in Renaissance Painting before Raphael', *Journal of the Warburg and Courtauld Institutes*, 42 (1979), pp. 104–21

VICENZA 2000
Valerio Belli Vicentino. 1468c.–1546, eds H. Burns, M. Collareta and D. Gasparotto (Vicenza, 2000)

VILLANO 1526
G. Villano, 'Croniche de la Inclita Città de Napole emendatissime' (Naples, 1526), in *Raccolta di Varii Libri, overo Opuscoli D'Historie del Regno di Napoli di Varii, et approbati autori* (1680)

VITZTHUM 1966
W. Vitzthum, 'Christina in Stockholm', *Master Drawings*, IV (1966), pp. 299–300

VITZTHUM 1970
W. Vitzthum, review of G. Scavizzi's *Luca Giordano* (1966), *Burlington Magazine*, CXII (1970), pp. 239–46

VOSS 1920
H. Voss, *Die Malerei des Spätrenaissance in Rom und Florenz* (Berlin, 1920)

WAAGEN 1838
G. F. Waagen, *Works of Art and Artists in England*, trans. H. E. Lloyd, 3 vols (London, 1838)

WAAGEN 1854
G. F. Waagen, *Treasures of Art in Great Britain*, 3 vols (London, 1854)

WARD JACKSON 1979
P. Ward Jackson, *Victoria and Albert Museum Catalogues, Italian Drawings, 14–16th Century*, I (London, 1979)

WHITTAKER AND CLAYTON 2007
L. Whittaker and M. Clayton, *The Art of Italy in the Royal Collection, Renaissance and Baroque* (London, 2007)

WINNER 1967
M. Winner, *Zeichner sehen die Antike* (Berlin, 1967)

WITCOMBE 2002
C. Witcombe, 'The Chapel of the Courtesan and the Quarrel of the Magdalens', *Art Bulletin*, 84 (2002), pp. 273–92

WITTKOWER 1967
R. Wittkower, *Masters of the Loaded Brush: Oil Sketches from Rubens to Tiepolo* (New York, 1967)

WOLK-SIMON 2002
L. Wolk-Simon, 'Two Early Fresco Cycles by Perino del Vaga: The Palazzo Baldassini and the Pucci Chapel', *Apollo*, 155 (2002), pp. 11–21

WREN CHRISTIAN 2010
K. Wren Christian, *Empire without End: Antiquities Collections in Renaissance Rome, c. 1350–1527* (New Haven and London, 2010)

ZERI AND CAMPAGNA CICALA 1992
F. Zeri and F. Campagna Cicala, *Messina, Museo Regionale* (Palermo, 1992)

ZEZZA 1994
A. Zezza, 'Documenti per la "Cona magna" di Sant'Agostino alla Zecca (Girolamo Santacroce, Polidoro da Caravaggio, Bartolomeo Guelfo, Marco Cardisco)', *Prospettiva*, 75–6 (1994), pp. 136–52

ZEZZA 2016
A. Zezza, 'Un Resto polidoresco nella Napoli antica: Il Fregio di Palazzo Pignone-Confalone', *Napoli nobilissima*, 73 (2016), pp. 17–22

ZUCCARO 1605
F. Zuccaro, *Il lamento della Pittura su l'onde venete* (Mantova, 1605)

Index

All references are to page numbers.
Those in *italic* type indicate illustrations.

Rosso Fiorentino 18, 26, 57, 84, 87
Rotterdam, Museum Boijmans Van Beuningen *41*
Rubens, Peter Paul 40, 131–2
Ruffo, Antonio 126–7
Ruviale, Pedro 61, 93

S
Sabatini, Andrea 69, 73
Saenredam, Jan 45, 56–7, *57*
Samperi, Placido 106, *106*, 119
Sandby, Paul 27
Sangallo the Younger, Antonio da 18
Sannazzaro, Jacopo 69, 80–82
Sannesio, Cardinal Jacopo 30–31
Sansepolcro 87
Sansovino, Jacopo 25
Santi, Giovanni 117
Scorel, Jan van 34
Sebastiano del Piombo 16, 35, 84, 93, 137
Seneca 118
Serra, Cardinal Alberto 43, 61
Soderini, Cardinal Francesco 43
Spinola, Cardinal Agostino 43
Spira, Petruccio 101, 113
Stagno, Thomaso 119
Stuttgart, Staatsgalerie 108, *110*, 115
Subba family 127
Summonte, Pietro 26
Susinno, Francesco 99, 126–8, 137, 149
Syracuse 89

T
Tamagni, Vincenzo 17, 41
Tanzio da Varallo 95
Tintoretto, Jacopo 131
Titian (Tiziano Vecelli) 131
Toronto, Royal Ontario Museum *40*
Trapani 96, 100
Turin, Galleria Sabauda 95, *95*

U
Udine, Giovanni da 14–16, 18, 85
Urban VI, Pope 34

V
Vasari, Giorgio 13, 18, 25–8, 30, 39–44, *42*, 56–7,
    61, 69–71, 73, 80–82, 85, 89, 101, 117, 120, 125,
    131, 149
Vatican
    Belvedere 56, 84
    Loggia 13–15, 18, 24, 28, 35, 41, 44, 56, 63, 66,
        79, 85
    Museo Sacro 26, *27*
    Pinacoteca 115, *132*, 133, 135, 143
    Sala del Costantino 16, 28, 31, 56
    Stanza d'Eliodoro 22, 66
    Stanza della Segnatura 84

Veneziano, Agostino 114
Vienna, Albertina 31, *31*, 32, 34, 35–6, *37*, *80*, 81
Vienna, Kunsthistorisches Museum 96
Voragine, Jacobus de 140

W
Washington, D.C., National Gallery 22, *23*
Weimar, Goethe-Nationalmuseum *60*, 63
Windsor Castle, Royal Collection 26, *27*, 73–5, *75*,
    81, 85

Z
Zeuxis 120
Zuccaro, Federico 40–41, *41*
Zuccaro, Taddeo 41